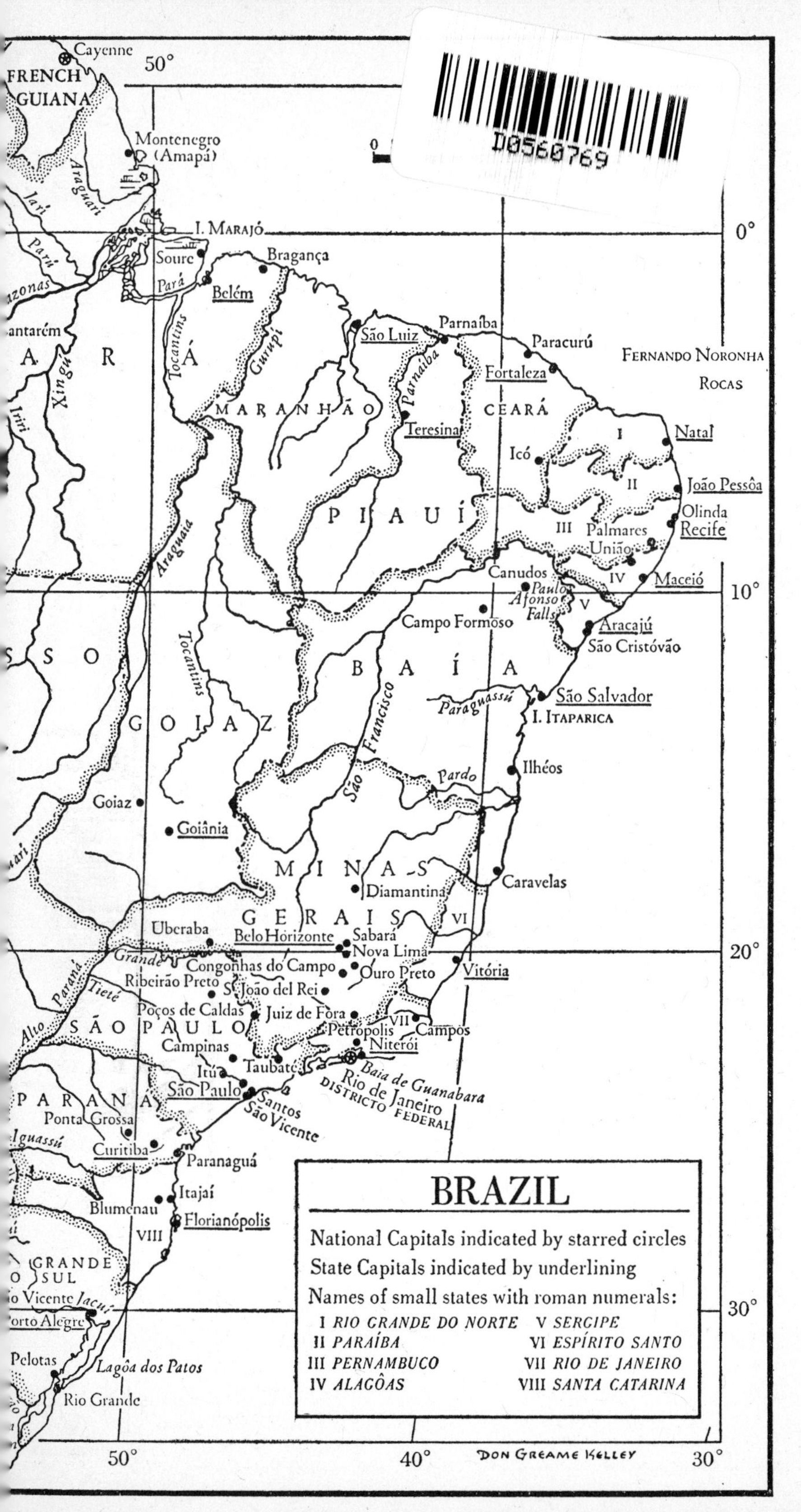

From *Brazil*, ed. Lawrence F. Hill, University of California Press.

The LIFE *of*
JOAQUIM NABUCO

Joaquim Nabuco

The LIFE *of* JOAQUIM NABUCO

BY CAROLINA NABUCO

Translated and edited by

RONALD HILTON

Director of Hispanic American Studies
Stanford University

In collaboration with

LEE B. VALENTINE FRANCES E. COUGHLIN

JOAQUIN M. DUARTE, JR.

STANFORD
UNIVERSITY PRESS
Stanford, California

STANFORD UNIVERSITY PRESS
STANFORD, CALIFORNIA

London: Geoffrey Cumberlege
Oxford University Press

THE BAKER AND TAYLOR COMPANY
55 FIFTH AVENUE, NEW YORK 3

HENRY M. SNYDER & COMPANY
440 FOURTH AVENUE, NEW YORK 16

W. S. HALL & COMPANY
457 MADISON AVENUE, NEW YORK 22

PRINTED AND BOUND IN THE UNITED STATES
OF AMERICA BY STANFORD UNIVERSITY PRESS

PREFACE

The Life of Joaquim Nabuco is more than a biography of a distinguished Brazilian, the great emancipator of the slaves of his country and the first Brazilian Ambassador to the United States. It is an excellent introduction for the serious student to the political life, social problems, and diplomatic affairs of the great southern republic during the latter part of the nineteenth century and the first decade of this century. The translation of this careful and detailed study by his daughter Dona Carolina Nabuco is Stanford University's contribution to the centenary celebrations of the birth of Joaquim Nabuco. It is fitting that Stanford should make such a contribution, not only because of this university's traditional interest in Brazil, but also because President John Casper Branner, who founded that tradition, was a friend and admirer of Joaquim Nabuco and named a mountain in Brazil after him. The publication of the translation has been timed to coincide with the Stanford Conference on Brazil, to be held on May 29 and 30 of this year. To judge by the number and the qualifications of the participants, this conference will be the most serious and significant general discussion of Brazilian affairs ever held outside of Brazil. The guests of honor will be His Excellency, Mauricio Nabuco, the son of Joaquim Nabuco, and at present Brazilian Ambassador to the United States, and his sister, Dona Carolina Nabuco.

The editor of this translation has provided an introduction which will give the nonspecialist the essential historical background for an understanding of the book. A few passages have been omitted, since they were of little interest to the non-Brazilian reader. A great many details have been checked and minor changes introduced in accordance with more recent research. In this regard, the editor must express his thanks to several colleagues on the Stanford faculty, who have advised him on points within their special field of competence. Among those who have been helpful are Professors Raymond D. Harriman, Hermann F. Fränkel, and Philip W. Harsh of the Classics Department, and Hadley Kirkman of the School of Medicine. The editor cannot praise too highly the work of his collaborators in this venture: Lee B. Valentine, Frances E. Coughlin, and Joaquin M. Duarte, Jr., all instructors in Hispanic American Studies at this university. Without the hours and hours of careful labor which they devoted to this task, the project could never have matured. As long as Brazilian studies in this country are carried on by such promising people, we need not worry about the future of this field of research. Miss Patricia A. Charlton deserves appropriate recognition for her careful and critical typing of the manuscript. Last, but certainly not least, we should mention the author herself, who has spared no pains to help the editor, and who has read the translation with a critical eye and incidentally proved her remarkable knowledge of the English language. We hope that she is satisfied that this translation of her book will be an effective instrument in making her father's life and times better known in the English-speaking world.

It is hoped that this translation may mark a small step forward in the progress of Brazilian studies at Stanford. The tradition begun by President Branner and developed by Professor Percy Alvin Martin continues quietly but steadily, and we are confident that Stanford University will remain a focus of serious Brazilian studies in the West of the United States. The Stanford Conference on Brazil has brought together a committee of faculty members who have worked admirably as a team—the editor of this volume does not remember having worked with a committee which showed an equally constructive spirit—and the unity of purpose exemplified by this group should reassure those who fear for the future of Brazilian studies. The editor would like to express here his real appreciation for the work of these colleagues: Charles F. Park, Jr., George S. Myers, Graham H. Stuart, Ira L. Wiggins, Carl E. McDowell, Juan B. Rael, John J. Johnson, and Weldon B. Gibson.

RONALD HILTON

STANFORD UNIVERSITY
April 1, 1950

CONTENTS

Part Three

MEDITATION, 1889–99

Part Four

THE LAST PHASE, 1899–1910

INTRODUCTION

THE BRAZIL OF JOAQUIM NABUCO

Until 1889, when Joaquim Nabuco was forty years old, Brazil, unlike any other country in the Western Hemisphere, was an empire. In 1807, when Napoleon's troops invaded the Iberian peninsula, Dom João VI, regent of Portugal on behalf of his insane mother, Dona Maria I, sailed out of the Tagus for Brazil with a large retinue, just one day before Junot's troops arrived. The capital of the Portuguese Empire was transferred from Lisbon to Rio de Janeiro. In 1815, the Congress of Vienna, which attempted to settle not only the affairs of Europe but those of South America as well, raised Brazil to the category of a kingdom, on the same level as Portugal. The inhabitants of the mother country were incensed by the newly gained equality of the former colony. Moreover, a constitutional revolution in 1820 made it clear that the Portuguese no longer wanted an absolute monarchy. A constituent assembly was held in Lisbon, attended by Brazilian as well as Portuguese deputies. The latter ridiculed their American colleagues and the assembly appeared to be about to end in chaos. In 1821, therefore, Dom João returned to Lisbon with his Spanish wife, Carlota Joaquina, leaving behind in Brazil his heir apparent, Dom Pedro, whom he warned that the separation of Brazil from Portugal might become inevitable. He added that in this event Dom Pedro should place himself at the head of the independence movement.

Dom Pedro was twenty-four years old at this time and, while he had real native ability, his rude manners and dissolute life lost him the affection of his subjects. His Austrian wife, Dona Leopoldina, was physically rather plain, but her devotion to her Brazilian subjects won her general esteem. However, her husband showed her no love. Her interest in things intellectual, especially botany and geology, was transmitted to her son, the great Dom Pedro II, who displayed a kind of Germanic encyclopedism.

Soon after Dom João's return to Portugal, the Lisbon assembly, in an effort to reduce Brazil to a colonial status by depriving it of a royal leader, ordered Dom Pedro to return to Portugal to complete his education. Although resentful, he was prepared to accede, but Dona Leopoldina persuaded him to resist. Encouraged by the powerful Masonic order and by appeals from all over Brazil, Dom Pedro announced on January 9, 1822, to the municipality of Rio de Janeiro, his decision to remain in Brazil for the good of the country. This gesture has remained famous in Brazilian history under the name "*O Fico*" ("I remain"). The Portuguese garrison in Rio de Janeiro protested, but was forced to return to Europe.

Dom Pedro undertook a series of journeys through Brazil to reassure the people. While he was at Ipiranga, on the outskirts of São Paulo, he received on September 7, 1822, dispatches from Rio de Janeiro which reported that the Lisbon assembly had taken measures showing complete intransigence. In the fashion of a Spanish American *grito* (proclamation of independence), Dom Pedro shouted dramatically "Independence or death." Thus this day, September 7, became independence day in Brazil.

Shortly afterward, Brazil was proclaimed an empire and its ruler took the title of Dom Pedro I. The Portuguese garrison of the north resisted, but the English admiral, Lord Cochrane, who had earlier served the cause of Chilean independence, forced this garrison to return to Portugal and thus achieved the stature of a national hero of Brazil. His tomb in Westminster Abbey has been a shrine for Brazilians visiting London, including Joaquim Nabuco, who is described in this biography as the organizer of a ceremony at the tomb during his office as Brazilian Minister in London. The civil "Patriarch of Brazilian Independence" was José Bonifácio de Andrada e Silva. Without his guidance, Brazilian independence would have been a much less peaceful process, and the Brazilian Empire might have fallen to pieces. His son was an active Liberal politician during Nabuco's youth.

Nabuco's home town, Pernambuco, had a liberal, revolutionary tradition, to which, in his fiery youth, he made frequent allusions in his speeches. In 1817 a revolution had broken out there and a republic had been proclaimed. In 1824, Pernambuco was the headquarters of a secessionist movement which proclaimed the "Confederation of the Equator." The second revolt was even more difficult to suppress than the first. While Nabuco admired the liberal spirit of these revolts, he was neither a republican propagandist nor anti-Brazilian; he was devoted to the Brazilian constitutional monarchy.

Realizing that the new Brazilian Empire would have international difficulties, Dom Pedro looked to his wife's father, Francis I of Austria and to his minister, Metternich, for support. However, the decisive influence in the period of Brazilian independence was that of England, which, instead of siding with its old ally, Portugal, succeeded in establishing peace between the old kingdom and the new empire. Thus Great Britain became the dominating influence in the international affairs and the trade of the Brazilian Empire. English political life and the English constitutional monarchy were regarded as models for Brazil, while English humanitarians and indeed the British Government exerted constant pressure on Brazil to abolish slavery. It is important to remember these facts in reading Nabuco's *My Formative Years* and in studying his career and his ideas. Bagehot was Nabuco's political bible, and his abolitionist campaign was inspired by the English humanitarians.

The United States was also active in fostering the independence of

Brazil. José Sylvestre Rebello was sent to obtain recognition, which President Monroe gladly granted on May 26, 1824. The United States was the first power to recognize Brazil, and this in part explains the pro–United States feelings of Brazilian liberals.

Brazil's first independent monarch ruled over a turbulent, inchoate body politic. Dom Pedro, by his lack of adroitness, soon found his position untenable. When his father, Dom João VI, died in 1826, he accepted the Portuguese crown as constitutional monarch, but lost it when an absolutist revolution placed his reactionary brother, Miguel, on the Lusitanian throne. All Dom Pedro reaped was the accusation that he was neglecting Brazil in the interests of Portugal. In pursuance of the traditional Portuguese aim of controlling what is now Uruguay, Dom Pedro fought an unsuccessful war with the United Provinces of the River Plate. It ended in 1828 with a peace, which established the independent republic of Uruguay, and constituted a virtual defeat for Brazil. Meanwhile, the popular Empress Leopoldina had died, while Dom Pedro's affair with the Marchioness of Santos had become a national scandal. Great Britain in 1826 forced Brazil to accept a treaty by which the importation of slaves into Brazil would be legally forbidden in 1830. Whereas the Brazilian abolitionists, including Nabuco, were later to blame slavery for practically all the woes of Brazil, at the time Brazilians blamed Dom Pedro for a treaty which they regarded as spelling disaster to Brazilian agriculture. In 1827, Evaristo da Veiga founded a newspaper, the *Aurora Fluminense*, which became a rallying point for Brazilian opinion, and implicitly damned Dom Pedro as a Portuguese who did not understand the spirit of the Brazilian constitution. In São Paulo, an Italian exile, Libero Badaró, ran a liberal newspaper which denounced the policies of the Emperor. He was assassinated, and the government was generally held responsible for his death. On April 7, 1831, Pedro I abdicated and returned to Portugal, where he was eager to take part in that country's effervescent politics.

The successor of Dom Pedro I was Dom Pedro de Alcántara, nearly six years of age, born a Brazilian, and as Pedro II destined to rule his empire with distinction until his abdication in 1889. Although a regency consisting of Costa Carvalho (later Marquis of Monte Alegre), João Braulio Muniz, and General Lima e Silva was elected, the most forceful public figure was Father Diogo Feijó, a liberal priest. The death of Pedro I in 1834 brought to an end the conspiracies of those who were planning to restore him to the Brazilian throne. The Additional Act of the same year established a one-man regency, and Feijó was elected to that post. In Rio Grande do Sul, a separatist war broke out, and was named the "War of the Farrapos" (ragamuffins). In 1836 the rebels proclaimed the "Riograndense Republic." Feijó's position was weakened by this protracted struggle. He resigned in

1837 and was succeeded by Pedro de Araujo Lima, who was later granted the title Marquis of Olinda. However, when President Rivera of Uruguay attempted to force Rio Grande do Sul into a greater Uruguay, the people of that province made it clear that their allegiance was to Brazil. In 1840, Dom Pedro II, although only fourteen years old, felt the urge to bring order out of chaos, and he gladly agreed to assume power himself.

In his speeches recorded in this biography, Nabuco alludes briefly to the intrigue behind this development. The threats to the territorial integrity of Brazil and the general unrest perturbed the whole people. The Liberals decided that the regency did not have sufficient prestige to govern and that the country needed a monarch at its head. There was one technical difficulty: Dom Pedro II had not yet reached the legal age at which he could succeed to the throne. The Liberals propounded the expedient of changing this part of the constitution by law, but the Conservatives were not willing to go as fast as the Liberals. Led by António Carlos de Andrada and one of his two brothers, a Liberal mob invaded the Senate and turned it into a kind of revolutionary convention. A commission was appointed to appeal to Dom Pedro to assume the office of emperor. Dom Pedro acceded to the request. His coronation was, therefore, the consequence of an unconstitutional act plotted by the Liberals. António Carlos became minister of the interior in the new government.

As a result of this episode, the Liberals held that Dom Pedro II owed his crown to them. While this view was clearly exaggerated, they resented any understanding between the Emperor and the Conservatives. As a militant abolitionist, Nabuco dragged up this issue and expressed anger that the slavocrat Conservatives should appear to be receiving support from the Emperor. But this indictment of the freedom-loving Emperor was unwarranted.

The initial years of the reign of Dom Pedro II were not pleasant, but it was a period of pacification and consolidation. The suppression of the slave traffic, on the insistence of Great Britain, was made more effective, the southern provinces of Brazil were restored to order, and the problems of the River Plate area clarified.

Such was the historical scene into which Joaquim Nabuco was born. What of the geographical scene? The immense country known as Brazil consists of an agglomeration of distinctive regions. Nabuco was, despite his internationalism, essentially a product of the Brazilian Northeast. Stretching southward from the hump of Brazil is a coastal strip, which was the center of activity in colonial Brazil until the eighteenth century, when the development of mining in the well-named state of Minas Gerais (General Mines) led to the growth of Rio de Janeiro and its broad hinterland. Only at the end of the nineteenth century did the coffee industry, combined with a heavy influx of Italian immigrants, make the progressive state of São Paulo economically and industrially superior.

The Northeast has as its focuses two major port cities: Recife (known also as Pernambuco, the name of the state of which it is the capital) and São Salvador (commonly known for the same reason as Bahia). A number of smaller cities dot the coast, among which the beautiful colonial city of Olinda, a few miles north of Recife, held deep charm for Nabuco.

The economic basis for the growth of the Northeast was sugar, and thus there developed a feudal society based on slavery which Gilberto Freyre has painstakingly dissected in his well-known massive volume, *The Masters and the Slaves (Casa Grande e Senzala)*. Nabuco was one of the "Masters" from the "Big House," although he rose to fame as the champion of the slaves crowded in their *senzalas*. Recife, the home of both Nabuco and his admirer Freyre, has a different character from sleepy, artistic Bahia. Ever since the Dutch occupation in the seventeenth century, which inspired the Pernambucanos to fight a war of liberation, it has been an active commercial center and its canals have always been busy with the traffic of the high seas. Perhaps its law school made it more aggressive intellectually and socially than Bahia.

It was on the political stage of Rio de Janeiro that Nabuco achieved national fame. The Rio of Nabuco was not the modernistic and healthy city of today, with its two million inhabitants. It was smaller, more rustic and, like most of Brazil then, subject to tropical epidemics—one reason why Nabuco, like other wealthy Brazilians, spent long periods in Europe. The Avenida Rio Branco and the other wide arteries of contemporary Rio had not yet been cut through the colonial city, with its narrow winding streets. The pulse of Rio could best be felt in the narrow but elegant Rua do Ouvidor, where still today traffic is forbidden so that it may serve as a kind of club for pedestrians.

Named after the great and good Pedro II, the aristocratic summer capital of Petrópolis lies quietly in the mountains back of Rio de Janeiro. In 1889, with the fall of the Empire, it was reduced to a pleasant shadow of its former self. As a young aristocrat Nabuco made frequent visits there, but because of his irrepressible character and his militant liberalism he did not secure the good will of that conservative community.

Apart from the Northeast and Rio de Janeiro, Nabuco did not know intimately the vast expanse of Brazil. Travel was difficult, usually involving a sea journey between two port cities. The vast interior of Brazil is still undeveloped, and few were the Brazilians in Nabuco's day who had actually seen most of the country.

What of the racial background of Brazil? There is in its interior a residual population of Indians and half-breeds who are of comparatively minor importance in their contribution to modern Brazil. In the areas where there were once great sugar plantations, particularly in the states of Bahia and Pernambuco, the population still has a high percentage of Negroes and mulattoes. The coffee state of São Paulo is inhabited largely by descendants of Italians who migrated there around the turn of the century. The population of the southern states of Paraná, Santa Catarína and Rio Grande do Sul has a special character because of the German and Polish colonies, which have been a positive and important force in the development of those states.

Despite these varied population strata, the ethnic basis of Brazilian society is Portuguese, just as the language of this vast republic is that of Portugal, with differences which only an unscientific nationalism has overstressed. Even in the Northeast, the region of Bahia and Pernambuco, the mass of Negroes receive their social and cultural directives from the Portuguese minority. This minority, despite the disappearance of the slave-owning landlords with abolition in 1888, still represents the traditional aristocracy of the region.

Joaquim Nabuco descended from the Portuguese nobility of the Northeast. On the paternal side, his family, the Nabuco de Araujo, came from Portugal to Bahia in the middle of the eighteenth century. During the nineteenth century, the Nabucos played an important part in the politics of the Empire. For three generations before Joaquim Nabuco, the head of the family had been a senator. José Joaquim, Baron of Itapoan, Joaquim's great-grandfather, took part in the constituent assembly and represented Pará in the Senate for many years (the senators during the Empire being appointed for life). Joaquim's grandfather and his father, both named José Thomaz, were likewise senators. The former was insignificant, but the latter was justifiably a hero in the eyes of his son Joaquim, who devoted to him a monumental biography entitled *A Statesman of the Empire.*

On his mother's side, Joaquim Nabuco descended from an even older family. The Paes Barretos had come from Portugal soon after the conquest in 1500 and had settled in Pernambuco, where they had owned a number of sugar estates, the best-known being that of Cabo. His mother's family was related to many of the oldest and most distinguished families of Pernambuco, such as the Cavalcanti and the Sá e Albuquerque.

Joaquim Nabuco's godparents, Joaquim Aurelio de Carvalho and his wife Dona Anna Rosa, were of similar background, and their sugar estate at Massangana was the scene of many episodes in Joaquim's childhood.

Nabuco's formal education followed the established pattern of that day. Nabuco studied at the best-known high school in Brazil, the Pedro II College in Rio de Janeiro, which still bears the name of that enlightened monarch, despite the advent of the Republic. Like many young Latin Americans who are undecided as to their future, he then entered law school. The

Brazilian higher education system is peculiar in that, even today, universities scarcely exist, although recent governments have tried to create them out of the heterogeneous and unrelated faculties which are the centers of advanced studies in all the major cities. In Nabuco's day there were two law schools in Brazil, one in São Paulo and the other in Recife. Nabuco studied at each of them in succession.

While Nabuco was studying law in São Paulo, the Paraguayan War (1865–70) was fought. Although conditions in Uruguay were originally responsible for the outbreak of hostilities, the struggle quickly developed into a struggle between a triple alliance, consisting of Argentina, Uruguay, and Brazil, and the power-crazy dictator of Paraguay, Francisco Solano López. The Brazilian Navy played an important part in the war. It sailed up the Paraná River, and on June 11, 1865, a Brazilian squadron under Admiral Barroso almost totally destroyed the Paraguayan fleet at Riachuelo not far from the junction of the Paraná and Paraguay rivers. Proceeding up the Paraguay, the Brazilian fleet finally succeeded on February 19, 1868, in forcing a passage past Humaytá, the Gibraltar of South America. Young Nabuco celebrated this victory with a speech in São Paulo.

The protracted Paraguayan War had an unfortunate effect on the internal politics of Brazil. The Duke of Caxias, Brazil's great military leader and a member of the Conservative party, was deeply offended by unfair criticism. Since he was indispensable, the Liberal government resigned and the prime minister, Zacharias, refused to collaborate with the Emperor, even though his party had a majority in parliament. The Emperor therefore felt justified, after a six months' crisis, in appointing a Conservative government. The day after this decision, on July 17, 1868, a motion by José Bonifácio (the younger) denouncing the Emperor was passed. As this biography relates, Joaquim Nabuco was among those who applauded this motion, although his father, the senator, who was the intellectual leader of the Liberals, warned his party that this campaign against the Empire, instead of weakening the Conservatives, simply strengthened the growing Republican party. His foresight was justified when in 1870 the famous "Republican Manifesto" was launched, demanding the abolition of the Empire.

In the preparations for Brazilian independence and later for the establishment of the republic, the powerful Masonic order played an important part and thereby inevitably came into conflict with the Catholic Church, which had an alliance first with the Portuguese monarchy, and later with the Brazilian imperial government. It was the official church of both regimes. Since Nabuco was actively engaged in this struggle, first on the side of the Masons and later of the Catholic Church, it is desirable that this civic issue be recounted, at least in its most critical moments.

At first, Brazilian Catholics were unaware of the real incompatibility of the Masonic order with their Church, and indeed a great many priests belonged to the Masons and even took higher degrees. Meanwhile, however, in Europe the Catholic Church was feeling the effect of Masonic influence. It was clearly to be seen in the anticlerical aspects of the 1848 revolutions, and it sought to undermine the temporal power of the Pope, which did indeed come to an end in 1870.

A crisis suddenly developed in Brazil in 1871 as an aftermath of the Rio Branco emancipation law. At a great festival held by the Rio lodges, a Catholic priest delivered an address which showed a greater adherence to Masonry than to the Catholic doctrine. This involved him in an argument with his bishop, who duly suspended him. The Masons, led by the Viscount of Rio Branco, who was both prime minister and grand master of the Masonic order in Brazil, took up the defense of the priest against the Church. The bishop of Rio, who was directly involved, showed extreme patience, but the new bishop of Olinda, a Capuchin friar named Vital Maria Gonçalves de Oliveira, was less tolerant and began to expel from the lay religious societies members who were affiliated with the Masonic order. His example was followed by the bishop of Pará, D. António de Macedo Costa. Although these bishops received no encouragement from their ecclesiastical superiors, they refused even to submit the issue to the civil authorities of the Empire and were therefore in 1874 condemned to four years' imprisonment. The Masonic problem was now secondary; the issue was regalism versus ultramontanism. By an unhappy coincidence, Pope Pius IX had just settled the problem with a special envoy from Brazil, Baron Penedo (whom Nabuco mentions frequently), when the news of the imprisonment of Dom Vital reached him. The Pope regarded this as a personal affront, and the entire Brazilian clergy was soon re-echoing his indignation. The Brazilian government was compelled to capitulate, and in 1875 granted an amnesty to the clerical prisoners. The Church had won a notable triumph.

The great constitutional issue after the Paraguayan War became the reform of that part of the Constitution of 1824 which established a system of indirect elections. The Liberals were especially active in demanding this reform, and in 1878 the government was entrusted to them, with the understanding that this reform was to be their major concern. The new president of the Council, Cansanção de Sinimbú, tried for two years to accomplish this, but his efforts proved unavailing.

From January to June of 1882, Martinho Campos was prime minister. His early downfall was the result of his policy of inaction. He was succeeded by Paranaguá, whose government lasted scarcely a year, while that of Lafayette Rodrigues Pereira lasted slightly longer (1883 to 1884). He was succeeded by Manuel Pinto de Souza Dantas, whose government survived barely a year. In 1885 José António Saraiva came to power, but he governed for only a few months. His successor Cotegipe remained in power until 1888. His resignation in this fateful year allowed João Alfredo Corrêa de Oliveira to form the cabinet which finally abolished slavery. This is perhaps the opportune moment to tell briefly the history of emancipation in Brazil. The subject has a special interest for us, as Nabuco was one of the leaders of the abolitionist cause.

Brazil was the last country in the New World to abolish slavery, indeed one of the last in the world. As we have seen, in 1826 Brazil signed with Great Britain a treaty by which the importation of slaves into Brazil was to cease in 1830. The Brazilian government was extremely lax in carrying out the agreement, and the slave traders showed great ingenuity in importing slaves despite the surveillance of the British Navy. They won wide support by whipping up popular resentment against the efforts of Great Britain to put an end to the slave trade. The British Government, urged on by a sincere group of humanitarians, decided finally that unilateral action was necessary to bring to an end the importation of slaves into Brazil, and in 1845 the famous Aberdeen Bill authorized the bringing to trial of Brazilian slave ships, not before mixed tribunals, but before the British admiralty courts. It was clear that the British Government was determined to use force to stop the slave traffic, and in 1850 the Conservative ministry of the Marquis of Olinda decided that the Brazilian government must act itself to put an end to the slave traffic. A law of that year, known by the name of its sponsor, Eusebio de Queiroz, ended the slave traffic by Brazilian law. However, this traffic was not entirely suppressed and, of course, slavery continued to exist within Brazil.

The victory of emancipation in the United States Civil War made the end of slavery seem inevitable. The Emperor Pedro II was well aware of the harm which the perpetuation of slavery did to the good name of Brazil. The war with Paraguay made emancipation a patriotic cause, since Brazil needed soldiers and slaves had to be freed before they could join the army. In 1867 the French Emancipation Committee wrote a famous letter to Pedro II, demanding the abolition of slavery in Brazil in the name of humanity. In its reply, the Brazilian government stated that emancipation was bound to come in due course and that the matter would receive proper attention at the end of the Paraguayan War. Zacharias, the prime minister, requested Joaquim's father, Senator Nabuco de Araujo, to draw up a bill which would forward the cause of emancipation. Senator Nabuco finished his task in 1868 and, with slight modification, Silva Paranhos, Viscount of Rio Branco, pushed it through parliament. It was finally approved on September 28, 1871, and was known as the "Law of Free Birth" ("*Ventre Livre*"), since its main clause declared that all children born of slave mothers should be free.

The Rio Branco law would have led gradually to the disappearance of slavery, but young Joaquim Nabuco was impatient and wanted a quick end to "the crime." In 1880 he introduced into the Chamber of Deputies a bill providing for the extinction of slavery at the end of ten years. The bill was defeated, and Nabuco took revenge by founding the Brazilian Anti-Slavery Society. A network of abolitionist clubs was established, linked together by the Abolitionist Confederation. The national government was hard to convince. Martinho Campos, who was prime minister in 1882, quarreled over the emancipation question with Nabuco.

By a curious series of circumstances, the province of Ceará took the lead in abolishing slavery before the national government did so. Fortaleza, the capital and chief seaport of the province, had poor harbor facilities. Ships anchored out at sea, and colorful rafts *(jangadas)* carried passengers and cargo to shore. The seamen who manned these rafts *(jangadeiros)* were violent abolitionists. They went on strike and declared that they would not transport slaves. At the same time they helped many slaves to land in Ceará and hide there. Ceará became the great haven for escaped slaves in Brazil, and in 1884, bowing to public opinion, the province officially declared the end of slavery within its boundaries. In the same year the province of Amazonas followed suit. Then it was the turn of Rio Grande do Sul. Acting not as a province but individually, many of the municipalities emancipated their slaves.

The national government realized that further procrastination was useless. One cabinet after another was formed with a view to ending slavery, but finally, on March 7, 1888, João Alfredo Corrêa de Oliveira, a Conservative, was made prime minister for the express purpose of bringing about emancipation. The next day, March 8, 1888, the Minister of Agriculture, Rodrigo Silva, introduced into parliament a bill which simply abolished slavery in Brazil and revoked all dispositions to the contrary. On May 13 the bill was signed, in the absence of Dom Pedro II, by the princess regent, Dona Isabel.

The abolition of slavery was almost a personal triumph for Nabuco, but one of its immediate consequences, the defection of the landowners from the monarchy, stimulated the fall of the Empire and the establishment of the Republic in 1889. Nabuco was in a dilemma. His family tradition and personal inclination, while Liberal, had been strongly loyal to the imperial institution. The Republic was largely the creation of army officers who knew some mathematics, were filled with the ill-assimilated positivism of Auguste Comte, and scorned as unscientific the learned and experienced lawyers of whom the imperial parliament was largely made up. Joaquim Nabuco belonged to this latter group. The opposition of the military to civilian control had become evident when in 1885 the Minister of War had, for good cause, punished a certain Lieutenant Colonel Cunha Mattos. The militarists chose as their champion an honest but mediocre soldier, General Manoel Deodoro da Fonseca. Dom Pedro II began in 1887 to suffer from diabetes, and his consequent lack of energy robbed him of his prestige and the Monarchists of their momentum. The landed gentry no longer supported him. The anticlericals spread the story that the princess imperial, Dona Isabel, was a mere tool of the clergy. Her consort, the French Comte d'Eu, was a most worthy person, but his unfortunate deafness made him the butt of widespread ridicule and criticism. In 1889 João Alfredo Corrêa de Oliveira was succeeded in the premiership by Afonso Celso de Assis Figueiredo, Viscount of Ouro Preto. However, General Deodoro da Fonseca, who had felt a great personal loyalty to the Emperor, was won over to militant republicanism by a middle-aged professor of mathematics in the military college, Benjamin Constant Botelho de Magalhães. Although he was the tutor of the grandchildren of Dom Pedro II, Benjamin Constant was a doctrinaire republican, and he was the brains behind the coup d'état which overthrew the monarchy. He relayed to General Deodoro da Fonseca a false rumor and thereby caused the old soldier to proclaim the Republic. The imperial family was put aboard the steamship "Alagôas" and sent to Europe.

The proclamation of the Republic had certain inevitable consequences. In January 1890, Church and State were separated. A new constitution was adopted in February 1891. Deodoro da Fonseca was elected president in the same month. Unfortunately he viewed the candidacy of a civilian, Prudente de Moraes, as a personal affront, and in consequence the army for several years regarded civilians as a menace to their control of the government. In November 1891, Deodoro da Fonseca highhandedly dissolved congress and thereby almost precipitated a civil war. He was shocked by the hostile reaction of the Brazilian people, and in the same month he resigned from the presidency. He was succeeded by his vice-president, Marshal Floriano Peixoto. Floriano's behavior provoked resentment on all sides and, added to the long-extant rivalry between the army and the navy, was the cause of the revolt of the fleet in 1893. The leader of this revolt was Admiral Saldanha da Gama, who had been a good friend of Joaquim Nabuco. It was unsuccessful, as was the federalist revolution which raged on land contemporaneously. Thus Floriano Peixoto can rightly claim to have consolidated the Republic.

In 1894 Prudente de Moraes was elected president, and thus began the period of civilian republicanism which was to be the Brazilian regime until after Nabuco's death. The presidency of Prudente de Moraes was disturbed by a fantastic civil war which has become world famous because of the account of it given in the monumental but excessively erudite volume of

Euclydes da Cunha, translated into English under the title *Rebellion in the Backlands*. A religious fanatic, António Conselheiro, gathered around him a mob of peasants who hated the "godless" republic and, in his stronghold, Canudos, located in the interior of the Northeast, withstood the attacks of government armies for several years.

The next president was Campos Sales, like Prudente de Moraes a civilian from São Paulo. During his period of office (1898–1902), his main concern was to stabilize Brazilian economy, and he succeeded admirably in this purpose. In 1900, the dispute over the boundary with French Guiana was happily settled, but the question of the boundary with British Guiana was submitted in 1901 to the arbitration of the King of Italy, with Joaquim Nabuco as the Brazilian representative. The verdict of the King of Italy, which was not pronounced until 1904, aroused no enthusiasm in Brazil and was an acute disappointment to Joaquim Nabuco. The story of these negotiations is told at length in the present biography.

Two successive presidents of Brazil were among Nabuco's friends and classmates in law school. Rodrigues Alves was president from 1902 to 1906. His regime was characterized by financial prosperity, which enabled him, with the help of the mayor of Rio de Janeiro, Pereira Passos, to transform the capital into the beautiful modern city we know today. At the same time he entrusted the famous physician Oswaldo Cruz with the task of eradicating diseases such as malaria, yellow fever, smallpox, and bubonic plague from the city.

Rodrigues Alves appointed the Baron of Rio Branco as his foreign minister, and it was during his presidency that Brazil won some of its most brilliant victories in its boundary disputes. It was, however, during the regime of Rodrigues Alves also that Nabuco suffered his aforementioned defeat in the arbitration case over the Brazilian boundary with British Guiana. Seldom in the history of government has so distinguished a son followed in the footsteps of so worthy a father as in the case of the two Rio Brancos. Since Nabuco was associated with both, the uninitiated should be warned not to confuse them. Both were named José Maria da Silva Paranhos. The father (1819–1880) was Viscount of Rio Branco; while the son (1845–1912) had the title of Baron of Rio Branco. The father is associated primarily with the previously mentioned Law of Free Birth (1871), but he had a great variety of activities, serving among other things as Minister of the Navy and Minister of Foreign Affairs. The son achieved even greater fame, and was a distinguished Minister of Foreign Affairs from 1902 until his death in 1912. During his period as foreign minister, he successfully solved most of Brazil's boundary problems. It was because of Rio Branco's extraordinary success that Nabuco's relative success in the question of the boundary with British Guiana seemed like a failure.

The next president of Brazil, Afonso Penna, was also a classmate of Nabuco's in law school. He was not as successful as Rodrigues Alves in the presidency and, after assuming power in 1906, he died in 1909 without finishing his term.

Perhaps the most distinguished political contemporary of Nabuco was Ruy Barbosa who, being born on November 5, 1849, was a few months younger than our protagonist. The centennial of the birth of both Brazilians was celebrated in 1949. Like Nabuco, Ruy Barbosa was from the Northeast—he was born in Bahia—and in general his background was similar to that of Nabuco. Of well-to-do and long-established Portuguese ancestry, Ruy Barbosa grew up in a liberal tradition and was a great admirer of English and American parliamentarism. He was indeed more sympathetic to Anglo-American Protestantism than was Catholic Nabuco. Like Nabuco, Ruy Barbosa spent many years as an exile in London, and like him he was one of the leaders of the abolitionist campaign. Yet, whereas Nabuco was slow to reconcile himself with the Republic after its proclamation in 1889, Ruy Barbosa drafted the new constitution, following as a model that of the United States. Ruy Barbosa's greatest international glory was at the Second Hague Conference in 1907, where his eloquence in several languages won for him the title of "the Eagle of the Hague." Seeing clearly the evils of the militarism which characterized the first years of the Republic, Ruy Barbosa fought successfully to introduce a civilian administration. Although he was actively involved in the Brazilian participation in World War I, political intrigues prevented his taking part in the Versailles Conference. He died in 1923.

Although he was an enthusiastic friend of the United States, Joaquim Nabuco remained always on close terms with the brilliant writer, Eduardo Prado (1860–1901), whose violent denunciation of the United States in a book entitled *The American Illusion* won him widespread fame in Brazil. However, the basic question as to whether Brazil should ally herself with the United States, as Nabuco wished, or with Argentina, as the proponents of the ABC (Argentina-Brazil-Chile) alliance recommended, was the cause of a disagreeable and permanent break between Nabuco and the distinguished diplomat and historian Manoel de Oliveira Lima (1867–1928), like Nabuco a native of Pernambuco.

Joaquim Nabuco was on friendly terms with most of the important literary figures of his period. He was ten years younger than Machado de Assis, who is hailed as the greatest Brazilian writer of the nineteenth century. Born in 1839, this child of a Negro house painter and a Portuguese woman led a simple life, but won fame through his novels such as *Dom Cazmurro*, *Posthumous Memoirs of Braz Cubas*, and *Quincas Borba*. Despite his humble background, Machado de Assis became a patriarch of Brazilian letters, and in 1897 founded the Brazilian Academy of which he was president until his death in 1908. His cordial relations with Nabuco began when he published an article encouraging young Joaquim, who at the age of fifteen had published a poem, "The Giant of Poland."

Just two years older than Nabuco, and his contemporary in law school, was the most eloquent of Brazilian nineteenth-century poets, the "poet of the slaves," Castro Alves. He supported the abolitionist cause in eloquent verses deliberately reminiscent of the sonorous music of Victor Hugo, and his poems "Voices of Africa" and "The Slave Ship" acquired a national character.

Joaquim Nabuco, as a polemist, was no respecter of persons, and as a youth he chose to criticize in his articles the romantic Indianist novelist José de Alencar, who was exactly twenty years his senior and who may in some ways be regarded as the father of modern Brazilian literature. His novels, *Iracema* and *The Guaraní*, reminiscent of Chateaubriand and James Fenimore Cooper, had won for Alencar immense popularity; but it was his iconoclastic book, *The Jesuit*, which involved him in a literary squabble with young Nabuco.

Nabuco likewise entered into verbal hostilities with another of the literary giants of the period, Alfredo d'Escragnolle, Viscount of Taunay (1843–1899), who is best known for his *Retreat from Laguna*, an account of a military expedition in the Paraguayan War, and his novel, *Inocência* (1872), which has been translated into many languages. It tells the tragic love story of a girl who lived in the conservative rural society of the Brazilian hinterland. Taunay wrote newspaper articles expressing doubts about Nabuco's abolitionist ideas. Nabuco did not hesitate to reply promptly and publicly.

The Graça Aranha to whom there are many references in this biography, and whom Nabuco regarded as his favorite disciple, was the well-known author of the novel, *Canaan*. There will likewise be found in this book, many references to the severe and learned literary critic, José Veríssimo, (1857–1916). Those unfamiliar with Brazilian affairs should be warned not to confuse him with the contemporary popular novelist, Erico Veríssimo. The former was from Pará, at the mouth of the Amazon River, whereas the latter is a native of the southernmost state of Brazil, Rio Grande do Sul.

The younger generation of Brazilian writers regarded Nabuco with respect, if not with veneration. The poet Olavo Bilac (1865–1918) admired his sincere oratory, and that internationally famous sociologist from Pernambuco, Gilberto Freyre, recently sponsored the parliamentary motion to establish in that city an institute named after Joaquim Nabuco and devoted to the study of the problems of the Northeast. The journalist, Levi Carneiro, wrote enthusiastic pages about Nabuco, as did the sociologist, Oliveira Viana; both were young and unknown when Nabuco visited Rio de Janeiro to attend the Pan American Congress of 1906.

Nabuco, the emancipator, was not merely a doctrinaire—he did indeed have many Negro friends. In the abolitionist campaign, he was closely allied with a sincere and able Negro, José do Patrocínio. Another beloved colleague was the Negro engineer André Rebouças who, after the fall of the Empire, showed such touching loyalty to the imperial family.

This biography of Joaquim Nabuco describes the public life of a national figure, and discusses his private life only in so far as it throws some light on his national and international activities. This introduction would be incomplete without some account of the family which Nabuco left behind. There are abundant references in the biography to Nabuco's happy marriage with Dona Evelina Torres Ribeiro. They had five children: three boys and two girls. There are in this book several references to Mauricio, so named because Maurice of Nassau renamed Recife, "Mauricea." Mauricio Nabuco was born in London on May 10, 1891, and his childhood years in England explain his excellent command of English. Since 1913, when he entered the Itamaratí (Brazil's foreign office), he has followed in the footsteps of Joaquim Nabuco, the diplomat. He has held a number of important posts, including those of Brazilian Ambassador to Chile, to the Vatican, and finally to the United States. The author of this biography, Dona Carolina Nabuco, is a sister of Mauricio Nabuco. Whereas Mauricio has chosen the career of diplomat and public servant, Dona Carolina has devoted herself to historical and creative writing. She gained international popularity by her novel, *A Sucessora* (1934), but there is general agreement that her most important work is this *Vida de Joaquim Nabuco*. It was first published in 1928 by the Companhia Editora Nacional. A second and a third edition have since appeared.

Just as Joaquim Nabuco's biography of his father, *A Statesman of the Empire*, is important as a picture not of one man but of a whole epoch, so this biography of Joaquim Nabuco unfolds before us not merely the life history of a great Brazilian but that of the whole development of modern Brazil. The affairs of Latin America are extraordinarily complicated for the ordinary reader in the United States or England, who does not have the background for reading a book about Latin American politics that he would have for reading a book about France or Germany. Moreover, Brazil is separated from the English-speaking countries by a language which unfortunately is little studied even in our universities. It is hoped that this Introduction may prepare the ordinary English-speaking reader for a book full of references which might otherwise escape him.

RONALD HILTON

The LIFE *of*

JOAQUIM NABUCO

Part One

THE FORMATIVE YEARS, 1849–79

CHAPTER I. ANCESTORS, CHILDHOOD—PERNAMBUCO, 1557–1857

The qualities which were to make Joaquim Nabuco outstanding were the same that had contributed to the prominence of his father, the third Senator Nabuco. Joaquim received from his father, besides stature and a fine presence, a splendid mind, a natural gift for speech, and an unfailing kindness. Joaquim often contended that he had inherited his imagination from his mother. While that was perhaps little in comparison with all the qualities he inherited from his father, it was sufficient to give a totally different aspect to the talents of the elder and younger Nabucos. The same lucid mind and power of clear argumentation which stood the father in such good stead as a jurist, served the son as an artist. In oratory, Joaquim's phrases were embellished with images, and the impetuousness of the apostle of abolition replaced the considered prudence of the "oracle" of the Senate. The third characteristic, kindness, is less subject to such transformation, but the imagination of Joaquim Nabuco revealed itself in the spontaneity and graciousness of the attentions he showed to his friends and in his acts of generosity.

On his father's side, Joaquim belonged to a family of statesmen whose honorable name had been made illustrious by his father. The Nabuco de Araujo family, of good Portuguese origin, came to Bahia about the middle of the eighteenth century. The first Senator Nabuco was Joaquim's great-granduncle, Chancellor José Joaquim, Baron of Itapoan, who took part in the Constituent Assembly and later represented Pará as a life senator. Joaquim Nabuco's grandfather and father, both named José Thomaz, also became senators. The grandfather lacked brilliance, voting systematically with the government, but Joaquim's father had the prestige and authority appropriate to one of the principal figures of his epoch.

On his mother's side, Joaquim Nabuco was descended from an old Portuguese family that had resided in Brazil for three centuries. The Paes Barreto family were the heirs of the estates of Bilheira in Portugal and Cabo in Brazil. João Paes Barreto, who founded the Cabo estate in 1560, the third year after his arrival in what is now the state of Pernambuco, not only was outstanding for his saintliness, which won him a place in Portuguese hagiology,[1] but he also excelled in temporal matters, so that he came to possess "so much property that he lost count." Referring to him as a "man of credit and opinion and one of the oldest residents of

[1]George Cardoso, *Agiologio Lusitano dos Sanctos e Varoens illustres em virtude do reino de Portugal e suas conquistas* (Lisbon, 1666), III, 149, 348, 349, 354.

Pernambuco," the Franciscan Friar António Jaboatão, in the chronicle of his order, says:

> In this land, João Paes Barreto was one of the foremost colonists, not only in nobility, but in worldly goods, and the richest man who lived in Pernambuco at that time . . . . João Paes Barreto was the owner of ten sugar mills, which he distributed during his life among his eight children. He spent most of his time at the sugar mill called Engenho Velho do Cabo. He died at the Hospital of Olinda, of which he had been a great benefactor, and among whose poor patients he wished to die. He was taken there a few days before his death and he predicted, correctly, to the monks that he would die on the day of the Holy Trinity.

A Noble of the Royal House, Knight of the Order of Christ, João Paes Barreto was also, in 1619, interim governor of the captaincy of Pernambuco, the most beautiful, opulent, and aristocratic captaincy in Brazil.

Pernambuco had been colonized by gentlemen from the very beginning. From Portugal came Jeronymo de Albuquerque and all the retinue of Duarte Coelho Pereira, the first to receive a grant of land. From Italy came Felippo Cavalcanti. Maurice of Nassau came with a choice following from Holland. The richness of the land permitted the illustrious colonists to continue their pleasant European way of life in the New World. Ships sailed away loaded with sugar and precious woods and brought back comforts and luxuries. Silver was used for everything, even the locks on the doors. The Jesuit, Fernão Cardim, who landed there in 1583, writes: "The women and children dress in all sorts of velvets, damasks, and other silks, and in this they go to great excesses. The women act very much like great ladies . . . . the men . . . . buy horses that cost 200 or 300 cruzados, and some of them have three or four expensive mounts. They are very fond of parties . . . . each year they drink 50,000 cruzados' worth of wines from Portugal. . . . . In short, in Pernambuco there is more vanity than in Lisbon."

The spirit of adventure which had brought the settlers so far from home was kept alert at all times through the necessity of defending by arms the enviable lands they had conquered. The owners of the Cabo estates always participated in these battles.

The family succession continued through the colonial period until the New Empire abolished the system of primogeniture as far as it applied to the land. The line ended with Francisco Paes Barreto, the ninth owner and Marquis of Recife. The opulent inheritance which had passed through so many generations was divided among his children and soon disappeared. Tradition, however, keeps bright the memory of the deeds of the last and most illustrious of the owners.

"Implacable enemy of the despots, the tyrants, and the hereditary enemies of his country," Francisco Paes Barreto unerringly chose the side of true patriotism in the struggles in which he became involved. In 1817, he was one of the leaders of the great revolution against the Portuguese oppressors, and in 1824 he preserved the national unity in the face of the menace of the Equatorial Confederation which threatened to dismember the Empire.

His leadership of the revolution resulted in his incarceration for three years with his companions in the prisons of Bahia, and later led to his being called to Lisbon to answer false charges concerning a subsequent uprising. When independence was proclaimed, he became one of the most devoted defenders of the Empire and of Pedro I, who made him a viscount and a marquis. Pedro I also named him president of what was then the province of Pernambuco, in opposition to Manoel Paes de Andrade, who was preparing the Confederate revolution, soon to break out. Paes Barreto resisted the movement for six months with the army which he gathered and maintained entirely at his own expense. When the government "solicited from him an accounting of the costs of war, the reply he gave to the monarch was that he wanted nothing." According to his admirer and biographer, "he did not brood over the widespread destruction of his properties . . . . where the fury of vengeance reached the point of setting fire to the residence house at the Engenho Velho do Cabo and of placing a keg of gunpowder in it. . . . . His wife became a fugitive, trying to escape the claws of these hungry lions."

At last, however, with the arrival of reinforcements sent by the Court, the master of the Cabo estate victoriously entered the city of Pernambuco, now known as Recife, with Brigadier Lima e Silva on September 12, 1824.

His niece, Dona Anna Benigna de Sá Barreto, daughter of his sister Dona Maria José Felicidade Barreto and of his cousin Francisco António de Sá Barreto II, another warrior of the "Martyrs," became the wife of Counselor José Thomaz Nabuco de Araujo and the mother of Joaquim Nabuco.

She was a woman of small stature and of slight build, and these features were accompanied by simple dignity and strict conduct, the result of her family tradition and of her Pernambucan education.

She brought to her husband's home in Rio the customs and principles of hospitality which were a matter of so much pride and honor in the North. At that time, everything in Brazil which was associated with elegance and refinement came to Rio from Pernambuco.

"The parliamentary representatives from Pernambuco," says Joaquim Nabuco in *A Statesman of the Empire*, "were from then on awaited eagerly in the capital. At various times the provincial deputies led by Boa Vista, Sebastião do Rego, and Maciel Monteiro set the fashion for the salons of Rio. The arrival of the 'lions of the North,' as they were called, was always a social event. They possessed a tradition of manners and gentlemanly conduct which set them apart from the rest of the world of politics . . . ."

Dona Anna Nabuco, whose husband's residence became the gathering place for these "lions," received them warmly, and with them, all of Rio de Janeiro regardless of political views. During his presidency of São Paulo, it was Senator Nabuco "who for the first time," according to his son, "brought together in the palace *luzias* and *saquaremas* (the names of the opposing political factions). Never before had the official world seen such heterogeneous company." The influence of Dona Anna dominated these gatherings, as indeed it did everything pertaining to the happy private life of the home. The same liberal, generous spirit demonstrated in São Paulo was evidenced in the gatherings in Rio. Only in the Nabuco home did all the members of parliament, including those of both parties and even the republicans, meet socially. Dona Anna was happy, elegant, and completely at ease. She hated formality and loved to receive. So the hospitality of her house on Princeza Street (now Corrêa Dutra) at the corner of Praia do Flamengo was famous for many years. While her daughters were young, it was a rare evening that passed without dancing. On Thursdays the receptions took on a more solemn aspect and were preceded by dinner. During the season of the lyric theater, the artists of the company performed at the Nabuco home, in some cases making their first appearance in Rio there. Later, the places of honor on the program were reserved for the daughters, and particularly for the voice of the youngest, which was said by contemporaries to be without equal. The weekly receptions were alternated with those of her friend, the Marchioness of Abrantes, and were frequented by the same people. Members of various diplomatic corps, in fact, any foreigners of importance who happened to be in Rio, were brought to these parties. Dona Anna spoke to them in Portuguese, the only language she knew, as naturally as if they understood her words as well as her obviously benevolent intentions.

Her constant eagerness to please her guests and the enchanting art of her hospitality, which were hers by birthright and by nature, were not sufficient to guarantee her toleration of those who might violate the tacit and generous precepts of that same northern hospitality. One Thursday night, while still at the dinner table, she reprimanded a guest who had gone too far in his references to a friend of the family, and she demanded that he retract his offensive statements. "She showed that she was from Pernambuco," exclaimed with enthusiasm that "lion of lions," her cousin, Sebastião de Rego Barros.

But it was not his mother who presided over the infancy of Joaquim

Nabuco and of whom he wrote: "Thanks to her the world received me with so sweet a smile that all the tears imaginable could not make me forget it." That task was reserved for his godmother, Dona Anna Rosa Falcão de Carvalho.

Joaquim Aurelio Barreto Nabuco de Araujo, fourth child of José Thomaz Nabuco de Araujo, was born in Recife, No. 39 Aterro de Boa Vista, at 8:30 on the morning of August 19, 1849. His mother asked, as she had with the older children, that he be given the name of the proper saint as indicated by the calendar. It was the third Sunday of August, the day set by the church to honor Saint Joaquim, who thus became his patron. On December 8, he was baptized by the local vicar in the chapel of the Massangana sugar plantation, which was the estate of his godparents, Joaquim Aurelio de Carvalho and Dona Anna Rosa de Carvalho.

That same day his father left for the capital to take his seat in the Chamber. The family accompanied him, except the baby, who, either because of his parents' fears of the effects of the journey or because of the desires of his godparents, remained with the latter in Massangana. Not until three years later did his parents come back to Recife, where the child was returned to them.

"We are sending your child as you request," wrote the godfather at that time. "I am sure he will arrive safely. He is very lively and mischievous. He is accompanied by a little servant named Marcos, whom we presented to him because he liked him."

However, the godmother was unhappy over this apparently definitive parting, and over the thought that the child also would suffer from the separation. She sent a messenger to find out "about how our little son has got along; for I have been very uneasy . . . . He was so small to have such a shock . . . . Forgive me for blaming you for the indisposition my son has suffered . . . . It will be well for him to come here for a change of climate; with the understanding that I will send him back (if I still live) whenever you wish."

Her ward returned to soften the loneliness of her widowhood, this time to remain until her death in 1857. "If it were not for the kindness of my son," wrote the adopted mother to the real mother, "I would be even worse, for he is so attached to me that he cannot bear to see me ill . . . . He enjoys his school work greatly and has progressed rapidly. The teacher is from Recife. I give him 400 milreis a year and breakfast, dinner, and supper."

Joaquim's foster mother lived only for him and was unable to deny his whims. "It is a work of mercy to punish those who err," said the kind lady when her sensitive ward would intercede for some slave who had exhausted her patience, "but the boy won't let me!"

She carefully saved gold doubloons for him, forming a small hoard which she kept secret from everyone. She built a schoolhouse for him, where he and the little slave childen were taught by the teacher she had brought from Recife.

Nabuco never forgot that school, nor the small plantation chapel dedicated to St. Matthew where he went to Mass, nor many other memories of his princelike childhood: swimming in the river Ipojuca; the oil painting for which he posed wearing the set of diamond buttons his mother had given him; the manger which they set up at Christmastime in the church; singing around the manger carpeted with cinnamon leaves, and the Negroes. But above all, he never forgot the desperate appeal of the strange slave who, fleeing from a cruel master, came one day to throw himself at his feet, begging to serve him. In this incident, which ended in the purchase of the runaway slave in Joaquim's name, as a gift from his godmother, there appeared to Nabuco in a most impressive way the tragic side, previously unknown to him, of the institution of slavery which had surrounded his infancy with devotion.

Massangana! "That background of my early life has never faded from my sight," wrote Nabuco in *My Formative Years*, as he recalled the patriarchal life of the little plantation and the gentle figure of his godmother. Those pages of reminiscences, pregnant with all the poetry of the old-time *fazendas* (plantations) and of the institution which he was destined to combat, are among the most enchanting he wrote; he preferred them above all others.

One night—he was not yet eight years old—he awoke to hear sounds of sobbing and praying. In the gallery, the Negroes were giving vent to their grief, and a forsaken feeling invaded him as well. His old godmother was dying, and for him as well as for the slaves a chapter of life was ending; uncertainty veiled the future.

Joaquim's parents sent a friend of the family to get him. It was through this emissary that little Joaquim, full of curiosity about his family, whom he did not know, sought to measure and calculate the benevolence of his brothers and parents toward him. The night of his godmother's death began an interminable cavalcade of new experiences. Recife gave him his first impression of a large city; then Bahia and Maceió. Everywhere, friends and partisans of his father showed their kindness and interest in him. Finally he reached the house where he was to meet his family.

In some unpublished notes he says:

My parents lived then in a large three-story house set back in a garden all decorated with china animals. It had the effect of a palace on me. I do not recall having felt any emotion at meeting them; I only remember being examined, observed, analyzed like some curiosity. The house was a meeting place for senators and depu-

and above all, politics; editorial staffs and literary and political societies attracted them in groups. Nabuco, with his qualities of leadership and his other attributes which attracted widespread admiration, was, from the first, one of the leaders in the full and happy life of the students.

His friend and classmate in São Paulo and in Recife, Sancho do Barros Pimentel, recalled in a letter something of those days, saying of Nabuco:

> . . . . from his first years in law school he demonstrated a natural talent for public life and for politics. He was destined to be a man of action, to live in a society that would applaud and exalt him. At that time there was a great deal of interest in current public affairs, and there were Liberals and Conservatives in the law school. In his first year, Joaquim Nabuco appeared in print and on the platform of the academic associations as the leader of the Liberals. He founded two papers, *Tribuna Liberal* and *A Independencia*, both political. The initiative behind the banquet offered for José Bonifácio after the sixteenth of July was all his; it was he who gathered together in the salon of the Concordia not only the Liberals from the law school, but also the great figures of the party in São Paulo:

These were the activities that filled Nabuco's life. As a student he was not unusually assiduous, but besides his work with the law school Liberal party and with newspapers, he wrote a pamphlet in defense of political crimes, using Charlotte Corday as his principal example, and he contributed to *Ipiranga*, which was not an academic sheet like the others, but the principal daily of the city. It was published by Salvador de Mendonça and Ferreira de Menezes. The latter, although no longer a student, continued to be one of their leaders.

Joaquim Nabuco spoke for his class in São Paulo at the celebration of the victory of Humaytá. From time to time he would defend a case before a jury in order to gain experience in speaking. A newspaper clipping with no name or date, but which he kept, notes with a certain relish one of those occasions: "Today the galleries came to life: . . . . Mr. Nabuco was going to speak for the defense . . . . and the people of the capital are already acquainted with his rhetoric since the occasion of our Humaytá celebration. The son of a fish swims without being taught."

He was called to preside over the Ateneo Paulistaro, the old student association, in whose directorate there was that year, by a curious coincidence to which time would lend irony, Ruy Barbosa as second orator. The first orator was named Moreira. Ruy Barbosa, unlike Nabuco, had taken his first two years in Recife and probably had not had time to become well known. At the end of the year, when Nabuco left for Recife, Ruy Barbosa became president and Castro Alves became the class orator.

Castro Alves was more than simply a student leader. He likewise had come to São Paulo for his third year, after already having tasted the glory that surrounds great poets. He represented all that the romantic public dreamed of in a poet: talent, youth, handsomeness, passion, melancholy. "He had no desire to be anything else in the world than a poet. To love and to sing—that was the ideal of his youth, the ideal with which he died," wrote Joaquim Nabuco in his first article about Castro Alves. "We saw each other daily for nearly a year and I never knew him to give a moment's attention to the realities of life, nor to the ambitions of youth." (*A Reforma*, April 20, 1873.)

Even his premature death, which prevented his talent from reaching its full perfection, only served to complete the aureole of romanticism that surrounded his existence. Well might Castro Alves believe that he had realized his one dream, "to be a glorious poet, and nothing else" (as Nabuco expressed it), when he, handsome youth that he was, recited in a warm baritone voice his own poems to an audience that acclaimed him, convinced beforehand of the immortality of what it was about to hear.

Nabuco went on to say:

> Whoever saw Castro Alves in one of those moments when he was intoxicated with applause, dressed in black to give his face a hint of sadness, with his brow contracted as if his thoughts oppressed him, with his eyes, so deep and luminous, fixed on a point in space, his lips lightly contracted with disdain or parted in a triumphal smile, would recognize immediately the man that he was: an intelligence open to noble ideas, a wounded heart that sought forgetfulness in the giddy whirl of glory.

Barros Pimentel said in the letter previously mentioned, "I never saw an audience carried into such ecstasy as it was in the São José Theater when Castro Alves recited one of his poems. J. Nabuco was always one of those who applauded most enthusiastically."

Years later, in September 1884, while speaking in that same theater on behalf of the slaves, Nabuco said: "I cannot help but see about me not today's audience, but the generation of my time, among which I seem to see the figure of the greatest of us all, the poet of the slaves, the echo of whose eloquent strophes still rings in this hall."

The third-year class of 1868 was probably the most notable that any school in Brazil can boast. Besides Nabuco, Castro Alves, and Ruy Barbosa, there were two future presidents of the Republic, Rodrigues Alves and Afonso Penna.

But in purely social gatherings, the center of which was the Concordia Paulistana, where the young people of São Paulo society went to dance with the students, it was Arthur de Carvalho Moreira, a "dandy" and an admirable waltzer, who triumphed over the intellectual leaders and the future notables of his class. He was the son of the Baron of Penedo, the outstanding figure in Brazilian diplomacy, and he enjoyed over his fellow pupils the advantage of his education in the capitals of Europe. He was one of Nabuco's closest friends and one of the finest spirits in the group.

José Bonifácio (the younger) was a professor in the school and exercised over these brilliant young men the prestige of his family traditions and of his own splendid talent. Poet, orator, statesman, exponent of every progressive idea, perpetually young in spirit, he could not help but inspire a special admiration in such pupils. The enthusiasm of the Liberals—and all the group were ardently Liberal—reached its climax with the famous movement of July 17, 1868. When José Bonifácio returned to São Paulo after the coup d'état, he was received as a hero. Castro Alves greeted him on his arrival, as did Nabuco, who embraced him in the name of the people. For the party's great banquet, Ruy Barbosa made his first political speech, which was to be so gloriously celebrated in the jubilee of 1918. Afonso Penna, Castro Alves, and Barros Pimentel also spoke. Nabuco, the first speaker, displayed the characteristic cadence of his oratory with this opening phrase: "In the name of youth, for they are not young who have not in their breasts the fever of liberal ideas, I come to salute a man who is an idea, a date that is worth a whole history, a party that is a people: Councilor José Bonifácio, the 17th of July, the Liberal party."

A spontaneous and appropriate comment made by Ferreira de Menezes at that banquet emphasized the fact that the young men truly idolized José Bonifácio. Bonifácio was saying in the course of his speech: "The present and the past belong to today's combatants; the future belongs to youth. Youth is the sun that is rising, the butterflies seeking the light ('You are the light,' commented Ferreira de Menezes), the swallows in search of Spring."

Another event of great importance in 1868 for the academic world was the first presentation of *Gonzaga*, Castro Alves' drama. Nabuco also made his debut that year as a dramatic writer, with *Fate* (*Os Destinos*), a tragedy, of which not a word remains. Intolerant of his early works, he purposely let it disappear. The critics, however, have traced its plot, and noted that it was clearly a melodrama.

The first performance of Nabuco's drama was on April 2, by the actors Furtado Coelho and Ismenia. "Mr. Nabuco was called to the stage more than once and applauded loudly," said the *Correio Paulistano*. Salvador de Mendonça wrote a eulogistic article in the *Ipiranga* the night of the farewell performance of the company in São Paulo. They opened with the play on April 12 in the Gymnasium Theater in Rio, where the Emperor saw it one night.

Nabuco's return to Recife in 1869 for his fourth year of studies had a decisive influence on his future. He was going to find his destiny as had his first Brazilian ancestor when he disembarked three hundred years before. Without this visit, the land of his ancestors and of his birth would have been nothing in his life but the enchanted picture of his first memories. He probably would never have represented Pernambuco in parliament; nor would that indissoluble bond have existed that made him say on one occasion: "If, by one of those terrible fatalities that I would give the last drop of my blood to prevent, that magnificent territory were broken in two, or in pieces, I would no sooner think of not being a Pernambucan than I would today think of not being a Brazilian."

He later came to consider this change of schools as one of the principal acts of his life, one of those occurrences which divide it neatly into periods of ten years and give a curious importance to those years ending in nine.

Recife had given him his first impression of a great city. He recalled that when at the age of eight he left the sugar plantation where he was raised, he went through Recife, "an unforgettable city, especially for one who saw it by moonlight, white as a cemetery, with its bridges, its towers, and the masts of its ships crowded against each other and anchored inside the city in the water of the rivers that cross it." He retained from that childhood night not only the memory of those ships, "resting in the city itself, but also a convent with great stairways and long corridors lined with tiles, which represented the life of St. Francis of Assisi." In other notes he added that Recife, "like Venice, is a city that rises out of the water and is reflected in it, a city that feels in its most hidden corners the beat of the ocean," that ocean which is seen "breaking before it in a sheet of foam, and which for centuries to come will kneel before the fragile grace of the coconut palms."

When Joaquim Nabuco returned to Recife at the age of nineteen, he still retained the appearance of adolescence, in spite of his unusual height. A soft down above his full lips foretold the mustache that was never to be shaven, and which the style of his day considered handsome. His strong, straight nose and firm jaw were admirably formed. He wore his hair thrown back in long waves which left the noble forehead free. His large brown eyes, which reflected his intelligence, added to the classic beauty of his features the human beauty of his expression. Nature was lavish with her gifts to him.

"I was most flattered to hear that you had been widely entertained there," wrote his father on May 16. And indeed, the young scholar was warmly received as the grandson of the owners of the Cabo estate returning to the land. He was more or less related to all the old families of Pernambuco, always closely joined among themselves by an infinity of marriages; and the Cavalcanti, the Paes Barreto, the Sá e Albuquerque, all his mother's people, showed a real interest in him, which he soon put to the test when he became gravely ill.

Typhoid fever spared his life, but it did cause him to lose that year at the Recife law school. "Your petition," wrote his father in the first letter which showed any reassurance about his son's health, "arrived here and is being processed in the Chamber of Deputies; but the decision will not be reached soon. . . . . It would be well for you to put forth every effort to fulfill the requirements and make the proper arrangements with the beadles." However, he had too many absences to be admitted to the examination, and the only recourse was the petition already mentioned. In it he had asked special authorization by law to take an examination on the subject matter of the fourth year, during the vacation period in São Paulo. Thanks to the special dispensation granted to him, he began the fifth year in Recife without being held back.

He found that the academic life of his native city was not as brilliant as that of São Paulo. Concerning the professors, whom he compared perhaps with José Bonifácio, he wrote these intolerant words in an article: "With some most honorable exceptions, youth belongs to the party of freedom, they [the professors], to that of power; youth thirsts for knowledge and eloquence, but they are wells of stagnant water from the Middle Ages, and like wells, they have an echo, but no voice" (*A Reforma*, November 15, 1871).

As in São Paulo, he attended political meetings and presided over a literary society which was magnificently installed in one of the finest buildings of Pernambuco. The solemn sessions of the Arcadia were social events: the officers wore dress coats and the ladies contributed the splendor of their presence.

During that time, reading was the great influence in his life. His developing mind avidly absorbed an immense variety of works, but in the album in which he transcribed the passages that interested and impressed him most, the predominant topic was slavery. It also inspired his first book, written during his studies in Recife. The only copy of this work, the original manuscript, is in the Instituto Histórico e Geográphico Brasileiro. That book, entitled *Slavery*, was never published, but it would do credit to a spirit even more mature than was his at that time. It vibrated with hatred and contempt for that institution, which he blamed exclusively for Brazil's backwardness, the institution which "slows down the advance of civilization, the knowledge of the arts, sciences, letters, of customs, of governments, of peoples; in short, of progress."

Only two parts of the three enumerated in the Index, "The Crime," and "The History of the Crime," appear in the manuscript. But even though incomplete, it is not a small work. It consists of 230 pages written in a small hand.

"History, in its simplicity, just as it refers to the sacred writings as 'The Book,' may refer to slavery as 'The Crime'," writes the author at the end of the first part. "We do not want it to be said that slavery is considered to have a moral basis among us; it does not. The present generation is not conscious of its position in relation to the slaves; if it were, it would not accept the situation." The author depicts his subject in the first part, which consists principally of descriptions. The pictures of slave quarters are easy to portray in vivid colors and to charge with emotion, but it is in the second part that the author distinguishes himself most. There, patiently and surely, always quoting authorities, he runs through the whole "History of the Crime," from its emergence in the infancy of mankind down to the modern traffic and its abolition, with all that had been done up to then in Brazil.

The third part, "The Reparation of the Crime," has been lost, or perhaps was never written, but Nabuco had definite ideas upon the subject. A letter to his father, written from Recife that same year, shows the radical means which the author advocated to remedy the matter:

My dear Father,

I am writing to tell you that I am enjoying good health, am studying hard, and getting along all right, except for my habitual "spleen."

The "Program" was received here and provoked general enthusiasm, as did also your letter about emancipation.

There is a unique glory that I dream of for you in this country. I want your name to be found under the decree which does away with slavery. If you should be called to the prime ministry, accept it for two days so that you may *dictatorially* extinguish the practice. . . .

. . . .

I dream of no other glory for you than that of Abraham Lincoln! ! ! It will be the greatest day of my life when your name is affixed to another proclamation of January 2 [*sic*].

Please give me your blessing and ask my mother to give me hers as well.

Your obedient son,

Joaquim

In Recife he did not find as much sympathy for his antislavery views as in São Paulo. Among his colleagues there was no one like Castro Alves, who electrified his companions with the reading of "O Navio Negreiro" ("The Slave Ship"). "The unrelenting hostility that he felt toward slavery," said Nabuco in São Paulo, "dominated all those about him in law school."

In Pernambuco, essentially a conservative capital, the atmosphere was different. The sugar aristocracy, to which he belonged, had very positive ideas concerning the need for slavery. All the wealth of the province and of its residents was based upon slavery and sugar cane. Nabuco lived in an environment where each person tried to be a more staunch defender of slavery than his neighbor, because conviction joined with self-interest, and the two united were unbeatable.

Braving the opinions of his time and place, Nabuco appeared before the law court of Recife to defend a slave accused of murder and to fight "hand to hand against slavery and the death penalty," as he said in the book he was preparing to write. Among the cases with which he illustrated and attacked "the Crime" in his unpublished work, he did not forget this rebel Negro whose deeds had just aroused the city. Those who had tortured him were declared guilty.

Thomas, the slave, got revenge for having been beaten in the public square by deliberately shooting at close range the officer responsible for his humiliation. Later he succeeded in escaping from prison, and, surrounded by police in the center of Recife, he defended his freedom for more than twenty-four hours, hiding in houses and on roofs, frightening the inhabitants, eating garbage, firing upon anyone who came near. The city was sleepless until the news of his capture came. "He was no longer a man but a tiger," admitted his own lawyer. The black man, terrible because of his physical strength and his savage violence, was imprisoned with great difficulty. He had already killed a guard at the time of his escape.

The court of Olinda had condemned him to death before this second escapade. However, the judge at Recife had granted an appeal, and it was with the added burden of guilt in the killing of the guard upon him that Nabuco came to defend him.

His crime was one of those that are judged beforehand. The death penalty, which still existed in Brazil, was for just such criminals. The Emperor, accustomed to commuting the sentence to life imprisonment, abstained in such cases. Royal clemency never dared to manifest itself in favor of a slave, murderer of an overseer or an owner. The landowning class demanded a "horrible example."

The planters, mostly motivated by their friendship for the young lawyer, were well represented in the audience the day that Thomas was tried. The news that Nabuco was to defend the notorious criminal did not cause him to lose popularity, and his name increased the interest and curiosity concerning the trial. It seemed incredible that anyone should appear to represent such an unsavory defendant. By doing so, Nabuco created a local scandal, which later turned into his first oratorical triumph. His own account of the case, in the book *Slavery* (*A Escravidão*), makes it possible to reconstruct the tenor of the discourse, which from the start aroused the enthusiasm of the listeners. According to the book, Nabuco began by pointing out that Thomas had been a model slave, circumspect, humble, frugal, and conscientious. Educated as a freeman, and considering himself to be one, he also possessed spirit, a quality to which slaves have no right. Respected in his position up to that time, even referred to as "seu Thomaz" ("Mr. Thomas"), he could not resign himself to being punished in the public square before a crowd of curious idlers. From that day on he was a wild beast. "In the beginning of this trial," wrote Nabuco in the book *Slavery*—and he must have said it to the court, "there were two social crimes. There was slavery and there was the death penalty. Slavery drove Thomas to commit the first crime, and the death penalty drove him to perpetrate the second." For the second offense the brilliant and passionate lawyer found ample excuses: "Obliged by natural law to preserve a life that did not belong to society but to God, he tried to escape when they came again to take him to the gallows. Then occurred his second crime. Either through overwhelming fear or a fierce desire for vengeance, he annihilated the man who seized him in order to subject him to the penalty of the law, just as he was about to begin to enjoy his freedom through flight." Before the jury Nabuco exclaimed: "He committed no crime; he removed an obstacle!" As he spoke those words of such dubious worth and ethics, the courtroom vibrated with enthusiasm, ample proof that he possessed even then the principal gift of the orator, the magic and impalpable power to sway the masses, not so much by the words spoken as by the force and seductiveness of his whole personality.

Sancho de Barros Pimentel, the witness responsible for the information about the statement and its effect, was then a colleague and roommate of Nabuco's. He pointed out in an article some of the characteristic traits of Nabuco's oratory: his truly remarkable ability to speak extemporaneously; his height, which served as a platform, in the absence of any other; "his clear and slightly metallic voice, which was heard without any apparent effort in the far corners of the galleries; his graceful bearing; his expressive and restrained gestures. But it was in his face that all the vigor of the orator was concentrated, and even more than the words themselves, that face expressed the emotions that possessed his soul by the gleam of an eye, by the movement of the lips, in the color that tinged his cheeks."

The culprit was condemned to the galleys for life. It was the best that could be hoped for, and Nabuco's speech was soon added to the long list of deeds that pass into tradition.

From his student days in Recife, the memory of still another oratorical success survives. This one was purely political and took place in July 1869 in the Liberal Club of Recife. At that time the party was laboring under the handicap of ostracism. The Conservatives, under Itaborahy, were in power and were strongly entrenched. In Pernambuco, the Liberals had split into two apparently irreconcilable groups. The meeting in the club was to elect the central committee for the province. Nabuco came late, purely as an observer, and found an important gathering. The discussion had already lasted for hours with no apparent effect upon the dissident radicals. They refused to proceed to the organization of the committee because they disagreed completely with the program of the majority. Those who were present became discouraged and began to leave. Suddenly a slender student leaped upon a bench and cried out: "*Quo vadis?*" It was Nabuco, who, uninvited, was making himself heard. He lacked neither enthusiasm nor suggestions. The meeting went on, and, after his speech was heard, the party was finally consolidated.

The next day the Baron of Villa Bella, one of the local party leaders, wrote a letter to his friend, Senator Nabuco, telling of his son's success. "I supposed him to be a young man of notable talents, but I did not know he was possessed of such eminent oratorical gifts. He dominated the audience, which warmly applauded him, and he made the radicals be silent." And Senator Nabuco, well informed from many sources, communicated his pleasure to Joaquim with emotion: "Dear son of my heart, accept my congratulations for the brilliant things you have done, which have brought you a great reputation and renown. You are my pride; you are the future of your family and the hope of your country."

CHAPTER III. EARLY ESSAYS. FIRST VOYAGE. 1871–75

Joaquim Nabuco received the degree of Bachelor of Arts in social and juridical sciences on November 28, 1870. He wanted to remain in Recife after graduation. His family, however, urged him to come to Rio and he agreed with reservations. "It is not beyond reason that I might come and establish myself in Recife at some future time," he wrote in 1870.

He was now concerned with choosing a career. Politics was undoubtedly his true calling, and it had always caught his imagination and his ambition. Nothing interested him so much as great social and national problems and the books which discussed them. Among foreign nations, England, the political nation *par excellence*, held a special fascination for him, because of its traditions, its parliament, and its political writers.

Furthermore, he had always lived in the atmosphere of state affairs, seeing Senator Nabuco, whose influence upon him it is impossible to exaggerate, completely devoted to political tasks. The Senator's principal preoccupation, at the time of Joaquim's return home with his Bachelor's parchment, was the future of the proposed emancipation law. On September 25, 1871, the son proudy attended the senate session in which Senator Nabuco made his most important speech.

But a political career was not a thing to be taken by storm at the age of twenty-one. If the Liberals had been in power, and if his father had not considered his entrance into politics a bit premature, Joaquim might have been able to secure a place in the House at once, rather than later. But in 1871, the most simple and logical solution for the new attorney was to enter his father's office. The great lawyer had one of the most frequented offices in Rio, but he was unable to hold his son there. Joaquim Nabuco's venture into the profession for which he had studied was brief and ended in the denunciation of a client.

One of the first cases given to him, and one in which he had become quite interested, was already before the judge when Nabuco learned something which changed the whole aspect of the case. His client had hidden from him the fact that there had been a legal heir to the legacy he was claiming. It was a child, who had lived only a few minutes but whose rights had passed to its mother. The young lawyer, paying no attention to those who were present, accused his client of deceiving him and said that the claim was unjust. The next step was to tell his father that a law career was not for him. For a time he tried journalism and literature.

The first newspaper to give him a place on its staff was *A Reforma*, the principal Liberal organ. He began writing philosophical articles, dealing with the existence of God and the soul, and demonstrating an ardent aversion to materialism. He had lost the faith of his childhood, but he retained all the foundations upon which to rebuild it later. He could hardly admit the hypothesis that the *ego*, which he considered immortal, had no life independent of the body, which he considered its mere instrument.

From metaphysics he passed to politics. He declared with characteristic frankness that he was not a republican. He considered the parliamentary monarchy, as practiced in England, to be the ideal form of government. On this point he entered into a controversy with the contemporary sheet *A República.*

Nabuco's antirepublican convictions did not prevent his criticizing the Emperor. On the contrary he wrote: "Having frankly accepted the monarchial form of government, we have the right to address the Crown without any misgivings." Confident in the rigid idealism of his twenty-odd years, he poured out counsel to the wise sovereign, whose reign, he unjustly said, history would call sterile. He wanted Dom Pedro to visit the United States, so that the king might come to know the privileges of a United States citizen, and in order to learn that "a country cannot be great with slavery." Enlightened by such a voyage, his mediating power, "which he had used only to destroy worn-out parties, and to wear out strong parties, if it were applied in the light and not the shadow of the constitution, with courage, not artifices, would bring about the emancipation of the slaves."

These articles had certain repercussions. From Bahia, Leão Velloso wrote to Senator Nabuco: "The *Diário da Bahia* today began printing our Quinquim's[1] excellent articles in his polemic with *A República*. . . . . Congratulate him for me on his brilliant, very brilliant work; that is how political positions are legitimately won." And later he said concerning the articles of the young writer in his debate on religious matters with certain bishops: "Quinquim had prepared us for his stand on the religious question; we are eager to have him as our spokesman; I hope he speaks as well as he wrote; I have never read anything better on the subject."

Later, Joaquim Nabuco gathered in a phamphlet his editorials from *A Reforma.* On all points of divergence between the State and the Church, he opposed the latter. His liberalism always defended the idea of absolute separation of the two powers, in the interest of Catholicism itself, which he felt should be "instead of the official church, the national religion of the country." He wanted to abolish from the constitution the articles referring to the taking of a religious oath by government employees, those

[1]In spite of Nabuco's repugnance for the infantile diminutives of his name, and of his constant protests, he had difficulty in curing his friends of the habit. In a circle much wider than that of his personal relations, the nickname of "Quincas o bello" ("Handsome Jack") stayed with him throughout his youth.

that prohibited the meeting places of other religions from having the exterior appearance of a church, those that prevented non-Catholics from belonging to parliament, and those that prohibited them from even using cemeteries. His obvious prejudice, although completely liberal, robs these writings of much of their force.

Several times he dealt with matters in Pernambuco, which he followed closely, and he severely criticized the president of the province. He became a literary and drama critic for the same newspaper, *A Reforma*. He devoted several studies to Castro Alves, and, although he showed in these a real admiration for the poet, he typified the youthful critic in search of unattainable perfection. In all these articles in *A Reforma*, the future "littérateur" is scarcely discernible.

It is evident that Nabuco was feeling his way, experimenting with his style and talent, learning by successes and failures to think freely, and during the two years with *A Reforma* his progress and his increasing assurance were noticeable. His youthful defects gradually disappeared. He learned to distinguish in his thinking between the new and original and what he had assimilated from his reading. The boldness that led him without reflection to oppose his personal impressions to generally accepted opinions was modified. But these faults had one quality sufficient to redeem them entirely—a vibrant sincerity.

Nabuco was not satisfied with journalism, and in 1872 he published his first book, *Camoens and the Lusiads*. The fascination which the great poet of Portugal held for him became a profound and permanent influence in his life. Nabuco frequently referred to him in his writings, and was chosen in 1880 to eulogize him in the observance of Camoens' third centenary in Rio. He wrote several still-unpublished sonnets to the poet, and in his later years he often lectured on Camoens before American university audiences.

In 1908, in one of those lectures in the United States, at Yale University, he declared that he was content to end his life as a rhapsodist of Camoens. "As soon as I read the *Lusiads* for the first time, I wrote a book to describe my amazement." In another lecture which he was preparing for Harvard University, but which death prevented him from delivering, he referred again to that book of his youth, quoting a phrase from a French critic: "Time has little respect for things done without it." Then he added, "The little book I wrote was done without time."

In the Preface to *Camoens and the Lusiads*, written with modesty, enthusiasm, and an independence as complete as it was ingenuous, the young author confessed: "Like a diver at the bottom of the ocean who does not need to read what has been written about it in order to be dazzled by the riches he sees, and by the new experiences, I decided that I did not need the help of anyone else to sense and understand the innumerable beauties of Camoens' poem." Under the circumstances the book could have no new documentation to offer to the learned. With respect to obscure points in the life of Camoens, the best the author could do was to explain his reasons for believing that certain familiar data were more probably true than others. However, in the analysis and discussion of the poem he found a broader field of movement than in the biographical portion. His personal judgment in *Camoens and the Lusiads* shows the same youthful courage as the articles in *A Reforma*, and, when he is wrong as well as when he is right, he always avoids mediocrity. That master of criticism, José Veríssimo, studied with rare pleasure the writings of Nabuco and was able to discern in this early work "with the indelible mark of the man who wrote it, many a sure and original view of our literature. More than one concept current in our national criticism might well be claimed by him." (*Jornal do Comércio*, April 7, 1910.)

The critics received the new book with such benevolence that one of his close friends wrote him: "What an ovation the press in Rio and in the provinces gave you! To enter by this means the ranks of men recognized by their country is doubly preferable to doing it by means of two or three eloquent discourses. *Scripta manent.* Your success almost consoles me for your not having entered parliament."

Even in a purely literary work such as the one mentioned, there are passages which show his obsession with the idea of liberty. In an unnecessary expansion of his own ideas he says: "The words that follow are painful to us. How could a poet as correct as Camoens call slavery happiness and salute Naples for becoming

> illustrious after so many years
> through the lordship of the noble Spanish?"

In the beginning of the book, while describing in a few lines the Brazil he knew as a youth, Nabuco had already said: "Several attempts, some of considerable worth, have been made among us with the intent to give us our own literature, but as yet it does not exist. . . . . The portrayers of our society have been as unsuccessful as those who have tried to portray our jungle life. In Brazil at present there is absolutely no originality in the arts, in construction, in customs, or in life. There are two things, however, that make Brazil seem new and different: the first, may it be said in our honor, is nature; the second, be it said to our shame, is slavery."

In the same year that he published *Camoens and the Lusiads*, he also wrote in French the brief *The Right to Murder*. It also condemns slavery: "Slavery, ignominious legacy from the past, a cancer which gnaws at the country's vitals and poisons its blood, only makes us appreciate more the worth of justice and feedom!" This small book was written in French, because it was intended to be a reply to the younger Dumas, who had published *L'Homme-femme*, sustaining the right of a husband to kill his unfaithful wife. His passionate cry, "Kill her!" had created a literary scandal and aroused other voices.

Intellectual Brazil had avidly read Dumas' book. Joaquim Nabuco, moved by it and by the imperious necessity of expressing his own opinions, wrote his ardent defense of woman. He did not address his essay to Dumas. He preferred to give it the form of a letter to Ernest Renan, his idol of the moment, for whom he professed an unlimited admiration. He wrote: "M. Alexandre Dumas fils has pronounced a decree against women; I appeal to you and your colleagues, who have no right to remain silent."

"A friend," wrote Nabuco in *My Formative Years*, "delivered with my compliments a copy of the brochure to the great writer, whom I almost considered a divine master. Now I am aware, literarily speaking, of the weak points of the Renanian manner; at that time I was the most completely hypnotized of our Renanists. My emissary was Arthur de Carvalho Moreira, of whom I have already spoken, and the letter he wrote me telling of his mission might have been signed by Chamfort. According to Renan, *L'Homme-femme* was nothing but a weak paradoxical work which was not worth refuting; a joke, not to be taken seriously."

In that same year (1872) Joaquim Nabuco went to Pernambuco to take possession of the property which came to him when he reached his majority. His godmother had dreamed of leaving him a more substantial fortune than he actually received, but she could not leave Massangana to him, since it was by right the inheritance of a near relative. She left him an estate without slaves. During her life she had tried to make up the difference by accumulating gold coins, saved from her household expenses. She called it her "invisible fund" in her letters to his parents. Her old and trusted servant, a free Negro named Elias, the only one besides herself who knew of the secret treasure, died before she did, and the money was never found. Years later, by mere chance, Nabuco received a confirmation of this touching solicitude for his future. While in London he was called to serve as a witness to a will, and he described the incident in these words:

> Upon reading my name, the sick man, Father António da Cunha Figueiredo, turned toward me and said: "It is very strange our meeting this way for the first time, after twenty years. It was I who drew up your godmother's will. She gave me a gold doubloon which I exchanged in Recife for 60 milreis. 'I have over a thousand of these,' she told me, 'for my godson to use for his studies and his marriage.' I advised her that she should mention such an important sum in her testament, but she answered that no one knew of it, and that she had a sure means of seeing that it reached your father in case of her death."

Of this mysterious gold Nabuco received nothing, although he was grateful. However, the land was real and its new owner promptly succeeded in selling it and used the proceeds to spend a year in Europe. He did not wish to consider his education finished without that trip, and in August 1873 he embarked for Bordeaux. Once on the Old Continent, he wanted to see everything, learn everything, and speak to everyone. He did not have time to travel through France, England, Italy, and Switzerland in the way he would have wished. Like a pilgrim, he went from museum to museum, from church to church, seeking out all the masterpieces of humanity. He made an excursion to Tours to see those gems of architecture, the castles of the Loire. In Paris he followed closely the trial and condemnation of Bazaine. In Rome he enjoyed new artistic emotions, the eternal vibration of Christianity, the pleasures of carnival, the palace balls, and the audience with Pius IX, whose extraordinarily kindly appearance seemed comparable only to that of Nabuco's father. He secured an introduction to the great names in politics and letters, whom his curiosity made him wish to observe. Renan, who already knew him through *The Right to Murder* and who enchanted him no less in conversation than he had by his writings, received him most amiably. He facilitated Nabuco's acquaintance with other notables, among them George Sand, who later wrote to the young Brazilian: "We thought that, since you came from so far away, you would amuse us, but in point of fact you charmed us. . . . . It is true that you will come back to us? Hurry up, for I am getting very old and you might not find me here when you return . . . . (it will not be for an hour next time, it will be for several days, won't it?). I don't know how you did it, but when you left—we all liked you."

During his trip he found time, in spite of so many occupations, to prepare a volume of verses in French, *Love and God*. It was long overdue, for the poetic phase was inevitable. It would be impossible to make a more precise, subtle, and artistic analysis of his poetic aptitudes than he himself made later, writing modestly in *My Formative Years*. With perfect good faith he expressed the judgment of his maturity upon that work of his youth. He said, "If what was in the pages of *Love and God* were new, I could certainly boast of my thinking; although even so, I would not be a poet. But it was not new." And again, "What deceived me in my verses, seeming sonorous and lofty, did not pertain to poetry: it pertained to eloquence." Unquestionably his small initial volume, although full of literary qualities, was not the revelation of a poet.

He returned to Brazil in September 1874, with his spirit enriched and his horizons broadened. At the request of the Emperor he lectured about what he had seen in Europe—about Michelangelo, Raphael, the great colorists of Venice; he called Titian "the painter of the magnificence of the flesh and the eloquence of matter." Nabuco's father attended the lectures, which were given in the Gloria School and published later in *O Globo*. "Of each of the pictures he saw," wrote Baron Homem de Mello, "he gave us his own judgment, bearing the mark of his individual feeling and always exhibiting the merit of originality . . . . Joaquim Nabuco did not make a debut; he obtained a triumph."

His interests at that time were more literary than political. In 1875, with Machado de Assis and two or three other friends, he founded a periodical which was worldly, light, and brilliant. It was *A Epoca*, and its few numbers reveal a consummate art. The paper was young and turbulent like its editors. It was devoted principally to society and letters and faced life without a care. Its program, the first number declared, was not to have a program; but it confessed one aspiration which it realized delightfully: "to present in a light manner a thoughtful opinion." It was written with finished literary taste. The elegant chronicles were a model of style and the verses and stories were on the same high level. Machado de Assis signed his work "Manassés"; Nabuco edited the political portion under the pseudonym of "No One" (Ninguém), maintaining the spirited and piquant tone the journal demanded. Adopting a farcical style, he criticized the careers and deeds of the ministers with the jocular and often cruel malice of an exuberant collegian. No name of editor or collaborator was given in the paper. Only much later did Machado de Assis betray the secret, when he included one of the stories from *A Epoca* in his book *Odd Papers* (*Papéis avulsos*), and wrote in a note: "The principal editor was an eminent spirit whom politics stole away from letters, Joaquim Nabuco. I can tell it now without indiscretion. There were few of us, but we were friends. Our program was to have no program, as the initial article stated, leaving each contributor with full freedom of opinion, for which he was exclusively responsible. The tone (speaking with the natural modesty of a collaborator) was elegant, Attic, and literary. The paper lasted for four numbers."

In 1875 Nabuco also wrote a number of articles for the Sunday edition of *O Globo*, the leading Brazilian daily at that time. According to José Veríssimo, these were much like those famous literary articles, the *lundis* of Saint-Beuve. Nabuco's articles dealt principally with literature and at times with society. They were immediately popular. José de Alencar, whose fame had by then reached its peak, added further to the interest the articles aroused by entering into a polemic with their author. Alencar's drama, *The Jesuit*, was published that year and was the motive for a whole series of articles by Nabuco dedicated to the works of Alencar. The literary supremacy of the great novelist seemed above discussion, but the young critic (to whom Alencar referred, with mixed humor and irritation, as "a cardboard Jupiter on Olympus, who wrinkles his brow and the earth trembles") dared to give an independent judgment of the great man. Alencar did him the honor of beginning a section called "On Thursdays" ("As quintas") in the same paper, in controversy with Nabuco's, called "On Sundays" ("Aos domingos").

From the very first, Nabuco irritated Alencar and criticized him irreverently. Nabuco wrote: "We do not recognize in the author of *Mother* (*Mãe*) a single quality of a playwright, and there is nothing more painful than to witness the downfall of a talented writer who insists on fighting against his calling."

José de Alencar did not need to answer him. Nabuco certainly had not sufficient authority to shake his reputation, and probably had no such purpose. But Alencar had no tolerance for the haughty though unconscious impertinence of Nabuco, who announced his intention of "studying the writer with the most perfect sincerity of which I am capable." Setting to work to refute one by one the criticisms of his young adversary, he succeeded only in giving them importance. Nabuco was following the worst method of criticism, scrutinizing everything, seeking tiny mistakes, some of which were typographical, as Alencar fully and uselessly demonstrated. The great man, for his own part, spoke of "certain favorite sons of fortune whose papa arranges the cradle of flowers where they emit their first literary wailings." He remarked on Nabuco's "Apollo-like appearance" in order to make fun of him by aiming cruel, sarcastic remarks about the futility of his handsomeness, his lack of merit, and his effeminate vanity.

It was a kind of criticism that was destined to pursue Nabuco all his life without ever affecting him. It was not possible to ridicule Nabuco's manly good looks, and his height of over six feet, but these attributes always attracted comment and served as the topic for much discussion. Because he was handsome and well groomed, his opponents assumed that he must naturally be vain. The nickname of "Narciso" arose spontaneously and was used for a number of years by his enemies, along with a swarm of absurd rumors in an attempt to belittle him. He was even accused of wearing bracelets and of using a curling iron on his hair!

These rumors were largely based on the excessive care which he devoted to his dress at one time. In Petrópolis and in Rio he got quite a reputation as a dandy, which was not pleasing to some of his friends, who preferred to see him distinguish himself entirely through his intellectual qualities. One day, one of these friends told Senator Nabuco that his son had appeared on the boulevards of Petrópolis, where the Emperor and his retinue were out riding, dressed in a plaid suit which was so "loud" that it would seem eccentric anywhere except in England, where it was in style. The elder Nabuco merely smiled, and predicted that the fad would pass, as his son's slouchiness during his school days had passed. And it did, but never to the point of his returning to his previous carelessness or of giving up his London tailors, and so his reputation persisted.

But Nabuco had no intention of filling his life with intellectual frivolities, worldly pleasures, or concessions to vanity. By 1875 he felt that he could no longer delay the choice of a career that would appeal to him more than his journalism or his amateur literary activities.

CHAPTER IV. DIPLOMATIC APPRENTICESHIP, 1876–78

Joaquim Nabuco dreamed of a life of political activity, but he was in no position to scorn a career of diplomacy to which circumstances led him. This life attracted him in many respects, while it offered him an agreeable future. He had no personal fortune. Senator Nabuco earned a great deal of money, but he spent it all on the upkeep of his large house with its tradition of hospitality. It was always at considerable financial sacrifice that he would temporarily leave his law practice to take an appointment as minister. His son could wait no longer for the seat in the House which would fulfill his dreams, but which depended upon the remote chance of a political change. The Conservatives were in power, and it was in the days of the single-party House. But he could accept a diplomatic mission, leaving his father to stay behind and watch out for his interests. So in 1876 he left for his first post, and soon afterward his father managed to have his name included in the third list of candidates which the Liberals organized in Pernambuco and pessimistically entered against the Conservatives. The elder Nabuco on that occasion wrote to one of the party leaders on behalf of his son, saying that Joaquim was an honor to his province and would be one of its glories in the future. The Liberal party had no success with its ticket, and it was not until two years later that the party of which his father was one of the leaders, came into power and Joaquim entered the Brazilian parliament.

His appointment as a legation attaché was dated April 26, 1876. He left at once, via Europe, to assume his post in the United States. Washington at that time was still a small city with little to offer as a place of residence. New York, on the other hand, was the heartbeat of the colossal American organism, which Nabuco never tired of observing and admiring. The extreme leniency of his chief, the Baron of Carvalho Borges, who himself lived principally in New York, gave him complete freedom in this respect and relieved him of any work. A friend of the two men, José Carlos Rodrigues, who at that time was managing a Brazilian newspaper in New York, remarked thirty years later: "At that time I met the then second secretary of the Brazilian Legation, of whom my late friend, Minister Borges, said to me that he would not have the temerity to give him dispatches to copy." "Rest assured," wrote the minister to Nabuco as soon as he heard of his arrival, "that you will find in me a colleague and chief who has received the best of recommendations about you and who will not be too demanding. When you come to Washington after residing in New York, it will give me great pleasure to know you personally and to furnish you with the information usually required by one who enters a new country and a new career." Another of the letters in Nabuco's files shows the unusually generous spirit of his former chief. After the young diplomat had left that career for politics and had revealed in his parliamentary debut such a brilliant talent that many fully expected to see him reach the highest positions in the land, the Baron of Carvalho wrote to him: "I have heard with great interest of the brilliant impressions you made in parliament, and I hoped that in the organization of the present cabinet you would be my superior in the Ministry of Foreign Affairs. The pleasure which that would give me would reflect the profound affection which you inspired in me through the goodness of your heart."

The President of the Council, Saraiva, explained to the House, soon after the date of the above letter, why he had not asked Nabuco to take part in his cabinet. It would have been strange to see a legation secretary suddenly promoted to the direction of the Ministry of Foreign Affairs. The pleasure with which his former superior had received the idea of such an exchange of roles was equally strange.

It was during the early days of his diplomatic career that Nabuco wrote most frequently in his diary, perhaps as a means of self-expression, living as he was among strangers. He published many pages of his diary in *My Formative Years.* These notebooks which he filled with observations of customs, political considerations, thoughts, conversations, and many things which reveal the manner of living and thinking of the American people, would furnish material for an interesting volume of criticism and analysis. *The Diary of a Diplomat* would be a title appropriate to the many light or skeptical sayings, which breathe the atmosphere of the diplomatic service. But alongside such witty remarks as: "To marry is to take root, and he who takes root vegetates, like any other tree," there are others of surprising vigor and profundity.

Joaquim Nabuco, who was all his life an indefatigable traveler, and one for whom no pleasure could equal that of seeing and learning new things, found in the United States a wealth of material for observation. He witnessed the debate in the House of Representatives over the vote in South Carolina. Dressed for the first time in his official uniform, he attended the reception at the White House on January 1, then made the official rounds of the homes of the cabinet members, which, like the President's, were open on that day. He followed closely the most exciting election in American history, the struggle between Hayes and Tilden, which ended with the Supreme Court decision giving the victory to Hayes by one vote. His live intellectual curiosity scrutinized profoundly the political organization of the great country in which everything was strange to him, from the material comforts which Europe did not even dream of to the characteristically hospitable society where a new type of woman was being formed, a type which he attempted to define in his diary. "It is curious," he wrote, "that the most perfect thing in this democracy is woman, who is more aristocratic here than anywhere in the world." He studied his subjects with fine psychology and sketched some with a romantic pen. Pretty Miss W., on whose perfect face "a smile is a luxury," represented American beauty, while Miss D. personified intelligence, and a third was kindness. Nabuco had a liking for society, a liking which was invariably reciprocated.

Nabuco's constant companion was Saldanha da Gama, the future martyr of the revolt of 1893, who at that time was in the United States on a naval mission. They both lived at the Hotel Buckingham on Fifth Avenue at Fiftieth Street, where under their windows the great cathedral of St. Patrick was being constructed. Nabuco, for whom writing was an absolute necessity, worked eagerly on his tragedy in French, *The Option.* Soon he was to leave it forgotten in his desk until thirty years later, when he again remembered it and began to polish its eloquent Alexandrines.

The war of 1870 gave him the action for this patriotic drama, vibrant with the emotion which he had suffered during the Franco-Prussian struggle. As a student in Pernambuco he was among those who always went to the docks on mail day to await the first news from Europe. "How grievous it was for us," says his letter to Renan, "to follow on the map of France the wave of the invasion!"

His diary for January 25, 1877, records the termination of *The Option*; in February it tells of a trip to Washington, D.C.; in August it describes his visit to the foot of Niagara Falls. Finally in October it tells of his departure for England.

After leaving Washington, he served in London, which seemed to him to be the ideal post. The minister was the Baron of Penedo, a diplomat of the old school, whose son, Arthur de Carvalho Moreira, at that time the secretary of the same legation, had been a close friend of Nabuco's since law school days. The Brazilian Legation in London, under the regime of Penedo, exercised a social prestige unequaled before or since. It was heightened by the magnificence of the standard of living which he maintained out of his personal fortune. He kept the same spectacular carriages, the same imposing staff of servants as was to be seen in the great English homes. His chef, Cortais, a true culinary artist, left him to go to the court of an important foreign country, but was soon considered too expensive to retain there.

Joaquim Nabuco attended some of the most brilliant parties given by the Baron of Penedo soon after his arrival and sent to *O Globo* some descriptive articles of the grand ball presided over by the most beautiful and elegant princess of Europe, accompanied by her husband, the Prince of Wales, and her brother, the King of Greece. Later he also described a banquet in honor of the Imperial Prince of France. These parties revealed to him a social system of which Brazil, with its democratic court and its simple patriarchal life, could give him no idea, outside of a few cases of great wealth. All the traditional trappings and feudal richness gave him new material to observe. At the same time, even in the midst of the splendid blond giants of the Horse Guards, Nabuco attracted wide attention as a handsome type of tall Latin. The guests always asked his name.

But the Penedo residence in Grosvenor Gardens was more than the center of a strange and interesting life to him. "In this foreign land," he wrote, "they are my family and my country, a little corner of Brazil." When he returned to London in 1900, after the house in Grosvenor Gardens had been closed, he noted in his diary that London "seemed an unknown city."

In all his later correspondence with the Baron of Penedo there is a note of nostalgia for those days with the legation, and even in the last months of his life he wrote from Washington to the widow of the Baron:

> I always recall with the same nostalgia our friendly relations in London, and your great hospitality, which no one in our diplomatic service has been able to match. We do what we can, but what a difference between our daily dinner with two or three secretaries or friends, and the daily banquet at Grosvenor Gardens! How Cortais would despise our table!

When he first saw London in 1874, he felt the "desire to live there always." But his stay this time was short. The year 1878 held two momentous occurrences for him: one public and happy, the rise of the Liberal party; the other private and extremely sad, the death of his father.

With the triumph of the party, Nabuco's candidacy in the forthcoming parliamentary elections was immediately arranged between his father, who was at that time alive, and his friend and relative, the Baron of Villa Bella, who was the principal Liberal leader of Pernambuco.

For a long time his friends had urged him to change his career. His intimates and his young contemporaries wrote him insistently, their letters full of unusual confidence in his future. In various letters he is urged to occupy "the position indicated by your character and talent," "the place which your name, your talents, your energy, and your youth reserve for you in the history of your country."

The rise of the Sinimbú ministry in January 1878 was to bring about the fulfillment of those desires, which were Nabuco's as well as his friends'. As soon as the new cabinet was announced, one of his fellow secretaries wrote him from his post in Rome: "The rise of the Liberals came about sooner than we supposed. I wanted so much to send you a telegram. . . . . You are now in a most favorable position. The foreign minister is on your side, the deputy job is just waiting for you; your father is powerful. With these elements and those you have in your own hands, the future, the very near future, appears in the most brilliant hues."

The Sinimbú ministry came to power in January of 1878. On March 19, José Thomaz Nabuco de Araujo died in Rio on the day of his patron saint. It is difficult to determine which was the strongest sentiment in the worshipful attitude which Nabuco had toward his father while he lived and toward his memory later: spontaneous affection, conscious admiration, a son's pride, or a disciple's veneration.

In *My Formative Years* he wrote:

> That influence, always present, no matter how far I was from it [*sic*], dominated and modified all others, which were invariably subordinate to it. . . . It was not exactly an influence of childhood, nor of the first bloom of youth, but of the growth and maturation of the spirit, and destined to grow constantly and to reach its full flower only after his death.

Nabuco was far from home and totally unprepared when he received word of his father's death. It was under the shock of this irreparable loss that he returned to Brazil and his family in April 1878.

The death of his father encouraged those in the province who opposed his candidacy and sought that position for someone who had already served the party. But Villa Bella was faithful to his promises, which he now considered sacred, and gave Nabuco his undivided support. Adolfo de Barros, the president of the province, was his personal friend ("I suppose I have something on my side, at least the friendship of the president," wrote Nabuco to Penedo on May 7). In any case, Nabuco entered parliament in last place on the list from Pernambuco, with only fifty-eight votes from Recife.

It was not without some sadness that he now abandoned the diplomatic service, which he had begun to like, in exchange for the uncertainties of politics. The diplomatic career offered a life of easy and brilliant successes to one who entered it with such complete gifts and aptitudes. On the other hand, politics appeared to be full of struggles and unknown factors to be overcome before a dubious glory could be attained. From Brazil, Nabuco wrote sincerely to the Baron of Penedo: "As I begin my political life, I feel sad and discouraged rather than happy and full of hope. I would prefer to be at ease in Half-Moon Street, near Grosvenor Gardens, enjoying the excellent company of your house."

But his calling impelled him. The ten years just ending were what he called pure intellectual dilettantism, the life of "an inquisitive man attracted by travel, by the character of different countries, by new books, by the theater, by society. An enviable life for me at that time would have been to watch from behind the scenes the great events of the time, to associate with the principal actors in them, and, as a distraction from the present, to have the right of entry to the excavations of Athens or Rome."

It is unquestionably at the end of this phase, at nearly thirty years of age, that the period of Nabuco's intellectual preparation may be considered closed. His spirit had, consciously or unconsciously, continued to reach out and grow, in preparation for his future political activity, but this period, in which he had produced little and enjoyed himself a great deal, had already become too prolonged in the eyes of his mother. She wanted to see him take his father's place in the public life of the country, and she also wanted to have him near her. It was the insistence of Dona Anna, overtaken by a cruel widowhood while her son was away, that settled his indecision between the two careers which attracted him so strongly with such different motives. "My sincere desire at that time was to continue in diplomacy," he declared in *My Formative Years*, notwithstanding the fact that he had just confessed the need for "a new provision of interior sunlight; I no longer needed dilettantism, but human passion, a live, palpitating, absorbing interest in the destiny and condition of others . . . . to aid my country, to put my shoulder to the work of my epoch."

He naturally went directly to his province to carry on his campaign in preparation for the election, which was set for September. There, in a meeting attended largely by students, he launched his program, which was a challenge: "The great question for Brazilian democracy is not the monarchy, it is slavery." The phrase provoked the principal incident, as far as he was concerned, in the easy campaign conducted by the party. When he heard himself hissed and booed for that declaration, in the very Santa Isabel Theater that was to be the scene of so many of his triumphs, he tasted consciously and with delight the pleasure of the orator who, in the midst of the storm, knows he possesses the truth and "foresees that those who attack him at that moment will be with him the next day."

That episode carried in embryo his entire parliamentary career. The dominant idea of his life, war against slavery, was presaged in that statement. His presentation showed all the independence which characterized him in politics, and the ambition which never sacrificed to the approval of the present his aspirations for service to the future.

Part Two

ACTION, 1879–89

CHAPTER V. PARLIAMENTARY DEBUT, 1879

About the middle of November 1878, Joaquim Nabuco returned to Rio from Recife to take his seat in the House, and on the eighteenth of that month he fell ill with typhoid fever. He nearly died of the disease, just as the first time he had it during his academic days, and it was not until January 22, 1879, that he was able to write to the Baron of Penedo, in a hand still shaky from his illness:

> After a fever that . . . . for more than forty days prevented my reading the letters sent to me, today I have the courage to write to you. My condition is such that any effort tires me, and especially any emotion or remembering. Please forgive me then, for such a short letter. I am in Palmeiras convalescing slowly. I feel that my whole organism is greatly debilitated. But I'm still alive!
>
> The other day I went to take my seat in the House, but nothing more. Politics interest me very little. . . . . It will be another month before I will be well. Therefore, I do not intend to go regularly to the sessions before the end of the summer.

As a result of his illness, his entrance into parliament was made in a mood of discouragement, reflecting the state of his health, and the spectacle he witnessed the day of his first appearance did not tend to correct that feeling. "As long as I live, gentlemen," he said later to his constituents, "I shall never forget the impression which the first session of parliament that I attended as a deputy had upon my spirit."

On that occasion the Baron of Villa Bella, his old friend who had just assured his election, was explaining to the House the motives which impelled him and Silveira Martins to retire from the ministries of foreign affairs and treasury respectively. They had not been able to reach an agreement with their colleagues concerning the eligibility of non-Catholics. The Brazilian government—for the moment a Liberal one—still maintained that only Catholics could be elected to office.

For Nabuco, who had returned from the United States and England imbued with the loftiest of ideas about individual rights, the discussion of such an elementary principle seemed absurd, not befitting the government of Brazil. It was a profound disillusionment, but it served to dissipate his lack of spirit. Renewed confidence in his great country followed easily, and with it the hope of seeing the Liberal party depart more and more from all such retrograde restrictions and adopt the principles of Gladstone and English liberalism which filled him with such admiration. He entered his country's legislature, where he represented the fourth generation of his name, with full freedom of action, for neither he nor his father for him had made any commitments with the party leaders. Nothing prevented him from expressing freely the ideas that he had absorbed early from his readings, and which had matured in him through his observations. The fervent interest with which he had followed the political questions of the whole world and his observant residence in foreign countries allowed him to view domestic matters with a clarity born of distance and perspective unknown to those who debated in the narrow field of politics and parties. His conclusions, of course, were always adapted to the use and circumstances of Brazil.

The reins of government were in the hands of Cansanção de Sinimbú, later Viscount of the same name. Sinimbú replied to the resigning ministers in a conciliatory tone. He denied "that any Liberal challenged the principle of the eligibility of non-Catholics. Our question, or rather our disagreement, concerned the opportuneness of the idea, not the idea itself."

Nabuco was unable to resist the temptation to mention the subject a few days later when he made his initial address. Not yet completely rested from his illness, he alluded to his weakness at the beginning. He discoursed upon freedom of conscience and showed neither timidity nor inexperience in the debate. His declaration: "It is necessary to recognize that we are in a Catholic nation, it is necessary to consider that the great majority, almost the totality, of Brazilians are Catholics," made an opening for the remark that was flung at him: "Then why not have a state religion?" Immediately he replied: "The right of the minority, the right of a single man in relation to his religion, is as perfect and complete as the right of all."

The portion of his first speech that shows youthfulness in abundance is the ending, full of ardor and hope: "I appeal to the initiative of the House, that we may do something for ourselves, that we may accentuate our responsibility . . . . that our Liberal party may discharge its mission, be an element of progress, as a modern writer has said, be the dynamic element of our society." Upon hearing him speak in this manner (". . . . with the sincerity and the passion I have in defense of the causes I embrace . . . . ," as he said in his speech of April 3), the skeptics probably smiled, or so it would appear from the final note in the official *Annals*:

> Very good, very good (applause).
> Mr. Zama: Very good, but he does not know the country he inhabits (Oh! Oh!).

In another of his early discourses he exclaimed with bold frankness: "I see a liberal situation, a Liberal party, liberal men, but I see no liberal ideas!" And indeed with him only ideas counted. "I am not concerned with men," he said on June 23. "Ministers last only a day (applause), and principles survive (loud applause)," he said on October 24, 1879. Days earlier, in his funeral eulogy of his friend, the Baron of Villa Bella, he had said: "There is only one way to resist this implacable fate; it is to replace the great men that we lose with great ideas (applause); it is, instead of placing our confidence in our generals, to place it in our flag."

He had already made a defense of the "Liberal flag" on April 8, in a speech which was much applauded:

> It is still the same banner which Pericles unfurled at the Pnyx, the same the Gracchi raised above the Forum; it is the banner of the Reformation, the banner of the Edict of Nantes, it is the banner of the Rights of Man . . . . it is the banner, gentlemen, of the emancipation of the serfs in Russia, and also of Washington before the walls of Richmond. In our country it was the flag of the Inconfidência, the flag of 1817, the flag of Ipiranga . . . . but the motto . . . . "Reform or Revolution";—on which we have written "direct election," "religious freedom," "the emancipation of the slaves," is not the flag that wavers in the hands of the President of the Council. . . . .

Direct election. Religious freedom. Emancipation of the slaves. In defense of that triple ideal, Nabuco fought like a paladin. A historian says of him that he came into the House "a new man, with the patrimony of a traditional name, whose eloquence quickly echoed throughout the whole country like a battle cry. There was something fascinating about him. Young (about thirty), large, strong, elegant, restrained in his gestures, with rare masculine beauty, his voice powerful, clear, and sonorous, he possessed also a touch of the exotic with which his travels had impressed his spirit and permeated his body; a touch of English manners and the passion for freedom of that unparalleled people, and at the same time the ardor of the Latin races, the exalted imagination of the Meridionals, the abnegation and quixotic unselfishness of a Spanish knight." (Tobias Monteiro, *Pesquisas e Depoimentos para a Historia*, p. 55.)

Religious freedom had already inspired his maiden speech, in which he was far from the Catholicism of his mature years. Freedom was his dominant passion, the prism through which he impartially viewed religious questions. He sustained the same ideas he had defended in *A Reforma.* Discussing the reform of education and the creation of free Catholic schools in the session of May 15, 1879, he spoke with such enthusiasm that he felt called upon for an explanation:

> Gentlemen, I did not wish to speak with so much heat as I was obliged to do, because the honorable members will think that I am an enemy of Catholicism.
>
> Felicio dos Santos: No, a friend!
>
> Jeronymo Sodré: Of such friends I say, "Get thee behind me, Satan!"
>
> Joaquim Nabuco: . . . . I am not an enemy of the Catholic Church, let the honorable members take note. It was enough for it to have favored the expansion of the arts, to be the factor it has been in history, to be the church of the great majority of Brazilians and of our race, for me not to be its adversary. When

Catholicism takes refuge in the heart of each one I respect it: it is a religion of the conscience, it is a great sentiment of humanity. But I am the enemy of that political Catholicism which allies itself with all absolute governments.

He defended the rights of non-Catholics and the secularization of cemeteries. He even advocated the selling of convent property to take care of the religious expenses in the budget. Afonso Celso, Minister of the Treasury, at that point directed toward him the just remark: "That is good liberalism; appropriate the goods of others, and long live liberty." But Nabuco's idea was less antiliberal than it appeared, for with the abolition of the novitiates in 1855 the religious orders, closed to new members, could do nothing but await the death of the last of the old ones. The properties were deteriorating day by day, so it was reasonable for Nabuco to say: "Gentlemen, it is absolutely certain that something must be done about the convent properties. . . . ."

On April 14 he returned to the subject:

From liquidation of the property of the religious orders, religious sentiment alone will gain, if the proceeds are applied for religious purposes. . . . . Within a short time those properties will be worth nothing. The honorable members cannot say that the convents in their present state satisfy the aims of their religion, nor the ends for which they were created (applause and protests).

Felicio dos Santos: That is none of our affair.

Joaquim Nabuco: Why is it not our affair? Under what regime are we living? We live under a regime of the union of Church and State, of a subsidized Church, of a Church leaning upon the budget. . . . . Beyond any doubt, the State has the right to decree the abolition of the religious orders and I am going to propose it in this House.

That threat appears to have been merely the result of the heat of the debate. Although later he had time to bring up every imaginable matter, never again did he consider such a proposition. On the religious question he departed from constant liberal principles, but apparently under the delusion that he was defending them. Perhaps his justification is found in other words he pronounced the same day:

Gentlemen, Lessing says in his *Laocoon*: "If God had in one hand the truth and in the other the aspiration for truth, I should choose the latter." The Liberal party ought to do the same with respect to freedom. Freedom obtained may be a benefit, the happiness of a country; but what makes a people free is simply the fervent desire for freedom, it is the instinct, the feeling that causes it to put forth every effort and to make every sacrifice in order to acquire and win it.

The great discussion of that legislature concerned the problem of direct election. The party in power had pledged itself to bring this about, and it was the main plank in the program of the Sinimbú government. It was the hope that carried the Liberal party to power after ten years of ostracism. The indirect election system was definitely condemned by public opinion to the extent that in the words of Sinimbú, the country "no longer views it as a party question." The Emperor, the people, even the Conservatives desired the great reform. But interminable divergences arose over the method of bringing it about. The government, in its anxiety to accomplish the change, was overly cautious. To gain support, it was willing to make concessions that disgusted true Liberals. "I understood, that since our principal mission was to bring about electoral reform, I should separate it from any other idea that at the moment might give rise to difficulties, and I could not expect the support of the Senate if I did not limit myself to the essential point of the reform," declared the President of the Council. The bill prepared by the government and presented to the House three days after those words were spoken on February 18, 1879, restricted the right to vote and was a disappointment to the progressive members. Sinimbú compromised on every point, and as Nabuco exclaimed in one of his outbursts of eloquence, "those Liberals who had set forth their ideas in the press and on the platform could find nothing to propose to the brilliant youth of this House, to the aspirations of all of us, but a conservative reform, a reform which did not grant complete suffrage, a reform that we cannot accept without renouncing all our principles." He had hoped for a complete reform of the system of indirect elections.

In the unanimous House that the party had elected—showing once again the great need for reform—the Prime Minister found only a small number of deputies against him. "We are few," said Nabuco on one occasion. "But you are good," remarked José Mariano. And indeed, the small group vigorously attacked each point of the proposal and proved its insufficiency. José Bonifácio, eloquent and conscious of his strength and of the support of the public, and Nabuco, impetuous and convinced, were the two main figures in the debate that arose concerning the right of illiterates and freed Negroes to vote, and the establishment of the poll tax. Silveira Martins left the cabinet to join his voice to theirs. The government was reluctant to make any concessions to them, but even if it had granted all they asked, the radical difference of opinion over the method of making the needed reforms would have remained. "We could follow one of two roads," declared Sinimbú to the House, succinctly pointing out that the change could be made by statute or by constitutional reform.

The solemn, occasionally brilliant discussion continued interminably, and the arguments for and against calling an assembly to alter the constitution multiplied and became more and more subtle. Nabuco said on April 29:

Our constitution is not in the image of those Gothic cathedrals built at great cost, which represent in the midst of our advanced civilization and the feverish activity of our time periods of passiveness and inaction; on the contrary, our constitution is a natural growth, it is a formation like that of the soil, where successive layers are deposited, where life penetrates everywhere, subject to eternal change, where the errors that occur remain buried under the truths that are born.

Our constitution is not a barrier raised across our path; it is not the tablets of the law received from the divine legislator, which cannot be touched because they are protected by thunder and lightning. . . . .

Our constitution is a great liberal mechanism, one provided with all the organs of locomotion and progress, it is a live organism that walks and adapts itself to the diverse functions that from time to time it must perform.

Then, after defending universal suffrage, but without expecting it for the present, he finished with an inflammatory peroration, asking the President of the Council to restore the flag he held "to the Conservatives to whom it belongs, to the crown which gave it to you, so that this electoral reform, this hateful restriction of the right to vote may not be remembered in history as the apostasy of the Liberal party."

This speech was his first great parliamentary success. The galleries burst into applause, offering him for the first time the tribute—prohibited by the rules of order—which was to be the final note of so many of his speeches. In the second discussion on May 27 came a new triumph, new applause, and even the imprisonment of one of the demonstrators. Days afterward, Silveira Martins gave a splendid tribute to the young representative from Pernambuco "to whom might be applied the words of Titus Livius about young Scipio Africanus: '. . . . Behold the young man whom Fortune prepares to save the honor of his country and avenge the defeats the Carthaginians have inflicted upon us.' The honorable member will one day be the glory of the Liberal party which you have so brilliantly upheld in this tribunal, recalling each time you rise the noble memory of your illustrious father."

As a matter of fact, the figure of the revered dead statesman and that of the promising beginner were inseparable in the minds of everyone. Joaquim Nabuco entered the Brazilian parliament in the revered shadow of his father. The elder Nabuco had been gone less than a year; his personality still lived, and his authority was invoked on every occasion, at times even against his own son. The Minister of the Treasury said, after hearing Nabuco cite an opinion by Pitt: "The honorable gentleman will permit me to cite in preference another authority, equally respectable to me, much more so to the honorable member and venerated by all Brazilians." That authority was Senator Nabuco. Similar comparisons were repeated and on one occasion a deputy exclaimed: "What is this we have heard from the son of that eminent man . . . . of that great soul who was our venerated leader and from beyond the tomb is still our guide?" (Franco de Sá, June 30, 1879.)

But the son did not bow before these opinions that were presented against him. He refuted them when necessary, with proof, and once he replied that Senator Nabuco was a progressive man and perhaps if he were alive he would no longer think in the same way. However, he was deeply moved to see the one of whom he was so proud constantly remembered. In one of his discourses he said parenthetically:

> The orators who have occupied this platform have really been so unanimous in their sympathy for me and their recollection of him that even at the risk of infringing upon parliamentary style with what appears to be the intrusion of a personal sentiment into these debates, I thank them from the bottom of my heart. . . . . The House will forgive me this expression of intimate acknowledgment, but there are moments when gratitude, silently accumulated, cannot help but run over, for in the words of the poet, "the heart, to hold it, is a narrow vessel."

To these few grateful words, which interrupted the consideration of certain marine matters, he added a brief and solemn pledge. ". . . . General Lee once said that while walking with his son along the seashore he noticed that the child was trying to walk in the footprints he was leaving impressed in the sand. 'From that day forward,' he said, 'I realized that I had no right to take a single step where my child could not follow me.' No matter how the political sands may shift, there are in them for me indelible prints, and if I have no other qualities, I have in my make-up sufficient fairness and unselfishness not to depart from the way that is marked for me."

Nearly all those present remembered well the oratory of Senator Nabuco de Araujo, so different in every way from that of Joaquim Nabuco at that time. The old Liberal leader had suffered from a trembling in his limbs during his last years, and was obliged to remain seated while speaking. He rarely took the floor, and then only on important occasions, bringing to the hall the crystallization of his thinking, of his knowledge, and at times the disillusionment of his experience. His son, on the other hand, vibrated with untested convictions and with an idealism that often bordered on the utopian and the impossible. Ardent, inflexible, he abused his oratorical facility, losing himself at times in rhetoric. He had no time to prepare his speeches, since he spoke daily during those first months. He took an interest in everything, was never at a loss for improvisation, and thought out loud before the House, which he could win over in an informal way as well as with his eloquence.

In *My Formative Years* he himself confessed that at that time "I did not know the 'is it worth while?' of the observer who restrains himself more and more. . . . .The public, the great audiences were for me what my waste basket is today or the fire that takes care of my superfluous exuberance of thought."

His aged father, a respecter of traditions and customs, had been essentially a party man, who guarded with care the bonds which joined him to his friends and party colleagues. He was an authority consulted with reverence. The son was young and without a proper sense of responsibility. He had not achieved a position of importance, and relied on his talent and the reputation which he soon won. He was independent of everyone and everything, perfectly willing to disagree with the party leaders. The father excluded fantasy from his speeches. They were solid as monuments and brightened only by the clarity of his keen intelligence. In the matter of embellishment, he was content with an occasional Latin quotation or a necessary historical reference. The son filled his discourses with images in which he transported his hearers back to antiquity, into the literature of all countries, into art or science. At times he recited verses; always he showed a naïve amazement at what he had learned and considered beautiful. On one occasion these digressions earned him the irony of the Minister of the Treasury, Afonso Celso. The future Viscount of Ouro Preto said to him: "I ask leave of the noble deputy from Pernambuco to allow Schiller, Charles V, Philip II, and Gambetta to rest in peace, dead or alive . . . . and deal only with the object under discussion." Immediately protests countered the criticism. "He had the right to speak about Schiller and Gambetta. What is wrong with that?" remarked Deputy Galdino das Neves. The next speaker, Manoel Pedro, likewise said: "The rhetoric of the honorable member from Pernambuco finds an echo in the country, which sees in him the worthy heir of a great name, and above any disdainful criticism of him are the manifestations which his words awake in the hearts of the Brazilian people . . . ."

In *A Statesman of the Empire*, Joaquim Nabuco studies his father and reveals his personal opinions of the art of oratory. Nabuco de Araujo seems to find that "it is not worth while to say what everyone is thinking—which is, however, the great opportunity of the orator—and that it is dangerous to say that which no one else has thought of. . . . . His training as a judge had made him incapable of eloquent tirades full of political passion. His eloquence was an exposition of abstract concepts. He felt that to be appreciated on the platform, one should use long pauses so that the audience could have time to think about what it had heard, as a reader may pause after each sentence he reads. Spoken eloquence, however, is by its very nature a torrent, and the more turbulent and sweeping, the stronger it is."

Farther on he says that his father was not a slave to any one theory or system. "His mobility is astonishing; those who see him pointing out the danger from one side and then the other are apt to judge him to be inconsistent, but the truth is that the way runs between precipices, and he looks to the right and to the left instead of seeing the abysses on one side only."

The same was not true of the son. Where the wise man hesitates and loses the opportunity, the inspired man of action dashes forward with contagious enthusiasm. Joaquim Nabuco did, of course, weigh the pros and the cons, but, after he once made up his mind, his doubts gave way to full confidence. Therein lay his influence with the people, stronger than that of his father. The audience is moved by the orator who excites its spirit, not by him who merely clarifies its mind.

In his portrait of his father, Nabuco includes solemnity as one of his characteristic traits: "The pauses and the silvery voice of Nabuco gave to his declamation a special solemnity." In this the difference between father and son is scarcely apparent. It is true that Joaquim Nabuco saw no necessity to strive for the exterior gravity proper for a senator. Where his father had majesty, he had impetuosity. His gestures were soberly harmonious rather than measured. His dress nearly created a scandal when he appeared for the first time on a hot day, under the severe stares of the President and among the traditional frock coats of his colleagues, in a light-colored coat of British cut. But though he easily dispensed with external solemnity, it was always apparent in his discourses, in the high level on which he maintained the debates, in his manner of approaching questions, in the noble cadence of his phrases, in short, in his eloquence, which is almost synonymous with solemnity. He was always a serious person. He may have used fantasy, delicacy, and finesse, but anything that was humorous, light, effervescent, or superficial was not natural to him.

"The *Official Journal* (*Diário Oficial*) must have shown you the reasons for my long silence," he wrote to the Baron of Penedo on May 8, 1879. "There is no deputy more assiduous than I, and when one is so assiduous one loses not only the time spent in the House; one returns home with his head full of what he saw, heard, or did—to think about the next day."

The most diverse matters appeared to interest him equally. During his first year as a deputy, the general budget and individual ministerial budgets gave him material for numerous speeches. He spoke on most of the questions that came under discussion, whether the subject was educational reform, the number of the land or sea forces, or the National Bank. He even spoke about matters of secondary or municipal importance, such as the renewal of the contract for public illumination and street cleaning, or the construction of a new slaughterhouse. A topic that gave him a chance to shine brilliantly was a proposed concession giving a group of individuals the exclusive right to explore and exploit the natural resources of the Xingú Valley for a twenty-year period. The first time the matter was discussed, on August 1, Nabuco declared his opposition:

Gentlemen, it is sad that in our country, after so long a time under a free government, a minister of state, with the signature of the Emperor, may make concessions, donations of hundreds of miles of completely unknown land, of navigable river channels, of all the products of the vegetable, mineral, and animal kingdoms which exist in an immense zone, which he himself does not know and of which he cannot present a map to the parliament.

I regret that the honorable members from Pará did not take the initiative. . . . .

Costa Azevedo: They will participate.

Joaquim Nabuco: They can no longer take the initiative.

It was Nabuco who finally introduced and carried the question to a conclusion.

Another opportunity for him to display his talent arose over the discussion of a special mission to China. Nabuco formally opposed the move, because one of its objects, according to the Minister of Foreign Affairs, was to bring Asiatic laborers to Brazil. He said:

If it were simply a matter of a trip around the world, or of an embassy to China, my only wish would be that our plenipotentiaries might go and dwell in that Peking street called "The Thousand Delights." But, gentlemen, it is not simply a question of fostering relations with China, or bringing closer together two of the greatest empires of the world. It is a question of a full-fledged Asiatic emigration to Brazil, and the diplomatic relations which are to be opened have no other object or design than to mongolize our country.

This was on September 1. On October 8, after the appropriation for the trip was passed, Nabuco remarked that the only consolation left to him was that cabinet positions were so transitory. "The noble President of the Council cannot be certain that, before his mission reaches China, he himself will not have left the ministerial bench."

He affirmed further: "Whenever the Chinese question comes up (let the House not deceive itself), it is merely the problem of slavery in another form." This idea had been from the first the main basis of his objection to the mission and one of the strongest arguments in his first speech about it:

What many of the planters of the south want is not Chinese immigration; none of them has spoken of it; none of them has confidence in it. What they wanted were coolies, Chinamen contracted in China for agricultural labor here, whose contracts, as in Cuba and Peru, constitute a temporary slavery, and would be a guaranty for the acquisition of manpower for labor . . . . and it is claimed that the coolies would be a means of transition from slavery to free labor. . . . . It is impossible to have free labor and slave labor, slavery and immigration, at the same time. We must choose. We must trust in slavery or trust in free labor. . . . .

African immigration, tried out at first as an inevitable expedient, was the cause of all our misfortunes, of the precarious state of the nation . . . . because slavery is the cause of all our trouble; the other, the Asiatic, is being born obscurely, unnoticed, today in this place.

Great rivers are so born; when they burst from the earth they are scarcely seen as they are mere threads of water, but they grow and increase imperceptibly until they become an Amazon or a Mississippi. It is possible, gentlemen, that this new attempt, like so many others, will be a great failure, which is what I desire. But it is likewise possible that Chinese immigration may develop greatly, and then this day, on which our protest against the mongolization of our country is making itself heard to the almost empty benches of this House, will be considered a fatal one for the nation.

The Minister of Foreign Affairs, Moreira de Barros, replied two days later with all the arguments he could muster on the advantages of Chinese immigration, and also with some personal sarcasm. Nabuco, in his magnificent and immediate reply, mentions how the minister

. . . . alluded in every possible way to my flights of fancy, to my youthfulness, saying that I was cutting a sorry figure and should go back to school. . . . .

Moreira de Barros: The translation is too free.

Nabuco: The honorable gentleman, throughout his entire speech was more concerned with the speaker than with the speech I gave, otherwise he would not have attacked me. Let me answer him; I shall not wound nor offend him. I do not wish to compare our two careers.

Moreira de Barros: I do not hesitate to compare my record with that of any man.

Nabuco: The honorable minister's career, like mine, began in parliament. The honorable gentleman rose rapidly to one of the most responsible positions that this country has to offer.

I have no desire to reach it (protests), nor do I have any hopes of being re-elected (protests); I simply desired in my perhaps ephemeral passage through this House always to place myself on the side of freedom, of justice, of progress, of humanity, which are to me the major interests of the country, so that any truly liberal man of generous sentiments could always shake my hand (applause, cheers). That is what I wished to reply on the matter.

He went on in the same vein. The applause from the gallery was deafening, and the crowd waited afterward for him to leave the building in order to greet him with a new ovation.

Nabuco's opposition to the Sinimbú government "which violated our principles and sacrificed the program of our party," became more and more violent. The *Gazeta de Notícias* supported him. Its publisher was Ferreira de Araujo; Ferreira de Menezes and José do Patrocínio were contributors;

they all fought by his side against the Xingú concession, the China appropriation, and the cabinet. They wrote glowing eulogies of the eloquent words of young Nabuco, "which would have the power," wrote Patrocínio, "to arouse the people."

"The first mistake of the honorable President of the Council was the organization of his cabinet," said Nabuco in the enumeration of his criticisms. The ministry, weak from the beginning, suffered continued loss of prestige with the successive resignations of several of its members. Silveira Martins, over the question of the eligibility of non-Catholics to vote, and Leóncio de Carvalho, Minister of Empire, over the matter of educational reform, had left their posts to join the opposition. These desertions had special repercussions. Nabuco welcomed Leóncio de Carvalho enthusiastically: "Today we are comrades in the same cause, and in the name of the opposition I can say that it welcomes with open arms the honorable ex-minister."

It was a double honor for Nabuco to be able to speak in the name of the opposition, because he was a beginner and because of the famous men who formed part of the opposition. Among them were the most notable of the House, including José Bonifácio, Silveira Martins, and Martinho Campos, a veteran oppositionist "by habit," and who "alone was a whole opposition."

Bonifácio had left the House just that year in order to enter the Senate, and Nabuco said: "José Bonifácio, through an unfortunate condition in our parliament, arising from the uncertainty of elections, which carries into the Senate men who never should leave this chamber, took his eloquence into a cold silent hall where it will have no echo."

According to an article by Rodolfo Dantas, another newcomer to the legislature and a close friend, it was Joaquim Nabuco who appeared to "fill the place in the House left by Bonifácio. . . . . The speaker's rostrum has never found him wanting. Whether Nabuco occupies it after previous careful study of the subject and considered reflection on the matter, or whether he approaches it impelled by an unforeseen circumstance or on the spur of the moment, complete success is always assured."

Speaking for the opposition and taking advantage of an opportunity "once more to explain its position before the House and the nation," Joaquim Nabuco said:

> From the beginning we say that this cabinet, in its aspirations as in its language, was not fulfilling what we supposed to be the mission of the Liberal party in the government, and from that time on we have said that, if the policy of this ministry is Liberal, we are not Liberals. But, gentlemen, no doubt is possible. We have the conviction of our ideas, of the feelings that animate us, and therefore, since we are certain that we are Liberals, it is the policy of the cabinet that is not! (Applause from the gallery. The speaker is complimented by nearly all the deputies present.)

The ministry continued to lose ground on all questions. The collecting of the new and unpopular tax called the *vintém* provoked a riot in Rio that revealed clearly the danger of the situation. The rejection by the Senate of the electoral reform bill approved by the House would have been enough to destroy all hope. Faced with such a possibility, the Emperor, instead of allowing Sinimbú to carry out his threat of dissolving the House, requested Senator Saraiva to organize a new government.

Nabuco wrote to his constant correspondent, the Baron of Penedo:

> I have not written you since your great friend gave way to Saraiva and a complete revolution took place in our policy and our party. I know how much the fall of Sinimbú must have displeased you, but since there are in the present ministry men who regard you highly, I think I may well say that his fall was a source of pleasure to me. Today the situation has changed, and the requiem which they were singing over my brief political career will have to be postponed for some time.

He was more than right. Some of the most important men in the party considered him a possibility for one of the ministries in the new government, and Saraiva himself felt impelled to declare from the rostrum that he had not invited him, simply because Nabuco was in the minority. It was a minority formed by himself alone, a minority of one.

CHAPTER VI. EMANCIPATION IN THE PARLIAMENT, 1879–80

The revolutionary note in Nabuco's speeches, the note which soon struck fear to the hearts of the whole class of landowners and farmers in a land as essentially agricultural as Brazil, was his attack on slavery. In his school days, the example of some of his colleagues such as Castro Alves, Ruy Barbosa, and others had drawn his attention to this grave and still completely unsolved problem. Later, when in 1871 the Rio Branco law was passed, all Brazilians, whether they favored total abolition, as did Nabuco and his friends, or preferred gradual emancipation, were more or less satisfied. The horrible institution had received a mortal blow. Never again would there be a slave born in Brazil.

The Rio Branco law fulfilled a national aspiration and was widely acclaimed. Even those who were injured by it could applaud it wholeheartedly; it did not touch their present property, it merely restricted their rights concerning the unborn children of slaves, and over a kind of property already condemned by humanity and civilization. But they were determined to fight any further steps.

Those who defended slavery and opposed the law of free birth later came to praise it after it was an accomplished fact; but now they had to defend their property, the source of their modest or large incomes. They predicted that to touch their slaves would be to bring about their ruin, as well as the ruin of farming and of the country. "Brazil is coffee, and coffee is the Negro," said Silveira Martins.

The wonderful law of "Free Birth" was only a beginning. One of the statesmen who did most for it in the Council of State, where he was the sponsor of the bill, and in the Senate, was the father of Joaquim Nabuco. On June 13, 1873, he called for a measure of freedom for the present generation of slaves, "for, having redeemed the future generations, it was necessary to satisfy the impatience of the present generation." His colleague, Senator Saraiva, added: "The great injustice of the law is its failure to care for the present generation."

In *A Statesman of the Empire*, Nabuco, the historian, speaks of "the torpor, the indifference which followed the law, as if the problem of the freedom of the more than two million slaves had been solved by the emancipation of those who were yet to be born." As a matter of fact, one whole side of the problem remained to be solved, and it was that side which came to concern Nabuco. As he was to say later at Recife in the campaign: "It is not our purpose to praise the law of September 28; that is the task of our adversaries." He cited against the law three points: first, the injustice mentioned by Saraiva of not doing anything for the present slaves; second, his most remote case, "a slave woman born September 27, 1871, may become a mother in 1911 of one of those innocents who would then remain in provisional slavery until 1932"; third, the situation of the "unborn" or "innocents," "those hundreds of thousands of persons who are slaves only to the age of twenty-one, that is, only provisional slaves. The repugnant spectacle of a great mass of future citizens growing up in the slave quarters, subject to the same system of labor, the same moral education, the same treatment as the slaves. . . . . Slave quarters and schools are poles that repel each other."

Since the passage of the law, nothing more had been done. When Nabuco entered the parliament in 1879 he found a curtain of silence over what he considered to be "the great question for Brazilian democracy." His declaration in Recife during his campaign showed clearly the attitude he intended to take in the Chamber. But his course had been marked long before. In 1881 he said to his constituents: "Whoever will take the trouble to read what I wrote and published in my student days, both in the field of literature and that of politics, will see that slavery is predicted clearly as the burden of any public career I might be fortunate enough to have."

That public career began on February 19, 1879, with a speech on the religious question, in which there was no reference to slavery. The voice destined to break the silence that had surrounded that matter since 1871 was not his but that of his colleague, Jeronymo Sodré, in a speech on March 5. The imperial budget was under discussion and Sodré asked for the floor to express his ideas on three different questions—education, religion, and the slave element. He left the slave question for the last, declaring that he well knew that it was the most difficult to deal with.

Sodré was a Catholic and was well known as an intransigent papist. His hatred of slavery was based on religious considerations rather than on a pure spirit of human justice. Moreover, from the practical viewpoint he failed to see any economic advantage in the institution of slavery. On the contrary, he called it "the cancer which corrupts everything." "I am a farmer's son," he said. "From my early years I have been accustomed to seeing the problem at close hand. I know that we, the owners of slaves, live wrapped in a mantle of riches, even while misery gnaws deeply at our vitals." It was a solitary cry of protest that touched those who heard it. It was short and stirring and yet suggested no means for solving the problem. Sodré asked "the public powers to look at the condition of a million Brazilians who still languish in captivity!" A chorus of protests replied: "They are not Brazilians!"

Sodré's speech was an important point in the abolitionist campaign. It marked the beginning in parliament of the agitation that was soon to spread to the press and to the whole country. Its consequences in the movement which culminated with abolition on May 13, 1888, were important, but many remained unaware of this fact since Sodré took little further part in that movement. To initiate it, and especially to keep it going, called for a persistent effort, an ever-increasing propaganda, in short, a strong man to lead the devotees. That was to be Nabuco's role.

During this his first legislative session, the future apostle of freedom was still a long way from the theory of total abolition without indemnization which he later proposed. In order to do away with slavery, he was willing to compromise on the questions of the date it would go into effect and the indemnity to be paid. He did not wish to sacrifice the gains secured in a long and risky campaign by making impossible demands. He saw clearly the difficulty of destroying slavery without injuring the whole country to which, after three centuries of common existence, it was so intimately, perhaps inseparably, linked.

His only remark injected into Sodré's speech of March 22, 1879, "England paid an indemnity," shows that his mind was not fully made up. In his own speech he declared positively that he did not ask for immediate emancipation. But he could not tolerate these words of the President of the Council, which he read to the House just as Sinimbú had pronounced them:

> Recognizing that the farmers feared some such measure, and that a certain spirit of malevolence attributed to the present government the desire to speed up emancipation, I declared that for my part I would not agree to any hastening of that fatal step.

"I know perfectly well," said Nabuco, protesting the statement:

> . . . . that immediate emancipation would mean the sudden cessation of all work in the country, and the stagnation of all our sources of income; but on the other hand, I wish to protest very clearly against the movement to make emancipation take a step backward; on the contrary, I shall always go along with any measure that may be proposed in this House with the purpose of advancing it. . . . .

No one could express an opinion in more moderate terms. Nevertheless, a shower of protests and indignant asides greeted his words, and he added:

> I can see, gentlemen, that there is no room in this House for moderate opinions, nor can one come here to say he does not desire the destruction of our agricultural property, that he does not favor immediate emancipation, but rather laws, measures that prepare us in the best possible way for total emancipation of the slaves.

"The honorable member was well applauded by most of the House," remarked Ruy Barbosa.

The following day the *Gazeta de Notícias* stated: "To each proposal of the deputy, and especially when he spoke of the emancipation of the slaves, there was a shower of remarks and asides, the cry of the interested parties, who fear more than anything else that the basis of their wealth will be affected."

From that time forward, Nabuco's speeches generally contained some reference to the subject. Many were insignificant, but they are symptomatic in that they reveal his constant preoccupation with the matter; others were more positive. Almost any topic could give rise to these remarks or offer an excuse for a brief digression. In this respect it is interesting to re-examine nearly all the speeches mentioned in the previous chapter. On April 3, for example, in view of an obvious intention to increase public revenues by a tax on slaves, Nabuco declared: "No taxes should be placed on slavery except for the purpose of freeing the slaves," and he repeated it again on April 14.

Again he had a word of criticism against religious orders that possessed slaves. On April 17 he submitted an amendment, which was approved, proposing a small tax on the slave commission houses. In the discussion on electoral reforms he said on April 29: "Not that I wish to compare the rights of freedom to electoral rights; not that I do not know that the first problem of this country is the freeing of the slaves." Concerning the Xingú River concession he stated on August 1: "I, who await the day of the emancipation of the slaves, cannot agree to the formation of companies that may threaten the rights, while they exploit without any guaranties whatsoever, the services and freedom of the Indians." The proposed bringing in of Chinese, which he saw as a "new calamity to strengthen slavery, that institution which will not surrender," permitted him to make even more insistent references to the matter on July 25 and allowed him to prophesy the acceleration of the abolitionist movement when slavery had reached its limits, and to declare that even though "we inherited slavery, which we cannot suddenly do away with," the least that could be done was to "try to develop and protect free labor." Finally, it permitted him to pose the dilemma, slavery or immigration, and to offer this solution on September 1:

> If instead of seeking this Chinese immigration [the government] would try to solve courageously the great problem by extinguishing domestic slavery and turning it into a sort of colonization program which would link the present slaves to the land, making them servants of the soil only during a short transition period, and opening a future in farming to the race that has been used as slaves in it, giving the slaves an interest in the land and a fatherland in the nation; if the many injustices which prevent our progress were corrected with humanitarian laws, I am sure that the country would receive a better return from that manly effort, and from the better understanding of its true material and moral interests, than by trying to renew the

source of the traffic by doing with Asia what was done with Africa, by seeking yellow slaves to mingle in the hovels, the fields, and the families with the black slaves.

Nabuco met the Foreign Minister's reply to this statement on September 3 with a triumphant improvisation:

The future of the measure, gentlemen, does not seem as sure to me as to the Foreign Minister; but there is reason to suspect that it is not an attempt at progress, but merely an effort to revive slave labor, and that the government to which the honorable gentleman belongs, the ministry he holds, has no free labor program, does not desire to hasten it a single hour, but rather, from the first, unfurled at the side of the white flag of capitulation already mentioned, the black flag of slavery and the feudal banner of large estates.

Several days later, on September 11, he again voiced the same tremendous complaint against the government, whose implacable adversary he was:

When the honorable President of the Council took office, his first word was that the government was disposed not to permit the hastening by a single day of the freeing of the slaves. Whom was that promise intended to reassure? Was the country in a state of alarm?

Ignacio Martins: It was.

Joaquim Nabuco: If it was rumored that we were going to attempt the immediate abolition of slavery, the government could say that we would not do it under any conditions; but for the party to join in a slavery program is a promise incompatible with the necessary evolution of the Liberal idea. (Applause from the opposition.) A Liberal cannot delay for a moment the great day of emancipation.

One of his colleagues and former schoolmates, Manuel Pedro Cardoso Vieira, also defended, on October 8, the cause of freedom, likewise linking it to the coming of the coolies, and also winning applause. Nabuco followed him to the rostrum to explain a sensational aside he had made: "The Viscount of Rio Branco has already abandoned the cause of slavery." He said:

If the Conservative party were in favor of abolition as we are, after having the honor of passing this law, it would have but one ambition today: to complete it, to perfect it.

Gentlemen, the law of September 28 will be considered in history as the glory of this reign. But the greatness of the law lies not so much in its having freed the newborn slaves as in having made of slavery a fact, and not a right. Where formerly the courageous stopped hesitantly before the monument which the profane hand was forbidden to touch, where slavery was previously inviolate, saying to all "*noli me tangere*," the main effect of the law of September 28 was to reduce it to a fact, demand its credentials and indicate its inevitable end. . . . .

. . . .

Once again, gentlemen, it is slavery that is in question. And so I warn the honorable President of the Council, although perhaps I lack the authority to do so:

there is in the House a group, which may not be a majority, but which is numerous. What does it represent? It represents the opinion which is arising within the party that the law of September 28 is not the final word on emancipation; that it was a great day, the glory of the country and of those who took part in it, but that it is necessary to go farther because the national aspirations demand much more.

The Liberal party is not willing to be accused and considered a reactionary party to be pilloried in the public square as a party incapable of any sacrifice for the good of humanity (applause).

The Liberal party, gentlemen, is not completely satisfied with the law of September 28, which is a law made by the Conservatives although with Liberal inspiration; the important improvements which we asked for, to make the effect of the law more rapid, were not accepted. Today the law is not sufficient. In this field we must go forward or back: we cannot stand still.

. . . . and the time is not far away when all Brazilians will be convinced as we are that the real hegira of our national life, the starting point of all our advancements, the day when we can enter the community of free peoples with our head held high, and take our rightful place, will be that day when in all the land there is no slave!

He had never spoken in such a categorical manner. Martim Francisco immediately took the floor in order to throw a bit of cold water on such fiery language:

I recognize the generosity and the good intentions of the honorable member, who represents an agricultural province, but I fear that his tender years may lead him into a course where the first-class talent he unquestionably possesses may serve to upset and disturb the peace of the nation.

". . . . In our province," said Francisco, "we will resist even with arms." Martim Francisco represented São Paulo, the land of the Andradas and of 180,000 to 200,000 slaves, and he feared that some plan for immediate abolition might arise from the young Pernambucan's words. He ended by repeating his request: "Do not place the great oratorical gifts which you enjoy at the service of a cause that might greatly harm our country."

Because of his efforts on behalf of the slaves collectively, Nabuco's aid was frequently sought to correct cases of individual abuses. He took up the case, for example, of the slaves of the São João del Rei Company which owned the mines of Morro Velho. This English company had acquired from its predecessors, along with the lands and equipment, about four hundred slaves, who according to express terms of the contract were to be set free at the end of fourteen years, or in the case of minors, at the age of twenty-one. Twenty years had passed since then, and Nabuco raised his voice in protest. The captives, registered by the manager with no mention of the obligatory clause, were still treated as slaves. Many had already died and the rest had no means of seeking their freedom. The crime had been exposed by the public prosecutor but no action had been taken. "I am not interested in whatever steps may have been taken, because they have had absolutely no results," roared Nabuco on August 26, in reply to an aside. The case, which until then had been kept quiet by the interested parties, now broke out with repercussions. Its scandalous echo was heard even in England, the country of those responsible. The *Revue des Deux Mondes* commented on it, saying: "It is particularly galling that the company, its directors, and stockholders all belong to that English nationality which has been so critical of Brazil every time the question of slavery has been brought up for consideration." When the slaves were freed, the Anti-Slavery Society of London sent thanks and congratulations to Nabuco. As an enemy of slavery and of the exploitation of coolie labor, it had double reason for felicitating the young Brazilian who had just completed so brilliantly his first year as a deputy. The session of 1879 closed in October. The calm, beautiful letter in which Nabuco replied to the message of the English humanitarian society is dated April 5, 1880. It was published in the English-language *Rio News* of April 24, 1880, and reads in part as follows:

> Thanking you once more for the gratifying message you sent me, I assure you that you will always find me at the fighting post I now occupy. I place the emancipation interest beyond any other, above any party allegiance. Compared to this great social reform, which should extend the right of property, freedom, family, and conscience to the race which produces more than two-thirds of Brazil's exportations, political reforms remain in the shade.
>
> In the approaching session of the Chamber of Deputies, besides a bill, the purport of which is to correct many of the inequalities and iniquities of the slavery covenant, I will introduce a bill establishing the 1st of January, 1890, for the entire abolition of slavery in the Empire. I know such a long period is a compromise, but it is a necessary one. It is the only means of surmounting difficulties which are still very great. The law of the 28th of September, 1871, sufficient for that time, has a slower action and gives a lower rate of yearly emancipation than the circumstances of the country and the steady progress of public conscience now both allow and require. An unchangeable term, such as the 1st of January, 1890, would leave time to the planters to prepare for the great evolution, while it would give rise directly in the hearts of the slaves to an invaluable hope, which would render life less and less hard for them at every step that should bring them nearer to freedom.
>
> That bill will not be converted this year into a law, but introduced every session, in a Liberal house by myself or some of my friends, and in a Conservative house by some prominent Conservative abolitionist, like Mr. Gusmão Lobo, increasing every time in votes, it will triumph at last.

During the parliamentary recess Nabuco continued to sustain and nourish antislavery propaganda. Early in January, the *Gazeta de Notícias* published an extensive letter by him, protesting against a slave market in Valença, where the sale of a large number of Africans was announced, many of them being advertised as under forty-eight years of age, which indicated that they had been brought in by one of the many clandestine shipments which arrived after the passage of the law of 1831. Legally they were free, as were a great part of the slaves of Brazil, under the terms of the law.

Parliament met again in May 1880. In the interval, the government of Sinimbú had fallen and had been replaced by that of Saraiva. Machado de Assis later described the scenes of the changing of the cabinet as follows:

> Oh, the fancy presentations of the ministers! It was a joy to see the full House excited, expectant, awaiting the new cabinet. Young ladies on the benches, here and there a diplomat, a handful of senators. Suddenly a murmur arose, all eyes turned toward the central door, the ministers appeared, led by their chief, compliments right and left. When they were seated, one of the members of the previous cabinet arose and explained the reasons for its resignation. Then the President of the Council stood up, told the story of his rise to power, and defended his program. A deputy from the opposition asked for the floor, spoke ill of the two ministries, found contradictions and obscurities in the explanations, and called the program deficient. Reply, rebuttal, agitation, a full day.

Saraiva came to power to accomplish electoral reform by direct law, a longer method than his predecessor wanted to use. Nabuco welcomed the new ministry gladly and with an eloquent speech. The cabinet change appeared to him to perform "a transformation as complete in the political situation of the country as if it were the accession of a new party, new men, a new situation," and represented "the Liberal party united after temporary divergencies," and re-established in the country "only two sides, the Liberal side and the Conservative side." As for his opposition and that of some of the others to the former cabinet, Nabuco declared that they had desired only "to create a condition that would appear acceptable to the whole Liberal party."

"Even if only the most extreme defenders of the recent ministry were now seated in those chairs, as long as the old policy was no longer in force we would be satisfied with them as if our own men were occupying those posts."

He pledged his complete support of the new government. Coming from one who had been such a turbulent adversary, this guaranty must have been somewhat reassuring to Saraiva. But his loyalty had the inevitable reservation:

> . . . . To be perfectly frank, I should announce at once the solemn obligation I have, whenever I occupy a place in the national assembly, to try by all means to hasten the day of the freedom of the slaves.

. . . . When the roll is called of all the nations who in this century have broken with slavery and have been civilized by free labor, I do not want Brazil to be the only one who cannot answer.

In this solemn moment I must make this important reservation, which leaves me with complete freedom of action with respect to my obligation. I cannot force the government to adopt my way of thinking, to make my project its own. But I ask the government not to put stumbling blocks in the way of that project; not to declare, as the last cabinet did, that it absolutely will not consent to shorten the time of emancipation a single day; not to unfurl the flag of slavery; but rather, if it does not wish to collaborate in our task, that it not obstruct, nor disillusion, nor torment those who wish to do something to shorten the captivity and better the lot of the unhappy slaves! (Loud applause from the floor and galleries.)

That speech, like Sodré's, marked an epoch in the abolitionist campaign. Emancipation, though its partisans were few, had taken a great step forward when it could be set forth as an indispensable condition for support of a government. As soon as Nabuco finished his speech, amid the usual applause, Martinho Campos arose. The veteran of the opposition, who with Nabuco had fought the former ministry and was now the real leader of the majority, was far from agreeing with such ideas about emancipation. Later, when he came to power, he declared openly that he was "a genuine slavocrat." Now, in an effort to moderate the effects of Nabuco's words and reassure the landowners, he began very carefully to smooth over the difference of opinion with words flattering the young orator and his cause:

Mr. President, the speech of my honored friend, who has no more sincere and enthusiastic admirer in this body than I, and whom I never see mount the platform without applauding the memory of his illustrious father, brings up the most serious of our social problems (applause), a subject of such a nature that before it, all questions of politics disappear (loud applause).

It is to be expected that a young man of the talent and culture of my honored friend would manifest only sentiments of horror toward slavery, the most fearful of the wounds that the past centuries left on the world (applause).

He said further, "I shall add my requests to that of my worthy friend," but, keeping his true feelings for the words that followed, he went on:

In the meantime, while the honorable President of the Council has the duty to lend efficacious protection to the most unfortunate and unhappy sons of this our country, he has also another duty no less rigorous: do not disturb, do not endanger, I will not say the property but the very existence of the most important part of our population until you have the means to put an end to slavery.

Now the orator felt himself on secure ground. The pacified deputies continued to voice their agreement. Finally Martinho Campos, with kid-gloved hand, gave to Nabuco a tacit reproof and a diplomatic piece of advice:

> The honorable member, whose talent and standing as a real statesman have been amply demonstrated here, as I am the first to recognize, should approach the question from this angle: For the good of the unfortunate slaves themselves, let him see if he cannot help them to live happily in their sorry state until the government has the means to help them, for it is not prudent to stir up questions of this sort, making promises that the government has no possibility of fulfilling (applause).

The President of the Council was in no haste to reply to Nabuco or to make known his manner of facing the problem. It was necessary for Deputy Freitas Coutinho, fearful that the government might agree with Nabuco's "dangerous" ideas, to insist that Saraiva state his position. Coutinho said:

> Shortly after the publication of the speech by the honorable member from Pernambuco, Mr. President, I received from a few of my constituents in the Province of Rio de Janeiro inquiries and objections . . . . I ask the honorable President of the Council to clarify this question, inasmuch as the honorable member from Pernambuco occupies one of the most salient positions in the majority (applause). His Excellency, who through his talents can lend unusual services to the government, which accepts him as one of the elements of its strength in this House, must, I suppose, enjoy a certain authority with relation to the bills presented here . . . .
>
> Felicio dos Santos: The honorable member has great talent, but no authority.

As a matter of fact, he had none. Saraiva, who on April 22 had already said, "Ministries do not have, and cannot have broad programs," now declared under the pressure of questioning: "The present ministry has not considered this question because it is too soon to consider it."

But the question was brought up again and again, and each ministry from then on had to explain its stand on the matter, and in general, each one was characterized in the popular mind by some phrase or slogan, quoted and discussed by the abolitionists, as was Saraiva's remark in reply to Nabuco. His government was referred to in the democratic press from that time on as the cabinet that "did not consider the question," just as that of his successor, Martinho Campos, was referred to as "genuinely slavocrat." Later, Paranaguá and Lafayette, trying not to hurt anyone's feelings on such a delicate matter, merely temporized on the issue. When Dantas, the hero of the abolitionists, came to power, he presented a slogan which was widely acclaimed: "Never stop, never hurry, never retreat." Although he was prevented from carrying out his program, he went down with the cheers of the abolitionists in his ears. Saraiva's second ministry managed to carry out a lame and odious caricature of Dantas' project; Cotegipe succeeded for a time in maintaining his program of the *status quo*, until finally João Alfredo brought about total abolition. Eight ministries and nine years of struggle between the beginning of the campaign in parliament and the great day of May 13!

The session of May 18, 1880, when Saraiva pronounced his "not considered," ended with a speech by Nabuco. Accepting the reply of the President of the Council, he reaffirmed his complete support:

. . . . If the honorable minister should occupy this position for several years, it will be from his own mouth, gentlemen, as he sits in that chair representing the executive power, that I shall hear read in this Chamber the proposed law which will mark the end of slavery in Brazil.

The honorable President of the Council cannot answer for the future, nor do I ask it of him. He, like any laborer given a certain task, answers for the work he has at hand and in mind.

Neither do I want His Excellency to answer for that which he cannot accomplish, but just as the honorable President of the Council is within his rights when he says the government is not now considering this idea, so am I within my rights as a Liberal when I promote within the party the formation of a sentiment favorable to emancipation.

Nabuco was superb in this extemporaneous reply. The applause was recorded as "deafening."

I wanted, and I still want not to let slavery go beyond the year 1890. . . . . Perhaps the living are not with me, but the dead are with me. The Marquis of São Vicente is with me, and the Viscount of Souza Franco, and my father—my father who expressed himself in the Senate in such a way as to leave no doubt as to where he stood.

This speech was still rather optimistic, but when he again spoke on the subject he understood better the resistance which the new cabinet intended to offer him:

The honorable President of the Council said of this question of emancipation that he was not considering the matter, and the honorable Minister of Agriculture repeated the words: "The government is not considering the matter," and from the benches of this Chamber came the voices saying: "The honorable Minister is reassuring the country."

Gentlemen, this is not a question that the government can fail to consider. The government may be of the opinion that it is dangerous to initiate any measures and that no further steps should be taken along this way. The government may think that this law is the statute of freedom for all Brazilians, that beyond it there is no hope for the slave; but the government cannot say that it will not consider a question of this sort, for it is a part of the very life of the country, and even if the government is not considering it, everyone else is. Even more so than the abolitionists and the slaves, you gentlemen yourselves, who see each day the wave of emancipation rising about you, should consider this problem!

Each time he discussed *his* question, greater firmness was noticeable in his tone and words. The fearless enthusiasm of his early ventures gradually gave way to an inexorable will, a conviction completely sure of itself. His whole speech of August 10 was calm, firm, and moderate. "Gentlemen, the idea of emancipation is an idea that is being treated with the greatest of moderation," he could say honestly in reply to accusations of being an agitator. Then he went on:

When a man presents a bill that has to do with slavery, should he be accused of throwing a torch into a powder keg? Gentlemen, when a society admits that its foundations are powder kegs, it is not strange that it sees the incendiary's torch everywhere.

I must compliment the honorable Minister of Agriculture for certain measures taken by him. Gentlemen, this question of emancipation needs to be handled with calmness and not hatred, it needs to be dealt with by common accord (applause); it is a question to whose solution should be called especially those whose great interests are linked to the slave group. . . . .

It has been said that the plantation owners should unite and not permit this question to be settled by others. It should not be settled without the plantation owners, and God grant that it may never be settled against them; but it cannot be settled by them alone.

It is not a matter, gentlemen, that can be dealt with by the agriculturists and the businessmen. No! Brazil is something more than a great coffee exchange.

In this speech he did not mention his bill, but merely several small matters connected with emancipation. He protested the reduction in the emancipation fund of the budget. He inquired about whippings and slave markets, and asked "whether an order had ever been carried out, which was published during Carnival by a previous chief of police, Sr. Pindahyba de Mattos, providing one hundred lashes for any slave who participated in the merrymaking."

As was natural, a small party gradually was formed around him. "We were very few in that legislature of 1879–81," he wrote later in an article about Joaquim Serra, "but even so we were more numerous than in later legislatures." (*O País*, November 1, 1888.)

The reason for this was clear. Those who were suspected of abolitionist tendencies were not re-elected, and Nabuco was among them. Joaquim Serra, another beginner in that legislature who was also later excluded, came to be the most tireless defender of "the cause" in the press. Sancho de Barros Pimentel, another beginner also defeated for re-election, said in the session of July 13, 1880: "I do not wish to retain from my passage through parliament the great regret of having failed at least to make clear my support of the cause so brilliantly defended here by the honorable deputies from Bahia and Pernambuco; especially the latter, for whom the greatest glory I wish is that in the future, when the book of parliamentary history of this country is opened, someone reading his name may feel that impression of sympathy, admiration, and recognition that many free Englishmen must feel today when they see on one of the pages of honor of their history the pure name of Wilberforce."

Nabuco later called the group of friends around him "one of the most beautiful communions that a social idea ever succeeded in producing in our country. . . . . On all matters relative to freedom, we could count on these ten votes, beginning with Amazonas: Saldanha Marinho, Costa Azevedo, Joaquim Serra, Costa Ribeiro, José Mariano, Joaquim Nabuco, Barros Pimentel, Jeronymo Sodré, Marcolino Moura, and Correia Rabello."

Sympathy for their cause attracted much interest to them, especially to Nabuco, who was the leader and the spokesman. Even the Conservative press applauded them for not adopting a radical tone, but appearing to want to help the slaves without injuring the country's institutions. The *Gazeta de Notícias*, published by Ferreira de Araujo, and to which José do Patrocínio ("Proudhomme") and Ferreira de Menezes contributed, consented to publish their bill. This paper, a most benevolent observer though not yet their ally, said on April 26:

> Joaquim Nabuco raised the banner of abolition and sheltered his political future in its shadow. Around him the whole nation, except the slaveowners, gathered its hopes and aspirations. The associations, popular discussion, the press, an increasing number of manumissions, in short, a pronounced antislavery movement, indicate the extent of public judgment on the question.

Nabuco rarely occupied the platform except when an opportunity arose to talk on emancipation. In contrast to his first year when he made so many important speeches, the *Annals* for 1880 show only two discourses of any length. He did not hasten to make a request of urgency in the discussion of his emancipation bill. When he finally did so on August 24, he reminded the Chamber that "since he had not abused the privilege of speaking that year, and had delayed the presentation of his bill specifically in order not to endanger the progress of our labors, he hoped to deserve the favor of the Chamber in conceding him the urgency requested."

It was granted immediately by thirty-eight votes, and seemed a routine matter. But the President of the Council considered it a serious problem. A cartoon of the time showed him running away in fear while Nabuco placed a bomb on the table of the Chamber.

The government decided to have the bill discussed in a secret session.

Martinho Campos sought out Nabuco to make the proposal, which was, of course, refused. The next day Saraiva declared in the Chamber that the ministry would resign "if the Chamber wished to go further than the government in this question." This was sufficient for the supporters of the government to accede to its wishes to prevent the session, and they agreed on a lack of quorum for the purpose. "Mr. Saraiva believes that by preventing the discussion he has solved the country's greatest problem," said the *Gazeta da Tarde* which Ferreira de Menezes and Patrocínio had just founded. ". . . . he has succeeded only in giving frightful proportions to the question of slavery, and in attempting to use pressure on those who represent in the Chamber the honest and liberal aspirations of the whole country. He has added colossal stature to young Mr. Nabuco, who has suddenly become the greatest figure on the political scene."

On August 30, with a quorum present for the first time, Nabuco demanded an explanation.

> The fact that the parliament frequently fails to meet, even without any specific bill on the agenda that might motivate the lack of attendance, might lead me to believe that there was no political reason for the lack of quorum on Friday, if it had not been made known the night before that the Chamber was not to meet that day.
>
> . . . .
>
> I wish, therefore, to know if the government, perhaps for the first time in this reign, intends to intervene in order to stifle freedom of debate in parliament (loud applause). I wish to know if a Liberal government intends to prohibit that which was allowed even in the Conservative parliaments; I want to find out if, at a time when the very institution of monarchy is attacked daily and the unity of the country is discussed, if, when nothing in our institutions is considered inviolable, Slavery alone has the right to be sacred and untouchable; a right that today not even the monarchy has! (A protest is heard.)
>
> The honorable deputy need not again call the attention of the President to the rules of the Chamber. The President of the Chamber understands that this parliament, where great questions are stirred up and the destinies of the country decided, cannot be governed by chicanery (cheers), that in the national parliament it is necessary that all voices and all causes have the right to be clearly set forth, and to fall or die according to the vote of the Chamber.
>
> Gentlemen, I wish to know the opinion of the government in this respect; I wish to know if the honorable President of the Chamber is willing to accept the vote of the Chamber which conceded me urgency, as definitive and still valid.

The rules of order prohibited such an occurence, however, and Nabuco feared that, if he requested a new declaration of urgency, the government would make of it a vote of confidence. He did not wish to place his friends, who supported the government, as he himself did, in a difficult position.

I am willing to withdraw my request if the government, by making of this question of urgency a vote of confidence, attempts to obligate the emancipators either to abandon the cause of emancipation, which depends upon them, or to vote against the government, to which they wish to remain faithful (protests).

I do not wish to place my friends in such a difficult position. As for my own position, it is clearly indicated. . . . . On the electoral law, I differed widely from the government, and voted against it, and I saw with great regret that the Liberal party accepted the reform as its own.

On the question of emancipation, however, in the conviction that it is necessary to go farther than the law of September 28, I would disassociate myself not only from the cabinet, not only from the Liberal party, not only from public opinion and the consensus of the nation, but from everything and everyone! On this point, I make an alliance with the future. Each year will be a victory for our ideas, and ten years from now today's session will stand as one of those historical examples of the divisions, fears, and jealousies of men who recoil from the great saving measures that transform the face of their country. I say in all frankness: it is not in the power of the President of the Council to prevent the fulfillment of this program; it is not in the power of any cabinet, a transitory shadow without reality, a creation of the fancy of the Emperor, to oppose the passage of a measure of this sort, when that very Sovereign knows that the time has come to confer the benefits of freedom upon a million and a half slaves who labor in his country.

The government maintained its intransigent attitude through its leader in parliament, Martinho Campos, and in a formal declaration by one of the ministers, Buarque de Macedo, who, although he had voted for the declaration of urgency, as he explained, "in order not to deny to any of the honorable deputies the opportunity to justify the ideas or bills that he might have to present," now declared to the Chamber that "the present ministers do not accept the declaration of urgency of the honorable deputy."

The request was put to a vote, and failed, seventy-seven to eighteen. The voting was by roll call, and besides the faithful, some of the opposition voted in favor, and one or two who were disgusted with the idea of voting simultaneously on slavery and on a motion of confidence.

"Events are becoming aggravated and accelerated," said the crafty *Gazeta da Tarde*. "Today the guard around the Chamber was reinforced with twenty-four permanent men. Why? The galleries were full. The words of the young abolitionist deputy were drowned with applause. Those of Mr. Martinho Campos were heard with visible signs of disdain."

Nabuco immediately resorted to the device of questioning the President of the Council about the motives which led him to make the matter a question of confidence. This interpellation, which began on September 2, offered new opportunities to discuss the great cause, which this silent war helped more than it harmed. Nabuco showed that he possessed the secret of maintaining the debates on an elevated level, and of being frank and sincere without attacking his adversary. He began his questioning with a tribute to the ministry, which had not lost his support: "In the present condition of the Liberal party, and perhaps of the country, I know of no combination that could possibly offer as full guaranties as that which the honorable gentleman presides over." Having said that, with a few more words of courtesy, he proceeded to prove that "a question cannot be arbitrarily attached to another one," and that the President of the Council "had no right to ask for a vote of confidence in the circumstances, because he was bringing to bear all his authority and prestige on a matter that was simply one for the individual members of the Chamber." He added:

> . . . . I did not want the honorable President of the Council to take on himself the burden of my bill; I merely wanted him not to create obstacles to the development of the idea of emancipation in the Chamber, and not to place the Chamber in the position of having to choose between rejecting the cabinet and rejecting a bill about slavery. . . . .
>
> By a vote of the Chamber, to which I must submit, I have lost the right to introduce my bill. I shall include some of the articles, those which are relevant, in the revenue bill and in the bill on interprovincial transportation of slaves, but my bill as I drafted it cannot again be presented in this session.

His adversaries replied with the most effective weapon of the slavocrats, pessimistic predictions. In 1880, with the future still uncertain, the example of the United States inspired natural fears. On August 30, Martinho Campos compared the position of Brazil with that of several countries that had faced the problem, and found it worse in every way. "The United States cannot be compared with Brazil. It had a slavery which was confined to a very few of its states, with a free population that provided a great industrial development and national wealth. The slave element represented a thirtieth part or less of the population, and a considerably smaller proportion with reference to the principal industries."

On September 2, the President of the Council also spoke, comparing slavery to a swamp, saying: "When we can see the bottom, then boldly, we shall do . . . . the rest . . . . ; as soon as we can dry up the swamp enough to see the bottom, the question will be solved."

Marcolino Moura of Bahia, one of the group around Nabuco, and another who would not survive the next election, arose to comment on the incident. He declared on September 4, 1880, "that the battle fought against the honorable deputy's bill in such an ungenerous manner was not worthy of a Liberal Chamber and did not represent public opinion. That victory was partial and represents the slavocrat interests. It will remain in suspense until the decisive battle, which will be one of ideas and principles."

The great body of slavocrats felt that Saraiva had done the country a great service in preventing Nabuco's action. Congratulations reached him from all sides, and the danger seemed to be over. The English Minister, in a note published by his government in its Blue Book of 1880, said that "praiseworthy as the efforts of Mr. Nabuco in the antislavery cause may be, it is hardly probable that any legislative action he might attempt would be successful, for the great sugar and coffee planters, who are strongly represented in both the Brazilian houses, would employ their best efforts to destroy his plans."

The *Gazeta de Notícias* was confident of the final victory of the cause, in spite of the defeat inflicted on Nabuco by the parliament:

> One glory no one can dispute him [Nabuco]: that of having brought up this question, which will now be studied, and which we are certain will be resolved in spite of the individual interests that oppose it.
>
> The movement recently aroused in favor of emancipation will bring more effective results than Mr. Nabuco's bill; its author may have withdrawn his bill from discussion; he has not, however, withdrawn from the country the conviction that it is necessary to do away with slavery.

Obstructed on all sides, Nabuco presented only the portions of his bill that had to do with taxes and could, therefore, be included in the discussion of the budget. As for the bill, on September 4, 1880, after the incident of the vote, he said he had hopes of "obtaining later from the Chamber permission to present it." The parts of the bill he did present dealt with the suppression of slave markets and the slave traffic between provinces, taxes on the leasing of slaves, emancipation of those captives whose masters left no direct heirs, enlargement of the emancipation fund through various fines, and the creation of relief funds at the request of José Bonifácio, the patriarch, whose name they would bear.

During the rest of the session the Chamber maintained a defensive attitude toward the abolitionist deputies and constantly placed obstacles in their way. Nabuco once asked why the rules of order were interpreted as they were only when it was desired to silence one of the abolitionists. Serra immediately added that they were "obliged to use any subject as a pretext for bringing the whole matter up for debate . . . . making it necessary for the deputy to employ strategic maneuvers in order to be able to exercise one of his rights. . . . . What we are trying to do is to raise the debate to the level which it deserves; it is that attempt that is called seditious and out of place . . . . those who take part in the debate are the professional politicians, the masters who contribute only intolerance or silence."

Rio Branco, author of the "Free Birth" law of September 28, died in that year, 1880. In the session of November 3, when the Chamber was commemorating his passing, Nabuco emphasized "the phase of his career, the high point of his life, which will be illuminated by history when all the rest is submerged in shadow," and added, "even if we did not go beyond the law of September 28, 1871, if we should forget the duty of our time and generation, even so, that law would be enough to light up the future." That was the only sentence in which the propagandist was evident. The speech was given in the elevated and serene tone of a historical judgment, but the slavocrats were watching closely and protested the next day. Martim Francisco declared that the speech did not express the ideas of the majority of the Chamber, that the press exaggerated the effect it produced, and that "since that great soul who has left the earth to ascend to heaven cried out in his last moments against the haste with which some wished to solve the problem of slavery, it is not right for others to try to use as weapons the talent, the thought, and the glory of that notable citizen, in order to attribute to him opinions that were not his."

With such words, Deputy Andrada appeared to be trying to prove that one cannot defend a bad cause without stooping to feeble means, and Jeronymo Sodré thanked him ironically for the "services that the honorable gentleman unwillingly lends every day in the parliament to the great cause of the freedom of the slaves."

Actually, the Chamber and the government would have exposed themselves if they had voluntarily taken a tolerant attitude toward the abolitionists. For simply having praised Nabuco in a literary gathering, Minister of Empire Homem de Mello was criticized by the slavocrat press. The occasion was a simple dinner given for the young defender of liberty at which the minister saluted his former pupil of the Pedro II School with a speech of friendship, alternating reminiscences with predictions of future glory; a friendly party to felicitate Nabuco for having added to his laurels as a parliamentary orator success as a speaker on literary subjects. Occasioned by the third centenary of Camoens, the Gabinete Português de Leitura had arranged a big celebration to be attended by practically all the cultured people of Brazil. Nabuco, master of the spoken word, author of a book about Camoens, and already at the age of thirty an eminent Brazilian, was invited to give the opening address.

Before an audience of four or five thousand, including the sovereigns, he uttered a literary masterpiece, which came to be quoted as a model, and which, even if it had not been so beautifully written, would still have been noteworthy for a phrase he coined which survived, as José Veríssimo said, as perhaps the "definitive wording of the glorious epitaph of Portugal": "Brazil and the *Lusiads* are the two greatest works of Portugal."

CHAPTER VII. THE BEGINNING OF THE PROPAGANDA, 1880

Abolitionist propaganda, which had been severely repressed in parliament, began to increase in strength and volume as its obstacles increased. It had been a long time coming, and never again would it be possible to restrain it. Its popularity was natural and inevitable, for whoever declared his hatred of slavery was merely expressing what everyone felt. The institution was definitely condemned in the opinion of the public, and it was only by an appeal to the right of property, to the need for order, and by emphasizing the threat to the very existence of the nation, that silence had been obtained on the subject for so many years. This blindness, born of familiarity and nurtured by the vested interests, was ready to pass away. The affirmations of the emancipationists, who were referred to by their foes as revolutionaries, anarchists, or incendiaries, needed only to be repeated a few times in order to triumph through their very justice and truth. The public opinion necessary for emancipation existed. The only thing lacking was organization. The group that got together in 1880 to prepare for action was, at first, rather small. "I already knew that you were my companion in this abolitionist campaign, which is beginning all too late," wrote Nabuco on May 8, to Domingos Jaguaribe. "Unfortunately, the good workers are still so few that they are all well known to each other."

These first apostles lacked a printing press. Then José do Patrocínio appeared on the scene with the recently established *Gazeta da Tarde*. The group already contained Joaquim Serra, one of the best journalists of his day. In the different papers for which he wrote, until the final victory found him on *O País*, Serra each day sounded his unique note, which was the defense of the enslaved. If he never dropped the abolitionist tune (topics of "importunate monotony," as he himself wrote in his famous "Topics of the Day," on May 14, 1888, soon after the law was signed), at any rate, as a consummate journalist, he knew how to execute an infinity of variations on the theme. There was no fidelity equal to his; no one wrote so much in favor of the great cause. "From 1880 until abolition," observed Nabuco, "he never let a day pass without a few lines on the subject. . . . . Undermined by a pitiless illness, each morning he salvaged enough happiness to smile on the hope of the slaves, which he saw grow day by day during those ten years like a delicate plant which he himself had cultivated. . . . . When abolition was a fact, when the flower unfolded, he died. . . . . And what a death! What sorrow for his wife and two children, his adored little daughter who did not want to leave his side a moment!" (*My Formative Years*, p. 240.)

The number of the abolitionists increased little by little. On July 9, 1880, André Rebouças, a well-known engineer, an incurable idealist, and a colored man, made this entry in his diary: "I allied myself with Deputy Joaquim Nabuco for abolitionist propaganda. I am to write the first article for the *Jornal do Comércio* on 'Carlos Gomes and Emancipation.' "

From then on Rebouças was one of the mainstays of the new party. "My life and that of Rebouças were one for ten years," wrote Nabuco to a friend in 1898. "Our friendship was for a long time the fusion of two lives in a single thought: emancipation," he said in *My Formative Years*, as he fondly sketched Rebouças' career. "The public thought that Rebouças was distinguished neither by his style nor by his actions; it might be said that in a movement directed by orators, journalists, and popular agitators, there was no outstanding role for him. Nevertheless, his job was the most important of all. Characterized by strictly internal, psychological action, it had the most important, most essential, though hidden, function of the motor, which distributed inspiration to all. He was almost never obvious, but each one of those, who was seen by the public, was looking to him, felt his influence, was governed by his gestures, which remained invisible to the multitude. . . . ." He had a curious complexity of spirit, this professor from the Polytechnical School, methodical, yet a dreamer, absorbed in the practical sciences by taste and profession, yet full of boundless idealism and blind enthusiasm. Well did Nabuco add to his sketch that "his center of gravity was the sublime." Engaged in the preparation of his lectures, in his mathematical research, in the study of astronomy, of botany, and of geology—his knowledge was universal—André Rebouças really lived on his dreams, his great plans for human brotherhood and utopia. He was always busy with some "idyll," as he himself called these projects, some idyll of a poet-philanthropist. "My idyll of this moment," he wrote to Nabuco from the exile he had imposed upon himself after the establishment of the Republic, "is rural democracy in Africa." The distribution of lands and the breaking up of the large estates were always among his most cherished plans. These plans were always vast, always important in their aims, and the details were worked out with scientific care. But first of all, dominating his whole life, was the emancipation of the slaves.

Nabuco testified that while the abolitionists were thinking: "The Negro is a man, he cannot be property," only Rebouças was thinking: "The Negro is a brother, he should belong to our family." Only he of all the abolitionists was moved purely by the human idea of charity, without any ambition for present position or future glory. As none had the fidelity of Serra, so none had the selflessness of Rebouças.

He was the treasurer of the Brazilian Anti-Slavery Society and of the Abolitionist Confederation. What "treasurer" meant in his case may be seen in this unpublished note of Nabuco's: "During the struggle for abolition, it was his pocket that paid secretly for the brilliant functions where the eloquence of others was displayed; he sustained the journals and the societies which were the organs of the cause. While still young, he had amassed a considerable fortune by his engineering labors. Part of it he gave away generously, part he spent for propaganda."

Abolition was his life, not only while the battle continued. It changed his whole course, his whole destiny. "He was a man of industry, a bold and successful engineer, who ended up practicing Tolstoyism. He was a mathematical genius, an alchemist who reduced all his science to a serpentine coil in which he distilled abolition from everything," wrote Nabuco in *My Formative Years*. He was also a near-republican who was to be transformed into an ardent monarchist by gratitude for the event of May 13, when the Princess Isabel signed the Decree of Emancipation. In a letter to Nabuco in 1886 he exclaimed: "It is necessary, however, for you to become convinced that Pedro II and company are your enemies, enemies of Joaquim Nabuco as well as of André Rebouças. They know that you enjoy merely monarchial *tolerance*. The Emperor's error made you as impossible for him and his dynasty as I myself am." But in 1890, what a different tone: "My dear Nabuco! You well know the whole truth. It was She who accomplished abolition, She alone!"

The fear that "She" and the Emperor, his "Holy Master," might suffer because of the glorious law, plagued his existence after May 13. The republicanism of his students, whom he had commanded during the abolitionist campaign, forced him away from the school where he had taught lovingly for thirty years and where he was the most eminent spirit. On November 15, without even bothering to ask the new government for leave of absence from his professorship, he exiled himself with the imperial family aboard the "Alagôas." He became their courtier in misfortune, and his diary became filled with simple pathetic notes such as: "Birthday of the Emperor Dom Pedro II: dinner in honor of the event; the Redemptrix offered a toast to 'Papa' . . . . The Emperor replied: 'Daughter! Hear my toast: To the prosperity of Brazil!' " Or this one: "Everything is just as in a good and saintly family, without the least prejudice. They never say: 'my throne, my kingdom, my empire, my dynasty!' It is always just: 'Brazil, my beautiful country . . . . How I long for beautiful Brazil . . . . for Petrópolis, my home, my garden, my friends!' "

To leave Brazil meant to sacrifice his profession and his means of earning his living, but it never occurred to him to act otherwise. When he left, it was never to return as long as the emancipating dynasty was in exile, even, as he wrote to Nabuco, if it meant selling his last share of stock. For a while he accompanied the Martyr-Emperor, as he called him, living only in the past, only in his reminiscences. "I spend my days," he wrote, "rereading what we did from 1880 to 1888 and I find not a word that should be corrected . . . . thanks be to God."

Of African descent, he carried his sorrow to that continent. Near the end of his life he settled in Funchal, on the island of Madeira, where he practiced his beloved profession, giving free lessons in integral calculus and geodesy to the Englishmen of the Cable Company. From there he wrote to Nabuco: "As for my daily life you may summarize it this way: André lives, and will probably die, in the pious remembrance of Brazil, of Dom Pedro II, and of our forefathers; he finds distraction from his patriotic and humanitarian obsession in astronomy, in botany, and in endless mathematical formulas." Death overtook him tragically. His fall into the sea from the top of a cliff had all the appearances of suicide. Abolition of slavery filled his life and gratitude sacrificed it.

In that sensitive heart with its childishly ardent enthusiasms, hopes, and disappointments, Nabuco occupied a cherished place. Taunay, another dear and intimate friend of Rebouças wrote: "One of the characteristic notes of the existence of that friend of ours was the warm affection he always had for *his* Nabuco. Not even you could estimate the intensity of that sincere veneration."

After their pact in 1880, Rebouças' diary recorded every step in the abolitionist propaganda. The two friends, after the coming of the republic, thought of writing a history of the movement based on that careful record. The book was to be written by Nabuco and—as Rebouças said in a letter—"barely colored by the vehemence of the *emotional race*."

In 1880, there was not yet unanimity of ideas among the abolitionists. There existed among them defenders of total abolition, like Sodré, and others, like Nabuco, who believed in more prudent methods. There was Patrocínio, whose tone was revolutionary, and there were also philanthropists, who, long before this political movement, had devoted themselves to the defense of the oppressed. One of these, Luiz Gama, had been discharged from his position in the police office as early as 1868 in the interests of the public service. Accused at that time of being seditious and a troublemaker, he continued to help the oppressed and the fugitives. He was born in slavery, the son of an African woman who would not accept Christianity, and who was deported as an insurrectionist. Luiz Gama's father was his master, who raised him in his own arms and then sold him as a slave. Luiz made his way in life by his energy and merit. He was practicing law in São Paulo when the abolitionist agitation began. Support such as his for the movement was especially valuable, and Nabuco realized it. That year he wrote: "The powerful contingent attracted to the discussion by a popular writer of great and rare talent, Mr. Patrocínio, and the intervention of a man who has placed his life at the service of the freedom of his race, Mr. Luiz Gama, as well as sentences from several courts, were invaluable aids to us."

As the ranks filled, the differences, both in tendencies and in ways of working for the common aim, increased. From the first, groups were formed according to particular affinities. Patrocínio was the popular leader, the orator and journalist, the representative of the people, and to them he always addressed himself. Nabuco's special group was more intellectual and philosophical. In *My Formative Years* he wrote: "Among those with whom I worked most intimately in 1879 and 1880, and who formed a homogeneous group with me, our own little chapter, the principal figures were André Rebouças, Gusmão Lobo, and Joaquim Serra. . . . . The frontier chapter was that of José do Patrocínio, Ferreira de Menezes, Vicente de Souza, Nicoláu Moreira, later João Clapp, with the Abolitionist Confederation." But they all worked in collaboration. On July 25, the first emancipation conference was held. It was one of the initial steps in the organization of the propaganda. On Sundays, simple little programs were presented. Ladies solicited donations at the doors of the São Luiz Theater, while inside professional artists and amateurs performed without remuneration. The real reason for these programs was the opportunity they provided to give a speech in favor of freedom.

Later the abolitionists were put out of the theater. Rebouças noted in his diary for April 17, 1881: "They refuse to let us have the São Luiz Theater for our emancipation meetings. The thirty-sixth had to be held in the Gymnasium Theater, which José do Patrocínio and I swept while the public waited to get in." Later they went to the Dramatic Recreation Theater. It was Rebouças, the part-time janitor, who always wrote the reports of the affairs for the *Gazeta da Tarde*. Later he wrote: "We became directors of public performances, at 500 reis per person; we swept theaters and posted bills; we were simultaneously editors, reporters, reviewers, and distributors; we were barkers at fairs; we were propagandists everywhere, in the streets, in the cafés, in the theaters, on the railroad trains." In another article he said: "In the São Luiz Theater, in the Gymnasium Theater, in the Dom Pedro II Theater, in the now historic Polytheama Theater, in the Dramatic Recreation, in all the newspapers, in three thousand pamphlets, in an endless number of banquets, at dinners, balls, parties, and even funerals . . . ." Indeed they did go to cemeteries, for the diary records for November 4, 1880: "I am promoting the abolitionist demonstration at the funeral of the Viscount of Rio Branco." Such manifestations were repeated at the graves of Ferreira de Menezes, Luiz Gama, and José Bonifácio, the younger.

One of Nabuco's problems, and that of his little group, was the formation of an antislavery society. Naturally there existed in Brazil emancipation associations and charitable institutions for the purpose of protecting and ransoming slaves. The Brazilian Anti-Slavery Society did not resemble these. Its object was not charity, but propaganda and action by all peaceful and legal means. The founding of the society took place September 7, 1880, at Nabuco's home in Flamengo. The waves could be heard pounding on the quays like "the fierce roar of the slavocrats," reported the *Gazeta da Tarde*. "When Joaquim Nabuco began to speak, the volleys in honor of September 7 began. He spoke to that heroic accompaniment. His pleasant voice, overcoming the roar of the governmental cannons, seemed to say to them: 'You lie! There is no freedom nor independence in a land with one million, five hundred thousand slaves!' "

Nabuco, the initiator of the society, was elected president. The title of honorary president was conferred upon several of the most illustrious persons present, including Muniz Barreto, Beaurepaire Rohan, and Saldanha Marinho, and the title of honorary member was given to the Viscount of Rio Branco.

It also fell to Nabuco's lot to write the manifesto which was widely circulated in three languages, thanks to the translations of the *Rio News* and the *Messager du Brésil*. The appeal made by the new society was written with great moderation, and was based on patriotism, charity, and justice, without invective or denunciation, without mentioning names or politics. It was addressed to the whole nation in clear and positive terms, in an effort to arouse its conscience: "Let our enemies not deceive themselves; we represent the modern right. At every victory for our side, the world will tremble with joy; with every triumph of theirs, the country will suffer a new humiliation. Brazil would be the most backward country in the world, if, having slavery, it had no abolitionist party. That would be proof that moral conciousness had not yet awakened in it."

The society soon took up the cause of the Africans imported clandestinely. "Innumerable Africans," said the manifesto, "are employed in our agriculture, who were criminally imported, and their sons constitute the new generation of slaves. Not even the excuse that slaves are legal property exists in favor of this condition; on the contrary, it is so obviously illegal and criminal that a mere review of the deeds of ownership of slave property would be sufficient to extinguish it."

"It is a question that reached great proportions this year," wrote Nabuco in December 1880 to Adolfo de Barros, vice-president of the Brazilian Anti-Slavery Society. He then enumerated the efforts of the abolitionists on behalf of these unfortunates, and added:

> None of our efforts had as much effect for our cause as the declaration made repeatedly by our adversaries, that to carry out the law of November 7, 1831,

would mean immediate emancipation. This was accompanied by the even more curious statement that the owners of Negroes were careful to register them as being old enough to have been imported before 1831. When the defenders of an institution confess that besides a crime, it is a fraud, that slavery is not only illegally constituted but also fraudulently registered, we have only one thing to do: ask the government to enforce the law.

Besides *O Abolicionista*, a monthly sheet started by the society to record its activities, and whose appearance, according to the first number, "signifies the progress which public opinion has made relative to slavery," Nabuco and his companions had the support of the *Gazeta da Tarde* and the good will of the *Gazeta de Notícias*. They had also definitely won over the able and witty pen of Angelo Agostini, whose brilliant political caricatures appeared in the *Revista Ilustrada*, and the applause, not resounding, but significant, of the foreign papers of Brazil. The *Rio News*, especially, edited by Americans, never tired of showing its admiration for Nabuco and promoting the great cause.

The controversies in the press helped greatly to keep the discussion alive. Taunay, the author of *Inocência* and *Retirada da Laguna*, wrote in the *Jornal do Comércio* combating Nabuco's famous and ill-fated bill. The latter replied in an open letter advising Taunay not to defend a "borrowed cause, against which his nature rebels, and which condemns the youth who embrace it to be spectators of the victory of the generation to which they belong." And further: "Your intervention surprised everyone I have met. It is always a mistake to disappoint public opinion. This explains your alternating affirmations and hesitations, your attempt to soften your blows with pleasant remarks, the real effort you make to hide your thoughts and the consequent lack of sincerity in your style and frankness in your spirit."

The letter was a model of lucid refutation, of subtle analysis and exactness of expression. Much greater interest, however—almost a scandal—was aroused a little later by the publication of another exchange of letters in which Nabuco's correspondent was the American Minister.

The example of the United States had been cited so many times that Nabuco decided to enlighten public opinion by calling upon the diplomatic representative of that country to express his opinions, with which Nabuco was familiar. He had previously obtained his acquiescence to the plan. Minister Hilliard, before becoming a diplomat, had been a slaveowner, had represented in Congress one of the principal slave districts, had fought for the Southern Confederacy, and now testified to the increased prosperity which had resulted from abolition. He replied to Nabuco's request with a long and carefully documented letter, attempting to prove the advantages of emancipation and to reassure the pessimists. He lent himself to the matter with true zeal, beyond the bounds of diplomatic propriety.

Later, in his memoirs, Hilliard spoke with satisfaction of the case, describing the splendid figure, the attractive manners of the young Brazilian deputy and finding words to define well his whole attitude: "Ambitious but unselfish, he devoted his fine powers to the cause of humanity. . . . . In all my life," he continued, "I had never met anyone with such a bright future. . . . . He shone like a star in his country's firmament, and his career subsequently bore out the promise of his youth." (*Politics and Pen Pictures at Home and Abroad*, New York, 1892.)

The *Jornal do Comércio* and the *Gazeta de Notícias* published this correspondence on October 31, and it was also distributed as a pamphlet. In his letter, Nabuco thanked the minister in advance for his reply, referring to it "as a service done to a million and a half human creatures whose freedom depends solely upon their owners' being convinced that free labor is superior in all respects to forced and unpaid labor."

In his reply, Hilliard dwelt upon the fears with which the idea of emancipation had been contemplated in the United States and upon the advantages which its realization brought. He said that as a diplomat he was not disposed to announce his views regarding any of Brazil's institutions, but as a man he was warmly in favor of freedom within an even shorter time than that set by Nabuco.

The Anti-Slavery Society offered a banquet in his honor. A portrait of Lincoln dominated the room. At the end of the dinner, cordial speeches were exchanged. Then the storm broke. Moreira de Barros asked in the Chamber "the meaning of the clear and manifest intervention of a foreign nation in an entirely domestic question" (November 22, 1880). Deputy Belfort Duarte, a sugar plantation owner, also made a speech on November 25, 1880, and questioned the government. He declared that he did not hate "with the holy horror that possesses the emancipators" the institution that "was perhaps the first element of civilization in Brazil."

The letters and the banquet caused such a sensation that on the day set for the President of the Council to reply, the galleries of the Chamber, and even the corridors, were filled with a curious multitude. Saraiva replied in a few words, but they were apt and well chosen: "The Honorable Mr. Hilliard appeared at the banquet in a private capacity. What he said in his letter and at the banquet cannot be construed as anything but personal opinion, which has no official character, and which, while subject to the judgment of the public, is not a matter for the approval or disapproval of the Imperial Government. . . . . If the honorable deputy from Maranhão is satisfied, I shall consider only one topic from his speech. He need have no fears that any foreign government will attempt to intervene in our internal affairs. If that should happen, this government has the assurance that all Brazilians would rally round it, including those fellow countrymen who differ with respect to the manner of solving the problem of slavery."

Propaganda outside parliament succeeded in doing what the emancipationist deputies failed to do from within; namely, to break the tenacious silence which was imposed upon the question in the Chamber. The abolitionist demonstration at Rio Branco's funeral, the articles, the meetings in the theaters, the Hilliard incident, had focused so much attention on the matter that there was no way to escape discussion of it.

On November 9, Joaquim Serra protested the public sale of illegally imported Africans. The slavocrat leader, Martinho Campos, was quick to reply: "Contrary to the request of the honorable deputy, I have more right to ask the Imperial Government to take the necessary measures to restrain the attempted slave rebellions that occur daily in the Empire. . . . . Does the honorable deputy wish to sacrifice the population of the whole Empire to half a dozen brutal and savage Africans? (applause)."

The discourse was a tirade against the abolitionists "who have nothing to lose," people who wear the "cloak of philanthropy at the expense of others," "reformers who admit no reply, who wish to subvert the whole world and upset the whole order of things without giving the victims the right to be heard (applause). What has happened all over the world in our day is not going to happen in Brazil, but the attempt is evident, on the part of a bold, but fortunately, small group." Evidently referring to Patrocínio and his followers, the government leader spoke of the "inflammatory gazettes" and the "unworthy exaggerations and falsehoods with which insurrection and sedition are openly fostered in the theaters of Rio de Janeiro."

The session of November 15 revealed the sharp dissension in the Liberal party over the issue of abolition.

Parliamentary debate on the question was finally permitted. In the session of November 22, one of the deputies most opposed to the abolitionists, Moreira de Barros, declared to the House that he had "changed his opinion radically. There is no reason for the intentional silence that we are observing." He then discussed Hilliard's opinions, opposing them with these words by an American "who is not a diplomat":

> I know how difficult it is to make noble and high-minded people understand that propaganda given out under such conditions can go on growing until it becomes irresistible. But it is unfortunately so, as the plantation owners of the South of the United States found out too late.
>
> The same fate awaits the planters of Brazil if they are not aroused in time. The propaganda which today seems insignificant, tomorrow becomes more imposing, and if it is not blocked, it will cause the complete ruin of the present agricultural class, the glory and strength of Brazil. . . . .
>
> Are the planters willing to wait impassively for this to happen? Would it

not be better to react at once against the propaganda and co-ordinate the elements of defense?

. . . .

Without ever descending to the level of the abolitionists, but instead, remaining on a high plane and fighting with worthy weapons, be vigilant and untiring in countering without delay the ignoble maneuvers by which they attempt to weaken you. And above all, develop among yourselves the spirit of association, strengthening more and more the bonds that unite you.

When the questioning of the minister took place concerning the Hilliard incident, the opinion of the Chamber was so surely and solidly against the abolitionists, and Nabuco's bill was so dead, that there was no cause for their foes to fear. This is seen in the assurance which Deputy Prado Pimentel gave, after Saraiva's explanation:

Mr. Joaquim Nabuco presented a bill which, I regret to tell him, was rejected with general enthusiasm (laughter).

Joaquim Nabuco: By all the slaveowners.

Despite the attacks and criticism ("We have been insulted here, in the press, and everywhere," remarked Sodré interrupting Moreira de Barros' speech), in spite of being what their adversaries called a party without members, or, in the phrase of Martinho Campos, "the party of those who have nothing to lose," the abolitionists saw all over Brazil the results of their efforts. The measures passed by the assemblies of São Paulo, Minas Gerais, and Rio de Janeiro, suspending, by means of a prohibitive tax, the entrance of slaves into those provinces, fitted naturally into the movement. The abolitionists had reason to rejoice over those resolutions, which to a great extent suppressed the caravans of slaves who were transported like cattle, and the cruelties arising from their owners' moving. The other parties likewise approved the measures. The concentration of all the slaves into the three great agricultural provinces, which process had been occurring over a period of time, did nothing to make the final and inevitable solution of the problem less difficult. The efforts of farseeing people toward that end had, until then, been defeated by the immediate needs of agriculture, and the victory of 1880 showed the imminence of the danger.

Another victory for the abolitionists was won that year in the Senate. There, also, the movement was discussed, and when the matter of increasing the emancipation fund came up, as well as the question of the eligibility of freed slaves, the abolitionist tendency triumphed. The majority, naturally, was against it, and Cotegipe protested: "If the government is an accomplice, let it say so, in order that our planters may know under what law they must live, but to live like this in continual unrest is impossible. . . . . Property menaced in this way loses value every day." However, some, like Cristiano Ottoni, made no attempt to hide their sympathy for emancipation. Speaking after Cotegipe about the insufficiency of the amount proposed for the fund, this senator, with the reserve natural to a member of that lifetime body, said: "The ideas that I advance do not mean that I join in the generous, but to my way of thinking more generous than wise, outcry of the illustrious heir to a name the Senate and the country revere."

Agricultural societies were formed to combat the dangerous movement. There were few planters capable of assuming the generous and sensible attitude which Martinho Prado Junior manifested to Nabuco in an open letter. Naturally he was not one of those who wanted emancipation at any price, but one who sought a possible solution. In the letter he declared himself to be not only an admirer, but an enthusiastic partisan of Nabuco, and not only from motives of philanthropy: "I yield, most of all, to an economic conviction that this country will be truly rich only on the day when there are no more slaves."

Outside of the occasional support of an individual such as this, the abolitionists encountered a tremendous resistance in the real centers of slavery, that is, in the most important zone of Brazil. On the other hand, strong support came to them from the provinces where the problem of the slave element could be most easily solved. In Rio Grande do Sul there was a veritable wave of interest in the cause. There the supporters of the movement united to found the Nabuco Abolitionist Society. The Vicar of Pelotas, Father Canabarro, in an outburst which contrasted with the impartial attitude maintained by the Brazilian clergy during the whole campaign, preached abolition from the pulpit, and praised the initiative of the Pernambucan deputy, confiding "in Divine Providence, which will certainly raise up, in every part of the Empire, a Joaquim Nabuco."

Nabuco wrote to one of the organizers of the movement, Alfredo de Mello, that the encouragement he received from the press of Rio Grande do Sul could not have been more helpful or more welcome. He felt that his name was too insignificant to represent so great a cause:

> . . . . But because of the seriousness of the conviction that moves me, the Nabuco Society, I am sure, will never have cause to repent having identified itself with the initiative that I am now taking . . . .
>
> I have always felt kindly toward Rio Grande do Sul; the movement now beginning there increases that feeling infinitely. The work of emancipation is for the present generation a work of sacrifice. Therein lies its greatness. That province, which so many times has spilt its blood for the Empire, will understand that there is another way of serving it that is just as noble: to raise over its territory the banner of emancipation, make its soil free, and give the first example of a province that rejects slavery and closes its frontiers to it, by means of prohibi-

tive taxes, thus creating on the map of Brazil, a bit of ground where no man shall be a slave.

This great example which Nabuco expected came not from Rio Grande do Sul, but from Ceará. There also the movement became affiliated with the parliamentary agitation. The Liberation Society of Ceará was one of the many associations of this kind, born of that first impulse, and did much to arouse the enthusiasm which was to liberate Ceará, town by town before the rest of the Empire. The true authors of this admirable page in the history of the province were the humble raftsmen, who later refused to transport from land to the ships the slaves which the south continued to recruit. Constant witnesses of the painful scenes of separation among the human merchandise they carried, they united as a class under the direction of Francisco do Nascimento, to place an immovable and victorious wall before the slave traffic.

At the end of that first year of struggle so productive of results, Joaquim Nabuco, before leaving to spend the parliamentary recess in Europe, turned over the direction of the Anti-Slavery Society to the vice-president, Adolfo de Barros. In the farewell letter he sent him, which the press made public, he emphasized the gains which had been made.

None of the steps taken seemed more important to Nabuco than having aroused public opinion, including that of their opponents themselves, who could no longer deny the permanent violation of the law of 1831 and the patent illegality of slave property under such conditions. "We forced slavery to recognize itself as illegal, to sit in the prisoner's box, to confess its crime, which is that of piracy and of reducing free people to slavery. This result should satisfy us: it contains within itself the complete solution to the problem."

CHAPTER VIII. TRAVEL AND CANDIDACY. THE INTERRUPTED FLIGHT. 1881

Joaquim Nabuco sailed for Europe at the end of December 1880. Ever since his return to Brazil he had been happily making plans for this flight, delayed so often, and frequently discussed in his letters to the Baron of Penedo. "I shall remain there a month," he wrote to the Baron in London in 1878. "Only one month, but it will be an entire month, minute for minute. If I had been born an Englishman, perhaps I would detest England; but as I was born a Brazilian, I adore it." Later he wrote again: "As September approaches, I find that everything pleases me, and it is likely that I shall take an even rosier point of view in my farewell speeches than I take now."

At the end of the year, he finally left on the trip intended to be a rest, but which was to be devoted to the cause that now dominated his life. Even while absent he wanted to continue working for emancipation, and he did not intend to return to Brazil without first having visited the antislavery societies of Europe and having studied their plans of organization and procedure. From Bordeaux he wrote to the Baron of Penedo:

> Among the motives that brought me to Europe, believe me, neither the last nor the least was the desire to see you. The news that you were in Nice came as a very unpleasant surprise. . . . . Please tell the Baroness how sorry I am not to see you there, and how much I thank her for her desire to have me visit Nice. Up to the last minute I hesitated as to whether or not I should go there at once to greet you, but the knowledge that I have of you and of myself makes me reluctant to come to Europe merely to visit Nice. Today I am a man with a purpose, not yet a fanatic nor a missionary, but a soldier faithful to his post, and in London I can do more for the cause than under the orange trees of the Mediterranean.

At the time of his departure for Europe, the abolitionist press and the party gave Nabuco a warm farewell. It was an occasion for extolling the merits of their chief, but even discounting partisan zeal, he well deserved the eulogy of Gusmão Lobo, written for the *Jornal do Comércio*, of being "the most brilliant parliamentarian the country possesses today."

In Lisbon the press welcomed him in the same effusive way in which his country had sent him off. Slavery was a human, rather than a national problem, and the entire world wanted to see it solved. On this trip through Portugal, Nabuco proved that foreigners did not have to be very familiar with the internal politics of Brazil in order to respond sympathetically to his name. He had brought about the creation of an abolitionist party, and represented, therefore, a humanitarian and universal symbol.

During his stay in Lisbon, Nabuco appeared once in the diplomatic gallery of the Chamber of Deputies. On seeing him there, one of the most accomplished orators of Portugal, António Cândido Ribeiro da Costa, proposed that parliamentary rules be dispensed with and that the Brazilian deputy be invited onto the floor. The Chamber applauded the idea of this unprecedented homage to Brazil, to Nabuco, and to the great cause, and stood up to receive the young abolitionist. The handsome tribute of António Cândido ended with the ardent wish that "in a short time his great work would be concluded and he would have the pleasure of enjoying the realization of the most pure and passionate of his desires—and that all of us, gentlemen, will see lifted and dissolved the last remains of the dark cloud that still hovers over America." The deputy Vilhena proposed immediately afterwards that, as a tribute to Nabuco's visit to the Portuguese parliament, whipping be abolished as a form of punishment in the army.

After leaving Portugal, Nabuco stayed a few days in Madrid, where he wanted to become acquainted with the antislavery society there which was working zealously for complete emancipation in the colony of Cuba. The parliamentary representatives from that island gave a banquet in his honor. Warmly received by his Spanish coreformers, he attended a session of the Spanish Abolitionist Society as the guest of honor, and was made an honorary member. He expressed his thanks to the society in an inspiring speech.

In Paris, he sought out the person with the greatest experience in the slavery question, one Victor Schoelcher, an old man who had dedicated his life to liberating the slaves in the French colonies and who had been entrusted by the provisional government with writing the decree of emancipation in 1848.[1] Nabuco finally arrived in London, whence he wrote to the Baron of Penedo: "Despite the lack of your companionship, it is to me the paradise of Europe." His old friend replied: "Unfortunately, I shall not be in London . . . . to meet you in Grosvenor Gardens, but Arthur [Arthur de Carvalho Moreira, son of the Baron of Penedo] is there and I

[1] Shortly after Nabuco's visit, when presiding at the great anniversary banquet celebrating the abolition of slavery in the French colonies, Schoelcher spoke of Cuba and Brazil: "The Emperor of Brazil, who is said to be a liberal man, ought to feel cruelly humiliated in being the only sovereign of the civilized world who reigns over slaves. Fortunately, the Abolitionist Society founded in Rio de Janeiro is vigilant; and its president, Mr. Nabuco, who a short while ago was in Paris, but sadly enough, could not stay until today, told me that the society was full of zeal and confidence, and fully determined not to rest until the monster was destroyed. Like that society, we also have well-founded hopes.

"Now gentlemen, permit me to interrupt my speech to propose for your approval the following motion: 'The Assembly, gathered on May 5, 1881, in Paris, to solemnize the anniversary of the abolition of slavery in the French colonies, sends expressions of most cordial sympathy to the Abolitionist Societies of Spain and Brazil.' "

hope that you are going to live with him." Nabuco answered from Grosvenor Gardens:

I cannot reconcile myself to the idea of not having you here. It is truly a desertion. To abandon London for an entire winter, with the Parliament open, with the theaters full, with the legation frequented by two illustrious visitors who like you so much! I do not know how to explain your absence. One month would not matter; but three months is an eternity. Do not forget to write to us.

Arthur has treated me very well in Grosvenor Gardens, but it is almost a strain to be there. If it were not ungracious for me to leave him now, when the house is empty, I believe I would look again for a small apartment so as not to be always in a mansion abandoned by its owners, where everything bespeaks past and future grandeurs. It is very lonely in your study, now that we no longer hear you commenting on the menu for the following day and see you with your passion for good cuisine.

Nabuco sent the Baron news of friends and of his daily activities, which were the same as when he had been an attaché:

In the evening we dine at the Club and then go to some theater. Tomorrow being Saturday, we go to the Gaiety. London, as you know, is always the same, except for the absence of the owners of this house, and that changes everything. If from now on all this does not lead you to devise a way of hastening your return, I must believe that your enthusiasm for this city was to a large degree but a reflection of other enthusiasms. I met Corrêa at one of Alfred Rothschild's soirees and had the honor of being introduced to his friend from Marlborough House [Edward VII, then Prince of Wales]. There I also met the beautiful Mrs. Roche, who is preparing to be the beauty of the season and is the same Miss Work whose portrait I have in the frame that was given to me, not by her, but by you.

Despite his enjoyment of worldly pleasures, Nabuco's chief interest in London was in those who could enlighten him about the problem of abolition. The Anti-Slavery Society, founded by the great English abolitionists led by Wilberforce and Buxton, had by this time achieved its purpose in the British colonies. It was still working, however, with the Egyptians and the Turks, and from afar followed also political events in Brazil, the last great stronghold of slavery. The society had already sent Nabuco a message of thanks for the liberation of the Negroes of Morro Velho, and now a great number of the most influential friends of emancipation—politicians, members of Parliament, and philanthropists—took advantage of his arrival in England to gather at a breakfast in his honor. Sir Thomas Buxton, heir to a name dear to the abolitionists, presided at the banquet, and in his speech recalled a similar meeting held to welcome the American abolitionist, Garrison, for work already accomplished. "Now," said Buxton, "it is a matter not only of congratulating, but also of encouraging Mr. Nabuco, conveying to him the sympathy that those present, as well as many of those who are absent, feel for his cause."

In reply, Nabuco reviewed the slavery question in Brazil. He explained clearly the spirit in which he received and appreciated foreign opinion on Brazilian matters. He could not believe that Brazilian abolitionists "need foreign aid, for lack of national support, when the truth is that they hold the attention of their country and receive the support of all elements which have no vital interest in slavery." Nor would he come to Europe to denounce slavery "away from the tribunal which has the right to judge it and will not fail to condemn it," although he was happy when "the liberal opinion of any country applauds the efforts of the abolitionists. We cannot scorn intervention which limits itself to the prayers of the entire world for the progress of our country."

In Brazil, where Minister Saraiva had been replaced by Martinho Campos, the papers naturally took notice of the homages given to Nabuco on his trip. From Lisbon especially, detailed reports reached Brazil concerning his activities and his person. Certainly the most brilliant of these reports were those of Ramalho Ortigão, in his *Letters from Portugal* (*Cartas de Portugal*), and one by Julio Cezar Machado, an ingenious reporter for the *Jornal do Comércio*, which draws a witty profile of Nabuco—"who has too much, really, for one man." The news from Europe increased the irritation of Nabuco's adversaries, who had fought him throughout the whole campaign with attacks in the press, anonymous threats, and the like. They attempted to depict him as being responsible for the depreciation of agricultural lands, and even for occasional slave uprisings which occurred. In the papers, criticisms like this one from a watchful *O Fazendeiro* regarding a plantation tragedy, appeared: "More blood is going to be spilled than the few drops on the laurel-crowned forehead of Mr. Joaquim Nabuco, while he, after having lighted the torch of slave insurrection in this country, courageously and disinterestedly waves his fine plumes in search of European ovations."

A singular accusation then arose among his enemies, which was heard even among those who were not, namely, that Nabuco was acting in a manner damaging to the name of Brazil abroad, and was undertaking imprudent commitments. His friends, on the other hand, rejoiced with him. They celebrated the events in Lisbon at a gathering in the São Luiz Theater, a gala festival with extravagant speeches. Later they met again, in the São Pedro Theater, to celebrate the happy occasion of his return, and organized an "abolitionist banquet" in his honor. Everything was used as a pretext for abolitionist propaganda.

After his return to the homeland, Nabuco continued to devote himself primarily to the advancement of the abolitionist campaign. As a literary distraction, however, he permitted himself to deal with lighter matters in his articles for the *Jornal do Comércio*. He spoke to the Baron of Penedo of "some insignificant articles that, when I feel like it, I write for the *Jornal*, just to kill time." In the first of the series he declared: "I am a volunteer, or rather, a free-lancer. I come in when I wish and when least expected, and thus I am not a clock which punctually marks the course of the week." He used the pseudonym of "Freischutz," but his friends guessed who he was. " 'Freischutz' can be only one person," Serra wrote to him. "The friend in the first row caught you. Your flowing Greek robes swirled about too much."

At that time, the abolitionist brotherhood and some other friends who had nothing to do with politics, used to gather in two rooms which they baptized the "New Club." The furnishings were simple; a table with the necessary writing equipment, two benches, a pitcher, and glasses. The club's chief attraction was its windows overlooking Ouvidor Street, where the members used to sit to look out and converse. All the life of Rio de Janeiro was concentrated in this street. On it, news was disseminated and discussed, and the ladies of the capital came in their carriages to look at the shops and let themselves be admired.

The atmosphere was not one of work. After the society was disbanded, Rebouças wrote to Nabuco with some relief: "We shall be free of the rascals of Ouvidor Street and we shall have only carefully chosen people in our work." In his diary, Nabuco continued to record festivals at the theaters, and the preparation of bulletins to be distributed by the Central Emancipating Association Against Slavery in Brazil, which was ever vigilant against any abuse. On March 28, for example, he notes: "With the approval of the Directing Board of the Brazilian Society Against Slavery, I delivered to Dantas, the Minister of Justice, a protest against the enslavement of Indians in the province of Amazonas."

The cause made rapid progress. Slavery still remained unshaken by the abolitionists' attacks, but the latter were unquestionably the talk of the day and served as the subject of serious discussions as well as newspaper gags. Nabuco was represented in effigy in Carnival floats and began to realize the effects of his great popularity. In his correspondence of 1881, the first sure sign of the fame that he had already won is revealed in the letter of a hat manufacturer requesting authorization to create a model that would carry his picture and be called "The Abolitionist." "If we relied upon our plantation owners to buy these hats," wrote the dealer, "we would really get nothing, for the name alone is enough to put them to flight. However, let us sell the hat in São Paulo and Rio de Janeiro, secure in the knowledge that as far as quality is concerned it will not be inferior to any foreign hat."

Despite all this, Nabuco found himself without support in the Liberal party. His term of office expired, and the party which had fostered his election in 1878, would have nothing to do with him in 1881. The other party which he had created was vociferous, but it did not have enough strength in any province to elect deputies.

The Chamber to which he belonged was supposed to have met for the last time in September. Its dissolution, decreed shortly after his arrival, put him in political retirement even earlier than he had expected. He did not take care of his own political future while there was time. With his name, his friends, and his talents, he needed nothing but a little excusable, self-interested prudence in order to obtain the positions which everyone predicted he would have. "Had Nabuco been a skeptic," says José Maria Bello in his excellent biographical sketch, "a simple worldling, or a mere intellectual, concerned only with gathering the pleasures in life that these things offer, he would have continued in a diplomatic career or he would have aligned himself with one of the political parties of the Empire, where, under the shadow of his father's prestige, he would have gained rapid access to the cabinet, to the Senate, and to the presidency of the Council itself."

He did nothing, even to secure definitely the seat that the party willingly offered him. In the meantime, however, he could show proudly that he had brought about the birth of a great campaign, which was responsible in large measure for the overthrow of a ministry and the triumph of direct election without constitutional reform; the same campaign which prevented the concession of the Xingú Valley and freed the slaves of Morro Velho. Finally, he could point to the fact that he had fascinated the Chamber with his oratory and had made a name for himself throughout the country. All this was well worth the sacrifice of a seat in parliament to one who always believed, as he once wrote to Graça Aranha, that "influence is worth much more than position."

From the very beginning his attitude left no room for doubts, so that, shortly after his first success, a friend wrote to him from Pernambuco: "There is no one in this land today who does not applaud your election, and those who did not help in it declare themselves repentant and have become your enthusiastic supporters. However, in the next contest, the government will win."

In February 1881, Nabuco wrote to the Baron of Penedo: "After all, it will be a consolation for me to know that I did not use the Chamber to prepare for my re-election. Governments know whom they choose." When he left diplomacy for politics, his desire had been to remain on the diplomatic list of personnel, so as to be able to return to his post if political life did not agree with him. In one of those moments of discouragement, which were not lacking in his political career, he had written to the Baron of Penedo:

It is not necessary to remain very long in politics in order to develop a profound disgust and an invincible aversion for it. Even though my position in the country does not correspond to that of an attaché in the diplomatic corps, it is so necessary for me to have a foot outside of politics, on less swampy ground, that I am obliged—not having a fortune nor any trade (the profession of lawyer is today a business)—to place myself again on the lowest step of the diplomatic scale. Nevertheless, the compensations are great. Among them are: fleeing from the summer, which was so nearly fatal to me last year; bathing in the spirit of England, so necessary after a period of absence; retempering myself in that much greater and vaster life that one finds in the capital of the world; attending the elections, the Derby, the Oxford and Cambridge boat race, which I have never seen; and above all, talking with you about all manner of things and living near Grosvenor Gardens and Hyde Park.

In spite of all these plans, two months after this letter was written Nabuco had requested his own dismissal from the post of attaché, because he regarded it as incompatible with his political attitude. It was not fitting that a legation attaché make accusations against the government, head the abolitionist campaign, and carry on a debate in the Chamber with the Foreign Minister regarding Chinese emigration, especially when the applause indicated that he, Nabuco, was right. If he had not requested his removal, it probably would have come anyway. The Sinimbú cabinet even proposed his dismissal in a dispatch, but it was not put into effect because the Emperor objected.

The liberalism of Pedro II prevented him from assuming an intransigent attitude toward the abolitionists. Arriving in Brazil in May 1881, Nabuco told the Baron of Penedo that he had been "the other day with someone who can do everything and command everything. The Emperor asked me about you and your whole family. . . . . We spent an hour conversing and several times he told me: 'Talk with our friend José Caetano' [Councilor José Caetano de Andrade Pinto, son-in-law of the Baron of Penedo]. He already sees that the issue is emancipation."

In October 1881, Pernambuco being closed to him, Joaquim Nabuco presented himself to the electors of the first district of the capital. Later he said to his constituents at Recife:

I knew that I would not be elected by any district, but it was my duty to fight. . . . . It was under such conditions that I presented myself as a candidate from the capital. . . . . At that time, emancipation was no more than an aggressive idea; it had not yet been accepted by the national conscience. The Liberal party did not take it into account, and therefore, in presenting myself in the name of that idea, I was placing myself outside of the party, with the abolitionist votes as my only resource. Even among my supporters, the necessary indoctrination was not complete.

What he meant by political indoctrination was described in his circular to the electors:

> The practice of begging for votes is absurd, pernicious, and completely out of harmony with the true principles of representative government. The elector's vote should neither be requested, nor given, as a personal favor. It is as much in the interest of the constituents to choose well as it may be in the interest of the candidate to be chosen. To ask a man of honor to vote in accordance with his conscience is an insult. The practice of secret bargains is reasonable in a system where men are sent to parliament to serve themselves. It is, however, the height of absurdity in the system where they are sent to parliament to serve the public.

With characteristic dignity and simplicity, he announced his stand in that circular, in a manner more likely to win the admiration of cultured minds than to gain the votes of tepid partisans. It deals primarily with the problem of the slave element, but the final sentence betrays the author's psychology. Nabuco, who was really a strong man, was also to a high degree a nervous and sensitive person. Despite his inexperience and despite a great disdain for what he always called "politics with a small p," the circular records one of the rare, short moments in which his political resoluteness weakened. Full of independent spirit and pride, its author says:

> I have no political ambition. Since the Andradas held power, I know that there has not been one man among those loyally serving the country who has found political life anything but a continual source of bitterness and sadness. I understand, however, that in the parliament where my family's name has appeared since the first assemblies of the Empire, I now have a part to play in the cause with which I am identified, and for this reason alone I am fulfilling a duty of honor by presenting myself to you as a candidate. If I merit your votes, worthy electors, I shall be fully compensated because of the benefits which your choice would give to an entire population of social foundlings, who should be entitled to a voice in the parliament, just as the accused has a defender before the court of justice. If, however, I am not elected, I shall leave political life without regret. If, during the period of Liberal dominance, I was unable to find a way to continue in politics, it was only so that I would not confuse the cause of my nation with that of slavery, for I have tried at all costs to separate the two issues.

On July 9 his diary notes: "I have seen evidence of the influence of my circular. At the same time that I write for votes, I am thinking of writing my farewell speech. Two careers sacrificed—diplomacy and politics. What next?" He continued in the meantime to defend in his articles in the *Jornal do Comércio* the candidacy which "represents, not an individual, but a policy," and to develop his ideas about slavery and the reasons for his fight against it:

One of the worthiest ambitions that the politician can have is that of assuming in the present an attitude which will be approved in the future; up to a certain point it even characterizes the statesman. This was not, however, the determining reason for my action. Service to the emancipation ideal today, for the one who wants to be loyal to it, is complete sacrifice, without compensation, not only of career but of name. It is the renunciation of the present and the future: renunciation of the present because of the antagonism that any of the phases of that great cause necessarily produce between those who wish to take a forward step and the powerful section of society which resists it; of the future because history shows that the achievement of a reform does not fall to the one who promotes it or discovers its necessity. Among us, glory has a bit of materialism in it and is accorded only to those who are in power. It rests in the hands of the Emperor, to be distributed to those persons of his confidence.

I was not led to combat slavery by any self-seeking motive, but by my own moral structure, which is incompatible with it. I did it, feeling within myself the only patriotism worthy of the name: that of a Brazilian who wishes to have the right to acknowledge his country without having to conceal, shamefully, that in the nineteenth century and in a free America, it is still a slave market.

Slavery is a word that may have lost all meaning for certain consciences, but for others it is like a branding iron, stamping the mark of degradation on the forehead.

To those accustomed to breathing the atmosphere of slavery, such reasons will not seem sufficient to determine the conduct of a politician; the electors of the capital, however, will understand and sense them. It is for them to say whether it is not yet time to do justice to the race which has made our country what it is, in such a way that one can say of it, in the words of the inscription on the great works of the Nile erected by myriads of slaves—"This task did not tire the arm of an Egyptian"—: "This task did not tire the arm of a Brazilian."

His colleagues in the Brazilian Anti-Slavery Society sent out to the electorate a request for them to elect the great defender of liberty. Councilor Octaviano, a very influential man in the district, did the same. Nothing, however, could help Nabuco. His condemnation was in his own platform, and the other candidates were so well aware of this that they fiercely resisted the sin of abolitionism. One of them protested against the accusation of such a sin with these words: "The slanderer, knowing that I was still ill in the city of Paraiba do Sul, took advantage of this circumstance to publish his perfidious insinuation at the late minute and in such a way that it was impossible for me to answer it in time. Since this calumny, read a few moments before voting, must necessarily injure me, I come to nullify it. To do this it is unnecessary to remind you of my conduct. In the Chamber, far from supporting Joaquim Nabuco, I have declared myself against his ideas with regard to the slave element."

Under such circumstances, it was not strange that the candidate of the abolitionist party should gain only a handful of votes, slightly less than Quintino Bocayuva, who was also defeated and also represented an insignificant party: the Republican. "When I think of the methods that I used to be elected," Nabuco wrote, as always to the Baron of Penedo, "of the way that I directed myself to an electorate of men of conviction, of ideals, and of great motives, it seems to me as if it were all a dream. I did not ask for a single vote, but they are few who can get something without asking." The election, the first in the whole country after the new law, disappointed the Liberal party. Nabuco continued in the same letter: "What a humiliating defeat for the Liberals. Two ministers are out, the Conservatives won in the province of Rio, and Pernambuco is threatened in the same way."

Of the twenty-one legislatures elected during the period of the Empire, this was the first and only one in which the name of the Nabuco de Araujo family was missing, a name which was represented in the Brazilian parliament from the time of independence up to the proclamation of the Republic.

The complete defeat of one who undeniably had been the most brilliant individual in the previous legislature was small honor for the Liberal party, and António Pinto, a deputy, had the audacity to say so on September 12, 1882, when the new Chamber met:

> . . . . this party, in order better to exclude abolitionist ideas from its confines, banished its best champion and most brilliant genius, the distinguished Joaquim Nabuco. Gentlemen, a party which excludes from parliament a figure of such stature, does not desire progress or reforms, much less the abolition of slavery.
>
> Mr. Escragnolle Taunay: Granted; it was a lamentable injustice.
>
> A deputy: It was not the Liberal party.
>
> Mr. Moreira de Barros: It was the first district of the capital that gave him only ninety or so votes.
>
> Mr. António Pinto: The Liberal party has no defense; it was bound by honor to bring about Joaquim Nabuco's election as deputy, come what may. . . . . My criticism is directed against the Liberal party, which sacrificed and condemned to ostracism one of its finest hopes, one of the richest ornaments of our national representation.

Removed from politics, Nabuco decided upon a plan of temporarily exiling himself from Brazil. His letters to his old friend, Penedo, document the entire development of this idea. On July 8 he wrote:

> Uncertain as the outcome of the election is, I must think of what I shall do if I am not re-elected. I have thought seriously of establishing myself in London. My reasons for not remaining in this country, in the event of an electoral defeat, are very strong, and those for not accepting a post or commission from the government, at least now, are obvious. Things being so, I should like to go to London on my own account to look for means of earning a livelihood. I suppose that if I

opened a law office to furnish information on Brazilian legislation, as much as to deal occasionally with Brazilian matters in London, and if I had your support and aid, as well as that of your friends, and of the companies already established there, I could make a living, keeping busy at the same time with other matters such as consultations, work on the story of my father's life, and the publication of two or three books that I have in mind, not to mention a paper that I could found for Brazil, which would be useful to all classes.

The idea for a paper disappeared, because the *Jornal do Comércio* invited him at that time to become its correspondent in London. Having accepted, Nabuco wrote to his old friend, Penedo: "I hope that our friendship will become even closer because of the kind of work to which I am going to dedicate myself, and for which I am taking a virtual library of manuscripts and documents." On July 21 he wrote:

After the stand which I took in the Chamber regarding emancipation, and the position in which I now find myself with respect to this reform, it would be impossible for me to accept public employment without losing my freedom of action. There remains to me, then, the prospect of working, and for work I prefer a place other than this, where any of my work would always be subject to politics, to the demands of friends, to the upsets of a new electoral period, and finally, to the temporary condition of a suspended, but not abandoned, career.

On September 23:

On October 31 the elections will take place. I am going to compose with José Caetano or Rodrigues a telegram that I want to send to you. . . . . What I ask of you is that if you receive the telegram saying "lost," be prepared to see me arrive in London soon after, as an emigrant, bringing with me the mission of erecting a monument to my father's memory by the publication of his works and life story, and proposing to accomplish this labor of love and devotion while engaged in earning a modest living.

He left Brazil on February 1 for an exile of indefinite duration. In his farewell to his former professor, Baron Homem de Mello, who later reminded him of the phrase in a letter, he said: "There I have a beautiful, pure wave to glide upon. Why should I stay here and become entangled in such picayune matters?"

During the two years that he was away, voices were raised against his absence on several occasions. It was called desertion and the abandonment of his post in the vanguard of the abolitionist campaign. Besides criticisms from his enemies, there were even some among his followers. At a great abolitionist festival, orators exchanged heated arguments about the matter, in the midst of shouts of approval and disapproval from the divided audience. José do Patrocínio was one of his enthusiastic defenders, and on the following day reinforced his speech with an article in the *Gazeta da Tarde* of April 23, 1883:

Vanquished at the polls, Joaquim Nabuco could live in Brazil only if he enjoyed complete independence.

Everyone knows that he is not rich.

He must, therefore, work, but in such a manner as to maintain the same position that he had before.

His profession is law.

Now, in this profession Joaquim Nabuco immediately had as an obstacle the animosity of wealthy people. These certainly would not bring cases to him, for that would be the same as entertaining an enemy who was sure to harm them.

Journalism remained open to him. He could use this as a means of keeping alive.

Who would hire him?

Which wealthy papers would have the courage to assume the responsibility of having his name on the staff?

I speak with the experience of one who has seen the list of lost subscribers being made up many times.

No one could defend his position better, however, than Nabuco himself. He did so on his return, in one of his historic lectures at the Santa Isabel Theater:

Those who attack me for having left, do me the honor of considering me a power in politics. Otherwise the accusation would have no basis. What they do not want is for this power to destroy itself, or be diminished. Very well, after my defeat I was convinced that the best way of maintaining this thing that they call power was to withdraw for a while from the country. Gentlemen, I did not consider myself to be the chief of the abolitionist party, but only a man who had a chance, by speaking about it in parliament, to call the country's attention to the most serious of its ills. This man had no soldiers at his command, he had companions as free of action as himself.

The best and most useful thing that he could do for his cause was to owe nothing to slavery, and to accept nothing from slavery. My duty was to safeguard my freedom of action, to be ready always to let my thoughts be known, and to speak the truth to the government. That duty kept me from becoming a public official, but for the same reason I could not live without independence and dignity. On the contrary, my obligation was otherwise. It was to make my life a continual protest against slavery, as Victor Hugo did against the Empire, to take an illustrious example and one that would have been in vain if it did not influence proceedings such as mine. I was not going to remain inactive in Europe. My method of action was the word and the pen. Being unable to speak—and he who has spoken in parliament always feels himself in a relative vacuum on other platforms, because on others one cannot be heard by the entire nation—I would write, and my book, *The Abolitionist Movement*, is the greatest service that I personally could give to our campaign. Not only that; from London I did not intend to lose sight of slavery, on the contrary, I intended to have eyes only for it. Proof of this could be heard in the great shout of alarm that I made against the sale of the freeborn in public auction, a shout that brought an end to that new market of free slaves. . . . . Furthermore, gentlemen, the work of the abolitionist chief, if we had and needed one, when on the contrary we need not to have one, could not always be done in the capital, for it is not there that the true abolition movement is developing; it is in the provinces (applause). The capital is refractory and nothing is attempted there. In compensation, one by one the provinces are burning themselves to be purified for the sacred call that attracts them. The abolitionist chief should not be only in Rio, but in Ceará, in Amazonas, in Rio Grande do Sul, and so on. The decentralization of the abolitionist movement, which I had thus foreseen, justified my action completely (applause).

Centrifugal force has increased the velocity of our course toward the future. I was a politician, and the time had arrived for men of action. They were the ones who could transform abolition into a consummated fact in the country before it was done by law. My absence favored, more than it harmed, the movement, giving it greater liberty than it would have had, had it been limited to accompanying me. We do not need chiefs, nor tactics, nor solemn meetings . . . . we have an opinion which is growing, we have a party free and open to all (applause).

CHAPTER IX. THE EXILE. JOSÉ DO PATROCÍNIO AND THE ABOLITIONIST CONFEDERATION. 1882–84

In writing about the city which he had chosen for his exile, Nabuco enthusiastically exclaimed: "The fact is that I love London above all other cities and places that I have seen. Everything in London strikes in me an intimate and resonant chord: its vast parks and woods, and the blackened bricks of its buildings; the giddy movement of Regent Circus or Ludgate Hill, and the dark recesses of Kensington Park, shaded by century-old trees; the warm summer days, when the asphalt softens under the feet, the leaves are covered with dust, and the air is like a Turkish bath; the delicious days of May and June, when the top-floor windows are transformed into hanging gardens, and the big flower beds in the parks are filled with tulips and hyacinths; the moonlit nights, which sometimes in the mist made Park Lane with its mansions seem to me like a bit of Venice, and which, as I looked from Piccadilly over the thick fog of Green Park toward the illumination around Buckingham Palace, always gave me the illusion of the other side of Rio Bay, seen from the Gloria esplanade; the dark, sad, foggy, winter days, which I would not have traded then for the blue of the Mediterranean nor the clearness of the Attic sky; the city's air of being the metropolis of the world; the magnificent beauty of its people; the smallest details of its own physiognomy; the counters of its luxury shops in Piccadilly and New Bond Street, with the hansoms stopped in front; the *Times*, the *Pall Mall Gazette*, the *Spectator*, together with the velvety paper, the large, clear type, and the smooth, soft, gilded leather of its books; the tranquillity of the clubs, the shelter of the churches, the silence of Sundays, as well as the confusion, the movement, the disorder of Charing Cross and Victoria Station created by the immense wave of all classes and ages that on Saturday afternoons pours from London to the seashore, to country homes, and to the banks of the Thames."

Everything contributed to the majesty of that metropolis which so fascinated him. "It is the silence that envelopes it; the calm, the tranquillity, the repose, the confidence that it breathes; it is the concentrated, collected, at times severe, air of its countenance, together with the urbanity of its manners; it is the seclusion in which one may live in the midst of its busiest streets . . . ."

As he wrote upon arrival, to the Baron of Penedo, it was not his own pleasure which he sought there in 1882: "Regardless of whether my absence be short or long, it is necessary that I utilize the time of my self-imposed banishment for work, rather than play. That is what I must do: work, study, and learn."

Nabuco's life in London was all work and study. He spent a great deal of time in the solitude of the British Museum. His notebook, his library, and his files all indicate that in those two years he read everything in existence about slavery, besides delving into political economy, finance, and all other subjects connected with the life of a nation. This, however, he did without sacrificing his reading of the literature of the day, those works of pure beauty which are pleasant as well as indispensable to the intellect.

It was only because he had such ease of expression, such instinctive eloquence, such a ready imagination, that his immense capacity for work could pass unnoticed. In London, in addition to the real and disinterested effort which he expended on the study of slavery, he had the essential work of earning his livelihood by writing articles for the *Jornal do Comércio* and letters for *La Razón* of Montevideo, as well as by rendering legal services, as a consultant on Brazilian law to English companies. For the latter he received twenty-five pounds per month. As a journalist, he earned forty.

His functions as correspondent for the *Jornal do Comércio* took a great deal of his time, but demanded conscientious work rather than the brilliant production of which he was capable. He had to be very careful not to leave out the smallest items of general interest, for he was writing at a time when such articles played the important role which the telegraph service would later assume. Nabuco's London letters are full of life and interest. Although they were written in an impersonal manner, his already characteristic style shone through. He became ironical in speaking of the latest original exploit to gain public attention, and commented with due dignity on great political events. He included society—at least enough to mention the great parties given by the Baron of Penedo—and also touched upon letters and art; but his principal concern was with politics. It was his true element. He referred to the business of state as if he followed it not through duty, but through pleasure; as if he were exploring it in the hope of one day putting its lessons into practice in another land; like one who followed the speeches and the gestures of Gladstone as a disciple and not as a journalist. No one was better informed and no one was more impartial than he. He gave the real history of contemporary England, with minuteness, comprehension, and breadth of vision. From Brazil, Machado de Assis wrote to him:

. . . . let me tell you that not only do I greatly appreciate your letters from London to the *Jornal do Comércio*, but that my friends and others with whom I have talked have the same feeling. I would point out that the difficulty, as you know, is great, because generally English affairs (not only those mentioned in your letters concerning local customs and interests, but even those of wider significance) are not well known in this country. To write so that everyone could follow them with interest was not easy, yet that was what you did. Your political reflections and your progressive and moderate spirit, in addition to your style and knowledge of the facts, lend much prestige to these writings. There is one passage which I consider as a warning, and though I do not know whether it has yet imbedded itself in the minds of our public men, I feel that they should always keep it before them: it is the one which refers to our debt, words of gold, which I hope are not gone with the wind.

Concerning the ten years of the abolitionist campaign, Nabuco later wrote: "By writing articles unwillingly for *O Jornal*, and at the same time doing research for *The Emancipation Movement*, and writing about slavery, I never renewed my literary powers."

Nabuco at this time announced to the Baron of Penedo that he had begun to write the afore-mentioned book, *The Emancipation Movement*: "As you see, I am a man with only one idea, but I am not ashamed of this mental narrowness, because that idea is the center and circumference of Brazilian progress."

Later, in 1886, he stated in his treatise, *The Eclipse of Abolitionism*:

> For eight years I did almost nothing else, and in this way my naturally erratic intelligence was restricted, not to thinking about that idea alone, fortunately, because that would have meant its confinement and death, but to producing nothing that did not have a direct and immediate relation to the country's organic sickness, its incurable ill.

Before writing *The Emancipation Movement*, Nabuco collected everything that he could find about slavery. He thoroughly examined all forms of that nefarious institution in every country in the world and in every period of history; he studied every aspect of its social and economic consequences; and he familiarized himself with the life, the ideas, and the methods of all the notable and obscure men, who in any epoch had defended the same ideal that he now did. Supplied with all this documentation and with every possible set of statistics, he created in *The Emancipation Movement* the gospel of his party, a book in which his discreet and artistic erudition furnished the necessary solid background, without ever making his rich, clear, sprightly style seem dry. There was no argument that was not skillfully presented in this book, which was a complete indictment of the institution which Nabuco accused of being in Brazil, "even today . . . . as hard, barbarous, and cruel as it was in any other country of America. By its very nature slavery is all this. . . . . Slavery, indeed, cannot be any other thing."

He gave the history of slavery, exposing its legal, social, and human flaws together with their influence upon Brazil, its society, and its politics.

He methodically pointed out and ardently denounced every danger and every weak point of slavery. In presenting the eager, young abolitionist party, he answered the accusation that it was unpatriotic by saying:

> The whole task of the advocates of slavery has always been to identify Brazil with that practice. Whoever attacks slavery is soon suspected of connivance with the foreigner, of being an enemy of the institutions of his own country. In this manner, António Carlos was accused of not being a Brazilian. To attack the monarchy, although this is a monarchy—or religion, although it is Catholic—is permissible to all; but to attack slavery is treason and a felony . . . . slavery, attacked in its most protected refuges, where it has become interwoven with everything in the country most dear to all of us, and wounded, so to speak, in the nation's arms, raises the cry of "treason" against the abolitionist.

The book did, in fact, establish the abolitionist party's code and, without praising individual efforts, made known the accomplishments that the abolitionist movement had already achieved:

> It is still too soon to give honorable mention to those who have contributed to the cause, and it should be the desire of all that the number of workers at the eleventh hour be so great that it will later become impossible to make personal distinctions. In order to combat the new idea, our adversaries need to transform it into the human form of individuals. . . . . What is significant for us today is only the country's suffering: as for the talent, the devotion, the enthusiasm, and the sacrifices that the abolitionists are now expending, our most ardent wish should be that no sign of all this remain, and that an amnesty of the past shall eliminate even the memory of the fight in which we are engaged.

The Emancipation Movement belongs unfortunately to the ephemeral literature of propaganda books. Once the goal is achieved, they no longer have more than a historic interest. It does, however, reveal the full activity of a strong mind, masterful argumentation, and such passion in defense that it is still full of life. Its vibrancy, created principally by its eloquence, outlives the subject and makes the book seem more like a speech before a living audience than the scholarly work that it was. For example, there is this passage, directed against the common objection that it did no good to attack slavery because the case against it was already won:

> Yes, it is won, but in the eyes of a dispersed, apathetic, and intangible public opinion, not of parliament and the government, the concrete organs of opinion; in the eyes of religion, but not of the Church, neither the communion of the faithful nor the constituted priesthood; in the eyes of science, but not of the scientific bodies, the professors, the men that represent science; of justice and right, but not of the law that is their expression, nor the magistrates who are the administrators of the law. . . . . It is won in the eyes of the political parties, but not

of the ministers, the deputies, the senators, the provincial presidents, all the candidates to the leadership of these parties, nor the electors that form the plebeian element of that aristocracy; in the eyes of Europe, but not of the Europeans established in this country who, in large proportion, either own slaves or do not believe in a Brazil without slaves and fear for their interests; in the eyes of the populace, but not of the people; in the eyes of the Emperor as a private citizen, but not as the chief of state; in the eyes of Brazilians in general, but not of Brazilians individually. In short, it is won in the eyes of theoretical jurisdictions, political abstractions, forces not yet in the realm of the possible, generous and impotent sympathies, but not of the only tribunal that can effect the freedom of the black race, that is, the constituted Brazilian nation.

Writing this book was the greatest service that he could have rendered his country while absent. His untiring zeal was not content with it, however, as his extremely active private correspondence demonstrates. He prepared a formal protest to parliament on behalf of those who shared his views, which was presented by Deputy António Pinto on July 14, 1882. "It was signed," Rebouças wrote to him, "by the 'Faithful'." In an eloquent letter to the President of the Council, the Viscount of Paranaguá, Nabuco denounced a scandalous placard from Valença announcing the sale as slaves of some young, freeborn, African men, and some octogenarians, a leper, and a blind man. The letter was published in the *Jornal do Comércio*, together with a note from the government declaring that it had taken the steps necessary to prevent a repetition of such sales.

Nabuco's letters to his friends are true proof of his unfailing interest in the cause. In those sent to Rebouças, he made plans for a publicity campaign. To Serra, speaking of the personal attacks to which the abolitionists were subjected, he said: "We must be tied to the pillory of public calumny, raised for the defense of society before the slave market. When the market vanishes, we may be sure, the pillory will also vanish." He wrote Gusmão Lobo to ask that the Brazilian Society, which had for the moment waned, meet at least once a month and not be permitted to die. On April 7, 1883, Rebouças wrote to him about the society: "You see that our beloved daughter has been reborn." Nabuco tried to get the European press to follow events in Brazil more closely, and to give due importance to the program of gradual emancipation in Ceará, whose progress his fellow workers communicated to him in letters and telegrams. The *Times* published a speech he made at a dinner attended by all of the Brazilians living in London and by some diplomats, to celebrate the emancipation of the slaves in Fortaleza.

In 1883, the eleventh Conference of the Association for the Reform and Codification of the Law of Nations met in Milan. Nabuco attended it in an unofficial capacity at the request of the Anti-Slavery Society, which considered him the most competent orator to call the congress's attention to the slavery problem. "I shall always remember," Charles Allen, secretary of the society, later wrote to him, "the visit that we made together to Milan in order to obtain from the conference the declaration that the slave trade should be considered piracy, and at which, as you know, a member of our executive committee, Mr. Alexander, skillfully supported the cause that you so powerfully advocated."

Nabuco delivered a long address to the conference, with, according to the *Anti-Slavery Reporter*, "all the fire and eloquence for which he was so noted." The papers in Milan christened him the "lion of the session." The resolutions that he suggested were acclaimed by the congress. He himself wrote to Rebouças, regarding these resolutions:

> You will note that one of them refers to that ignominious clause for the extradition of fugitive slaves by which Brazil can obtain their return from the government of Montevideo, and which is null before the human conscience. You will also note that the clause relative to extradition is copied verbatim from the very praiseworthy protocol in Brazil's extradition treaty with France, which I made public in my book. The article concerning the possession of slaves by foreigners is based upon the terms of the Second French Republic's immortal decree of April 27, 1848.
>
> On the following day, Mr. H. Richard proposed that the resolutions voted upon the day before be sent to London to the representatives of all the powers there, to be transmitted to their respective governments. The proposal was unanimously passed, its sponsors justifying by the urgency and special nature of the subject, this notable distinction conferred by the congress on one series of resolutions among all those voted upon in the session this year.
>
> At the municipal banquet, my toast to Italy became a eulogy of the abolitionist idea in Brazil, and I returned from Milan very well satisfied with the results obtained.
>
> Good-bye, my dear friend. Courage and confidence! One day we ourselves shall have a free homeland. Already we can see that this is not to be reserved for another generation, as was imagined when we began the campaign.

Whether absent or present, Nabuco had the problem of maintaining his complete independence from the government of Brazil in order never to interrupt his propaganda campaign. A note from his diary states:

> May 13, 1884. P. asked me if I wanted to earn £4,000 (100,000 francs) in the Waring dispute. It is outside of my plan of conduct, which is to have nothing to do with the government. If I am not *here* a political man, I have no reason for being here. Complete abstention.

In the legal work which he accepted in London, he was careful not to touch any lawsuit that might be connected with the Brazilian government. "It is true," he wrote to a friend, "that I gave *advice* about *legal* questions to the Central Sugar-Mill Company of Pernambuco, but when I accepted the commission I expressly declared that I would have nothing to do with the company's disputes with or claims against the government." One may imagine the indignation with which he included in one of his articles to the *Jornal do Comércio*, a contradiction of a deputy's statement that his collaboration in *O Jornal* was of "semiofficial character, because its author had a government stipend."

In the meantime, his family and some friends, desirous of having him in Brazil, conceived the idea of securing for him the position of director of the National Library, a post which was vacant. Things soon seemed to be going along very well, and a solicitous relative wrote to Nabuco, who knew nothing of the plan: "The Emperor told José Caetano [José Caetano de Andrade Pinto, chamberlain of the Emperor] that he would be very glad to know your thoughts about returning to this country, where your presence is necessary and you would have a brilliant role to play."

Immediately rejecting the idea, Nabuco wrote: "The position of librarian, despite being scientific and therefore independent in every way, is no less political than the position of legation attaché." His letters to his friends dispelled any doubts about his attitude. The *Gazeta da Tarde* published one of them, in which he said:

> I hear that *O Globo* is talking about my appointment as librarian. My library is already numerous enough, consisting of more than a million and a half volumes [a reference to the million and a half slaves in Brazil] in which every day I read of the country's opprobrium and shame.

With all this, Nabuco's exile lay heavy upon him. The desire to return to Brazil under conditions that he could accept became a real source of suffering. "I understand your nostalgia," Machado de Assis wrote him, "and no less do I understand the consolation that absence brings you. If there is any consolation for us, your friends, it is the tempering that you will receive from this exile, as well as the advantage of not being bound to a vain fight or a voluntary truce. Your hour will come . . . . You have the youth, the faith, and the future; your star will shine, to the satisfaction of your friends and the confusion of those who envy you."

Letters from his friends gave him a faithful picture of what was happening in Brazil, and of how much he was missed in abolitionist circles. Serra wrote to him, "Your name appears constantly in my articles in *O Globo*. In parliament, no orator has yet appeared who can be compared with you. . . . . There is no one who is not conscious of your absence. . . . . Our position is still the most uncomfortable in this world. No decision on the part of the abolitionists who are in the parliament. . . . . In the press there is some activity, but the press here attempts to produce action and does not reflect public opinion. It has, in fact, roused few." Nevertheless, Serra did not rest. "Our Serra has outdone himself in the *Gazeta da Tarde*," said another letter to Nabuco. "Our faithful ones," wrote Rebouças, "are always Adolfo de Barros, Serra, Alencastro, José Américo dos Santos, and Clapp. All the rest are more or less dissident and wavering."

The elections finally drew near. The party, naturally, had the greatest interest in returning Nabuco to parliament and now possessed the powers to gain this victory. The Abolitionist Confederation announced its intention of presenting him as a candidate for Rio de Janeiro. As the Liberal Club's candidate, he was offered the first district of Goiaz. Some friends wanted to see him represent Ceará, which was working so valiantly for emancipation. The seat that he would win was discussed, but not the need for his presence.

"The first general election has to be dominated by the abolition question," Jaceguay wrote to him. And Rebouças, on March 10, wrote: "Everyone says that you will return to become the leading statesman of Brazil . . . ." But in order to return, he had to give up his means of livelihood, and it was the party that paid for the trip. Rebouças, as treasurer, wrote to him: "We need you by the first of May at least. Rodrigues will send you £100 for the expenses of the trip, etc. There are excellent hopes in the second district. We need you in parliament in 1885. It is fitting that you should have the last word on abolition as you did the first."

His exile ended just in time. Nabuco's health had really been affected by too much work, and even perhaps, by his homesickness: "What disturbs me most is not knowing what I have, and why I have become so thin in a few weeks. One of the doctors said that I was missing the sunshine of Brazil and the active life that I led there. It is possible. I believe myself literally ill of nostalgia. My heart is in Brazil."

"My friend Joaquim Nabuco arrived from London, on the 'Tamar,' in a state of extreme nervous debility," wrote Rebouças in his diary on May 17, 1884. Rest and the sun of his homeland effected a cure in Nabuco in a few days. He discovered with happiness that he had not been forgotten during his two years of absence. In Alagôas he was received with the classic political festivities—rockets and a band—and led on to the floor of the Provincial Assembly, where he expressed his thanks. To the Baron of Penedo, Nabuco himself wrote from Rio de Janeiro:

> In Bahia I distributed various statements regarding emancipation with the object of stimulating a popular demonstration, as you will see by the papers. In Rio, all street manifestations were prohibited by the police, for which I was glad, because I did not come as an uncompromising member of any party and today I can speak calmly rather than as a party firebrand. . . . .

While Nabuco, in the period of exile and study, completed his evolution as an uncompromising abolitionist, the party in Brazil was consolidating around the same unyielding principles. The Abolitionist Confederation was in full bloom. Founded on May 12, 1883, it had infused new life into the party and new spirit into the abolitionist societies, uniting them into a single body. From the beginning, twelve societies were affiliated with the Confederation. Patrocínio and Rebouças, speaker and treasurer respectively of the new union over which João Clapp presided, wrote its manifesto. It was immediately read and signed by fifteen confederated societies meeting in general assembly, after which it was made public at a gathering in the Dom Pedro II Theater, and finally presented to parliament and published, at the request of Deputy Severino Ribeiro, in the *Diário Oficial*.

Thanks to the new organization, the abolitionist campaign now entered its really popular phase. The same methods were used as before, but the Confederation's many affiliated branches, working through their membership and their organizations, swelled the number of abolitionists to huge proportions. On important occasions, these groups showed their strength when they marched in civic processions. João Clapp, as the Confederation's president, worked unselfishly and untiringly beside Patrocínio, who was the soul of the organization. In everyday life, Clapp was a businessman with a china shop on Ouvidor Street. Privately, however, as a philanthropic conspirator and protector of fugitive slaves, he was one of the cornerstones of the Confederation.

The members of the Abolitionist Confederation came to be regarded as heroes. Their public activities included the planning of speeches, of liberty parties at which certificates of emancipation were ceremoniously delivered, and of banquets such as the one honoring the Rio Branco law on September 28, 1883; this banquet was regarded as a gesture of opposition to one given by the Conservative party. In private the abolitionists also carried on an active program. Their secret agents incited slaves to escape from the plantations. They created hiding places for some of the fugitives, and sent others to Ceará. They arranged false documents declaring the fugitives to be free Negroes. They used passwords and had salaried personnel. They sent thugs to punish the secret agents who were trying to catch them in the flagrant theft of slaves. They undertook, in short, a series of exploits that made the public, which followed their activities with great interest, as enthusiastic for the cause as its apostles. The people were intrigued by the clandestine savor and the unexpected audacity of the abolitionists' deeds, as well as by the humorous spectacle of authority being deceived. They were sympathetic, moreover, to the beauty of the abolitionist ideal, the emotion of pity which it aroused, and the dignity of protection generously dispensed. The members of the Confederation experienced the intoxication that comes from receiving praise for the performance of charitable work done for the glory of the country, as well as, perhaps, for their own. They had no consideration for the masters, nor any scruples as to the means employed to gain their ends, because they refused to admit the ownership of man by man. Patrocínio had chosen for their motto: "Slavery is theft."

Being absent, Joaquim Nabuco had not followed the Confederation's early activities very closely, but his services were given special mention in the organization's first yearly report. He was referred to as a "delegate in Europe," and both his splendid book, *The Emancipation Movement*, and his work at the Congress of Milan were mentioned. Following the Congress of Milan, the Confederation had held a festival which it proclaimed was in "homage to the free, united and abolitionist Italy." The theme of the celebration was "President Joaquim Nabuco and the International Juridical Congress of Milan." The speaker was Patrocínio.

Patrocínio dominated the public meetings and was the journalist of the people. As such, his role in the abolitionist movement was different from Nabuco's, although it was of equal importance. Joaquim Nabuco's aristocratic temperament would have been reluctant to light the revolutionary torch which Patrocínio brought to the campaign and which contributed so powerfully to final victory.

This almost black mulatto, who rose to prominence through his ability, was proud of the fact that he belonged to the lowest levels of society, that he represented all, and could, in his speeches, recall that he was a poor, common, black man. Sylvio Romero, an authoritative critic, put Patrocínio beside André Rebouças as one of the greatest representatives of his race in Brazil. Romero very aptly concluded that Rebouças had depth but lacked form, while Patrocínio, on the contrary, had form but no depth.

Patrocínio's eloquence was based upon an appeal to the emotions rather than reason. It was emotion which inspired him to great performances, such as throwing himself, sobbing, at the feet of the Imperial Princess in an irresistible impulse of gratitude. He did not deliver his speeches. He acted them out with extraordinary dramatic power, but they possessed a communicative ardor and a vibrant spontaneity which hid his exaggerated dramatics. As a man, he was certainly neither handsome nor well proportioned. Short, stout, with impetuous gestures and a slightly nasal voice, he was, nevertheless, a fierce and invincible natural force. The intense sensitiveness of the African race was inherited by him. To express it and to direct the torrent of his eloquence, he had the educational advantages of the white race, and the combination fascinated people.

It was Patrocínio, the great popular orator, ever ready to speak and always received with ovations, who, with Patrocínio the irreverent and zealous journalist, achieved final victory for the abolitionist movement.

In the *Gazeta da Tarde*, he attacked the plantation owners and the government with violence, openly advocating revolt.

The revolutionary note which characterized Patrocínio struck no responsive chord in Nabuco. The latter, even in his most impassioned speeches, always respected his enemies and, unlike the Negro leader, was unable to avail himself of the formidable weapon of invective. Nabuco even thought that there was such a thing as too high a price to pay for emancipation, and his closest friends agreed with him. That price was the irremediable destruction of order. One of the followers of this theory wrote: "It is not true that the cause of emancipation must be won by provoking hatred and persecution of the masters, or by personal and shameful attacks against the Emperor. The cause must be won in parliament."

Despite certain differences of opinion, the alliance among the leaders of the movement was at all times as close as possible. The only disagreements concerned the methods of procedure.

The advocates of violence and the advocates of moderation worked hand in hand. At times, the latter would become inflamed by the former, while at other times they lent them the necessary calm. In certain periods, Rebouças' diary records almost daily meetings with Patrocínio and many other signs of fraternal work: "May 15, 1883. I take over the direction of the *Gazeta da Tarde* because of the illness of its owner, José do Patrocínio." Clapp also, whom Nabuco mentions in *My Formative Years* as one of the members of Patrocínio's "church," calls Nabuco "my illustrious chief" in all his letters.

The co-operation was real. There was room in the campaign for every type of mentality, and the common ideal united them against all enemies.

CHAPTER X. THE RISE OF THE ABOLITIONIST MOVEMENT, 1884

Because it marked the conversion of the Liberal party to the cause of abolitionism, the year 1884 is one of the most important in that great campaign which was to end on May 13, 1888, with the final conversion of the Conservative party. The Republicans, led by Quintino Bocayuva, had already joined the abolitionists, resolved to pursue their own ideal, abolition of the monarchy, only after the achievement of emancipation. Even with this contingent, however, the abolitionist group was insignificant beside either of the two major parties, in whose shadow there was no room for other, lesser bodies. The young party loudly declared itself to be the representative of a national aspiration, but its adversaries could say with equal assurance that, politically, it did not exist. Then in 1884 a Liberal leader, Councilor Dantas, carried the abolitionist party with him to power. Thus the Liberal party which, in Nabuco's words, "had affronted reason and good sense during the past six years by becoming a beggar for the patronage of slavery shook off the tattered mantle with which Sinimbú had vested it in 1878 and presented itself clothed in the noble colors of conscience and human dignity. Thus it contended for power with its adversaries." (*Jornal do Comércio*, July 30, 1884.)

During Joaquim Nabuco's absence in London, the Paranaguá ministry, which on July 3, 1881, had succeeded Martinho Campos' short-lived, slavocrat government, ceded its place to the ministry of Councilor Lafayette. This was the fifth of a series of Liberal cabinets whose presidents, Sinimbú, Saraiva, Martinho Campos, Paranaguá, and Lafayette, tried to resist the abolitionist threat, either by means of direct opposition or by compromise.

Nabuco, who was not yet a historian, but a journalist full of campaign ardor, wrote (*O País*, May 12, 1885):

> It was because of the Emperor's private insistence that, after five pro-slavery ministries, a previous consultation of the three Liberal leaders was held, with the result that Dantas was called to power with his well-known program. Thus it was only the Emperor's intervention which gave the Liberal party the opportunity to acknowledge in a weak and timid fashion its tardy concurrence with the abolitionist movement.

After Lafayette's fall, the Emperor turned first to Saraiva, whom he called to the palace on June 6, 1884. But even that statesman, who had succeeded in establishing the system of direct election during his first administration, was unable to organize a homogeneous ministry capable of solving the slavery problem. In 1886, Nabuco wrote (*O País*, December 15, 1885):

> Following Saraiva's failure, however, the Emperor, as if he had been stung by his conscience or as if he thought that the Conservative party smelled too strongly of the slave quarters, conceived the idea of listening to the three architects of that Tower of Babel called the Liberal party, Sinimbú, Afonso Celso, and Dantas. It is known from the papers of the period that the Emperor subjected the three to a real contest whose theme was the emancipation issue, and that Dantas won the prize in the competition.

All credit for the great step belonged to Dom Pedro II. Each of the leaders upon whom he called gave the parliament an account of his interview with the Emperor and of his motives for not accepting the honored position.

After these explanations, the slavocrat Andrade Figueira said in the Chamber: "You [Sinimbú, Afonso Celso, and Dantas] left the Crown completely free with regard to this question (applause from the opposition but none from the majority) by not assuming the responsibility of refusing to the Crown the role that it wished to assume, of placing itself at the head of the abolitionist propaganda campaign and directing it."

On June 9, Dantas, the new President of the Council, presented to both chambers a program whose cornerstone was the solution of the slavery problem:

> We have reached a point, Mr. President, where it is necessary that the government intervene with the utmost seriousness in the progressive solution of this problem by putting it frankly into the hands of this parliament, whose duty it is to bring about a solution (applause). In this matter, we must not retreat, nor stop, nor be precipitate.

He then enumerated the measures which he considered feasible for "fixing the line which prudence permits, and civilization enjoins us to reach." The first was to extend to the entire country zoning restrictions on slave property, a measure already adopted in several provinces. The second was to increase immensely the emancipation fund, and the third was to liberate all slaves when they reached the age of sixty.

These measures were certainly not designed to fill with happiness those who dreamed of immediate abolition. "I confess," Nabuco later wrote, "that when I heard of the program of the Dantas ministry—providing for the emancipation of sexagenarians—I wanted to laugh." (*O País*, December 15, 1886.) From London he wrote to a friend about the matter: "When even the Shylocks are ready to spare the slave that last bit of flesh, which is his due, will that be the solution of the problem?"

In the press Nabuco became one of the principal defenders of the Dantas ministry, whose accession to power was considered by all to be an abolitionist victory. In one of his vigorous articles, he explained the relations between his party and the government leader:

> The Dantas cabinet represents nothing more than the conversion of the Liberal party to the national principles proclaimed by the abolitionists six years ago.
>
> Our present situation is characterized by the fact that precedence is given to the slave reform above any other, the necessity of satisfying the public conscience regarding the hereditary crime of slavery is recognized, and all minor interests are absorbed by the supreme interest in national emancipation. These things which give the present situation its predominantly abolitionist form, are not the work of the Liberal party alone, nor of its senatorial leaders. They are the work of the abolitionists, of the abolitionist minority in the legislature from 1879 to 1880, and of the press that supported it. They are the work of the *Libertador Cearense* and of the assembly of Amazonas; of the Abolitionist Confederation and the *Gazeta da Tarde*. They are the work of all those who for years have kept repeating that, despite the law of September 28, slavery as a political power was still intact, that it was our country's greatest enemy, and that above and before all else it had to be crushed.
>
> The loyalty with which we have supported the Dantas ministry proves our sincerity. We support, in reality, a statesman who asks much less than we do; one who offers a slow, illogical, inadequate solution to a problem which we should like to solve by prompt, rapid, efficacious means; one who, fourteen years after the Rio Branco law, proposes only immediate liberation for persons sixty years old, for the most part contraband slaves.

The government could not be expected to have the abolitionists' zeal, but the truth was, as even Nabuco said, "that Dantas' simple language, breaking the molds of the traditional veneration with which our council presidents have always referred to slavery, produced a great stir throughout the entire coutry. . . . ." Dantas proceeded with care. On June 17 he told the Chamber: "The present ministry does not seek battle, but rather debate and the exchange of ideas." In the Senate on July 1 he said: "I am not an abolitionist, as they now wish to paint me." No doubt remained, however, as to which road he had entered, and the slavery party itself, by unanimously rising up against him, tightened even more the bond of union between the President of the Council and the abolitionists. According to one of the first articles signed by "Garrison," even the farmer understood that "abolitionist and emancipator are synonymous and the difference between synonyms in politics is very insignificant, compared to its greater importance in ideology."

"Garrison" was a member of the brilliant guard of honor which immediately arose in the press to support and defend Dantas. The members' real names were not known, but the vigor and the genius of their writings won them fame and forced their adversaries' attention. They were concentrated in the purchased space of the *Jornal do Comércio*, the editor of which was Gusmão Lobo, who had been an abolitionist from the very first. Unable to advance the cause sufficiently in the editorial columns of the old conservative paper, Lobo made up for the loss in the articles for which space was purchased. It is necessary to remember that these subsidized articles of the *Jornal do Comércio* were a tradition. No one thought of not reading them. In those paid columns, the turbulent life of Rio de Janeiro was reflected through the long years. They constituted a tribune where those who were interested came to examine the questions of the day, both public and intimate. Personal justifications, banal greetings, insulting articles, alternated with political declarations of all types. Gusmão Lobo installed his strategic center of activities there. He filled the paid column "with a great number of articles written with infinite skill and cunning and under every possible disguise. The purpose was to present the full and accurate picture to those who were concerned solely with the reform, and at the same time influence the rest of the public more in its favor."

In this skillfully conducted campaign which continued uninterrupted during the entire Dantas government, the authors of the commentaries signed themselves as Grey, Clarkson, Garrison (the three most feared and constant contributors), Chatham, Wilberforce, and Buxton.[1]

At last they proudly disclosed their identities, when the opposition in the Chamber began "to hurl insults against those of us who supported the government in the press, and to denounce as salaried writers men with names like Gusmão Lobo, Ruy Barbosa, Rodolfo Dantas, Barros Pimentel, and Joaquim Nabuco."

Lobo was "Clarkson." Ruy Barbosa, the most valuable addition brought by Dantas to the abolitionist movement, was "Grey." Nabuco was "Garrison." When *O País* was established, they all moved over to it. The assault of the "English," as they were called, occurred almost daily. Nabuco's first article appeared on June 12, three weeks after his return to Brazil and five days after the change in ministries. On June 10, Rebouças, who took upon himself the responsibility of bringing Nabuco to *O Jornal* and of removing the last editorial objections, recorded in his diary: "I deliver to *O Jornal*

[1]Charles Grey, second Earl Grey (1764–1845), who in 1833 brought about the passage of a law abolishing slavery throughout the British Empire; Thomas Clarkson (1760–1846), active pamphleteer and abolitionist agitator, inspirer of Wilberforce; William Lloyd Garrison (1805–1879), president of the American Anti-Slavery Society, founder and editor of the *Liberator*; William Wilberforce (1759–1833), leader in the English Parliament of the antislavery movement; Chatham, William Pitt, Earl of Chatham; Sir Thomas Fowell Buxton (1786–1845), great and able aid of Wilberforce in his efforts for the abolition of slavery.

Joaquim Nabuco's first article entitled 'Abolitionist Movement.' It was accepted with great difficulty, and published under the pen name 'Garrison'." Gusmão Lobo had already used this name. "It is not fitting to forget it," the latter wrote to Nabuco, "because various articles under this pen name honor and exalt Joaquim Nabuco, whom I then called the Precursor, the St. John of the Jordan of liberty and more, much more, for at that time we were, though it was unbeknownst to them, the hope and the faith of the slaves. At that time, how few were the combatants! Today there are so many victors! What a prodigious harvest! But how arduous was the sowing!"

A great number of new enthusiasts did indeed arrive to swell the ranks of the abolitionists, as soon as the sun of power shone upon them. As Nabuco wrote to the Baron of Penedo on July 23: "No one imagined the moral effect that the government's intervention would have."

The Dantas plan was not presented until a month after the new government had assumed power. As Dantas explained in the Senate on July 1, it was necessary to prepare it carefully. The parliament awaited the measure in a state of electrically charged expectancy. Irritated by the triumphal tone that the abolitionists' propaganda was acquiring, the farmers' clubs tried to arm more strongly against it, injuring themselves with their own violence in the process.

On June 9, Cristiano Ottoni attacked these clubs in the Senate, protesting against the inclusion in some of their statutes of articles like this: "All those who receive abolitionist papers will be considered suspect." Radiant at such intervention, "Garrison" forthwith proclaimed that an eleventh-hour recruit of Cristiano Ottoni's valor ought to receive for this speech alone a "salary double to ours and rise immediately to the top rank. . . . . Unfortunately, he is still afraid of being called an abolitionist. . . . ." (*Jornal do Comércio*, June 1884.)

The Senate had occasion to take a stand in regard to the abolitionist propaganda campaign. It was discussing a report from a legislative committee concerning several formal declarations in which farmers had requested that public peace and individual security be guaranteed. In the June 28 session, the abolitionist movement's most inflexible adversary, Martinho Campos, made a four-hour speech in which he declared himself to be a slavocrat. Furthermore, he claimed again the most advanced and dangerous post in that group for himself. In his opinion, the abolitionist campaign "was becoming more and more odious to the nation." The President of the Council, on the contrary, felt that the campaign had always remained within the bounds of legality. In case it ever exceeded them, however, he declared himself ready "energetically to fulfill my duty and inexorably to use the means of repression which the law gives me." Silveira da Motta and, once again, Cristiano Ottoni continued to speak in favor of the abolitionists.

Formal declarations for and against the abolitionists' propaganda were made in the Chamber. José Mariano, an ardent abolitionist, declared that "the abolitionists neither wish for nor approve of excesses." On two occasions, Mariano presented parliament with formal declarations from the Abolitionist Center of the Polytechnical School. On the first of these occasions Andrade Figueira, deputy from Rio de Janeiro, protested that "the Polytechnical School cannot have an abolitionist center."

Andrade Figueira defended the evil cause of slavery with conviction and loyalty. He was one of the deputies of whom Dantas said that "when the members of parliament received him, they put on their best arms and charged at him with the utmost force." Up to the very end, even in his vote on the Golden Law, his sincere and tenacious voice, intrepid and firm, was raised against the abolitionists. Like a good prophet, he declared from the beginning of the Dantas government that the President of the Council would be unable to obtain the freedom of the sixty-year-old slaves: ". . . . it is robbery. The worthy minister will be unable to drag it from the Chamber. . . . . he will not force a favorable vote on such a law from this group." Dantas, President of the Council, replied: "I do not wish to force it, I wish to obtain it spontaneously, and I shall obtain it." (Session of June 13, 1884.)

On July 15, Dantas' plan was finally presented to the Chamber. Since it included the creation of new taxes, it could not be initiated by the government. It was introduced, therefore, by Deputy Rodolfo Dantas, the Council President's son, who declared that in so doing he expressed the government's opinion concerning the slavery reform.

On the following day, "Garrison" significantly entitled his excellent article "The Resurrection of the Liberal Party." In his opinion, Dantas "breathed new life into the party by raising it from the decay of long apostasy and by restoring to it the dignity of a national people's party. He washed away the stain left by so many consecutive ministries that refused to look at slavery because it was disconcerting to the majority of them. The spectacle of the resurrection of a party in the Chamber yesterday was magnificent."

The Dantas plan had been endorsed by twenty-nine deputies. It included the measures already announced in the program, plus a requirement to register all slaves in Brazil. It was not much, but "Garrison" had spoken well to the point during the first days of the liberator government when he expressed the fear that "if the President of the Council is firm and resolute, even to gain so little, he will be abandoned on the eve of the general elections by all who hope for the farm vote."

The parliament's ill will toward any measure which injured the farmer became evident at once. The reading of the plan had scarcely finished before the President of the Chamber, Moreira de Barros, rose to request its dismissal.

Afonso Celso Junior and Severino Ribeiro made enthusiastic speeches in favor of abolition. In the voting conducted to determine whether or not the measure should be rejected, as the government requested, considering it to be a vote of confidence, fifty-two deputies voted against the request of their slavocrat colleague. In the words of Ruy Barbosa this request was "the first attempt to strangle the plan." The government won, with fifty-five votes in its favor, but such a small majority was not one to inspire confidence. The favorable vote of the two Conservative abolitionists, António Pinto and Severino Ribeiro, was generally considered political suicide.

The situation was becoming noticeably dangerous, a fact confirmed by each voting. The minority, although it felt itself strong, did not seem to have the courage for the decisive blow. "Garrison's" article in the *Jornal do Comércio*, suggestively entitled "The Battle for the Graves," clarifies the politics of the moment and will serve as an example of this notable series of articles.

The power of a moral idea, of a principle universally accepted by the human conscience, has never been better demonstrated than in the recent sessions of the present parliament. From the time that Rodolfo Dantas introduced into the Chamber the bill concerning the slave element, up to the present, the ministry has been faced with a slavery coalition which could have overthrown it twenty times. This formidable opposition seems to be headless, however, and incapable of movement. Not daring to declare its victory, it does not know how to terminate the new drama of slavery of which it has made itself the protagonist.

The involuntary homage that the advocates of slavery thus render to civilization and to justice could not be more eloquent. It would seem that, like the warriors of old, the prime minister is protected in his fight by an occult divinity, that his adversaries stand in fear of the infallible blows of the immortal, and that it is the invisible lance of the guardian goddess that keeps them at a respectful distance. Each day of the session is one more triumph for the cause of the slaves, the national cause par excellence.

The drama offered in the Chamber is enough to show that the power of right is not a vain thing to be laughed at by those who believe only in the right of power. What do we see there every day? The same solemnity always: The seats of the Chamber all occupied, the floor, the galleries, the platform, filled with an audience eager to witness the great fight. The majority are waiting for the battle signal; the ministry is prepared for the execution prophesied for it so many days ago; but the opposition prolongs the anguish because it dares not assault the positions in which the cabinet is entrenched: On one side are the enthusiasm of a noble dedication to the principles of social morality which raises fallen nations and blots out the saddest stains of traditions, the certainty of the approbation of the future, the conviction that a page of honor is going to be written into the history of the country, and the aspiration that our homeland may compete on an equal basis with other states. On the other side are an alliance with a disgraceful institution for party motives, the repudiation of the steady transformation of a slave country into a free country, the pain, that must be poignant to stout-hearted men, of flinging again into the gloomy prison of perpetual captivity the old slaves who were beginning to see a ray of light; the suppression of the liberal, American, humanitarian feelings of compassion, equality, and justice which the men of our party cannot sacrifice to the incoherent necessities of the moment. These are the diverse motivations which animate the two phalanxes. One fights for national aspirations, while the other fights for ill-conceived class interests. One is ready to abandon power, because power ought not to be held a single day by the party that wants and assumes the responsibility to accomplish a reform, yet is hindered from so doing. The other desires nothing save power, and in order to gain and retain it, subscribes to the creed of the property owners of the interior, to the system of agricultural fiefs, and to the secret articles of the agricultural clubs. In doing this, however, it assumes an attitude and employs phrases that make its position reflect the low degree of civilization that we possess. Thence comes the fatal paralysis at the moment of attack. Masters of the situation, the advocates of slavery do not dare to plant their flag in the battlements of the Chamber because it is a black flag. They are ashamed of their victory. They know that they won it on grounds on which only barbarous people fight in the nineteenth century: the personal liberty of man. They are aware that their triumphal chariot will be followed by more than a hundred thousand old and worn-out slaves, snatched away from the temporary liberty already conceded them by the ministerial proposal. They realize that their names will be written in the pages of our history in letters of bronze as those who perpetuated the captivity of the victims of the slave traffic.

They know that the news of their inglorious triumph in Brazil will reverberate throughout South America as the proof of our backwardness, and as the sentence which, through national discouragement, pusillanimity or cowardice, we have brought against ourselves, namely that without slavery we are a dead nation.

They realize all this, and thence come their forced indecision and the state of expectant inactivity to which they have condemned themselves after each numerical victory.

The attitude of the slavocrat opposition to the Dantas ministry demonstrates in the most positive manner the intrinsic power of the abolitionist cause and the support that it has among the civilized opinion of the country. As has been the case on other occasions, it is not the number or the eloquence of the adversary, the national prestige of the prime minister, or the critical condition of the country which prevents the opposition from giving battle to the government. It is the idea, the cause, the aspiration with which the government had the courage to identify itself. "I call myself emancipation and you call yourself slavery," says Dantas to his enemies. It is the invincible force of the first of these words and the irrefutable odiousness of the second that explain the dilatory tactics of the opposition. The President of the

Council challenged the opposition to a decisive duel. It may be fought immediately if they wish, just as long as the field is emancipation, and this stipulation is made for the honor of those who say they are fighting the government only because of the Dantas bill. Up to now the opposition has found no way to obtain a vote of no confidence which, by condemning the project, would immediately dismiss the cabinet. To whom does victory belong? To the government or to those who failed to destroy the supposedly defeated enemy because they were ashamed to cross the line it had marked as sacred?

The conscience of the slavocrats themselves answers, since the country cannot but admire the courage and the resolution with which Dantas has proceeded. He does not cling to power for its own sake, but for the sake of the cause. In this case it is not a matter of a ministry that does not comprehend the extent of certain votings, rather, it is a matter of a ministry that demands that each of its adversaries have the same frankness it has. It demands this first, in the interest of the reform initiated by it and for which it must sacrifice all, and second, in order that public opinion and the Crown be informed as to what must and can still be expected from that Chamber. Under these conditions the government in its role has no other motto except, "More light!" It has the right to demand that parliament dispel all the darkness and that each side accept the responsibilities of its opinions by declaring them.

Enough, therefore, of hesitation.

There are human lives at stake. It is necessary that the advocates of slavery in parliament be convinced that the question of slavery involves the aspiration, the sufferings, the hopes, the rights, the tears, the death of thousands and thousands of beings like us. It is a concrete, not an abstract, question and involves what is most sensitive and sacred in the human personality. Let them not delay, then, by a single day this cruel fight which is to be waged over the tombs of the slaves, as in 1871 it was waged over their cradles.

Finally, in a moving session on July 28, Deputy Lourenço de Albuquerque sent a motion to the committee reproving the ministry for continuing to take the initiative in public matters without the Chamber's support. Another deputy, João Penido, offered a motion whose terms were even more categorical: "The Chamber, condemning the government's project concerning the slave element, denies it its confidence."

The lack-of-confidence vote passed fifty-nine to fifty-two. The idea of emancipation as represented by Dantas met defeat in the Brazilian parliament. The plan ceased to figure in the discussions of the Chamber, although in the session of August 4 Ruy Barbosa presented an excellent report on the subject. It had been prepared as a joint project by the civil justice and finance commissions.

The possibility of an appeal to the Emperor still remained, and Dantas confidently requested of him the dissolution of the Chamber. Dissolution was a reasonable solution, since the majority was too small (it consisted of only two votes, discounting the four re-elected ministers and the President, who did not vote) to permit any one of the coalition parties to organize a ministry. It was, moreover, a solution which met the desires of the Emperor and the nation. On July 30, Dantas announced the dissolution of the Chamber, which meant that thereafter it could vote only upon matters concerned with the budget, being obliged to complete such business as quickly as possible. On the following day in his customary paid space, "Garrison" wrote:

> Yesterday's session in the Chamber of Deputies was a memorable one. Some of the reflections which it inspired in the majority of those present deserve to be kept for posterity. The crowd of people, the presence of all the deputies in their seats, the long silence which preceded the entrance of the cabinet, the short and imposing solemnity of the explanations offered by the government and the chiefs of the opposing coalition, and the enthusiastic and spontaneous applause with which the people saluted the prime minister after the session produced in all, whether actors or spectators in this drama of our politics, the impression that they were witnessing the development of a national crisis. Indeed that was what the dissolution was.
>
> Another thought which occurred to all was that the Emperor had deliberately made it clear that as far as the issues of emancipation and slavery were concerned, it was the former, not the latter which the country ought to examine. Honor to the Chief of State who made this decisive statement in favor of liberty, who gave the nation credit for generous sentiments, and who preferred the national manifesto of Ceará and Amazonas to the secret articles of the farmers' clubs!

The year 1884 contained many important dates for the abolitionists. Aside from the events in parliament, which regardless of any voting results represented victories for "the cause," none is more important than March 25, the day the last counties in Ceará emancipated their slaves, and June 20, when Amazonas, whose provincial assembly had voted three hundred *contos* to pay for the liberation of its slaves, also became free. It is true that the Lafayette ministry was able to dismiss President Teodureto Souto, who had obtained that measure from the assembly and issued an order setting the legal time limit for the slaveowners. The slavocrat press was able to call the emancipation in Ceará a bacchanalia. Andrade Figueira could declare in the Chamber of Deputies that "there is no law to decree emancipation in Ceará, that it is not true that slavery is abolished there . . . ." because "the president of the province could neither proclaim this law nor prevent the entrance of slaves." The majority in the Chamber could stifle discussion about the vote of approval which Severino Ribeiro proposed in honor of the liberation of the slaves in Amazonas. But the facts caused rejoicing in all Brazil.

A series of popular celebrations was held in Rio de Janeiro, as well as a triumphal procession of the Abolitionist Confederation. On April 11 the Confederation, which had undertaken the task of liberation in the capital, celebrated the achievement of emancipation in the Uruguaiana Street district where the *Gazeta da Tarde* was located. The slaveowners there granted freedom without indemnification. In September the slaves in the counties of Pôrto Alegre, Uruguaiana, São Borja, Vamão, and Conceição do Arroio in the state of Rio Grande do Sul, and those in the São Francisco Square section of São Paulo where the law faculty stood, were liberated.

The students were always devoted defenders of the cause. In Rio the Polytechnical School succeeded in obtaining liberation for the slaves in the São Francisco Square and Teatro Street district, where placards were posted proclaiming it to be a free square. The government ordered these posters pulled down. On July 21, Rebouças recorded in his diary: "Under senatorial pressure, the Minister of the Empire prohibited the functioning of the Abolitionist Center in the Polytechnical School, and the issuing of my propaganda articles from there. June 22. Dantas, the President of the Ministers, asks me not to start a conflict between the Polytechnical School and the Minister of the Empire."

Joaquim Nabuco, who had returned to Brazil to lend his party aid at the most opportune moment, continued to win followers with his eloquence. Beginning with his speeches at the celebrations given in honor of his return by the Nabuco Abolitionist Fund and by the Confederation, he showed himself to be the same fine orator he had been before and won the same applause. To one of his adversaries that year he said, "You may believe me when I say that I feel highly rewarded. I have reached the only position attractive to me: that of being simply a private citizen who is listened to by the entire country. In or out of the Chamber, in Brazil or in Europe, I consider myself today to belong to a greater and higher parliament than that of the General Assembly, that is, the parliament of public opinion."

In September he went to speak in São Paulo. The São José Theater was filled to its maximum capacity for his lectures and afterward the people, accompanying him to the hotel, proved that even in a slavocrat province the cause of abolitionism was strongly alive. In that fine speech Nabuco stressed again that "there was no personal glory for a son of the Latin race in being an abolitionist at the end of the nineteenth century in an American country," and he offered to the abolitionist, as a parable, an episode from the *Odyssey*:

> "Ulysses told Polyphemus that he was named No One. Then the Cyclops, his eyeball consumed with flame and the air thundering with the shouts of his blindness, responded to the giants when they asked him who had caused him such suffering and torn such lamentations from him in the stillness of the divine night: 'It was No One.' 'If it is no one,' answered the Cyclops, 'if you are alone, we cannot succor you against the blow with which Jupiter wounds you.' " Gentlemen, it is not we who kill slavery, it is the spirit of our time. Therefore, the name of the true abolitionist is No One, and for myself I wish no other in this cause.

The abolitionist campaign itself was certainly an Odyssey, an epic poem in several cycles. According to José Veríssimo, it was "the most remarkable social movement that Brazil has ever had." Abolitionism created one of the most singular epochs in Brazilian history. It was a movement which, in its antagonisms, resembled a civil war, though in its ardent zeal it was more like a religious one, resting as it did upon drama, sacrifice, and magnanimity and composed of the efforts and struggles of all Brazil. On one side were ranged the defenders of "the cause," the leaders who were rewarded with glory, and with them the anonymous multitude of humble martyrs who have been forgotten. On the other side were the adversaries who kept the abolitionists' spirits alive.

In order to arouse the warm interest of all, it was sufficient that the question affect, as it did, the life of the entire nation. It involved individual circumstances so directly that it would have been impossible to surround it with the indifferent atmosphere proper to abstract questions. By its very nature, it aroused passions and hatreds and lent itself to fantasy and legend. The abolitionists rightly sought to bring about the birth of a wave of feeling in which all would commune, and the people would become inspired with the orators' words and with their own efforts. "Although," says one of Nabuco's unpublished notes, "emancipation was not achieved by saints, it was achieved by poets, wounded in their human sensitiveness. Our agitators were writers, and the abolitionist movement produced an ephemeral literature."

The arguments which the abolitionists put forth, strong and clear as they were, could not move the whole nation in the way that their eloquent appeal to the emotions did. They preferred to take advantage of the emotional beauty of their cause—the poetry of the plantations, the misfortunes of the blacks, and the growing ardor of the fight. They used the descriptive talent which many of them possessed and which the subject favored to overcome the inertia born of habit and the blindness inherited from other generations. Thus the abolitionists created the galvanic atmosphere of those ten heroic years. After May 13, 1888, Nabuco wrote (*Jornal do Comércio*, August 24, 1888):

> We, the abolitionists, who from the beginning fought for abolition, what did we lose? Nothing. We won everything. Above all we won what can be most precious in life, the reason for living, as Lucretius said, *vivendi causa*. For ten years we filled each day with the same thought, which rose above our souls every morning with the regularity of the sun, illuminating, warming, and giving life to them. For ten years we lived with the dream of an emancipated and free homeland, ten years of hope crowned by a reality which has exceeded all the finest anticipations. . . . .

CHAPTER XI. THE ORATOR. ELECTORAL CAMPAIGN. 1884

In the coming elections in which the country was to decide the fate of the ministry of June 6 and the emancipation issue, the candidacies which most interested the government were those of Joaquim Nabuco and Ruy Barbosa.

It was not easy to find an electoral district for either candidate. Ruy Barbosa had been re-elected in 1881, when not a single abolitionist had been returned. Now, however, he hesitated, or rather they hesitated for him, between a district in Goiaz and his own district in Bahia, which no longer regarded him in the same light since he had declared his liberal ideas concerning slavery. Nabuco, also hesitating, almost decided to stand for election in the second district of the capital, to which he sent a campaign circular, but he finally went to Pernambuco to try his luck in his own province. From there he wrote to the Baron of Penedo: "I do not send you the message 'I came, I saw, I conquered,' only because the battle has not yet occurred, but 'I came, I saw, I conquered' in the first campaign, which was to have myself included on the ticket of the Liberal party as a candidate in the first district of Recife."

Every bit of the energetic campaign was carried out in close co-operation with José Mariano Carneiro da Cunha, who was presenting himself for the first time with an exclusively abolitionist platform. Representing the same idea, each man was as much interested in the other's victory as his own. José Mariano was a resident Pernambucan and, when Nabuco arrived there in 1884, already had a devoted and numerous following in which the humble class bulked large. The Conservatives and the clergy, enemies understandably enough of this declared anticlerical candidate, spoke with ironic scorn of the "people of José Mariano," but they did not question the popularity of this democratic leader. In the provinces even more than in the capital, politics was discussed in every hall, on every street corner. Orators were public heroes, and no one else in Pernambuco had the prestige of José Mariano.

Mariano's election was more or less guaranteed by his personal strength. Nabuco's chances at that time, however, had a very different aspect. His long absence had almost broken the natural ties that bound him to his province. He presented himself, as the *Jornal do Comércio* stated, without "any weapon other than his powerful eloquence put to the service of an incomparable cause," and with it he accomplished the miracles that one should expect from such a cause. The Conservative candidate against whom he had to compete, Manoel do Nascimento Machado Portela, was a man of great authority in Pernambuco. He had always held political positions there, he was a professor on the faculty, and he had made himself deservedly respected as a just and good man. Emancipation, and only that, was the platform on which Nabuco presented himself. It did not offer much hope for votes, although it did provide a brilliant theme for meetings and speeches. Nabuco undertook the task of transforming ephemeral applause into certain votes, and of attracting with his eloquence all the representatives of abolitionist opinion. He planned and carried out an electoral campaign in accordance with his theories. The method of secret agreements and requests for personal favors he left to his adversaries, preferring to fight by proclaiming his ideas and to conquer only with them. On the eve of the election, in the Santa Isabel Theater, he could declare with assurance in his last lecture:

> Now that we have reached the end of this campaign, it is our right to announce the methods by which we conducted it. It was, as you see, a fight against an adversary who shunned publicity and worked only in the secretness and silence of intrigue (repeated applause). In this battle everything that we said and did was before you, in front of thousands of witnesses. We have not fought upon personal grounds, discussing individuals, but on impersonal grounds, discussing ideas (applause). I preferred propaganda to secret agreements; I preferred winning public opinion to begging for votes (applause). In this month of November I spoke almost every day. My speeches were heard by thousands of persons. They can tell whether I spoke two languages, whether I hid my thoughts, whether I promised anything that was not in accord with the promises, or better, the commitments of the abolitionist movement.

And in a message to his electors, he said:

> I had to choose between many languages and a single language, between valueless and contradictory promises and solemn public commitments, between private visits and repeated public gatherings.

Thus lacking the time to do everything, Nabuco chose, instead of secret agreements "which are transitory and at most bring about the triumph of mere individuals, a propaganda campaign which is enduring, which serves as an example, and brings about the triumph of great ideas." His campaign was noteworthy, not only for its oratory, but for the method by which it was conducted. His example, even though it did not bear fruit, awoke general admiration. Rodolfo Dantas wrote to Nabuco from the capital: "You are setting a new example and giving an excellent lesson to this country, where electoral campaigning has been reduced to either accepting orders from public leaders or begging for votes to the candidate's great humiliation. An election carried out in the manner of Gladstone is truly a benefit, both to the electorate and to future candidates."

From one district of the city to another, Nabuco went giving talks, accompanied always by a great mass of people and surrounded by an unforgettable atmosphere of support and admiration. From his first speeches it was apparent that the cause was won. "An enormous crowd from this capital gathered Sunday at Afogados to hear the speech of Joaquim Nabuco and then paraded on foot, stretching out for almost a league, from Afogados to the city, with Joaquim Nabuco and José Mariano in the lead. Anyone who saw this cannot deny that the abolitionist cause is victorious," stated the *Jornal de Recife* on November 10.

It was under similar circumstances on November 16, speaking at the Passagem da Madalena after a long address in the Santa Isabel Theater, that Nabuco said:

> Gentlemen, I suppose that many of those who are listening to me here were present at the address which I delivered a few hours ago in the Santa Isabel Theater. Those people can appreciate the fatigue which I feel at this moment. However, I must not postpone until next Sunday the meeting convoked for today. Since you are not tired of listening to me, I hope I do not tire while speaking to you. I thank the thousands who have come so far to hear me, after having just listened to me for a long time, for the applause they give me everywhere.

Even though he made so many speeches in such a short space of time, Nabuco found the means of constantly renewing himself. In his speech at the Passagem da Madalena, "speaking in the wealthy section of Recife, as on the previous Sunday he had spoken in the poverty-stricken section," he declared that slavery as a source of wealth as well as a social system was dead, and its maintenance meant "the ruin and bankruptcy of everything." To the men of capital and wealth who were afraid to abandon the "rotten ship of slavery in which they sailed," although they should have been the first to aid the abolitionist movement, he pointed out the interest they should have had, "a material interest, it is clear, in leading the movement. It follows that in order to lead it, it is necessary to be prepared to accelerate it. If they do not do so, it is because in them wealth does not make up for lack of intelligence and does not correct ignorance."

At another meeting he showed commerce the reasons why "slavery is its greatest enemy, the cause of its decadence and apathy. . . . . As for me, I fear that the destruction of slavery would affect property as much as I fear that the ending of some form of piracy would destroy commerce."

At Campo das Princezas he plainly showed the workers that the first step in the rehabilitation of labor was the abolition of slavery. "Slavery and labor are as repellent to each other as slavery and liberty. What is slavery if not the robbing of labor and the degradation, from the cradle, of the laborer? . . . . slavery has retarded the emancipation of our working class for two centuries. . . . ."

On all of Nabuco's journeys, at all of his speeches, at the historic addresses in the Santa Isabel Theater, at the various gatherings, and at the meetings in the public square, students formed his guard of honor. From the first, the university group was completely won over by the cause and its orator. In the streets they sang an abolitionist hymn whose refrain declared: "Nabuco is our guiding light." They formed a guard of honor which surrounded him always, listening to all of his speeches in the two months of their apostleship. One of them, inspired by the ardent feeling of that time, later drew this sketch of the orator of abolition:

> He is a legendary image who will remain in our memories and be transmitted into the future as the essence of Brazilian eloquence.
>
> When Joaquim Nabuco appeared on the platform, it was as a crusader, clothed in the shining armor of his eloquence. His clear, loud, and vibrant voice, sounding like a clarion, gave one the physical impression of actually seeing the walls crumbling down. . . . . In the midst of the battle he was the knight-errant who tried to pull them down. Then they assaulted him, turned on him personally, and there were no insults, no calumnies, no treacherous or malicious weapons with which his irate enemies did not attack him. Hardly a blow touched him. Fiercely and impetuously he threw himself upon his adversaries. It was not the pounce of the jaguar, which is characteristic of the people of our jungles, since there was nothing feline in his nature. Rather, it was the attack of the cavalier, the answer of the sure and avenging sword, the invincible sword forged of the immortal steel of justice. As he charged, he smiled. Scorning his enemies, he turned back to that chorus of the slaves' petitions and gathered up again the captives' grievances and sorrows, sung in the heavy melopoeia of the torments of hell. Then, his eloquence loosed the torrents of sympathy and compassion which pity nourishes in us, and he ascended to the heavens of poetry, climbing, climbing as in the ascension of an archangel, as in the flight of a bird, which like the lark, "the higher it goes the more it sings and the more it sings the higher it goes. . . . ."
>
> He was an impressive figure—tall, slender, and graceful. He had a powerful head, fiery pupils in his large, dark eyes, gestures which recalled the elegant majesty of great birds, a bold mind, and a musical voice. On his lips, a wave of eloquence mixed with the spirit of victory vibrating in the air and broke out into a copious flow of images. . . . .
>
> One might say that our tropical grandeur in all its strength and splendor was being embodied in human nature, was becoming eloquence itself! He went from the Chamber to popular meetings, fascinating the multitudes, carrying them away in his enthusiasm and scattering the spark of redemption, which spreading throughout the entire country, became the lightning ray which mutilated the old tree of slavery. . . . . Such is the power of the feeling which Nabuco aroused with his oratory, that by it a pure intellectual magnetized and swayed the gross multitudes.[1]

[1] "The Heroic Youth of Joaquim Nabuco," a lecture by Graça Aranha for the Society of Artistic Culture, in São Paulo, April 22, 1915.

It is not easy to characterize Nabuco's oratory, which like everything else in his personality was complex and variegated. While it was not popular like Patrocínio's, nor academic like José Bonifácio's, it had some of the qualities of both, plus an air of graceful fancy and an unexpected touch of imagination which was his alone and which was enchanting.

Nabuco was a born orator and owed most of his prestige and his fame to his eloquence. Everything helped him, beginning with his physical endowments. "To be the bearer of a humanitarian and noble idea," wrote Ramalho Ortigão when Nabuco passed through Portugal, "is a fine thing, but the possession of a countenance full of the clearness of a conviction is a quality essential to the circulation of an idea which is represented by an individual. . . . . Joaquim Nabuco has the physical aspect of the kind of man in whom the multitudes instinctively believe, because they think he is strong, the first condition for being sincere. Moreover, he has the attractive manners, the intelligent look, and the witty smile which attract sensitive souls."

In physical appearance he had in his favor a commanding stature, stately bearing, an energetic and inspired countenance, eloquent yet discreet gestures, and a beautiful, vibrant voice, capable of effortlessly filling great spaces without any loss in its velvety and sonorous timbre. Within he had all the fire of his conviction and all the resources of his genius, which by 1884 had attained its full development.

The inflammatory orator was also a thinker who carefully weighed his words, studying and preparing them as if unable to rely upon extemporaneous addresses, as if in these he did not always shine. "On rereading his speeches," wrote Magalhaes de Azeredo, "one finds a quantity of suggestive ideas and arguments which suddenly clarify a problem or situation. At every step are some of those typical, synthetical phrases which run instantly from one end of the country to the other, engraving themselves upon the memory of all, just because they sum up an entire program or complex group of sentiments to which no one could remain indifferent."

The Recife speeches, like all his written ones, abounded in images and owed much of their success to them. People always have a tendency to applaud such things, and Nabuco, exuberantly imaginative, did not resist the temptation to use them constantly. He realized that comparisons were one of the best methods for making his ideas clear, and that a simple audience could be enchanted by them as it could not be by definitions. Moreover, Nabuco was as much at home in one method as he was in the other, just as he was also equally at ease in an appeal to emotion or in logical demonstrations.

The addresses at the Santa Isabel Theater represented the height of his eloquence. The adversaries of abolition did not attend them, but its partisans filled the theater to capacity. Several thousand persons thus formed a remarkable audience filled with an unequaled enthusiasm.

The 1884 series of addresses was recorded in shorthand, transcribed, and the following year published as a volume under the title *Abolitionist Campaign in Recife* (*Campanha Abolicionista no Recife*). A reading of these speeches amply demonstrates the reason for the ovations which punctuated them. One can easily imagine the effect of passages such as these, spoken by an actor like Nabuco in a moment of inspiration:

Yes, gentlemen, it is the abolitionist movement with which you find yourselves confronted. Wherever I turn, I see the horizon covered with the waters of that enormous flood. I saw that great current, which today inundates the country like an equatorial river at flood tide, when it first descended as a stream of crystalline water from the heights of a few minds and the fountains of a few hearts, both equally illuminated by the rays of our future (applause). I saw it, now a river, open its way like Niagara through the heart of the rock, through the granite of secular resistances (applause). I saw it when, once past the falls, it gained the open plains of public opinion (continued applause), growing constantly wider, fed by the innumerable affluents of thought, honor, and national feeling which came from all sides. Like the Solimões, the river's name changed as it pursued its course, being first Ceará, then Amazonas, then Rio Grande do Sul (applause drowns out the orator), and today I see it ready to flow out into the great ocean of human equality, divided into as many branches as there are provinces and carrying on its waves the shattered dam of a legislature and the wreckage of five ministries (applause). I say to you, gentlemen: I do not fear the strength of that flood, the volume of those waters, or the damages of that inundation. Because the Nile deposits upon the arid soil of Egypt the loam which yields great harvests, it is said that Egypt is a gift of the Nile. The abolitionist current also carries suspended in its waters the fertile silt of free labor and human dignity, the physical and moral soil of the future Brazil, whose prosperity and greatness will one day be called a gift of emancipation (enthusiastic applause).

Ah! Pernambuco has a great past, but it seems that its sons do not wish it to have a great future! It once led the nation. In the seventeenth century it lighted two great beacons, freedom of conscience and freedom of commerce, which illuminated the seas of this continent. Over two hundred years ago, amidst the convulsions of the Portuguese monarchy and the supreme struggles of Holland, alone and unaided it hoisted on the fields of Guararapés that flag of Brazilian nationality in whose center the great American symbols of independence and the republic were later traced in the blood of its martyrs (applause).

But today those great beacons have gone out. This center of so much noble activity no longer radiates any movement. The blood no longer flows from this virile heart of colonial Brazil. The city of Maurice of Nassau has lost its prerogative in the initiation of heroic resolutions, and in the midst of such decay the Lion of the North disappears among the rivers of the American Venice like the great Lion of St. Mark's, symbol of that powerful Adriatic republic, among the canals of its lagoons (more applause).

Well, Pernambucans, let us revive our patriotism. In order to lift this province once again to the heights of its past, let us begin by inscribing it among the free provinces, in the enlightened, rather than in the dark portion of the country. Remember it was in Pernambuco that for the first time in our history a government —a government of dreamers and of martyrs, in an hour of revolution and on their way to the scaffold—had the courage to promise liberty to the slaves, feeling that they too longed for the desired independence. Do not scorn that testament of the heroes of 1817 simply because their government was a spontaneous expression of the Pernambucan soul instead of a tyranny imposed from without. Let us begin from there, and let us make a pact, all of us who cry out in pain upon seeing the political decadence of our province, let us make a pact to effect a second Pernambucan Restoration in order to restore Pernambuco to its historic role. To do this, before we attempt the still doubtful solution of the federal problem, let us complete the achievement of the recognized solution to the major problem, which is the social equality of all Brazilians. This solution, to be productive, must be twofold and may be summed up in this slogan: "Liberty and Labor"—the labor which gives dignity, the labor which gives value to life! (Deafening applause.)

The series of addresses ended with these words:

But, gentlemen, I forget that we are on the eve of the battle and that you and I must reserve our strength for tomorrow. Tomorrow, in fact, the city of Recife is going to be called upon to proclaim its stand in a solemn judgment between two irreconcilable ideas, between two principles which, like the good and the evil in the theogonies of the Orient, have been in perpetual conflict throughout the ages (applause). See the somber procession with which slavery intends to oppose your votes, the retinue with which it presents itself in your elections. Look at that multitude which marches behind the triumphal chariot of the American Moloch, which during its three centuries among us has feasted upon the victims from Africa sacrificed to its thirst for blood (applause). They are the old slaves of sixty burdened with age and with work, who not only gave to their inexorable master great crops of sugar and coffee, but another harvest of children and grandchildren which further enriched him. They are the galley slaves of a life whose entire history is the tragedy of the slave quarter, a life devoid of any consolation or support outside of itself and its own tortured heart and bruised conscience, devoid of any of those external supports which we all possess, having neither family, nor friends, nor authority, nor religion, nor law. They are the bearers of a life which is stolen from them completely, body and soul. One by one the days of their lives fall, cast in copper coins, into the hands of the owner. . . . . You may imagine what the suffering must be of the man whose days are molded in this fashion, without any regard for the physical and moral needs of the thinking being, which we are. . . . . See that whole retinue of weary individuals, followed by their children and grandchildren, slaves as they are, the first fruits of their own blood whom they offered to the cupidity of their master without, however, thus redeeming themselves from slavery (applause). Slavery is the traffic in what is most holy, most mysterious, and most inexplicable in nature: motherhood! (Applause.) It is that barbarous and atrocious law which says to the woman who conceives: "Your child is going to be a slave like you; you are going to enrich your oppressor with the product of your womb." . . . . Do not say that among us that monstrous principle is abolished, because it is not. By virtue of it alone slavery exists in our country, and to abolish it in fact would mean the emancipation of all those slaves, sometimes the children of crime and violence, who constitute the gratuitous and unwilling present which the female slaves make to their masters! (Prolonged expression of emotion.) Ah! gentlemen, for the honor of human nature in our country, why did it not happen that, as is the case with some species of animals, the human species did not reproduce itself in captivity! (Further emotion.) It looks as though I shall be unable to reach the end of my sentences, I am so carried away by the torrent of impressions created in me by that situation which, when not piracy, became the law of Herod. . . . . But not only the old slaves of sixty appeal to you; every generation cries out, including the freeborn who are slaves until the age of twenty-one, "What manner of men are you?" Pernambucans, such great injustice does not revolt you, and such great suffering does not move you! You, poor men, how can you expect the powerful to sympathize with you, if you have no compassion for beings even more unhappy and forsaken than yourselves! No . . . . that is impossible. Your votes will not maintain any longer an inhuman and cruel institution in constant violation of the fundamental truths of science and religion, of civil and moral law. You will not support slavery, which is the cause of the atrophy which for centuries has retarded the development of nations! It is an institution which destroys and degrades everything that it is the purpose of social institutions to build and develop! (Prolonged applause.)

No, gentlemen, the city of Recife has awakened from the profound sleep of many years of indifference and callousness. In this place where I now speak, the center of so many traditions and so much heroism, which were it not for slavery would today be a strong and respected republic, but which with slavery is beginning to forget the past and doubt the future, it might be said that we hear a voice shouting: "Enough persecution, enough suffering!" It is a voice rising from the soil of your nationalist battles and your liberal revolutions, and, listening to it and echoing it at this solemn moment, I denounce slavery to the Pernambucan people with all the strength of my soul! (Applause.) Yes, in the name of the past and of the future, I denounce to the people of Recife, gathered together in their public assemblies, that institution which to be condemned by the human conscience needs only to be named: slavery! (Applause.) I denounce it as a violation of every article in the penal code, of every commandment in the law of God! (Prolonged applause.) To you who are workmen I denounce it as the theft of work; to you who are priests, as the theft of the soul; to you who are capitalists, as the theft of property; to you who are women, as the theft of motherhood; to you who are free men, as the theft of liberty; to you who are military men, as the theft of honor; to you who are men of color, as the theft of your brothers; and to you Brazilians, as the theft of the motherland. Yes, to you all I denounce that cursed institution of slavery as the fratricide of a race and the parricide of a nation! (Long and spirited applause, lasting many minutes.)

There was not a vulnerable point in the conscience of the people which Nabuco did not touch in his magnificent attempt to convert Pernambuco to the abolitionist cause.

The conversion was real and complete. On the eve of the election he could well say: "You know what has been the result of that endeavor in which, day by day, I have made such great efforts, always encouraged by thousands of people. The Liberal party in this city has become abolitionist en masse, and the abolitionist cause, which before had been but the opinion of a few, has become the popular party."

The addresses in the Santa Isabel Theater brought together and permanently united the energies and opinions of the dispersed segments of abolitionist opinion. The strength of that wonderful Pernambucan abolitionist movement which did so much for the liberty of Brazil dates from them. "It alone of all the abolitionist groups in the Empire could win elections, and what elections! With nothing but the uncompromising banner of abolition."[2]

The Termite Club (Clube do Cupim) was certainly the most picturesque incarnation of Pernambuco's abolitionist movement. What Patrocínio and his companions did in Rio, and what António Bento did in São Paulo to aid the escape and alleviate the sufferings of the slaves, José Mariano and his compatriots in the Termite Club did in the northern province. Their activity was secret and the society's watchword, in accordance with the symbolism of its name, was "to destroy without noise." Their joy derived from the number of slaves that they succeeded in helping escape to Ceará. They notified friends there of the remittance of so many "pineapples," the name they had agreed to give the human merchandise which they "dispatched" to liberty, or as Patrocínio used to say of Ceará, to "the land of light." According to a note in Nabuco's papers, the fugitives were sent "in vessels used to transport sugar between the small ports. Through their knowledge of the coast, the small crews of those large barks were especially adept at aiding the escape of the slaves and their placement in other localities. The abolitionists in Recife made use of these crews in carrying out the exodus that they organized. The fleeing slave hid himself in one of those boats, thanks to the universal complicity of the poor class, disguised as a sailor, a sugar loader, or a water seller, and was put off in a safe place." In an article about one of the most zealous leaders of the Termite Club, Barros Sobrinho, Nabuco said:

While Ceará used rafts, Pernambuco used barges. The only difference was that the rafts of Ceará refused to transport to the ships slaves who had been sold to the South, while the Pernambucan barges transported to the North slaves who escaped

[2] Article about António Bento by Nabuco in *O País*, August 22, 1888.

from the province. . . . . The barges do not fight passively but with their sails. They do not reject the proposed passengers; they receive as many as their tonnage allows, even doubling it. They smuggle out the free with the same audacity that in other times the slaves were smuggled in. That was the work of the members of the Termite Club, whose fame will live forever in the tradition of the province. The Club's most famous names were João Ramos, José Mariano, Barros Sobrinho, Numa Pompilio, Guilherme Pinto, Nuno da Fonseca, the characters of the popular play of the actor Tomás Espiuca. . . . . As the abolitionist movement was a vast network spread throughout the entire city, it is impossible to evaluate all the dedication shown and the services rendered.

In *My Formative Years* Nabuco gratefully recalled many of the devoted souls whose names, "even the principal ones, were not heard outside of the province," but which in his private correspondence recurred many times. "It seems to me," says a letter of 1905, "that I see them all as at the time of our campaign. I read in one paper of the death of Barros Rego, in another of the death of Corbiniano. They were all veterans of that legion which victory dispersed sixteen years ago."

A writer whose impressions are interesting to consider because he was a foreigner has drawn a picture of that legion which is photographic in its lifelikeness. Count Prozor, who was then secretary of the legation and later became the minister of Russia in Brazil, formed a lasting friendship with Nabuco. En route to Europe, he spent several hours with him in Recife. In an article "Joaquim Nabuco and Brazilian Culture," in the *Revue Hebdomadaire* of Paris, written after Nabuco's death, he said:

At that moment he was surrounded by his followers, old doctrinaires, emaciated and long-haired, and vibrant young men of concentrated zeal, all with flaming and resolute eyes, abundant and precise words, sober gestures, decided manners, and all more or less disciples of Comte, at times bearing names from the Positivist calendar which they had substituted for their own with the facility conceded by habit and Brazilian law. I remember that one of them, a pharmacist by profession, called himself Numa Pompilio. In a tavern at the port, where I went to wait for the boat which was to take me out to the steamer, the fat Portuguese innkeeper, dressed in shirt sleeves, was serving some Negroes. Between strong shots of cane brandy and with tremulous gestures, they were carrying on an animated conversation in which the name of Joaquim Nabuco constantly recurred to the exclusion of any other. He was already the popular hero, unique, the same one whom I saw being toasted a quarter of a century later in exactly the same way at an inn in the Santa Teresa section, while another group of followers waited for him on the quays of Rio de Janeiro. A legend was growing side by side with history.

Prozor even sketches the figure of Nabuco himself in the midst of the crowd, "striding through it with big steps, a smile on his lips, and extending his broad hand to the friends who came to meet him. From the beginning, he exercised great influence over the masses, thanks to his tall stature, his fine features, his sonorous and clearly enunciated speech, his ideas and his life, vibrant with noble determination. To win those children of the sun, it was necessary to give them heat and light. These things he spread in profusion, being rich and prodigal in mind and heart."

No one could predict with certainty the results of that battle of 1884, a struggle which everyone recognized to be one of ideas, not men. "An election of such significance for the future has never before been held in Brazil," said the *Jornal de Recife*, and Liberal orators and papers repeated this refrain in every key. It took on a proud note when they appealed to patriotism, and a pathetic one when they spoke in the name of the captives, particularly of those eighty thousand old ones whose liberty hung in the balance. Thus they succeeded in making some ray of beauty radiate from the humanitarian cause itself.

The press of the province seemed indifferent to any subject that did not deal with the election or the candidates. On both sides there were fears of disorders, and, among the more enthusiastic partisans, veiled and isolated threats of violence were even heard. When the decisive day arrived on December 1, however, everything seemed to be in perfect order. The legal representatives for both parties in the election had nothing but a few insignificant objections to make. It was announced early that José Mariano's majority in the second district was over two hundred votes. In the first district, however, Nabuco was declared to be beaten by a majority of less than twenty votes at the very most.

These were only the first reports, spread confusedly by the people stationed in front of the government building or wandering about the streets in large groups. Curiosity was intense. Rumors were promptly picked up and enlarged, and those charging fraud and treason seemed to the Liberals to be especially credible. Only thus, according to them, could Nabuco's overthrow at the polls be explained. With or without reason, the names of false abolitionists who betrayed their party were cited. They were accused of passing out antiabolitionist ballots to faithful electors who mistook them for abolitionist tickets. The equality of the fight and the insignificant difference between the Conservative and Abolitionist votes excited fiery tempers. José Mariano was in the city hall when a fraud detrimental to Nabuco was discovered. Many were eager to get at the truth and to check the honesty of the elections but he advised them to be calm.

On election day both Nabuco and Mariano went through each other's districts. Leaving the city hall, José Mariano went to the parish of São José, where similar cases of fraud had been reported. He was followed by a crowd of people, who set out on foot in the direction his carriage had taken.

On the door of the church of São José, a district where Nabuco's triumph had been considered certain, the results of the election were posted: Portela 94, Nabuco 76. The election committee had already begun to write its report on the voting. José Mariano had been there for several minutes when the approaching wave of the populace, shouting for Nabuco, could be heard arriving. There were no police present. The committee's first move was to bar the doors against the entrance of the mob, whose numbers were so great that no one would have been able to safeguard the ballots. By thus establishing the clandestineness of the elections, they only confirmed the suspicions of the approaching crowd. "They are falsifying the ballots," shouted the people outside. The legal representative for the Conservatives, who was illegally armed, waited for the mob with revolver in hand. He paid with his life for that insolent defense but before he fell he twice forced the crowd to scatter back down the stairs. The assailants, who at first had no weapons, finally climbed up armed with knives, clubs, and even cobblestones. The Conservative legal representative, Major Esteves, commonly called Bodé, continued to defend the precincts with the aid of his brother and a nephew. The nephew was killed instantly, while Esteves was mortally wounded. José Mariano, who was unarmed, was slightly wounded in the fray. The election books and papers were destroyed.

At the Santa Isabel Theater, before he left Recife, Nabuco stated:

> I cannot express my sorrow at having to associate the savage scene of São José with the memory of my election in Recife. I have a right to say that such a scene should not be the result of an electoral campaign such as mine, which was conducted entirely in the open, without any hidden methods, secret agreements, or frauds, and of which it may be said that the candidate was merely a symbol of the abolitionist movement.
>
> I have a right to mourn when the memory of a campaign as fairly conducted, as pure, as patriotic, and as far removed from any idea of fraud, corruption or violence, as was the Abolitionists' campaign in Recife, is associated with the bloody stain of São José.

On the night of the tragedy, the president of the province, Sancho de Barros Pimentel, sent this communication to the President of the Council:

> Immediately after the incident, a great crowd led by Dr. José Mariano came to the government palace. They explained that when they went to the church to check on the results of the voting upon which the election in the first district depended, they were received with bullets. Several shots were fired at Dr. José Mariano, who received only a light wound in one hand. The Conservatives, on the other hand, affirmed that the group had come for the purpose of invalidating the election because the Conservatives had received a majority.

Mariano answered the unjust accusation that he and the populace acting under his orders were responsible for the disturbance, with the declarations, sworn before the law and supported by Nabuco, that neither he nor Nabuco would accept office if their friends had intervened in the election in any illegal way. As proof of his innocence, he cited the advice that he had given the people in the municipal chamber before they followed him to São José. He pointed out that he had not arrived with the crowd, whom his carriage had outdistanced, but with a friend and the latter's son, and that he had been completely unarmed and unprepared in every way.

The whole country, and particularly the Emperor, was impressed by the news of that swift and bloody scene. From the first to the twenty-first, the Emperor sent the President of the Council no less than thirteen letters about the matter, writing twice on the day of the election.[3] All the testimonies were heated and contradictory and failed to establish sufficient responsibility. Above all, they failed to prove any premeditation on either side. Their only result was to furnish new fuel for heated discussions in the papers. Both parties, particularly in Recife, now found reasons for indignation against their adversaries. In the Santa Isabel Theater, Joaquim Nabuco denounced all those who, "lacking a party banner, today raise the bloody clothes of their unfortunate compatriots as a standard. . . . ." According to him, neither party had the right to impute the guilt for the scene to the other, since the responsibility "belongs, unfortunately, to that bold partisan who, alone, faced the unarmed and enthusiastic multitude that entered the church and died a victim of his courage and his odious politics."

The known stubborn fanaticism of the Esteves family greatly favored the attackers. Since, however, no one among the attackers was killed or gravely wounded, it might in justice be concluded that perhaps the voluntary defenders of the polls merely tried to frighten the people off by firing into the air. The dead bodies of the Esteveses, whose assailants were not discovered, and the destruction of the records were concrete evidence against the people. But there were strong arguments to prove the peaceful intentions with which they had arrived. If their intention had been only to burn the polls, they would have gone, for example, to one of the Conservative bulwarks where Portela had a real majority, such as Afogados or Mártires. The parish of São José, besides being far from their point of departure, was a Liberal parish where everyone had expected Nabuco to win and where Portela had finally won by only a few votes. If the people had not gone to São José solely to investigate the rumors of fraud, as José Mariano maintained, what would they have sought? A recounting of the votes at the very most.

[3] Tobias Monteiro, *Pesquisas e Depoimentos para a História*, pp. 94–95.

Since the Conservatives' small numerical advantage disappeared with the crime of São José, a new election became necessary. The Liberals awaited it with confidence, but the Conservatives, having won an advantage at the polls, wished to dispense with it, even though they lacked the results of one of the parishes. Ten days after the election, the Conservative committee members from the first section of São José drew up a new election report and signed it at their homes, although this made it void. To the Liberals, such action was but another cause of provocation and complaint. Nabuco wrote to the Baron of Penedo that the small majority which the adversaries seized upon, those three or four votes over the legal quotient, "were not a tenth of what was stolen from me. In the opinion of this whole city, it is I who was really elected, and that is the cause of the popular excitement."

On December 20, immediately after the meeting of the examining board, Nabuco wrote again to his old friend:

The legal board, presided over by the local judge, decided that there should be a new election. I believe that the Conservative committee members, who withdrew from the board, will give a mandate of election to Portela, but the mandate is a document which must be signed by the judge. I do not think that the Conservatives will have a candidate in the second election, but will leave me a clear field. Under such conditions, elected by over half of the registered voters in a legal election, I shall go to the Chamber like the best of them. The election is on January 9. You may consider me a deputy, unless the Chamber bars me.

Through the papers Nabuco declared:

My friends well know that I would not go to the Chamber with a mandate which lacked the vote of one section if that vote were annulled by an act of force done to my advantage. With such a mandate I should not have the moral authority in the parliament which my word must have for me to feel that I am really strong.

Nabuco said the same thing at a last address in the Santa Isabel Theater on January 6, 1885:

. . . . I did not want a mutilated mandate which had a single spot of blood on it. On the other hand, I did not want to draw any advantage from the events of São José, whoever was responsible for them. . . . . At this moment I could have in my pocket a mandate which would at least be better than Dr. Portela's. It is the mandate which the election board members favorable to Portela requested the judge, who was president of the board, to give to me! I rejected that mandate, which gave me the right to run in the third election under better conditions than my opponent, because I had the law in my favor. I rejected it in order to subject myself to a revolting, and thus submit my cause to the only judge who can decide it in a manner satisfactory to me and to the Pernambucan people: the same electorate which Dr. Portela and I both claimed to have had on our sides on December 1.

The dissident members, however, as Nabuco had predicted in his letter to Penedo, set themselves up in another room as a vote-counting board. By including the election report drawn up by the first section of São José several days after the election, they recognized 839 votes plus 2 questionable ones for Portela, and issued a mandate to the candidate of their party. Fortified by this testimony, Portela declared that the first district did not have "the caprice to claim two mandates" and asked his followers to abstain from voting in the second election.

For Nabuco it then became a question of honor to be elected by over half the effective electorate of his district. The method adopted by Portela for destroying interest in the election was excellent, however. The failure of his followers to appear at the polls made the voting of those who did obvious, and placed the poor and humble electors whose livelihood depended on the Conservatives in a difficult position.

Nabuco's diaries at the time of the election carry many curious items about those constituents and partisans who gave him their votes at the cost of real sacrifice: "a woman had my picture and one of José Mariano, which a fearful voter asked her to keep! . . . . Coutinho, dismissed for not wanting to vote. With ten children . . . . one old elector's son-in-law hid his clothes. He went to vote in rags."

The second election, held on January 9, was precisely the triumph that had been expected. The vote for Nabuco not only amply exceeded his own and Portela's in the first election, but represented undoubtedly, as he said in his last speech in Recife, the "real majority of any half of the effective electorate of the capital [Recife]."

It was a complete ratification of Nabuco's claim, and the Liberals celebrated it with a parade of rejoicing. The happiness was not unanimous, however. A stone, thrown at Nabuco from a second story window, wounded one of his companions in the arm.

CHAPTER XII. RETURN TO PARLIAMENT. THE FLAG OF FEDERATION. 1885

The abolitionist forces put on a splendid display at the popular reception given for Nabuco in Rio de Janeiro upon his arrival from Recife. In his final speech of that day, delivered in São Francisco Square as the great procession which had followed him from the quays was about to disperse, Nabuco declared: "What is done, is done; and what remains to be done is virtually done."

The abolitionist societies, with their banners, led the demonstration, which assumed particular importance because of the great mass of people who took part in it. The students tried to unhitch Nabuco's carriage in order to pull it themselves. The windows were filled with spectators. The speeches were moving. Patrocínio, speaking from the building of the *Gazeta da Tarde*, the day and evening issues of which were devoted entirely to Nabuco, caused the simple people to shed tears. One of his most effective oratorical devices was to forget his role as general of the movement, and remember only that he was a Negro. Turning to Nabuco he exclaimed: "At this moment, the representative of one and a half million slaves kneels at the feet of the redeemer of his race." Quintino Bocayuva was also waiting for Nabuco with flowers in front of the building of *O País*, where he had had placed a large inscription with the greeting: "Joaquim Nabuco, Glory of His Country." The parade stopped in front of each of the buildings of the abolitionist papers, as well as before the *Jornal do Comércio*, which was not declaredly abolitionist, but where they wished to greet Gusmão Lobo. The oppositionist papers received a contrary treatment. Said *Folha Nova*, before which the crowd passed "without vivas or greetings": "At the window of *O Brasil* were some gentlemen from the editorial staff who must not have been flattered with the crowd's shouts. In vain Nabuco, hat in hand, requested calm; the excited crowd did not calm down until the parade continued, and another explosion occurred in front of the *Diário do Brasil*. . . . ." The Baron of Penedo wrote to Nabuco: "I read about everything connected with your arrival at Rio in the papers. The absolute silence of *O Jornal* did not surprise me. It fears losing the good will of the farmers of Rio." He also wrote: "Despite what may be done in the Chamber by way of conspiracy against you, I do not fear your debarment."

Not only in Pernambuco, but in all Brazil, the elections had been extraordinarily closely contested. The government, after honestly attempting to maintain complete electoral freedom, was not sure of victory at the end. Almost indispensable friends like Ruy Barbosa were overthrown, as well as one of the ministers, Mata Machado. At the same time the abolitionist movement, which won some victories, such as that of the ex-president of Amazonas, the emancipator Teodureto Souto, also suffered some defeats, such as Patrocínio's in the capital. The net result for a long time remained doubtful.

While still in Recife, Nabuco wrote to his old friend Penedo:

> Because of my name and the enemies that I made in the last Chamber, plus the interest that Dantas took in my candidacy and Recife's importance, the confirmation of my election is going to be the great battle, the main battle of the new Chamber. I expect, however, to win. At present, we have a majority of deputies and we expect to increase it.

However, the already precarious government majority tended to diminish. Besides the Conservatives, the President of the Council had various dissidents from his own party against him. They represented what Nabuco called a "hybrid liberalism, allied to the cause of slavery, and exceeding in zeal and audacity of vituperation the Conservatives themselves, for the latter did not need to make such an effort to recommend themselves to slavery."

With the Chamber still waiting for many deputies to be formally seated, the government's partisans found themselves reduced to the expedient of not making up a quorum, but it was impossible to hide the liberator ministry's dangerous situation. The crisis broke on April 13, when a discussion of the Dantas project was announced. Moreira de Barros presented the following motion: "The Chamber of Deputies, not accepting a solution of the slavery problem that does not include indemnification, refuses to give its support to the Cabinet's policy." Afonso Celso Junior sent to the committee an opposing motion endorsing the ministry's emancipatory policy. Rising in the midst of profound silence and absorbed attention, Dantas asked that his adversaries discuss his project frankly. "If you have confidence in your ideas," he said, "if your cause is better than ours, why do you flee from the battleground of the July 15 project?" "You do not have the courage to say that you wish pecuniary indemnification for the emancipation of the sexagenarians!" broke in Almeida Oliveira. In the roll-call vote which followed, a fifty-to-fifty tie resulted.

The battle's equality roused the passions of the public. There were always displays of general interest going on outside the Chamber as well as in the galleries. If the popular opinion of the man in the street and of the masses represented the nation's thinking, no one could deny that Dantas embodied a national aspiration. In spite of the decisions of the parliament and the polls, popular support backed him tenaciously, as it backed abolitionism in any form. When, however, that sympathy began to take a militant form and people jeered at slavocrat politicians on the street, the superior indifference and the tolerance of the upper classes toward popular demonstrations disappeared.

Pretext for a parliamentary crisis was found when Moreira de Barros, president of the Chamber, was booed in the streets as he left the building; about the same time, a rock was thrown at a deputy who had gone over to the opposition. In the session of the Chamber on May 4, Antônio de Siqueira, the deputy at whom the rock had been thrown, proposed with his dissident colleagues the following motion:

> The Chamber of Deputies, convinced that the ministry cannot guarantee the order and public security which are indispensable to the solution of the slavery problem, denies it its confidence.

The motion was approved by fifty-two votes against fifty, thus overthrowing the ministry by two votes. Overthrown also was the emancipatory ideal represented by Dantas, whose popularity merely increased. That night, thousands of his partisans gathered in front of his house to give him a noisy demonstration of their support. Dantas declared himself consoled, "because I have fallen into the arms of the people."

The Emperor chose Councilor Saraiva as Dantas' successor. Saraiva's name commanded the greatest respect in the Liberal party, and he was the only person capable of consolidating it once more. On May 11 the new President of the Council announced his program to the Chamber: "the solution of the slavery question and the improvement of our financial state, which is grave."

The problem which Dantas had been unable to solve could not fail to be the first point in the program of any Liberal ministry. On terminating his April 3 speech, Dantas had said to those who had fought him because of the issue of indemnification for the aged: "Remain with that glory and may it satisfy you completely. As for us, we fall with dignity, embracing the project of July 15." On taking over his post, Saraiva rendered this tribute to Dantas before the Chamber: "The retiring minister performed a great service by bringing the question from the street to the parliament (applause) and by sacrificing himself in order to find its solution. This is undeniable."

Dantas' successor was prepared to come to terms with the desires of the abolitionists and the interests of the farmers. He was willing to modify the Dantas project until it satisfied both factions, inviting "Liberals as well as Conservatives, radical abolitionists and moderate nonabolitionists," to co-operate in its solution. But the progressive abolitionists, who considered their acceptance of the Dantas project the extreme in conciliation, could not view such a pact favorably. In the sarcastic words of Joaquim Serra, it was a pact "between the timid and the obstinate," a "concession of those that ask little and those that refuse absolutely, ... the happy medium between the minimum and nothing."

The Chamber was still incomplete. Because of Saraiva's assumption of power, Joaquim Nabuco was among the number who were still waiting to have their mandates approved. The Chamber debarred him, fifty-one to forty-eight, in the following week.

The Chamber's decision concerning the numerous contested mandates had aroused indignation in many cases, but never such as now. While the building of the Conservative organ, *O Tempo*, was stoned in Pernambuco, *O País* reported that the government was obliged "to send two warships to Recife to convince the Pernambucan people that their elected candidate was Dr. Portela and not Dr. Joaquim Nabuco."

Reserved for Nabuco, however, was a revenge which could not have been more honorable, either for him, or for those who made it possible. On May 12, he was excluded from the parliament, where his party judged him indispensable. On the 14th, as an election was pending in the fifth district of Pernambuco, he received a telegram announcing the withdrawal in his favor of the Liberal candidate for that post, Ermirio Coutinho. The abolitionist crusade needed nothing more to ensure its glory than the inspiration of such gestures of abnegation. Coutinho, whose withdrawal was followed by that of the second candidate, Joaquim Francisco de Melo Cavalcanti, sent this generous circular to his electors:

> I turn to the press to declare solemnly that I have taken the firm and unshakeable resolution to sacrifice my political aspirations in favor of the great Pernambucan Joaquim Aurelio Nabuco de Araujo.
>
> I say only: it is not in favor of an individual, it is upon the altar of a holy cause, of which Joaquim Nabuco is the incarnation, that I sacrifice my aspirations.
>
> I withdraw, then, bowing respectfully before the man who carries the sacrosanct banner of the redemption of the captives. The only remaining thing for me to do is to beg my good and devoted friends, and all the Liberals of the fifth district not to listen to the calumny which seeks to stain the great man. It is necessary that the farmers see in Joaquim Nabuco, not the destroyer, nor the incendiary and the enemy of property, but the mainstay of law and order; the man predestined by Providence to play a great role in the social and political world.

On June 7, 1885, less than a month after his debarment from the Chamber, Nabuco was brilliantly elected by the fifth district, with a majority in every precinct. "Never," said *O País* on June 9, "has any other deputy ever entered parliament with more moral strength, or surrounded with greater prestige."

There had been no time for Nabuco to go to Pernambuco before the election to present himself personally to the fifth district, but he left immediately afterward to thank his new constituents. He found the capital of the province decorated with flags, and the population rejoicing in his victory. The reception in Recife surpassed all his expectations. He made triumphal excursions to Nazareth and Bomjardim, the counties that had elected him.

By 1885 Nabuco's popularity had reached its peak. Photography had made his face well known throughout the entire country. His picture appeared as a trade-mark on products of all types: on cigar and beer labels, on handkerchiefs, on pieces of cloth and packages of tobacco. His name was given to new flowers, and served as a source of inspiration for unknown poets and composers of dance tunes. These were ingenuous methods, as well as excellent ones for promoting the cause. The large correspondence that Nabuco received testified to his position in the country. Many letters came from admirers congratulating him, and expressing happiness with the progress of the cause, and with each of his elections ("happiness," said one of the letters, "such as I have never experienced in my life"). Others told him of the pleasure with which their writers endured acts of malice because of their being abolitionists. In addition to these, there were many special appeals. Unhappy victims of slavery, or charitable souls moved by pity, wrote to tell Nabuco about individual cases of misery, punishment, abuse of the law, or illegal enslavement. From the midst of the self-seeking requests for employment or promotion, there arose from that correspondence a characteristic lamentation, a supplication from the unfortunates to someone who was interested in their misery. From the mass of the supporters of the abolitionist movement, there arose a generosity and an exaltation of spirit which did honor to the Brazilians.

On July 3, Joaquim Nabuco took his seat in the Chamber, "under a shower of flowers," according to the diary of Rebouças. On the same day he made his first speech which, in the *Annals* of the Chamber, is concluded with the same note found on former occasions: "Prolonged applause in the galleries." The time arrived for a second discussion of Minister Saraiva's project for the gradual extinction of slavery, which was replacing the Dantas plan. The project was based upon the idea of paying an indemnity to the slaveowners, a principle which the abolitionists could not admit, and which was going to be a burden on the entire country. Proposed on May 1 by Padua Fleury, the government's new plan retained some of Dantas' ideas. Among the provisions that were kept were the prohibition on transferring slaves from one province to another, and the requirement of registration. However, the declaration that slaves were natural citizens of Brazil, a clause which abolished the abuses of the law of 1831, was omitted.

The plan raised the age limit for the emancipation of the old slaves, which Dantas had fixed at sixty, to sixty-five. As a guaranty to the owners against any excesses of the abolitionist movement, a fine of from 500 to

1,000 milreis was to be imposed on anyone who lured away or sheltered another person's slaves. In short, the project was one which fully justified the reasonable fears of the abolitionists, even though it had many adherents in the Chamber.

Joaquim Nabuco declared:

I am sorry that my voice is a discordant note amidst the almost unanimous acclamations which the President of the Council has received from this Chamber, but I am consoled by the thought that in this matter both he and I have a great compensation. His is that my speaking against the project materially fortifies it, and if perhaps I should succeed in taking one Liberal vote away from it, that imperceptible void would immediately be filled by two or three Conservative votes. Mine is that by making the sacrifice of personally displeasing the worthy President of the Council, I help as much as I can to prevent the small reform that he presents to the parliament from killing the great reform that the nation desires.

I am not one of those who congratulate the worthy President of the Council by contributing to the quasi-unanimity which supports him. In order to obtain it, he has had to create the coalition government under which we now live, converting the previous Liberal situation into a Conservative situation, even though the Liberal party really has responsibility.

To achieve this, it was necessary for him to make the Liberal party, which was already pushing ahead with the great reform, turn back to welcome not only its own outdistanced rearguard, but foreign auxiliaries as well.

. . . .

. . . . Let the worthy President of the Council take note of an invariable law of political science. A law like this one, presented to solve a problem, must not be such that, upon being passed, it is already out of date. The law must anticipate, it must provide beforehand for the nation's inevitable advance. It must look forward, not backward. The worthy President of the Council will see within perhaps five or six years this living, efficient, national propaganda bear its final fruits. Behind him he has three centuries of slavery. Yet, instead of a forward-looking law, he gives us a bill that falls short of the point which the nation has already reached. Gentlemen, this is the same as wanting to fill up a crater that is ready to erupt at any place on the surface of the Empire.

. . . .

I give credit to the honored President of the Council for all his hopes and illusions, ... but I reject his proposal (applause).

I reject it because I believe that the nation, in less time, will do more and better. Public opinion is perfectly prepared, for example, for a law that forbids any further buying or selling of slaves in Brazil. Despite being limited and narrow, such a measure would have more morality and justice than the bill of the worthy President of the Council. I reject his plan because I believe that the social transformation through which we are now passing will continue with increasing velocity. I think that the disbelief in the future and the lack of faith in the vital elements of our country which his project reveals, could only be detrimental to that transformation.

This was the first of four speeches, all equally successful and admirable, in which Nabuco unmercifully dissected the Saraiva bill, censuring it, as he said in one of them, "with the rude frankness with which I am certain history will censure it." All of the speeches abounded in the most effective images.

I do not ask why Mr. Saraiva has changed the age of the slaves who were to be emancipated without indemnification from sixty to sixty-five! It was a sacrifice made to gain coherence among the former dissidents. A bridge was necessary to enable them all to accept the same project and thus restore party discipline; the President had no scruples against building that bridge with the sixty-year-old slaves. By means of that bridge of intertwined human lives, the former opposition has climbed to power. Those sexagenarians are of no worth under the law, but they have been of worth to the law, because it was they who made the law possible.

The July 24 speech concluded with these words:

But I for my part deny to that sinister institution the funeral rites that are requested for it. I refuse to give it the honor and the tribute of national recognition. I vote that it be buried in unhallowed ground, next to the fratricidal and bloody institutions which throughout history have trafficked with the honor, the liberty, and the equality of men.

The defeat of Dantas had shown that the abolitionists' ideal could not yet be realized in Brazil, and that their efforts had not yet made victory possible. The President of the Council, in his reply to Nabuco, declared with reason that it was not up to him "to modify the project to suit his pleasure," when he found himself "deprived of the aid of some of the leaders and influential members of his party." The country would have the law that it deserved and that slavery imposed upon it. The abolitionists and their partisan press fought ardently against the bill, which was soon nicknamed "the monster." Ruy Barbosa attacked it in two notable addresses delivered at abolitionist celebrations in the Polytheama Theater. In the Chamber, however, the measure was opposed only by the abolitionist group which Nabuco had organized, and by some intransigent Conservatives, represented by Andrade Figueira, who thought that it was premature. After long debate, the bill was finally approved, by seventy-three to seventeen votes, in the third discussion on August 14.

Dominating every party, slavery forced them all to unite in order to vote for a law that meant repression to the abolitionists, a continuation of their present status to the slaves, and indemnification and an increase in the value of slaves to the masters. It is a law that attributes the usury of Shylock and the hypocrisy of Tartufe to our legislator, and makes him appear before the world in the pay of slavery, as the captor, the jailor, the plunderer, the executioner, and the grave-digger of the slaves. [1]

On the same day that the Chamber approved the new law, and without waiting for the approval of the Senate, Minister Saraiva recognized that his mission was finished and sent his resignation to the Emperor. In the Chamber, according to Nabuco, there was "a Conservative predominance under a Liberal government." The government admitted this inconsistency and the impossibility of its continued existence. As Nabuco wrote, slavery "divides the Liberal party and unites the Conservative party," so that in spite of having a majority in the Chamber, no Liberal leader would dare accept the untenable heritage. Paranaguá, who was invited to take over the ministry because of that majority, declined the commission. Thus, on August 20, a Conservative ministry assumed power with all the signs of a long life.

The Baron of Cotegipe, João Mauricio Wanderley, was the leader of the new government. He was one of the shrewdest and most skillful statesmen, and one of the subtlest and most flexible minds, to be found anywhere in the politics of the Empire. The Liberal majority in the Chamber was naturally united against him. In the session for the presentation of the new ministry on August 24, Cotegipe faced the Chamber with the malicious familiarity that characterized his oratory, and the political experience of a long apprenticeship. Confident of his strength, and sure of the fact that the Emperor could not refuse to grant him dissolution if he asked for it, Cotegipe answered the vehement questions of the deputies about the great problem of emancipation, but he refused to say anything more before the bill was discussed in the Senate. He brought a witty note to the debate, which was becoming heated because of the Liberals' disappointment, but he did not give an inch.

The only alternative remaining to the condemned Chamber was a motion for a vote of no confidence, which was immediately proposed by Deputy Maciel and passed by fifty-five votes. This did not cause the President of the Council to change his humorous tone, however:

What does that motion say that I have not already said? Does it say that the Liberal majority or the worthy Liberal deputies have no political confidence in ministry. Is that it?

Voices: Yes, certainly!

The Baron of Cotegipe (President of the Council): Well that is what I say, too. It is the truth! (Pause, prolonged hilarity.)

[1] Speech by Nabuco at the Abolitionist Celebration of September 28, 1885.

Cotegipe did not call for dissolution, which was the only solution to the problem. He wanted the Chamber to give him first the proposed legislation about slavery. At the end of the session Nabuco delivered a memorable speech:

> There are in this nation two institutions, and no one knows whether they are held in esteem or hatred. These institutions have formed an alliance for the purpose of ruling the country completely. They are the monarchy, which means the government of a single man, and slavery, which means the dominance of a single interest. Whenever the destiny of one becomes endangered, the other thinks that it hears the funeral knell of its own extinction. That is what we see today on this floor, that is the spectacle which we are witnessing.

The blow at the monarchy was really directed solely against the person of the Emperor, who was responsible for the rise of the Conservatives at a time when the country was being swept by a pro-Liberal wave.

> . . . . We have nothing but a parliamentary form of government. Like the thick spider web placed at the entrance of the cave of David to fool the enemy into believing that he was not there, its sole purpose is to conceal from the eyes of the country the real government of the Lord's Anointed behind an appearance of popular authority. Under such circumstances the country wanted action and freedom. It wanted reforms that by their very daring would stir the indifferent masses, reforms inspired by sympathy for the destiny of the poor. That virtually unknown American country, Brazil, was rising in a tremendous effort that was beginning to be noticed by the world. It was demonstrating that it had within itself something of the spirit, the enthusiasm, and the ideals of the new races. When Brazil was expecting to see on the horizon, illuminated by the dawning light, a flock of morning birds greeting the break of day, the old Conservative owl appeared before us, bothered by that premature light. It was the owl from the towers, the mansions, the prisons, and the slave quarters, come to release the pious soothsayer from the Liberal illusions of the country! (Applause in the galleries; the President calls for attention.)

The entire first part of that speech was directed toward the throne:

> That throne, when we found it on the seventh of April [Pedro I abdicated on April 7, 1831], was a cradle like that of Moses on the Nile, placed on the edge of a stream which was rising to carry it away. In 1831, with the aid of Evaristo da Veiga, we rescued that cradle. In 1840, with the aid of António Carlos [de Andrada], we ignored the constitution and dressed the fifteen-year-old Caesar in the robes of imperial purple in which we had found him. But never, Mr. President, in spite of the vast liberal irradiation of the American continent, has it been possible to reconcile that orphan of absolutism with the democracy that adopted him and saved the crown for him.
>
> In the forty-five years of the present reign, the world has passed through such a

tremendous transformation that the human spirit is dazzled when it stops to inventory all its progress. In those forty-five years, steam has replaced sails on the surface of the seas. News travels around the globe in incomparably less time than it took the cry of independence to go from the fields of the Ipiranga to the capital. Everywhere the machine has been substituted for muscular energy and human skill. Electricity, although still in the cradle, has already asserted its primacy as a source of energy in Brazil. Industry and science have transformed social dynamics to such an extent that the problems of existence, individual or collective, are no longer the same. In the meanwhile, none of this has suggested to the Emperor at least the idea that all this progress could have been imagined just as well in Bôa Vista by the illustrious friar who educated him [Pedro de Santa Mariana, a Carmelite who had a reputation for both virtue and ignorance], as in the convents of the Middle Ages by the genius of an Abelard or a Roger Bacon.

This was probably a polite way of saying that the Emperor had a medieval mentality. The last part of the speech was about the Liberal party and its future attitude:

But, Mr. President, one must not think that I personally lament the end of a situation favorable to my party, nor that I believe the sacrifice made is lost. . . . . There is a moral law that has been pointed out more than once and that confirms the absolute value of disinterestedness. It is that no organism, individual or collective, be it a man, a party, or a nation, can do anything really great and universal without destroying itself in the process or without expending its energy in that act which thus becomes an act of complete consecration. The Liberal party has not destroyed itself entirely because it has not achieved the realization of its goal, but even at the beginning it has sacrificed itself to it.

I do not bemoan that sacrifice, but those who dared to enter this battle against the landholding slave interests, a battle that could have had no other outcome, have the right to lament at finding themselves repudiated only to be replaced by the partisans of that monopoly of the soil and of man, of money and of blood.

. . . .

The Liberty party entered this battle under the protection of the abolitionist movement. If the worthy President of the Council will look at the other side of the case, he will see that the provinces, like the former colony under the yoke of the mother country, are beginning to feel that their only choice now is between independence and death (applause).

. . . .

We are all preparing ourselves with the same feeling of individual liberty with which Cromwell's soldiers steeled themselves for the great religious battles that established the supremacy of Parliament, and with the same unselfishness and abnegation with which the first Puritans left the shores of old England to found New England in America. Knowing what we want and holding our hearts high, we are making ourselves ready, Mr. President, to give some day to this nation a government in which, as in the Roman consuls and tribunes, the world may see both the sanctity of the country and the inviolability of the people represented (noisy applause in the galleries; the orator is congratulated).

The unfortunate Saraiva project occupied the Senate's attention throughout the whole month of September, and was finally approved without any change, as the government had requested. The efforts of Silveira da Mota, Afonso Celso, Cristiano Ottoni, Dantas, and José Bonifácio, who was the hero of the discussion, could not prevent its passage. On September 28, the date of the famous law of 1831, the bill received the approval of the Emperor, who had already signed a decree dissolving the Chamber of Deputies on the 25th. The Baron of Cotegipe was all-powerful, and the problem of emancipation was considered solved.

It was probably with the idea of giving the Liberal party one more worthy aspiration to encourage it in its ostracism, that in one of the last sessions Nabuco had presented his plan for federation of the provinces. The idea was not new, having been introduced as early as 1831. The system of centralized government did not permit the provinces of Brazil to use their own resources to their advantage and sent them presidents alien to their interests. Freedom from this yoke was most necessary. A federal system was the only one that the Republicans conceived of in their dream for the future nation, but there was a certain originality in seeing the idea presented now by an inflexible Monarchist. Nabuco's wish was simply to have the Empire carry out every possible reform and thus, in the full expansion of its liberty, make the change to a republic become unnecessary.

The federal plan had been growing in Nabuco's mind for some time. The year before in the Santa Isabel Theater in Recife he had said:

> The greatest of all the political reforms to which I intend to devote myself after the completion of emancipation is a quasi-federal decentralization of the provinces.

On September 14 Nabuco introduced his bill into the Chamber with the signatures of thirty-nine deputies. Convinced of the importance of the idea, he declared solemnly:

> I thank this august Chamber for allowing the bill to be classified as urgent. I shall be the first, Mr. President, not to see in that act, on the part of the few Conservatives who were generous enough to associate themselves with it, anything more than the deference shown between adversaries who take leave of each other on the eve of a battle. . . . . As for the Liberal party, however, that act signifies its resolution, at a time when the government benches of parliament are occupied by the forces of personal government, to plant on the battlements of this building a great national flag, that of federation (applause).
>
> I ask my worthy colleagues to do me the honor of keeping silent. The subject

that I have to cover is so grave that it is necessary for me to measure each of my words. It is so serious that I really feel, like the orators of old, that the platform is a sacred place. At this moment I am assuming the greatest responsibility that a Brazilian, whether a public or a private individual, can take on himself. That is to discuss the integrity of his country in order to ask that it be recast in a pattern different from the one which has existed since we became an independent nation. In short, Mr. President, I propose the monarchical federation of Brazil, within the limits that I shall have occasion to justify. This means the revival, today in this Chamber, of the bill that the Liberal party sent to the Senate in October 1831; a bill that expresses the quality of strong, masculine, and patriotic liberalism of the generation that made the 7th of April possible [a reference to April 7, 1831, when Pedro I was forced to abdicate].

Nabuco then recalled in a comparison the Cretan legend in which the Curetes protected the infant Zeus (Jupiter) by dancing about him and clattering their weapons so that his cries were not heard by Kronos, his father, who wished in vain to destroy him; Kronos was overcome and Jupiter became king of the gods:

This shows, Mr. President, that the same thing happens to great ideas intended for the government of the world as happened to the infant Jupiter. They may be hidden in the cradle from the wrath of the power that they will one day be called upon to dethrone. They may have to seek refuge in some obscure place on the earth and in humble hearts. It may be necessary for the Curetes [priests of Jupiter in the Cretan cult] to drown out the infant's crying with the rattle of their shields so that it will not be heard. But on the day set by destiny, the new power will appear in all its strength and virility to reclaim the empire that belongs to it (applause).

. . . .

In fact, Mr. President, although the abolitionist movement, with rare exceptions, is a recent phenomenon in our history, federation is a phenomenon of our whole past. We find it in the slow and gradual growth of our country. We find it associated with the old captaincies. We find it before independence, and even after it throughout the reign of Pedro I and the regency. In order to lose sight of it, it is necessary to pass through the forty-five years of this reign, during which time the process of centralization has been completed and has caused the spirit that enlivens all Brazilian history to disappear completely from the surface.

The solid reasoning of that long speech was based upon four points which Nabuco enumerated thus before elucidating them:

There are four reasons why the independence of the provinces is demanded by all Brazilians. In the first place, there are the enormous distances that separate the provinces, a reason sufficient in itself.

In the second place, there is the diversity of interests, which it is quite unnecessary to stress. It is as absurd to maintain that there is an identity of interests between the people living along the Amazon and those living along the Paraná, as it is to affirm that there is no difference between the interests of the people on the coast of Great Britain and those on the coast of the Black Sea.

A third reason is that as long as the government of the provinces is conducted by a delegation from the central government, it cannot be truly provincial.

Still a fourth reason is the impossibility of preventing, without absolute autonomy, the increasing absorption of the provinces by the state. By reason of the weakness that the state imposes upon the provinces, the more the central government needs money, the more the provincial resources will be absorbed by the collectivity called the state.

In open debate, Nabuco was, as always, invincible. He had just read an article by Agassiz about the immensity of the Amazon region and the advantages of its decentralization, when MacDowell, a deputy from Pará, interrupted him thus:

That is a worthy aspiration of the learned traveler. However, if you knew the locality better, you would see how much he has exaggerated.

Sr. Joaquim Nabuco: You forbid me to touch this subject because I do not know the locality. Mr. President, this is an argument in my favor. I have occupied myself with these matters of the Amazon Valley for a long time. Ever since I was a boy, the vastness of that region and its marvels have fascinated my mind and imagination. I have read almost everything written about the nature and the present state of this wonderful territory. In the meantime, the worthy deputy considers me incapable of forming a judgment about it. In saying this, does he not see practically demonstrated the fact that his province cannot be governed from such a distance, by a Chamber composed of men like me? (Applause.)

The press found ample material for speculation in the bill. It was received as an event of major importance by those who thought its realization was possible. It was considered an assault upon the Republican platform by some journalists of that party. Others, such as Rangel Pestana, believed it acceptable under this principle: "We shall find the practical means of achieving the victory of a federated republic." Public opinion, however, found the idea entirely irreconcilable with the monarchy, it being impossible to find utopia under an imperial regime. The *Gazeta da Tarde* itself took that position, although in announcing its decision to combat the measure, it asserted its "fanatic admiration for the character and genius of the proponent." *O País*, which was frankly republican, affirmed that "the monarchy in Brazil will be centralized or there will be no monarchy." It accepted the proposition, however, because "it brings into question the very form of government that rules us, and has so long sufficed for us." It saw in the project a sign that Nabuco "is fatally yielding to the two opposing currents that are drawing his brave and sincere spirit toward different poles." It said:

> As a political event and as an oratorical success, the speech of the illustrious deputy will remain as one of the finest pages in our parliamentary history and one of the most brilliant victories eloquence has ever won.
>
> If the Liberal party, that is, if the old Liberal party, has died, we must in its honor say that it falls on the field shrouded in a glorious flag.

On September 15, the Republican deputy, Prudente de Moraes, declared in the Chamber:

> If the worthy deputy succeeds in gaining the conversion of the provinces into confederated states under the monarchy, I shall cease to be a Republican, so that I may enlist in the ranks of the worthy deputy's party. I have the right to ask some compensation, however. If the worthy deputy encounters in our present institutions, especially in the omnipotent crown, an invincible obstacle to the realization of his patriotic dream, I ask him on that day to come and enlist in the Republican party. Thus, with his talents and his training, he may aid it in this campaign which will finally extirpate from American soil that anachronism called monarchy, and give us the federation whose necessity and advantages the worthy deputy has demonstrated so convincingly.

Nabuco replied: "The pact is made."

CHAPTER XIII. THE JOURNALIST. ECLIPSE AND RESURGENCE OF THE ABOLITIONIST MOVEMENT. 1886–87

The elections for the new Chamber took place on January 15. Faithful to its program, the Liberal party in its seven years of power had made direct election the law and had presided over two completely free elections. Dantas had permitted the election of a chamber that as soon as it met overthrew him. The Conservatives, however, did not resist the temptation to return to the old system and made up a chamber of friends of the government, where only a handful of Liberals were permitted to enter by tolerance.

Nabuco perceived the difference in the atmosphere upon his arrival at Recife, where, as in the previous year, he came prepared to battle by means of the word. He found his first district under the Conservative iron glove. The methods which the party had always used and was going to employ once again were in full operation. Positive orders on how to vote had gone out to all public employees and their dependents, and districts were arranged to suit the candidate.

In Recife, Nabuco encountered obstacles at every step. He was denied the use of the Santa Isabel Theater for electoral speeches. The building had also just been refused to the Commission to Redeem Slaves, which wanted to use it for the solemn delivery of eighty-three certificates of freedom. The abolitionist movement was being visibly oppressed, and in the January 15 elections, Nabuco was defeated, as was foreseen by Councilor Portela.

He had one consolation: "If I had been elected, my fate would have been the same as that of José Mariano." In fact, José Mariano, who was elected, was debarred by the Chamber (where only nineteen Liberal deputies were permitted to take their seats). With the Conservatives' return, Brazil relapsed into the regime of unanimous parliaments.

Slavery was in power, and few voices were raised against it in the first months of the regime. The semblance of a solution, which the Saraiva-Cotegipe law brought, created a relative calm about the great problem, and the government's severe restrictions against all demonstrations reduced even the echo of the abolitionist movement.

The abolitionist movement and Nabuco's political career both underwent a definite eclipse. Deprived of the Chamber as a sounding board, the leader of the oppressed party turned to the press, which had already served him so many times before. Only now, however, did journalism become the principal activity of his life. His wish, as well as that of his companions, was to create a paper of his own, a great abolitionist organ over which he would have exclusive control. It looked for a moment as though that dream was going to become a reality. The name *O Século* had already been chosen. The party's finances did not permit it to materialize, however, and the expected outside support failed. It was then that Quintino Bocayuva, the director of *O País*, found a solution just as acceptable. He asked Nabuco to come conduct his campaign of uncompromising abolitionism from there.

The paper *O País*, founded in the previous year, had already achieved a certain popularity, which the name of the new editor enhanced even more. With his daring, but never offensive, frankness and his concentrated and steady fire against the government, Nabuco attracted a great number of readers. At the same time he brought on a storm of anonymous attacks from every side. His only reply, made in *O País* on July 26, was to declare himself "armed with a profound scorn against that type of projectile."

Nabuco, the propagandist, completed his work as a journalist with the publication in 1886 of a series of pamphlets entitled "Liberal Propaganda." Among them were *The Error of the Emperor*, *The Eclipse of the Abolitionist Movement*, *Liberal Elections*, *Conservative Elections*, and *Slaves*. In addition to the article that gave it its title, each of these pamphlets included some comments about the political events of the previous fortnight. The opposition published a series of parodies, which met with better success. These were called "Propaganda of the Truth," and included *The Error of Joaquim Nabuco*, *The Eclipse of Patriotism*, etc.

There was a great sale of the Nabuco pamphlet, *The Error of the Emperor*, whose title alone awoke curiosity. The error that Nabuco pointed out was the fact that after Dom Pedro II, stirred by a desire to aid the movement, had called upon Dantas, he desisted from his intention, and upon seeing Dantas overthrown by only one vote, immediately called upon Saraiva.

> On the previous day, emancipation was in power, while on the following day, slavery was triumphant. That was the first, the great, and the fatal error of the Emperor. It was the error of changing his mind, of making the work that was begun useless, and of paralyzing the national movement.

Dom Pedro, on reading the pamphlet, made various notes in the margin which many years later came to the attention of Nabuco. Their dispassionateness contrasted with the severe tone of the author, who, on the other hand, had excused himself by saying: "The one who writes these lines is neither a partisan enemy nor a personal adversary of the Emperor, but just the opposite." His Majesty noted in the margin: "I believe this. I have always liked Nabuco."

While parliament was in session, Nabuco wrote a daily article in *O País* which was always entitled "The Parliamentary Session."[1] That column was his personal commentary. It was less a parliamentary review than a platform from which, while excluded from parliament, he could voice his appeal for abolition. He looked at parliamentary questions and discussions exclusively through the prism of abolitionism. With his finger ever on the wound, he analyzed cases as they occurred while he was still under the emotion of the news. "There is not a single fact about slavery," said one of those commentaries, "that does not sum up them all."

Sometimes he aroused pity with the publication of letters that he received, telling about unpunished cruelties on plantations. Until complete freedom came, he asked that all the mercy consistent with the cursed institution be shown.

The paper was for him a platform, from which he directed successive campaigns like the one against the punishment of whipping. This campaign was carried to a successful end within a few weeks. Nabuco revolted against this form of punishment which, in the Brazilian penal code, existed only for criminal slaves. At the end of his column on July 29, 1886, he exposed the case of four slaves condemned by a jury in Paraíba do Sul to three hundred lashes. Two of the four died as a result of the punishment. He concluded thus:

> It will be sad for the Imperial Princess to have to read this news on her birthday, and I am profoundly sorry to have to publish it today. However, that picture will enable the future Empress to recognize the condition of our slaves and to understand the mission of the abolitionists in her father's kingdom.

On the following day in the Senate, Dantas quoted that article and requested information about the case. The Minister of Justice replied in a speech which the fiery editor of *O País* called "a justification of the penalty of death by whipping, or in other words, of a disguised death penalty, secure from imperial clemency and cruel in the last degree."

The Senate immediately went about putting an end to the degrading

[1] Many of his articles in *O País*, written in 1886 when parliament was closed, had the title, "Letter from Petrópolis." The Russian minister, Count Prozor, recalls: "In 1886 I made the acquaintance of Joaquim Nabuco. I had been named legation secretary in Brazil and, as the whole diplomatic corps did then and does now, I had taken up residence at Petrópolis, a thousand meters above the furnacelike heat of Rio de Janeiro and the yellow fever which still raged at that period, despite which there was never any truce in the political struggles. Deeply involved in the fight, Nabuco used to come often to refresh himself in the midst of our little colony, where he was always welcomed. Radiating intelligence and life, always alert and interested, he possessed at the same time a natural kindness which allowed him to adapt himself to our various mentalities and made him as welcome to children as to grownups." (*Revue Hebdomadaire*, June 20, 1912.)

punishment. José Bonifácio lent his eloquence to the discussion. With vibrant appeals, Nabuco pushed the matter toward a definitive solution, complaining of any delay. ". . . . it was discussed one day in the Senate . . . . no one remembers any longer the victims of 'public justice' . . . . The minister of that 'justice' can turn his attention back to the elections of Minas." To Nabuco, it seemed to be "preaching in the desert." Several weeks later, however, after the Chamber had approved the Senate bill, he jubilantly acknowledged: "Our campaign, which began on the birthday of the Imperial Princess, will be finished tomorrow, on the birthday of her son, with the approval of the law that we demanded."

It was the Senate which, by taking upon itself the mission that fell more naturally within the competence of the temporary Chamber, breathed some life into the abolitionist movement. On June 1, 1886, Dantas introduced a bill which placed a five-year limit on slavery. It was not discussed, however. "It was just a flag," protested Nabuco in *O País*. "A battle never took place." But the Senate found other ways of pronouncing itself.

On July 6, the former President of the Council, Councilor Saraiva, protested against the violation of the law of 1885, for which he had been principally responsible. It had proved to be an elastic law, and making use of Nabuco's words, he said:

> . . . . The leader of the abolitionists asserted that the law could be good, but that he found it bad because it would have to be carried out by ministers who did not believe as he did in immediate abolition, and he added: "If we were to execute the law, we would, with ordinances, make the law grow. . . . ." Now the ministry has followed that advice, but in the opposite sense: with ordinances it has restricted the effects of the law. But, if the abolitionists who thus intended to amplify the law are revolutionaries, will not those who seek to attenuate its beneficial effects be equally revolutionary? To falsify the law, whether in one sense or another, is always a revolutionary proceeding.

Several days later, Otaviano proposed that, in the reply to the Speech from the Throne, there should be omitted the sentence beginning with the words: "The law of September 28, 1885, is being faithfully and loyally executed." The Senate approved this change. On July 13 Nabuco commented on the news in *O País*: "The government was defeated yesterday in the Senate, on grounds on which defeat means disgrace."

Later the Senate approved two additions proposed by José Bonifácio to the budget of the Ministry of Agriculture. Both dealt with the execution of the law of September 28, 1885. This time Cotegipe refused to accept the new censure. From the Senate, he appealed to the Chamber which he controlled, and which saved his pride by reasserting its support of him. The Chamber refused to give its approval to the Senate's additions. It supported the budget presented by the Ministry of Agriculture, and called for a general assembly of the two houses to resolve the conflict. With the huge majority that Cotegipe had proclaimed and that everyone expected in the assembly, the cabinet's policy would be fully reaffirmed by the direct representatives of the nation. "In a few hours the ceremony will terminate in this manner and the sentence of the slaves will be definitely wrought," wrote Nabuco on October 7. On October 9 the two houses meeting in joint session rejected the amendments of José Bonifácio by a vote of ninety-two to thirty-three. The editor of *O País* consoled himself by looking to the future: "The voting was a flood, but of what use is the flood to the drowned man save to carry him more quickly to the sea?"

The first anniversary of the August 20 ministry found that body as strong as on the day it came to power, and occasioned a shower of eulogies, praising primarily the cabinet's financial success. On the same day that the vote in the general assembly demonstrated the supremacy of the cabinet over the rebellious Senate, however, the ministry received the first effective blow from another side. Carrying its restrictions on public opinion a bit far, it had severely chastised some army officers for expressing their political views in the press. As a result, the cabinet now saw all the armed forces take the side of their colleagues who had been disciplined. This was the beginning of a military incident which was to terminate in February 1887 with the removal of the penalties. The dignity of the ministry was left visibly shaken and the resentment still seething.

In October 1886, Fate delivered a hard blow to the Abolitionist party, which had suffered so much under political domination. The sad event was the death of José Bonifácio. The tribute of a truly national sorrow was shown at his funeral, where Joaquim Nabuco, standing before the tomb in São Paulo, expressed the gratitude of the abolitionists.

At the beginning of 1887, Nabuco was in Recife again, still trying to bring about a resurgence of the cause that he represented. "In any case," a friend wrote to him, "you must not withdraw until you have succeeded in re-establishing at least one of the numerous abolitionist clubs which have been closed. This must be done in such a way that the club will last as long as is necessary." Before his departure, Nabuco did indeed found the Pernambucan Society Against Slavery. His short stay in Recife, which was marked by the most significant sort of tributes, satisfied him fully as to the perspectives for the future. Among the Pernambucan abolitionists he caused a great renewal of enthusiasm, as he had wished to do. His address on federation in the Varieties Theater, and his address to the people of Palmares planted seeds which were not long in germinating.

Still remembering the government's severe repression at the time of the last election, it was with some fear that people gathered to hear Nabuco.

Once they began to disband in disorder, hearing a horse neigh and thinking that it might be the sign of a cavalry charge. Ready to begin his speech, Nabuco detained his alarmed listeners with a gesture: "Gentlemen," he exclaimed, "it was the whinny of a horse that announced the victory of Pharsalia to Caesar!"

On that same day, with feelings of nostalgia for Europe, Nabuco embarked for the Old World as correspondent for *O País.* Faithful to his old love, he spent the greater part of his short absence in England. At this time, the Association of International Law was meeting in London. Nabuco proposed there a motion that was accepted by acclamation. In it the conference renewed the resolutions approved by the Milan Congress of 1883. At the banquet for the lawyers in the Guildhall, the Lord Mayor toasted the cause of freedom in Brazil, and Nabuco replied. His friends in the Anti-Slavery Society, which continued to follow solicitously the progress of the cause in Brazil, received him as affectionately as ever. The announcement of the meeting that was sent to members on this occasion carried this note: "It is hoped that Senhor Nabuco will be able to be present."

In August he was on his way back to take part in the electoral struggle in the first district of Recife, a struggle brought about by the entry of his constant rival, Councilor Portela, into the cabinet of Cotegipe. The new minister of the Empire had to ask the voters to confirm his seat in the Chamber. Once again Nabuco presented himself against Portela.

"Arrived in Pernambuco. Six rainbows," he wrote in his diary on August 26. Never has a poetic sign foretold the future more accurately. The bad weather was definitely over and the brilliant election which awaited him was a decisive and permanent triumph. The irresistible wave of the abolitionist movement was overcoming the resistance of the Conservative ministry. The schism in the Liberal party caused by the slavery problem was being firmly mended, to the advantage of those who refused to compromise with slavery. Nabuco's candidacy in 1887 was a victory for the progressive elements of the Liberal party in Recife, which were led by José Mariano. The enthusiasm with which the people received Nabuco clearly showed that government coercion would gain nothing this time, even though it was exercised with particular vigor.

The fate of the Conservative candidate, Portela, who was now minister of the Empire, had a direct effect upon the life of the ministry. Alarmed by the news of the abolitionist enthusiasm, the Baron of Cotegipe ordered the warship "Imperial Marinheiro" to Recife, but it was shipwrecked on the way. Not only was Joaquim Nabuco prevented from speaking to the people, but by order of the chief of police, groups of over three persons were forbidden to gather in the streets and squares of the towns. Nabuco, who had scheduled a meeting in Afogados, asked the people to join him in complying with the illegal prohibition. "Those who disregard my request," he declared in his manifesto, "will aid in the election of the minister of the Empire." The warning did not come in time, however, to prevent the gathering in the square of Afogados of a group which the cavalry dispersed. In the ensuing confusion, there was one accidental death. The solemn burial of the humble victim, Eduardo Borges de Siqueira, with its large attendance of people, was a tacit and energetic protest against the government's imposition. In the Senate at Rio de Janeiro, the representative from Pernambuco, Luiz Felipe de Souza Leão, declared: "If the government, not content with these measures, wishes to secure the election of the minister of the Empire at any cost, it is quicker and more decisive to order a decree drawn up granting him admission into the Chamber of Deputies."

In the Senate, Dantas, Cândido de Oliveira, Franco de Sá, and Otaviano, and in the Chamber, Deputy Pedro Beltrão, commented energetically upon the events of Pernambuco.

On September 14, Nabuco was elected by a majority of over a hundred votes. The result of the election had such a direct influence upon the slavery question and the ministry that not only Recife, but all Brazil anxiously awaited and noisily celebrated the news that arrived from the north. Ouvidor Street was crowded with the curious who were waiting for telegrams. Those from Recife brought news of an extraordinary enthusiasm, accompanied by fireworks, acclamations, and the liberation of slaves. Telegrams from São Paulo, Fortaleza, Ouro Preto, and everywhere announced similar rejoicings. With reason *O País* declared:

> It is not the victory of Joaquim Nabuco that we are celebrating, it is the glory of the province of Pernambuco and the victory of the abolitionist ideal.
>
> The defeat of the minister of the Empire, vanquished at the polls by his eminent competitor, does not mean a personal rebuff to Councilor Machado Portela, as much as it means the condemnation of the policy of the present cabinet. By accepting the position of minister, Portela had espoused that policy, and by so doing placed a humiliating yoke upon the neck of the Lion of the North and hitched it to the cart.
>
> In making this protest, which is as solemn as it is peaceful and proud, and full of nobleness and dignity, Pernambuco has washed out the spot with which some sought to stain the escutcheon of its glorious traditions.

All the abolitionist press exulted. In *O País* even some of the advertisements bore titles like "The Government" or "Joaquim Nabuco and Portela," in order to call the reader's attention to a cough medicine or a hat.

Of the hundreds of telegrams sent to Nabuco from all parts of Brazil, and visibly inspired by pure patriotism, at least one had unpleasant consequences. Nineteen students of the Military School of Rio Grande do Sul sent a collective message that stated: "We hail your triumph. As an abolitionist deputy, you represent Pernambuco with pride despite government pressure." For upholding the terms of the message before the disciplinary council, the students were sentenced to twenty days in prison and sent to regiments on the frontiers.

All of the young people were for Nabuco, even though, because of military discipline, only the students in civil schools were able to display their feelings. The director of the Naval School received a warning from the government regarding the ovation made by the students in the Naval Arsenal at the passage of the launch in which Nabuco was going ashore at Rio. That arrival in Rio was a new consecration of Nabuco's popularity, amidst the general rejoicing for an election that interested the entire country and whose significance was appreciated by all.

The ministry was not overthrown. It was reconstituted without Portela and for several months continued to resist the movement which two years before it had considered to be definitely crushed. Now, still active, it was becoming a threat. Everything was converging toward the final victory. In 1887 several bishops, in eloquent pastoral letters, brought the support of the Church to the cause of liberty. Since the beginning of the year, the efforts of the government to repress abolitionist meetings had been causing isolated but symptomatic disorders. A gathering scheduled by the Confederation for August 6 in the Polytheama Theater ended in an armed conflict between police thugs and part of the people in attendance. The Abolitionist party had some disorderly members who simply sought to make trouble. Speaking in the Chamber on October 8 concerning some abuses and property destruction that occurred in Campos, Nabuco called them "the necessary baggage of all parties."

On October 5, Nabuco had been recognized as a deputy and had taken possession of his seat to the accompaniment of applause that the police thugs, who were stationed in the galleries, were unable to restrain. Only ten days were left until the year's work would be finished, at which time Nabuco had to return to Recife. He wrote: "I go to Rio only to obtain from the military the assurance that they will not capture slaves." On October 7 he declared in the Chamber: "Is there any profession that is higher or more honorable than the profession of the soldier? Is there any profession that is lower or more degrading than that of the slave-catcher?"

On the 8th he said:

> Not a soldier goes out upon those tasks without a heavy heart and the feeling that he is playing a role beneath his dignity. . . . . The worthy deputy for Rio de Janeiro, who has requested me not to bring burning questions into the Chamber, will permit me to make a solemn appeal to the Brazilian Army, and to all those

who have dignity and honor, to cross their arms and refuse absolutely to participate in those lamentable and tragic man hunts.

The deputy for Rio here mentioned was the principal advocate of the opposing camp, Andrade Figueira. Nabuco treated this meritorious adversary with special deference. He distinguished "his political role from his feelings" and recognized him as "the most notable man in the Conservative party of Brazil." Figueira replied that Joaquim Nabuco

was not the most suitable person to try to increase lack of discipline by preaching the dangerous doctrine that the army ought to refuse to comply with its duty to maintain public order and security, because it considered it beneath its dignity and mission. This mission of catching slaves who have been seduced away by the criminal propaganda of the abolitionists and of delivering them to their owners can never dishonor the uniform of a soldier. It is a mission of order and peace, whose purpose is to restore tranquillity to unhappy families and to attend to the interests of production, without which there will be no soldiery (laughter).

The Nabuco of that year, striking the last blows at a moribund institution, was not the same parliamentary orator who in former times had bravely challenged it in its fortress. His inner conviction had not changed, but already the difference was noticeable between the daring denunciations of earlier days that were flung from an almost solitary post, and the formal condemnations which now seemed more like those of a judge who was backed by public opinion. One of his colleagues in the Chamber, Afonso Celso Junior, described the orator of that final phase:

Nabuco's appearance constituted in itself the best introduction of all. It was only necessary for him to appear on the platform in order to gain attention and sympathy. Very tall and well proportioned, with finely chiseled head and features, magnificent eyes, and an expression that was both gentle and manly, Nabuco was an admirable combination of strength and grace, a handsome giant who stood out in any crowd. A noble figure, he was one of those creatures that nature seems to fashion as a model, with care and love.

His clear voice was like a clarion. Penetrating and powerful, it imposed silence and cut short interruptions. It ordinarily rang out in sonorous bursts. Instead of growing hoarse with time, it acquired with practice increasingly powerful and metallic tones.

It was a voice of combat, the voice of the commander instructing his soldiers as the battle approached. Nabuco's elegant gestures and his stance also contributed to the impression that his speeches produced. One of his customary gestures was to put his hands in the pockets of his trousers, another was to run two fingers of his right hand into the pocket of his waistcoat. These and other mannerisms gave him an advantageous air of ease and informality. He enunciated his words syllable by syllable, emphasizing the most significant ones.

In addition to so many splendid qualities, Nabuco also possessed an immense facility of speech and a lively and poetic imagination which, strengthened by his careful literary studies, produced an abundance of radiant metaphors and waves of enthusiasm, natural eloquence, and inspiration. Furthermore, Nabuco always chose lofty subjects for his themes; social, philosophical, and religious problems of universal scope. He avoided individual controversies and political intrigues. He did not submit to party discipline nor did he recognize a chief. The abolitionist question had attained its impassioned and brilliant peak. Nabuco had linked his name with the captives' cause, and was the victims' consecrated spokesman. In 1887 he re-entered the Chamber in an unusually triumphant manner, after routing at the polls the minister, Machado Portela, a good and influential man whose defeat was a surprise to all.

At that time Nabuco was a composite of many and varied qualities. He was the hero of society, the traveler who had associated with important foreigners, the journalist. He had great popularity and was regarded as the personification of Brazil. The abolitionist press continued to deify him. Everything, in short, co-operated in pointing out and enhancing the unforgettable oratorical triumphs of that time. Nabuco was a fascinating figure. Even his adversaries, who were irritated by his superiority, recognized and proclaimed his great qualities. People of all conditions, including numerous ladies, came to see and hear him. The galleries of parliament acclaimed him. As soon as the president uttered the formal phrase: "Joaquim Nabuco has the floor," a shiver ran through the excited audience and the atmosphere was electrified.

The speech did not follow a continuous and uninterrupted course. It was delivered in spurts. Nabuco spoke for a while, then concluded that part of the speech with a precise quotation, a fine image, or a witticism.

He stopped, rested, and permitted the remarks and the applause to flow around him. Olympic, and towering above the multitude, he slowly fingered his notes. With his eyes half-closed, he smiled and reflected, waiting for the noise to cease. He disdained the comments that were made, or encouraged those that pleased him. Then suddenly, he set out upon a new onslaught.

Silence was restored as soon as he began to speak.

It was impossible to hold him back any longer. If the noise continued, it was swiftly stilled by Nabuco's extraordinary voice and his dizzying speech. His concluding remarks, full of vast lyric overtones, were carefully and skillfully prepared.

In them he employed his most majestic images, his most comprehensive assertions, and his most theatrical gestures. They provoked thunderous ovations in the galleries. Nabuco seated himself, and for several minutes all work was virtually suspended while the undying echoes of his powerful and mighty tones reverberated in the most elevated and sensitive parts of the mind and heart.[2]

On October 15 the Chamber recessed. Nabuco had missed no opportunities to speak during the ten days after he took possession of his seat. On

[2] Afonso Celso, *Eight Years in Parliament* (*Oito anos de parlamento*), Rio de Janeiro, 1901, p. 150.

one day he made no less than four speeches about different subjects. He also fought untiringly from his other platform in *O País* throughout the entire month of October. While he was appealing to the army to dispense with its humiliating mission, the latter was engaged in a particularly tragic hunt which served to add to the reality of Nabuco's words.

Sixty slaves, armed with scythes and cudgels, had fled from the county of Capivari. With orders to capture them dead or alive, an armed force pursued them to the hills of Cubatão, where a bloody battle ensued. On October 19 Nabuco wrote in *O País*:

> After having been morally deposed by the national army, Sr. Cotegipe contrived to defame that body by putting it at the command of the owners of fugitive slaves. There is no denying that the revenge is bloody and the humiliation complete.

He continued to say that the soldier who fell while capturing slaves did not die for his country.

> At the most, he is the victim of discipline. The slave, however, dies for his freedom, his family, and his race. He dies defending himself, not attacking others. He dies like the martyrs of the greatest of all religions, like the hero of the greatest of all battles. He dies as all men have the right to die, since he cannot be free save at the cost of his life.[3]

Knowing that the majority of the army was with him, Nabuco did not fear the attempts of those who sought to embroil him with the military. In his article on October 21, he justified his use of a violent expression that had caused some scandal, and proudly answered the attacks and scorn that rained upon him from all sides.

> The new cause for incrimination is that I called the Brazilian Army slave hounds. I called all those who help to seize fugitive slaves slave hounds, from the President of the Council who leads the pack to the last police soldier.

The delicate question involving military discipline with which Nabuco dealt gave his words a revolutionary tone that was new in him. "It seems incredible," said one of his adversaries in the newspaper *Novidades*, "that Sr. Nabuco now intends to take the place of Proudhomme [Patrocínio's pen name] by advising trickery, theft, fighting, and murder as the means for reaching freedom." It was strange, continued the article, that the deplorable madness of the slaves of Capivari had drawn words of applause and congratulations for the victory of the fugitives. "With all the responsibility that his name implies and all the authority of the mandate he now holds, Sr. Joaquim Nabuco expressly used words to that effect in *O País*, the official organ of the nation's anarchy."

[3] *O País*, October 21, 1887.

Since the Emperor was gravely ill in Europe at the time, the case was solved with a petition from the Military Club to the Imperial Princess, respectfully requesting that the army be allowed to confine itself to its proper high mission. On October 26 Nabuco returned to the province, thus terminating his mission. His friend Rebouças wrote in his diary: "J. N. [Joaquim Nabuco] returns to Recife after twenty-six days of herculean labors in the parliament and in *O País* on behalf of the captives."

Slavery had entered its final phase. The slaves began to be interested in the movement. Nabuco's diary referred to a black named Ciriaco who belonged to the Viscount of São Clemente. "He had killed himself because I was defeated and gave that as his reason." In the province of São Paulo, where the problem was greater than in any other part of Brazil, the disorganization of labor was no longer a terrifying threat, but a living reality. It was impossible to restrain the exodus of the slaves who were abandoning the plantations with the connivance of the slave-protecting societies. The task of those secret, philanthropic associations, which were like those called in the United States the underground railroad, was easier and more fruitful in São Paulo than anywhere else in Brazil. With their help, an estimated ten or twelve thousand slaves succeeded in escaping to the hills of Cubatão. The leader of that stirring service was António Bento de Souza e Castro, an abolitionist whose devotion knew no limits. He wrote to one of his fellow workers: "To me, Dantas and Nabuco stand above all else, even my political beliefs. Nothing else is of any value."

Two men, he and António Prado, represented São Paulo's role in the abolitionist task. Bento sheltered slaves. Prado led the landowning class, as one of its wealthiest and most important members. He was conservative in his beliefs, but progressive in spirit. Although a member of the Cotegipe ministry, he was resolved to face the inevitable emancipation patriotically, and advocated a prohibitive tax on slaves. Led by him, the plantation owners of the province freed their slaves on condition that they continue to work until Christmas of 1889 in order to safeguard production. Not even that term was sufficient, however. In giving Nabuco the news of that decision, António Prado's brother, Eduardo Prado, wrote:

> I understand how this will hasten the solution of the crisis: the province of Rio will complain, but it suffers on account of itself. I want to know your opinion in that regard.
>
> If it should happen that the great majority of the farmers of São Paulo promise to free all their slaves by the end of '89, will your party be satisfied? Can it limit itself to exerting pressure upon the slaveowners of Rio de Janeiro in order to get them to imitate the example of the Paulistas?

The abolitionist movement had nothing to fear. It was doubtful whether the slavocrat ministry would be able to maintain itself until the reopening of parliament. In his last speech in parliament on October 15, Nabuco insinuated that the movement was capable of destroying the monarchy itself, should it try to do so. He feared "that in the interval between sessions, a great cyclone of indignation might sweep before it not only slavery and the ministry, whose continuation the speaker does not desire, but something else as well, whose existence and conservation the Liberal abolitionists value as highly as does the Conservative party."

CHAPTER XIV. THE LAW OF THE 13TH OF MAY, 1888

The end of the year 1887 found Nabuco, that untiring traveler, again in Europe. The itinerary with which he had left Brazil was out of the ordinary. After several weeks in England, he intended to visit the Southern states of the American Republic, then Cuba, Jamaica, Haiti, Puerto Rico, Martinique, St. Thomas, and Barbados. The slavery problem occupied him constantly, but his primary concern on this trip was not propaganda. On the eve of abolition, he wanted to study the effects of emancipation in other parts of the world in order to assure himself that abolition would not mean the death of agriculture in Brazil, as its enemies prophesied. He also wished to prepare himself for the task of building up a free labor supply, a task that would naturally fall to the abolitionists after the destruction of slavery.

Victory for the abolitionist movement in Brazil was assured, but at that time no one was able to predict that the emancipation law would come as soon and be as complete as proved to be the case. The Emperor, who was gravely ill, was seeking a cure for his health in the Old World. Nabuco conceived of an infallible means of forcing the Princess Regent to take, without delay, the action in favor of the slaves to which her motherly heart inclined her. That was to confront her with her duty as a Catholic. As soon as this inspiration came to him, Nabuco left London for Rome armed, thanks to his old friends in the Anti-Slavery Society, with letters of recommendation from Cardinal Manning. He found Rome full of pilgrims, brought there by the jubilee of Leo XIII. On February 10 he was received by His Holiness, and on the same day he sent a description of the audience to *O País*:

The Pope receives his visitors in private audience, without any witnesses. No one is in the room except him and the person to whom the audience is conceded. A secretary and an officer of the guard are in an adjoining room, but once he is introduced into the small salon, the doors are closed and the visitor finds himself alone in the presence of Leo XIII. The Pope was reading a book of Latin verses when I was announced. He ordered me to be seated in a chair beside him and asked me what language he should speak. I preferred French.

The impression that I had throughout the audience, which lasted not less than three-quarters of an hour, was not like the feeling one has in the presence of one of the great sovereigns of the world. The Brazilian throne is an exception. Never in Brazil has there been a man as accessible as the Emperor, nor a house as open as São Cristovam. But because their condition is superior to that of other men, monarchs in general are educated and brought up in the belief that they are better than the rest of humanity. One of the most notable advantages of the papacy as a monarchical institution is the fact that it is an elected monarchy. Other sovereigns are born, live, and die on the throne, while the popes only attain royal dignity in the last years of their lives. As a result, they spend all their lives as men and do almost nothing on the throne except to crown their careers. That human character of the pontifical royalty is the principal ingredient of its prestige, just as election is the reason for its unlimited duration, and religious spirit is the condition of its moral selection. I would even say that alone with the Pope one has the impression of being before the confessional rather than the steps of the throne, if at the same time there was not something in the frankness and the reserve of His Holiness that excludes from the very beginning the idea that there is the confessor, interested in uncovering the depths of his interlocutor's soul. In the meantime, the predominant impression is one of absolute confidence, as if, within those four walls, everything that one might say to the Pope took on the character of an intimate conversation with God, whose interpreter and interceder was there.

The words that fell from the lips of the Holy Father are engraved in my memory. I do not believe that they will ever be erased, nor that I shall ever cease to hear the voice and the firm tone with which they were spoken. The Pope began by commenting that he had delayed me for a long time in Rome, but that his duties at that time were numerous. I answered that there was no better way to employ my time than to spend it waiting for the words of His Holiness. "I was going to the United States," I said to Leo XIII, "where the greatest part of the Negro race in America is located. But then our bishops began to speak with determination and in common accord about the jubilee of Your Holiness and to ask for the emancipation of the slaves as the best and highest means of solemnizing that event in Brazil. When I heard this, I thought that above all else I must come to Rome to ask Your Holiness to complete the work of those prelates by issuing a condemnation of slavery by the Church. This action on the part of Your Holiness would give the abolitionists a point of support in the Catholic conscience of the country that would be of the greatest advantage to the complete realization of our hope."

His Holiness replied: "What is close to your heart is also close to the heart of the Church. Slavery is condemned by the Church and should have ended a long time ago. Man cannot be a slave to man. All are equally children of God. I am keenly touched and I completely approve of the action of the bishops in choosing, with the agreement of the Catholics of Brazil, my sacerdotal jubilee for the initiation of that great attempt. . . . . It is now necessary to take advantage of the bishops' action in order to hasten emancipation. I am going to speak on that matter. Whether the encyclical will appear in the coming month or after Easter I cannot say yet. . . . ."

"What we wanted," I observed, "was that Your Holiness speak in time for your message to reach Brazil before the opening of parliament, which will be in May. The words of Your Holiness would have great influence upon the government's purpose and on the small part of the country that does not yet wish to go along with the national movement. We hope that Your Holiness will say something that strikes the conscience of all true Catholics."

"I shall speak that word, you may be sure," answered the Pope, "and when the Pope has spoken, all Catholics will have to obey."

The Pope repeated these last words to me two or three times, always in the impersonal form and not: "when I have spoken," but always "when the Pope has spoken."

I believe that I was absolutely loyal toward my adversaries in the explanation that I then gave His Holiness about the progress of the abolitionist movement in Brazil. The Pope asked me various questions, to each of which I replied with the complete loyalty that I owe first to the Pope, and then to my countrymen. I described the abolitionist movement in Brazil as having become pre-eminently a movement of the landowning class itself. As I should, and as is just, I gave the unselfish workers of the last hour credit for playing the greatest part in the final solution of the problem which without their generosity would have been insoluble.

I referred to the brilliant work of Sr. Prado and to the moral effect of Sr. Moreira de Barros' pronouncement as factors of the greatest importance. I explained how there was not, in the history of the world, another example of the humanity of a great class equal to that of the Brazilian masters who renounced their titles to slave property. I said that that was the real proof that slavery in Brazil had always been a "foreign" institution, alien to the national spirit. That statement is even confirmed (I did not say this to the Pope) by the fact that of the whole community the foreigners in Brazil were, and still are today, the ones showing the least sympathy for the emancipation movement. As for the Imperial Family, I repeated to the Pope that whatever is favorable to the slaves in our law, even though it is little, is due to the initiative and imposition of the Emperor. "A dynasty," I added, "has certain material interests that are dependent upon the support of all classes. It cannot afford the ill will of any group, much less that of the most powerful of them all. The papacy, however, is not dependent upon any class. Therefore it is placed in a position to take the point of view of absolute morality, which no dynasty can take without destroying itself." Speaking of the present President of the Council, I told His Holiness that he was a man to whom the Church in Brazil owed much, since he was the principal author of the amnesty which ended the conflict of 1873. As for the question of slavery, however, we had no reason to suppose that he wanted to go beyond the present law, which was positively contrary to the unanimous desire of the nation. "However," I added, "I do not ask Your Holiness for political action, although the political consequences that will undoubtedly result to the nation are undeniable. Fortunately, Your Holiness is in a position where you do not see parties, but only principles. A moral commandment is what we want, the instructions of the Church concerning the liberty of man. No government in the world can claim that the Pope, when he establishes a principle of universal morality, is acting either for or against the political interests of that government. Recently a Brazilian priest was arrested for sheltering slaves. Everywhere we abolitionists are sheltering slaves. We are doing what the bishops of the Middle Ages did with the serfs. I can assure Your Holiness that public opinion is unanimous. The word of the head of the Church would not be disputed by anyone."

Then the Pope repeated that his encyclical would be inspired by the principles laid down in the Gospels. The cause was his as well as ours, and the government itself would see that it was good policy to recognize the freedom to which all the children of God were entitled by birth. At the same time that he dealt with emancipation, the Pope said he would also speak about the necessity of giving religious education to that mass of unfortunates who until then had been deprived of moral instruction. . . . .

. . . .

Throughout the entire interview, the Pope listened to me with the greatest sympathy, and I felt justified in having asked for more than what Cardinal Manning had thought would be reasonable. Indeed, His Eminence had advised me to ask the Pope for the repromulgation of some of his predecessors' bulls. Instead I asked for personal action by Leo XIII. "Circumstances change," the Pope told me, "and times are not the same. When those bulls were published, slavery was strong in the world, but today it is fortunately finished."

. . . . I did not see the least vacillation, or the slightest attempts to twist moral doctrine to suit political circumstances in Leo XIII's manner of expressing himself. I saw only moral conscience shining like a beacon light, shining like a light that is indifferent to the shipwrecks of those not guided by it.

The encyclical was not immediately forthcoming. Through the Brazilian Legation at the Vatican, the Cotegipe ministry asked the Pope not to publish it. Some delay resulted from the negotiations, but the moral effect of the Pope's decision upon the country was complete from the day Nabuco's interview appeared in *O País*. The Pope's interest spread from Brazil to other peoples. In 1888, Leo XIII announced his support of the cause of the enslaved. He gave 300,000 francs to help the work of the antislavery movement, and canonized Pedro Claver, the apostle of the Negroes. He appealed to all men, independent of religion or country, to support the cause of the victims of slavery. He gave his entire backing to the great work of Cardinal Lavigerie in Africa.

In Brazil, support for the emancipation movement grew. Slaveowners made mass liberations. On February 12, the birthday of Antônio Prado, all the slaves in the city of São Paulo were set free. By means of subscriptions and charity balls, the Imperial Princess initiated and directed a movement for emancipation in Petrópolis, which was successfully culminated on April 1. Her sons, the little princes, showed frankly abolitionist sympathies in the ingenuous little paper that they printed in the palace for their parents and friends.

Patrocínio had left the *Gazeta da Tarde*, but only to go to work with increased zeal on his new organ, *Cidade do Rio*. Although the Cotegipe ministry realized that its days were numbered, it continued to resist the abolitionist movement. The chief of police, Coelho Bastos, had won a notorious unpopularity in his faithful execution of the government's repressive policy. The detention of a naval officer by the Rio police for dubious reasons gave the press and the navy a pretext for insistently demanding the dismissal of the police chief.

The Princess made a special point of requesting the government to take action against Bastos. Parliament, which would have been the legal expression of the national will, did nothing since it was not in session. Faced with the Regent's letter regarding the incident, however, the Baron of Cotegipe preferred to submit his own resignation.

"It is apparent from the context of your letter," the resentful minister replied, "that Your Imperial Highness gives more credit to other sources of information than to those provided by your constitutional councilors. The cabinet has no other alternative but to request respectfully that Your Imperial Highness dismiss it. We regret having to do this now, however, when we know that we lack neither the support of public opinion nor the necessary resources to preserve order."

Another Conservative leader, Councilor João Alfredo Corrêa de Oliveira, organized a new ministry. He was ready to carry out in the widest terms, without limit or conditions, the measure demanded by all Brazil. By taking on the responsibility of a change in government during the parliamentary recess, the Imperial Princess hastened and simplified the final action of the long abolitionist battle. Such a step also gave her a much more active and decisive role in the creation of the law that she was to have the glory of signing.

The Liberals were very disappointed by that violent change in political custom. As a result, they saw destiny deliver into the hands of the Conservatives the glorious realization of an ideal which they claimed as their own. A section of the Conservative party, led by Paulino de Souza e Cotegipe, regarded itself as doubly unfortunate. In the first place, it had to pass a law which it considered contrary to the interests of Brazil. In the second place, that law, which was really a revolutionary act, robbed the Conservative party of its traditional source of unity and strength.

The sincere abolitionists, naturally, placed themselves above such political disagreements. Upon his arrival from Europe, in the Santa Isabel Theater before thousands of people, Joaquim Nabuco declared his intention of supporting the ministry, since its program contained the idea of immediate and unconditional emancipation. "Our obligation," he said then, "is to free the slaves. They are neither Liberals nor Conservatives and they do not question who their saviors are." In the Chamber that progressive Liberal came to be the leader of a Conservative government.

The parliament which was to decree abolition was opened on the traditional date of May 3, amidst general enthusiasm, by the Imperial Princess Regent, who, acclaimed and covered with flowers, was moved to tears by the occasion. On May 7 the new ministry presented itself and announced for the following day a discussion of the plan that was to serve as the basis for its program. "Sublime speech by Joaquim Nabuco," recorded Rebouças in his diary. The galleries greeted Nabuco's superb oration with prolonged applause. First he welcomed the new ministry; then, "for the realization of its great program," he guaranteed it "the unselfish support of at least a part, if not all, of that fraction of the party that has always been, above all else, abolitionist." He added:

No, Mr. President, this is not the time for listening to the voice of political parties. We are at the brink of the cataract of our national destiny. Near it, it is as impossible to hear the voice of the parties as it would be to perceive the buzzing of the heedless insects that fly over Niagara Falls! (Applause.)

This is incomparably our country's greatest moment. The present generation has not yet experienced anything similar to it. We must remember that our parents, who saw April 7, listened to our grandparents, who witnessed the declaration of independence. Then we realize that in this Brazilian land there has been from generation to generation a chain of emotions similar to these (applause).

Within the limits of our national life, and discounting the progress of a whole century, 1881 is a greater event for Brazil than 1789 was for France (applause, bravos). It is literally a new country that is beginning. When the form of government changes, the institutions that give strength or life to it remain automatically in a vacuum. Therefore, Mr. President, we should question whether our old parties, stained with the blood of a race and responsible for the horrors of a barbarous legislation, barbarously carried out, ought not in the hour of national liberation to be expelled into the desert, sent out like the sacrificial goat in the feasts of Israel, burdened with the failures and the curses of the purified nation. . . . .

. . . .

After emancipation, the old parties may return with their leaders. If I had to ask them for something, I would certainly not ask, Mr. President, for the rigorous continuity of policy that my illustrious friend at the end of his speech urged as the first condition that a politician should fulfill to win the support of public opinion. I would ask for exactly the opposite. I would ask for such a lack of continuity that they would seem like other parties, and the nation would be unable to recognize them as the same ones that made the people lose faith in parliamentary government.

Yes, Mr. President, if it is the Conservative party that is going to declare slavery abolished in Brazil, I say without recrimination that the blame for that substitution of roles will have to fall entirely upon those Liberal dissidents of 1884. They prevented the Dantas ministry from winning the elections of that year, from dragging all the electorate of the country with it, and from accomplishing a much wider reform than they proposed (applause).

There has always been a minority of timid men in the Liberal party. On account of them, the issue that most interests the Liberal party, the question of abolition, on which depends the formation of the Brazilian people, is studded with great names which are Conservative instead of Liberal. It was they who prevented António Carlos de Andrade e Silva from doing what Euzebio de Queiroz did [in

1850]. They prevented Zacarias de Goes Vasconcelos [who was the dominant figure in Brazilian politics from 1863 to 1868] from doing what Rio Branco did [in 1871]. They prevented Dantas from doing what João Alfredo Corrêa de Oliveira is going to do. They have never had faith, either in the people, or in liberal ideas (applause). But slavery has already been exploited too long. . . . .

In Gustave Flaubert's *Salammbô* there is, Mr. President, a scene of great descriptive power that is an admirable portrayal of Carthaginian life. It pictures the chief of the mercenaries who have revolted against Carthage being guided into the temple of Tanit by a slave. There he stole the goddess' mantle to which the fate of the city itself was linked in the popular belief. . . . . Covered by the sacred mantle, he passed through the numberless crowd of Carthaginians. Driven by vengeance, but dominated by terror, they dared not touch him, because to touch him would be to provoke the goddess that protected him. It could have been an assault against the sacred symbol upon which it was sacrilege even to gaze (applause).

Mr. President, I had wanted the Liberal party to realize that at this moment the honorable President of the Council is also wrapped in the sacred mantle to which the fortunes of our party are linked. That mantle confers the privilege of inviolability to all who possess it.

For Nabuco it was a week of triumph. He experienced the glorious sensation of attaining the goal that he had set and for many years had never let out of his sight. While still young he had achieved the end which, in the campaign's blackest days, he had thought he would not reach in an entire lifetime. On May 8, the government's proposal was presented to the Chamber, couched in the simplest and most complete terms: "Slavery in Brazil is declared extinct. All dispositions to the contrary are revoked."

The enthusiastic crowd naturally was not disappointed when it heard this generous proposal read. Prolonged and noisy acclamations greeted it both on and off the floor.

Joaquim Nabuco then rose. In this scene he was certainly the principal figure, and it was natural that happiness should illuminate his earnest face:

Mr. President, I ask you and I ask the Chamber to be tolerant of this demonstration that the Brazilian people have just made within the walls of parliament (applause). There has never been a day like this in all our annals! (Applause.) There has never been a moment like this in the history of our nationality! (Applause.) It is as if Brazilian territory up to now had been occupied by a foreigner. This act has suddenly evacuated it and left us masters of our national life! (Applause.)

I wish that the heart of each Brazilian deputy would beat as mine does at this moment, so that the Chamber might attain the glory of being the liberator government; so that it might pass and send to the Senate as an emergency measure and a great public necessity, the bill providing for the total abolition of slavery! (Applause.)

Nevertheless, Mr. President, it seems that, for the benefit of the slaves themselves, and in order to prevent this great decree from being disputed in any corner of our land, it must be vested in great solemnity. The painful delays which the elaboration of the laws may demand are inevitable.

This law, Mr. President, cannot be voted upon today. However, by a reasonable interpretation of our rules, to which I am sure no one, not even the brass heart of the worthy deputy for the eleventh district of Rio de Janeiro, could take exception (applause in the galleries), ... it can be voted upon tomorrow, because we can name a special commission to deliver an opinion on it. We can suspend the session for a half-hour, because five minutes, or even one minute, is enough to reach that opinion. We can suspend the printing of the law simply for the length of time necessary for the discussion to take place. We can dispense with the recesses so that the day after tomorrow we can send the law to the Senate, passed by acclamation and covered with the blessings of the country! (Applause and bravos in the galleries.)

So it was done, although Andrade Figueira, the deputy whose opposition Nabuco had foreseen, did raise his expected protest against dispensing with the printing and the minimum time limit, claiming that such action was a violation of the rules. Valiant defender of a lost cause, on slavery's last day he made a useless but coherent outcry. With some irritation, which was excusable at that moment of the defeat of his cause, he protested against the enthusiastic people who had come into the Chamber itself to applaud, "converting the august majesty of the floor into a circus" (some applause and some boos from the galleries).

Taking advantage of this opportunity to speak, I shall say to the worthy deputy from the first district of the province of Pernambuco, that I do not know if he has judged correctly the material of which my heart is made. Although I do not know whether it is a heart of brass, I prefer it to be brass rather than clay!

Those ambiguous words surprised Nabuco, who had had no intention of offending. Above all on such a day, he was in no mood for mean personal disputes. Disregarding the insult, he immediately replied:

I do not believe that this remark about a heart of clay was aimed at me (applause).

If it was, I shall leave the worthy deputy's insult on the carpet of the discussion, because it is not worth picking up (applause). Neither do I believe that it was aimed at the people, because the worthy deputy must realize that at this moment, the predominant feeling in all hearts is one of true patriotism (much applause).

I think I did justice to the worthy deputy's feelings by calling his heart brass in regard to this question. The worthy deputy, in characterizing the extraordinary and exceptional events that have taken place, compares the greatest session of the

Brazilian parliament to a circus. In this matter, I believe that the Brazilian people who are gathered in the Chamber can give no better proof of respect save to defend the inviolability of the worthy deputy from Rio de Janeiro in the duty that he has just performed, wanting to prolong what is no longer possible, namely slavery.

There was room in the galleries for only a very small part of the jubilant Brazilians. The rest surrounded the legislative palace from whose windows the government leaders and members of the Chamber came to greet the people. "Joaquim Nabuco came to the window," said Patrocínio in his new paper, *Cidade do Rio*, "and the people applauded him with the enthusiasm that only fidelity to principles can inspire. He was the victor. His hair was still plastered with perspiration and petals. Erect, motionless, immovable as a statue, he stood there, grand and solemn, as he was to be preserved in the memory of a grateful nation, in the statue that he himself had cast with the fire of his speech and the bronze of his character. After a long pause, he became himself again. Then he saw the people, with their heads uncovered as if before an idol, and he led a bravo to the Imperial Princess."

On the following day, during the second discussion of the bill, Andrade Figueira still came "to plead the cause of good sense confronted by unruly passions. In view of the apoplectic eagerness of the abolitionist movement, which is worth about as much as the apoplectic anger of the opposition, all discussion should be avoided. The scenes that took place in the other Chamber at the time of the opening of the general assembly, and the scenes that were witnessed on this floor yesterday have sufficiently shown the speaker that all discussion is useless, if not impossible. In the face of these facts, however, the speaker cannot keep from voicing the protest of a solitary person which the Chamber ought to expect from him."

He confessed that, "a long time ago, he had considered himself isolated in the discussion of those questions." However, a deputy exclaimed: "You will see that you are not!" Indeed, in the roll-call voting, nine voices joined him, against the eighty-three that triumphantly passed the bill.

On May 11, the measure was presented to the Senate. There, Cotegipe and Paulino de Sousa were the leaders of the dissident Conservatives. They raised their voices against the swelling, irresistible wave, against the law that contained, according to them, the germ of all revolutions. But there too the fraternization was general. It was seen on the floor, in the corridors, where Paulino himself good-naturedly greeted Nabuco with a "Hail Caesar!" and on the street, where the shouting people waited. There, as in the Chamber, printing and debate were dispensed with upon Dantas' proposal, and the bill was passed without them. Dantas was the great victor on the floor of the Senate. When the voting was finished, he was carried into Ouvidor Street on the shoulders of the people.

The day, May 13, fell on a Sunday, but Brazil could not wait for twenty-four hours. The Senate met in special session, and the Regent came down from Petrópolis to sign the law which was to consecrate her in history as Isabel, the Redeemer.

In the palace, the accumulated emotion reached its peak. On his knees before the Princess, Patrocínio, weeping, delivered a speech. Eight days of festivities followed throughout all Brazil. There were processions, torchlight parades, and bands of music installed in the offices of the newspapers or roaming through the festively lighted streets. There were speeches from windows, student demonstrations, balls, and popular amusements. The major events were the Abolitionist Confederation's parade and the field Mass held on the Field of São Cristovam, which was attended by the Princess and a great crowd of people. The city was full of expansive, acclaiming people and overflowing with visitors who were attracted by its amusements. The heroes of the moment could not appear without the enthusiasm doubling. Patrocínio was always in the streets, exuberantly acclaiming the Princess or receiving his just share of ovations. More than once Nabuco was carried about in triumph. Everywhere the banners of the abolitionist societies were solemnly received and collected by museums and institutions as historical trophies.

The news echoed jubilantly abroad. "Abolition was the first emotion that Brazil gave to the world," Rebouças once wrote. In Argentina above all, the matter did not seem like an event in a foreign land. Thirty thousand persons paraded before the Brazilian Legation. Criminals were pardoned. Everywhere, in the streets and in the theaters, the people rejoiced with Brazil upon hearing what to Nabuco seemed, "the most beautiful tidings that God could send to the world."

Among other ways of celebrating the event, the minister João Alfredo distributed some titles of nobility, including among them the names of known slavocrats. They seemed to be consolation prizes, or, in the ironic words of Nabuco in *O País*, "they seem inspired by the Argentine Republic's generous idea of pardoning some criminals in celebration of our great day."

As if it knew enough not to put Nabuco's name next to those, the ministry waited months before offering him the title of viscount. Nabuco placed little value on titles of the Empire. At the beginning of his parliamentary career he had proposed in the Chamber, "that the unclassifiable nobility that we have in Brazil be abolished," but he did not pursue the idea.

In refusing, he had his father's example to follow. As the son tells us in *A Statesman of the Empire*, his father had never accepted a title for himself, "because he saw the delusion of a nobility without inheritance or fortune, and also because he liked the name that he had always used." Like him, Joaquim Nabuco refused to exchange for a new title a name that he too bore with just pride.

CHAPTER XV. FEDERALIST CAMPAIGN. MINISTRY OF JOÃO CORRÊA DE OLIVEIRA. 1888–89

In a letter written many years later, a friend of Nabuco's recalled a casual conversation that took place early in 1888 while they were waiting for a streetcar in Recife. The correspondent, A. de Souza Pinto, recorded Nabuco's words thus:

> The João Alfredo cabinet had been made up, and complete and immediate emancipation without indemnification was assured. In the midst of the expansive joy which that expectation created in us, my dear friend said more or less the following:
>
> "So we are going to be in opposing camps, those of us who up to now have fought under the same flag!"
>
> "How is that?" I asked.
>
> "Because after abolition there will be room for only two parties in Brazil, the Monarchist and the Republican."
>
> "And also because I shall not see you in our front line?"
>
> "No. I love liberty too much to wish for the Republic in my country."
>
> I have never forgotten that dialogue.

Abolition, as it was carried out, almost through the imposition of the people, was really nothing but the first victory of the whole country's budding revolutionary tendency. The institutions and the parties, deeply undermined, remained the same in appearance, but the shadow of the republic was approaching threateningly. The 13th of May, which for Nabuco had been a final objective, was only the first step for almost all of his companions. During the eighties, Brazil had entered into a period of reform and agitation for which the abolitionists were greatly responsible. Nabuco did not boast about this. He was still hopeful that the wave would soon exhaust itself and would respect the throne. In 1889, speaking in Buenos Aires about the three points of his political program, Abolition, Federation, and Peace, he said:

> We intended simply to free the slaves, but in doing that we got all this: the formation of a sovereign public opinion, the influence of the press, the autonomy of the provinces, and arbitration. Begun as a work of pity and compassion, abolition became the focal point of a vast ideal of justice. Like a lofty beacon, this ideal illuminates the four cardinal points of our political system: moral life, civil life, political life, and the international life of the nation.

With abolition accomplished, there still remained for Nabuco and for a great part of the Liberal party the ideal of federation, which was also equivalent to a revolution.

After May 13, all of Nabuco's energies were concentrated upon it. A faithful monarchist from his earliest youth, the idea was to him both a desire of his liberal spirit and a guaranty for the endangered monarchy. It seemed to him to be "in the popular favor, a strong rival of the republican idea itself, and one which was going to take precedence over it as the abolitionist idea had already done" (session of December 3, 1888). "The truth," he wrote in *O País*, "is that today there is only one reform that can hold back the coming of the republic, and that is the autonomy of the provinces." He believed that the throne, having already satisfied the people's demands about slavery and on its way to complying with those on federation, would thus be definitely established. "I recommended federation, which, I am sure, would have saved it," Nabuco said, speaking of the monarchy many years after its fall (speech in the Casino Fluminense on July 20, 1906). As soon as abolition became a reality, many of Nabuco's partisans began to call him the federalist leader, instead of the abolitionist chief. He confidently declared that "the interval of rest and observation between two great national campaigns has passed, and the same effort that was made to free the slaves will be used to liberate the provinces."

He made himself the champion of federation, in the Chamber and in *O País*, and sought to gather about him all the elements that had fought with him for the freedom of the slaves. "Liberals and Republicans," he asserted in *O País* on August 4, "are in agreement on one point: the most urgent of all reforms is the autonomy of the provinces."

However, the two aspirations, a republic and federation, were inseparable in the Republican program and almost synonymous in the minds of many Monarchists. The Republican party, which had left its own ideal in the background to gather all its forces about Nabuco's abolitionist banner, was unwilling to come to enlarge the ranks of his federalist campaign.

In 1885, the first plan for federation had been introduced into parliament by Nabuco, whose speech was heard only as an eloquent exposition of an impractical dream. In the following year it was not thought worthy of consideration. One newspaper reported that when the reform was put to a vote on May 26, there was such hilarity on the floor and in the galleries that Andrade Figueira had to call the deputies and spectators to order. Patrocínio, commenting on the session in his paper, remarked that the Chamber with a yawn "turned again to the project, presented by Joaquim Nabuco and almost all the Liberal deputies of the last legislature, as though it were doing a great favor, in the manner of one giving alms. The fate of the provinces, where they were born, did not merit even a glance."

Despite the indifference of parliament, however, the idea was gaining great impetus, particularly in the provinces. In the different provincial assemblies, indications of profederation sentiments began to appear.

Nabuco's proposal, which had had thirty-nine signatures at first, reappeared the second time with seventeen. Many of the names were the same. However, as it was a Conservative Chamber the second time, the names of those who supported Nabuco then were in the minority. The Liberal party in the Chamber significantly continued to support federation.

The form of the proposal was also different. Nabuco now believed that federation ought to be achieved by reforming the Constitution. In 1885 he had magnificently expounded upon the necessity of federation. In 1888 his speech was an explanation of the reasons for the new form of government and an attempt to prove that monarchy and federation were not incompatible.

That was his great difficulty. The idea of federation split the Liberals but united the Republicans, proof perhaps that the aspiration belonged to the latter. Nabuco's struggles became more difficult, as he saw the federalist campaign gaining ground at the expense of the monarchy. Moreover, fresh opposition in the Liberal party itself suddenly appeared before him.

There were, among his opponents, leaders that he respected, as Rebouças' diary records on August 7, 1888:

> A conference at night in the home of Senator Dantas, who sides with me against Joaquim and favors the evolutionary method, beginning with a law of provincial privileges.

Nabuco also found opposition among his most recent friends, such as the Baron of Rio Branco, who wrote to him:

> . . . . I am very much afraid of the new flag that the lord of Cabo's grandson has raised, and particularly of that word "Federation," which among us has been forgotten and which has already cost us much blood and many battles.

However no disagreement was more interesting than that shown by Dom Pedro II, although it was quite tolerant. In his diary, Rebouças recorded the conversation that he and Nabuco had with the Emperor when His Majesty was passing without pomp through the streets of Petrópolis, exchanging ideas with members of his household or with acquaintances that he met. On November 2, 1888, Rebouças wrote: "Joaquim Nabuco, in Petrópolis, discusses his favorite topic with the Emperor: federation and the autonomy of the provinces." And on March 4, 1889, he set down these truly memorable words:

> I discussed federation with the Emperor while we were in the station. Showing deep feeling, he said to me: "I am a republican. . . . . Everyone knows it.

If I were an egoist, I would proclaim the Republic so as to have the glory of Washington. . . . . I would only be sacrificing Brazil to my vanity, because the small provinces do not have sufficient population for federation. Federation would cause general disorder, ending in separation."

There were many signs favorable to the Republicans: the disagreements among the Liberals; the support, on the other hand, of some Conservatives, notably António Prado; and the decline of the old parties, which came as a result of the abolitionist propaganda and was aggravated by the federalist campaign. Already Silveira Martins had asked this question concerning the abolition that the Conservatives had brought about: "Where are the Liberals going to plant their flag, if the Conservatives desert theirs?" He also prophesied that the road to all reforms, even federation, was open, now that the major issue of slavery had been settled.

In Nabuco's case, this indifference to parties was long standing and was nothing more than a complete scorn for what he called "politics with a small 'p'." His popularity now permitted him to have the complete independence that, at the beginning of his career, had cost him his seat as a deputy. Even in his province, however, where he was regarded as an idol, serious difficulties arose with fellow party members. The fraternal union of the two most widely publicized names in the hostile parties, Joaquim Nabuco and João Alfredo, caused perplexity in the local politics of Pernambuco and took the enthusiasm out of debates. The people had understood Nabuco's immediate support of the ministry that was going to accomplish abolition, but they were surprised to see him continue at the side of a Conservative government after May 13. Many times did Nabuco have to explain that it was his duty as an abolitionist to support this government.

By making the emancipation of the slaves the first task of his government, Councilor João Alfredo had assumed the responsibility for the disastrous consequences that everyone foresaw. He had accepted, so to speak, the heritage of abolition itself, with all its difficulties. Thus he found himself faced with silent discontent, labor instability, and agricultural problems which were the necessary consequences of the Golden Law, as the abolition act was known. It would have been a display of narrow partisan spirit, false to the true abolitionist ideal, to have overthrown him at once, without wanting to know the remedies with which he proposed to relieve the crisis. At least that seemed to be Nabuco's understanding. The Conservative ministry found him on its side in *O País*, where he respectfully quoted the words of Lincoln, "Don't change horses in midstream." In the Chamber he maintained that an election at such a time "could suit only the disgruntled slavocrats, who were anxious to take their revenge."

Nabuco explained his motives in the session of July 4, 1888. He recalled that on the eve of abolition he did not say, nor would he have been able to say:

". . . . as an Abolitionist I support the government. As a Liberal I oppose it. When the question of abolition is raised, it will have my vote; when any other matter is proposed, I shall vote against it." What I would thus do, as an Abolitionist, would be to betray the honor of my flag. Such action would encourage all the conspiracies that might tempt the partisan spirit, and consequently it would reduce the Liberal party to following the triumphal chariot of the President of the Council, instead of placing itself in the lead, with the flag that belongs to it. . . . .

. . . .

I am a party man. Nothing is more difficult than founding new parties. Therefore, what I want is not a new party. I want the Liberal party to become a truly democratic union to work for the defense of the institutions that we believe are necessary. This union should unite the democratic elements that come from the real Liberals, the Republicans, and the Conservatives. The great neutral mass of public opinion adheres to this democratic group. These elements should unite in order to obtain the realization of great social reforms which are much more necessary than the political reforms inscribed on the forgotten banners of the dethroned parties over half a century ago. . . . .

We must sound the currents of opinion, and enter a campaign as great as the abolitionist campaign. That is the campaign for the autonomy of the provinces, the campaign for federation, and for provincial rights and privileges. . . . .

This is the reason why I have not hastened to overthrow the present cabinet. It is a Conservative government, but it is a Conservative government which has accomplished a Liberal reform. Unfortunately, it did not fall to the lot of any Liberal government to carry out this reform. I do not know what path the government is going to take. I do not know whether or not the government prefers to maintain the unity of its party, consequently destroying the national patrimony which it possesses today, and thus diminishing its own glory. The government has become acquainted with the courage of its friends, it has seen the nullity of the resistance that is opposed to it, and it has sensed that there is no other really strong and loyal support except that of the nation. However, I do not know whether or not the government, as it has already done in the question of emancipation, will raise the banner of great national reforms. If it does, it has the right to demand of the Liberal party the same aid that it asked for and obtained with regard to abolition. I do not know which of these two roads the government will take and therefore I do not know yet what my position with respect to the cabinet will be. . . . . For this very reason, however, I desire and am trying to prepare for the rise of a Liberal party which will represent organized democracy and liberalism in action. The disillusions and the misfortunes of that other Liberal party, which has not yet succeeded in being anything but the oligarchy which the country is familiar with but which real Liberals are repelled by, are therefore a matter of complete indifference to me (prolonged applause; the speaker is warmly congratulated).

There was one question, however, on which Nabuco differed with the government. He declared in *O País* that, given the choice between the ministry's fall or the carrying out of its policy, [the writer] is forced to prefer the lesser of these evils, which is the first one, even though it is a very great evil." He saw in the government's plan for creating banks of property credit only a new disguise for the idea of indemnification, to which the slaveowners still clung. Agriculture had entered a crisis, particularly in the province of Rio. The irritated plantation owners exploited the situation by alarming the country and exerting a pressure which was difficult to escape, especially when it took the form of a threat to the monarchy. On June 26, 1888, in an effort to conciliate those elements, the President of the Council read to the Chamber the government's proposal to found banks in different parts of the country. The special purpose of these banks would be to loan property owners, using their lands as security, the means for reestablishing the balanced labor supply that was upset by the law of May 13. It was neither the first nor the last of the propitiatory measures presented in parliament, the most important of them all being the one suggested by Cotegipe in the Senate. In his speech on July 10, Nabuco attacked both bills, calling them the "two armed giants named the Cotegipe indemnity and the João Alfredo indemnity. For the good of our country, I trust they will cancel each other out."

Nabuco voted against Andrade Figueira's motion in the Chamber to give the government a vote of confidence for its conscientiousness in "relieving the present agricultural crisis." The motion was passed by seventy votes to forty. On July 10 and 23, Nabuco fought the bill with two technical speeches on the measure's financial shortcomings. In *O País* he passionately attacked the theories of indemnification in general, and those of Councilor Lafayette Rodrigues Pereira in particular.

To José Mariano he wrote:

> I am today where I was yesterday. I oppose João Alfredo on the matter of the mortgage banks for the same reasons that I supported him on the matter of abolition. However, I do not wish to overthrow him by joining the reactionary partisans of slavery in any way. . . . . I am fighting today for ideas and not for parties. In ideas I am uncompromising. As far as parties are concerned, I will no longer attempt to stimulate them. They are dead, quite dead. New tools are necessary to do something new. Those that have come to us from slavery are only whip ends and bits of whipping posts that are of no use in the reorganization of the country.
>
> Thus I occupy a solitary position in the Chamber that corresponds to my ideal, which I shall not call political, but popular. . . . .
>
> I know that my attitude has been very displeasing to those who believe in strict party discipline. . . . . Today I am beyond personal party politics. I work in the realm of ideas. I have always considered that these ideas had a sufficient breadth

to permit all men to serve them willingly, regardless of their political baptism. Therefore I shall no longer be a candidate for office.

The bill providing for banks of property credit was finally approved by the Chamber in the last days of the legislative session. It did not become law, however, because when the parliament opened in 1889 the situation was changed. The ministry's days were numbered and its last hours darkened by an atmosphere of criticism, in painful contrast to the prestige which had lifted it to power to accomplish abolition and kept it there for more than a year.

Irregularities in the open bidding on contracts for improving the port of Pernambuco had provided the press with material for a scandal of tremendous importance. The bids had been won by the Loyo industries, and in addition, the most important contracts that were granted by the government in several provinces had been conceded to the same gentlemen, who were linked by marriage to the family of the President of the Council. The personal probity of Councilor João Alfredo was not in doubt, but the administrative error from which the Loyos benefited was great. It was impossible to satisfy public demands and the tradition of honesty in the Empire upon the crucial point of the accusation, which was the matter of favoritism to friends. The outcry was general. Nabuco thought it unjust, and years later, speaking of João Alfredo in a letter to a friend, he wrote:

With a clear conscience I defended him, alone, against my furious party on the Loyos matter, which the party wished to use, and did use, as a staircase to power.

On May 15, Deputy Afonso Celso, son of the Viscount of Ouro Preto, had called the attention of the Chamber to the matter. On May 22, in a long and heated discourse, Nabuco excelled himself in the difficult defense of João Alfredo:

The position that I have always assumed has been one of censuring acts without making the act the basis for general criticism of the moral character of anyone. That is what I am doing with respect to the present ministry. I am charging the serious events denounced in this parliament to the account of administrative errors, and I maintain that they are part of a system of errors from which no administration among us has yet been free.

Evidently he did not have precise proofs with which to refute the accusations. Therefore he skirted the subject and stayed on the more comfortable grounds of general assertions. He plainly showed that favoritism could occur within the law and that all past administrations had fallen into similar errors, without being guilty of dishonesty. Finally he pointed out that if there had been dishonesty, the action taken should never have been to overthrow the ministry, but first to impeach the accused or to fix the responsibility for the offense that had been committed.

He concluded by exclaiming:

At least I shall not contribute to the staining of a name that will live in the history of our country when all of us will be forgotten.

In his will João Alfredo gave proof of his gratitude by leaving a legacy to Nabuco, who, however, died before João Alfredo. The choice of the legacy "was made by my whole family. It indicated their feelings of friendship and grateful appreciation to my loyal and unselfish ally in the battle to free the slaves. Nabuco is one of the most generous friends I ever met in adversity, the one who first consoled me in political misfortune, and the one most faithful to me in my retirement. In addition he possesses an intelligence, a kindness, and a character which do honor to Brazil and of which all we Pernambucans are justifiably proud" (will dated Rio de Janeiro, February 1, 1895).

Although Nabuco's speech was brilliant and was applauded by the galleries, it did not convince his peers. None of them joined their voices to his. Ruy Barbosa, who was a passionate adversary of the government in this matter, as he was in all matters, refuted the arguments of the speech in the *Diário de Notícias*. He labeled them the "dialectics of lost causes and of desperate bosses." Only Nabuco's eloquence, he said, was:

. . . . capable of fragrantly perfuming the most impure places and wringing enthusiastic applause from the audience by defending the clients least worthy of sympathy. His spotless name, his personal honesty, and his magic genius were what enabled him to create the idyll of the Loyos in the session of the twenty-second of this month without bringing a storm of ridicule and stones, instead of applause, from the audience.

The Chamber discussed the question widely and passionately on May 22. It returned to the subject in the following session, in compliance with the requested urgency, and immediately afterward it set up a passive resistance to the ministry which it was impossible to withstand. The majority refused to make up a quorum. For some time the ministry's weakness in parliament had been perceptible, and the President of the Council had tendered his resignation to the Emperor, but it had not been accepted. Once the resolution not to make up a quorum became known, however, no more positive proof was needed to show that the ministry and the Chamber had become incompatible. The Emperor then accepted the resignation of the minister who had retained all his confidence. He called upon three Conservative statesmen in succession. The first was Senator Corrêa. Of the second, the Viscount of Cruzeiro, Taunay wrote in *A Notícia*: "When I asked the Viscount of Cruzeiro why he had excused himself from organizing a cabinet, he replied . . . . 'Because I could only undertake this task in one of two ways: either by dictatorship, without which it is no longer possible for this country to govern itself, or by the union and agreement of the two constitutional parties. How could I count upon the support of parliament, when the first two men invited into my cabinet would have to be you and Joaquim Nabuco!' " The third Conservative statesman whom the Emperor invited to form a cabinet was the Viscount Vieira da Silva. As none of them succeeded in organizing a cabinet, he resorted to the distinguished leader of the Liberal party, Councilor Saraiva. Saraiva also tried, then declined for reasons of health. At his suggestion, the Viscount of Ouro Preto, Afonso Celso de Assis Figueiredo, formed the ministry which was to be the last one under the monarchy.

The Liberals returned to power. One might suppose that Nabuco would view the accession of his party to control of the government with the same approval that he had shown for the liberator ministry. Before pronouncing himself, however, he waited for an indication of the government's attitude toward the subject which he now considered to be of prime importance: the matter of federation.

The great idea was constantly growing. It had little support in parliament, however, where the bill for federation was still not thought worthy of consideration. "No one expected its fate to be any better this year," wrote the author of the bill in *O País*, "and it was introduced into this session only so that parliament would have to declare its position on the autonomy of the provinces every year."

It was outside of parliament that the propaganda campaign was flourishing, particularly after the appearance of a great prophet. On March 7, 1889, Ruy Barbosa began to write a series of daily articles in the *Diário de Notícias*. They were the inspired articles of a utopist, the destructive articles of a fighter. In them resounding echoes of patriotism and violent personal thrusts alternated, with an effectiveness perhaps unequaled in Brazilian journalism. It was a success achieved by innuendo and skill. Barbosa demanded liberal reforms, attacking first the João Alfredo ministry and then the Ouro Preto ministry. The excellent literary form in which he penned his vehement denunciations was unique in Brazil, and guaranteed his articles a sensational success and long reverberations. The attack was of great violence, but it was couched in a style so admirably cadenced and so picturesquely colored that it seemed to acquire serenity from its own harmonious beauty. It rang with tones of tremendous authority. Federation was gradually taking first place among the ideals of which Barbosa had made himself the champion.

Ruy Barbosa and Nabuco could not head the propaganda campaign together. Although they defended the same aspiration, the differences between their formulas for achieving it were irreconcilable. Nabuco demanded federation with monarchy, in other words, a federated monarchy. Ruy Barbosa merely wanted federation, however it should come. Barbosa's motto was "Federation or Revolution," a formula that was gaining the support of the great majority of the voters. Nabuco's monarchism could not accept that. "If the monarchy does not wish radical reforms," said Ruy, "the Liberal party will become a Republican party: that is the Liberal solution."

On May 1, 1889, the Liberal leaders convoked a Liberal congress which met in Rio to put the new ideas into effect under a monarchical form. It was a vain attempt to restore to the great decadent party its former vigor.

The Viscount of Ouro Preto presented himself in parliament with a program of important reforms that were in harmony with the resolutions of the recent congress. He was an adversary of federation, which had gained few votes in congress, and he proposed in its place a relative autonomy for the counties and provinces. In addition, he advocated freedom of religion, the reform of the Council of State, and having senators no longer appointed for life, but elected for a relatively short period.

Sr. Pedro Luiz: This is the beginning of the Republic.

The Viscount of Ouro Preto (President of the Council): No! It is making the Republic unnecessary!

According to one of Nabuco's notes, the session of June 11, when the ministry was presented, was "a continual tumult in the midst of a wave of suffocating people." Nabuco made the last speech of the day.

I am obliged to speak by the responsibility that falls upon me as the initiator of the federal idea, since the President of the Council has torn up the federal flag with his first words! [This was denied by the President of the Council, who declared that he said only that he would carry out the program of the Liberal party.] . . . . The federal flag has passed from my hands to those of Ruy Barbosa. As a result of the attitude that I thought I ought to take after May 13, I have lost the confidence of those sections of public opinion that have always listened to me. Unfortunately, Ruy Barbosa, who is playing the role of Evaristo, is at heart a Republican while I am a Monarchist. This prevents me from accompanying my illustrious friend in his campaign for a federation with or without the monarchy. My position is one of great difficulty. I must let the federal idea become a weapon for the Republicans, since the Liberal party repels it. Under such conditions, I do not believe that I shall present myself again for election in Recife. I do not wish to bring about the Republic, and without the Liberal party it is impossible to create a federated monarchy.

As a Monarchist, I shall continue to be as firm as a rock. . . . .

. . . .

The monarchy, however, which I believe is beneficial and popular, cannot support itself with bayonets or favoritism. It can exist only by means of national reforms such as abolition was. Federation would be the same sort of thing. However, I see unhappily and with surprise that the Liberal party renounces federation at the same time that the Emperor accepts it. It is a grave responsibility for the President of the Council, who is, in effect, the dictator of the Liberal party (denials from the President of the Council).

. . . . I do not see how the monarchy would be able to resist the Republican agitation if the latter were to double its strength with the almost explosive power of the provinces' anxious desire for their autonomy.

Since reaction is impossible, it is necessary to take advantage of the concessions. I vote for the program of Ruy Barbosa, which is today that of Sr. Saraiva. However, I do not want to divide the Liberal party, without hope of obtaining federation. Even united, the Liberal party would need outside help to put the idea into effect completely throughout the country.

It is a work for all sincere Monarchists. After making this protest, I leave the matter in the hands of the President of the Council. He said that he well knows what he wants. I believe that he knows what the Liberal party and country want. Given certain circumstances, and the intervention of an unforeseen action, it would not be impossible for the monarchy to find itself condemned by the very elements of public opinion that still support it. I have a great responsibility in the chance that the institution is running. However, I have a firm conviction that abolition gave the monarchy popular strength, and I am convinced that if federation were accepted with the same sincerity, it would guarantee the imperial institution's stability. Simulations of autonomy, however, are of no avail. Under such circumstances, the honorable President of the Council must carry on patriotically, so that his ministry may not perchance be the last one of the monarchy.

These were Nabuco's last words in the Chamber. On the same day a motion for a vote of no confidence in the ministry was presented by Deputy Gomes de Castro. The motion was passed by seventy-nine votes against twenty, Nabuco voting with his party in favor of the government. Gomes de Castro characterized the ministry's program as "frankly liberal, progressive, and almost revolutionary." It had certainly displeased the Conservative Chamber. The Emperor granted Ouro Preto the dissolution of the Chamber. He then convoked an extraordinary session for November 20, which was never to meet.

CHAPTER XVI. ADVENT OF THE REPUBLIC, 1889

When Nabuco handed over the federalist flag to Ruy Barbosa, it was not the first sacrifice that he made for his monarchist ideas. He had already sacrificed to them his position as a collaborator in *O País*, because the paper's republican tendencies displeased him. Moreover, *O País* restrained its tendencies only because, as one of the principal organs of the Brazilian press and one with great responsibility in the forming of public opinion, it could not adopt revolutionary attitudes. Underneath its respect for order, and despite its confessed neutrality toward the growing movement, it was certainly traveling the road toward declared republicanism. That was the natural direction of its editor, Quintino Bocayuva. Like Ruy Barbosa, Bocayuva was a perfect incarnation of the national aspirations which Nabuco liked to call Abolition and Federation. These aspirations were normally expressed as Abolition and Republic. Shortly after abolition, *O País* prudently published Bocayuva's program in a first article entitled "Social Agitation," on June 20, 1888. Nabuco, whose daily article Bocayuva had cut out in order to print his own, immediately offered his resignation. As Nabuco wrote to Quintino, his action was motivated by "my beliefs, which I find are irreconcilable with the spirit, the implications and the purpose of the program that you outlined for *O País* in your article yesterday." Bocayuva replied:

> Let us stop writing letters. I am asking that you come and get the one that you wrote me and to talk with us. You know that all of us here are your sincere friends. Nothing can be more agreeable to us than to advance by every means the brilliant public career to which your talents and fine qualities entitle you.

The solution was a new column entitled "No Man's Land" ("Campo Neutro"). It was considered Nabuco's exclusive responsibility and was written under his signature. His articles in this new tribune did not differ essentially from those of the past. He continued to concern himself with the politics of the day, which he followed with an intense interest, being thoroughly familiar with all its phases. But his position on *O País* was false. Patrocínio's pun in calling the column "The Graveyard" ("Campo Santo") was not inappropriate. He found in the sentences of the new section "the mournful solemnity of the colonnades in a temple of monumental nostalgia to a dead faith. Only through the magnificent inspiration of the architect could one imagine the greatness of the god who formerly had his cult there." (*Cidade do Rio*, January 4, 1889.)

"No Man's Land" could not last very long. Not being a professional journalist, Nabuco was not given to concealing his thoughts in order to please the public or the editorial office. Bocayuva, who tried to respect the ordered neutrality of *O País*, despite his secret republican convictions, did not always succeed in resisting temptation. In consequence, the men were two irreconcilable forces. Within six months, another greater example of Bocayuva's unfaithfulness to the principles of the paper caused Nabuco to resign again, and this time it was irrevocable. He wrote to the Baron of Penedo: "I was obliged to leave *O País* because of its republicanism. The fact that its republicanism was rather intermittent increased rather than diminished the difficulty of my position."

The farewells were affectionate. On January 5, *O País* paid tribute to the political scruples that were removing Nabuco from its editorial staff. Once again the paper affirmed that it did not indulge in republican propaganda, despite the fact that its chief editor was a Republican. "As for *O País*," Nabuco wrote later to Bocayuva, "I do not need to tell you that I shall never be able to erase the years of '86, '87, and '88 from my heart. The remembrance of the hospitality that I found there, and the memory of the incalculable services, that under your direction the paper rendered to the abolitionist cause, will never leave me."

Nabuco was now a spectator watching the passage of that surging movement of which, until May 13, he had been the center and the voice. Now it was headed by his former companions, Bocayuva and Ruy Barbosa, and had attracted the majority of his own soldiers.

In a letter written in November 1888, he made plans to remain

> . . . . quietly in my own province in Pernambuco, trying to convince my countrymen not to become Republicans! . . . . I must fight for the Princess, who is our Lincoln, as I fought for abolition. It seems very strange that I should find myself in this role at the head of the Monarchist coalition. Although I have no faith in a Brazilian republic, I have no desire to support the monarchy against democracy in our present phase of feudalism and the quasi-vassalage of the working classes. All of my efforts are bent toward making the monarchy the creator and the protector of the only democracy that we can have in Brazil, that of the people themselves.

His position in the Liberal party since his youth had been so extreme that at any period both his allies and his adversaries would not have been surprised to see him cross the abyss that separated him from the Republican side. At a conference in October 1888, Bocayuva prophesied that, "despite the respect which the beliefs of the glorious Pernambucan deputy merit, in all justice to his valor, I believe that he will be obliged to evolve with the Brazilian people."

Nabuco's plans were so sweeping and his independence of the traditional parties so complete, that, to many, his ideas seemed to have no logical place in a monarchy. No less than the Republicans, the Monarchists were surprised that so many revolutionary plans did not place him in the Republican fold. Despite his fundamental loyalty, Nabuco did not have the confidence of the Emperor, and no one could have foreseen that, with the fall of Pedro II, few would suffer as would this habitual adversary, whose advanced liberalism the Emperor had always feared. "Your monarchism," they wrote to him from Recife, "is classified here in every way, from hypocrisy to unbecoming flattery."

Spirits became inflamed as the Republican propaganda expanded and grew stronger, protected by complete freedom of press and speech, as was the Emperor's wish. The most dangerous of the preachers for revolution was Silva Jardim, who made many speeches against the monarchy. Step by step, he followed an excursion of the Count d'Eu, consort of the Imperial Princess, through the various provinces of Brazil, making the Count the principal object of his insults. Jardim also preached in Rio de Janeiro, where he refuted the arguments of Nabuco. José Leão said in his biography of Jardim:

> He found no one in the arena with whom to fight because his soul was remorseful at going to battle against the "Isabelists," who had formerly been Republicans. For the theme of his discussion, he took the speeches offered by Joaquim Nabuco in the Chamber of Deputies. With these, he opened a series of addresses to reply to what he considered to be the single living force that had risen in favor of the dying institution of the monarchy.

The *Gazeta de Notícias* reproduced at length the addresses of Silva Jardim, with headlines the entire width of the page. The monarchy, aloof and tolerant, thus permitted the first seeds of its destruction to be spread to the four winds.

The people, however, did not refrain from expressing themselves. The first address had passed off peacefully, but in the second, Silva Jardim faced a theater full of angry adversaries as well as of faithful followers. Jardim continued to concern himself with Nabuco, and in order to add prestige to the dispute, he emphasized the merits of the enemy, whom he believed he had defeated. "It was not I who injured the reputation of Joaquim Nabuco. It was not I who demonstrated the smallness of his political ideas. No, it was not my word; it was your applause, representing then, as now, the Brazilian nation." Interruptions and protests rained down. Taking on the air of a prophet, the speaker exclaimed, "I represent you, because you wished it so. Cease your comments, they only interrupt your own words!" Then he took on the air of a martyr when he said: "Let that shot come! Let that much-announced bullet pierce me! Why then do they make comments. . . . .

If the bullet with which they threaten me, and which I have been expecting for an hour, were to come at this moment, it would do much more for the Republic than a million speeches!" The bullet was not shot, but disorder reigned. A group outside fired on the building, which was immediately overrun by the so-called "Black Guard," a large band of police thugs who were the imperial bodyguards.

The speaker permitted himself to be interrupted, but not intimidated, and after an hour of fighting he again took up his speech. Rebouças made a note of the scene in his diary, recording as well the impression of the Emperor, with whom he was on intimate terms:

> January 2, 1889. While walking with Dom Pedro Augusto, the Emperor censured the Minister of Justice, Ferreira Viana, for the behavior of the police in the conflict. . . . . As always, Pedro II supported the doctrines: "not to kill" and to permit discussion.

"We are," wrote Nabuco to the Baron of Penedo, "in a time of much uncertainty for one who, not having in politics a current bank account, has something that is called conviction. I am a convinced Monarchist, and I am beginning again, on account of the problem of the monarchy, the life of sacrifice that I had on account of the question of abolition. My only hope for rest is to lose one day the sacred fire and to find that I have already done enough. When will that day come?"

Nabuco received that year much correspondence advising him to become a Republican. He received also anonymous letters from admirers and adversaries, and some of the more violent ones brought threats. One warned him not to make Monarchist addresses, saying: "Nowhere in these two provinces will there fail to be a backwoodsman or a free slave to throw a knife or discharge a blunderbuss against those who oppose liberty."

Nabuco was accustomed to such communications and did not consider them of great consequence. During the abolitionist campaign, after receiving threats of death, he took the precaution of going about armed for some time. With respect to this practice, he told the following anecdote. While walking one day in Petrópolis with a member of the British Legation, the weapon that he was carrying accidentally went off in his pocket. The discreet and phlegmatic Englishman showed no surprise upon hearing the unexpected shot, and they continued their walk, resuming their conversation without commenting on the occurrence.

In 1889, Nabuco married Dona Evelina Torres Ribeiro. They went on their honeymoon to Argentina. Despite the private nature of the trip, it took on a somewhat official stamp because there were so many demonstrations of every type.

Being fond of travel, Nabuco took his bride up the River Paraná to

Asunción, and then visited Humaitá. He was received in the Paraguayan Senate, where he spoke with sincere and noble eloquence about the Paraguayan war.

> You suggested that I take a shell from Humaitá as a souvenir; I wish that all cannon balls that fell on Paraguayan soil could be removed from it. However, since this cannot be, I desire that such a moral and material harvest grow from the soil they have pierced, that it will be impossible to find the slightest vestige of past disagreements.

The elections, presided over by the new government, were held on August 31. Nabuco was not interested in his own candidacy and had not returned from Argentina until just two days before the elections, after an absence of over two months. He purposely did not consider going to Pernambuco. He had written to his friends there that he would no longer be a candidate and he had already said in the Chamber on June 11, in reference to his delicate political situation, that he did not intend to present himself again to the electorate. The Liberal papers of the province denounced his support of João Alfredo as treason to the party. *A Província* described his defense of the Loyo cases as the "disastrous crash of the leafy jequitibá tree which seemed to shade the modern generation." All strict party followers showed themselves to be deeply resentful of Nabuco's attitude toward the party. He was denounced as a representative who seemed pleased to break the ties that united the party. He was constantly claiming to speak as a "Liberal," yet in every case he permitted himself to decide personally what Liberal ideas were. He did not give any chief or any political force the right to influence his vote. At the very moment that the Liberal party was making its great effort to present a united front against the imminent Republican danger, he proclaimed with his enemies the decadence of the old parties, and demanded reforms. After having persuaded his district to raise the abolitionist banner above the standard of the party, he now intended, instead of resting upon his laurels, to raise the flag of federation in the shade of the organized party. After prolonged support of the Conservative ministry of João Alfredo, he had proclaimed his independence in the Chamber when a ministry of his own party came to power. For all of these reasons a heavy atmosphere of intransigence and mutual incomprehension enveloped him, even in his native province. Nabuco sensed that lack of confidence, and it was precisely in his moments of greatest independence that, as a reaction, he always experienced a real repugnance for politics, and an indifference toward his own career which permitted him carelessly to contemplate the fate of his candidacy.

Even though Nabuco was absent, indifferent, and had left his interests to go by default, his habitual rival, the Conservative candidate Machado

Portela, could do nothing against him. "An election almost without an opponent," Nabuco recorded in his diary on the day of victory. Later he reminded his electors: "When I supported the Conservative cabinet on March 10, I understood that I would not be able to accept from my fellow party members anything but an unsolicited mandate, yet you have elected me with a truly moral unanimity."

António Carlos da Silva, who was always Nabuco's right arm in elections, told the latter's brother-in-law, Hilário de Gouvêa before the election:

> I cannot predict the result of the election, with Nabuco being absent, but there is no cause for discouragement at present. We have some "great" Liberals and "patriots" who are irreconcilable with Joaquim, and according to them he has betrayed the Liberal party. We have no leader in the first district, since the one who should be here is absent. We have a group of kitchen politicians who vote only for money, which we do not have. We have to suffer the apathy of chiefs who have no reason to put themselves out for Joaquim. We have to endure the intrigue and envy of his old enemies and his new. In compensation, we have a great, united, and strong electorate, sincerely and unselfishly devoted to Joaquim.

After he was elected, Nabuco went to Recife to express his thanks. The members of the Liberal party directorate abstained from receiving him. The party papers did not celebrate his arrival, nor did they print his speeches. But the people welcomed him as always, and his customary audience went to applaud him in the Santa Isabel Theater, where he explained his political attitudes before four or five thousand persons.

> I have no difficulties with the Conservatives. I am again ready to applaud them if they carry out the new reform. That is what has separated me from my friends: I applaud my adversaries on such occasions, while my friends shout that they were robbed. The country prefers the Conservative reforms of the 13th of May to the Liberal reforms of the 9th of January. . . . .
>
> It is possible that the directorate of the Liberal party of Pernambuco is in favor of the ministry. However, when Sr. Ouro Preto presented himself to parliament, I declared myself to be a federalist. I know that my support of the João Alfredo ministry was exploited here. In disgust, I decided not to be a candidate any more. I became one only because the party directorate, upon sounding public opinion . . . .
>
> A comment: Out of fear (general applause).
>
> . . . . put me on the ticket.

The silent rancor of the slavocrats, engendered by the agricultural crisis, soon turned into an active hatred. A real epidemic of republicanism appeared in the agricultural clubs, not only as a direct, but as an immediate consequence of the 13th of May.

"At that time I was writing for *O País*," Nabuco said in a letter, "and

I shall always remember a night when Quintino Bocayuva told me with great happiness: 'I have just been to a Republican meeting with men whose total income amounted to over twenty thousand contos.' The great property-owning class had gone over to the Republic. With the issues of the *Jornal do Comércio* for May, June, and July of 1888 and all the accounts of the agricultural clubs of Rio and of the counties of Minas Gerais, it is an easy story to write."

The agricultural clubs were not the only element that rose up against the monarchy. The army also remained in a state of irritation. The solution of the military question and the fall of the Cotegipe ministry had removed only a part of the armed forces' difficulties with the government. Resentments still survived. The military tried out their strength, continued to harbor some of their grudges, and severely censured the acts of the royal house.

Another important element on the Republicans' side was the youth of the country. Ardent applause for the Republican propagandist Lopes Trovão started a demonstration in the Military School. Nabuco was provoked into making one of his speeches in the Chamber, a speech which Silva Jardim was later to refute.

Jealous of their political influence, the students expressed themselves with their customary freedom. More than once they cheered for the Republic in the presence of the Imperial Family. With great sorrow, the sensitive Rebouças recorded these facts:

> July 15. Wretched lack of respect shown to the Emperor and the Imperial Family on their leaving the Santa Ana Theater.
>
> Great agitation and revolver shots in Ouvidor Street, those responsible being students in the pay of the proslavery Republicans.
>
> July 16. More disrespect shown by the medical students to Princess Isabel, who freed the slaves.
>
> October 31. With tears I note the Polytechnic School's declaration of affection for the Emperor, which was cynically received by P—— and other Republicans because the attempted assassination failed . . . . !

It was with great disgust that Rebouças then lectured to that iconoclastic youth, drunk with revolution, which formerly had eagerly allowed itself to be led by him when the cause was different!

> October 31. I finished the term at the Polytechnic School . . . . The students offered me a great bouquet of artificial flowers which I ordered kept in a cupboard in the civil engineering office. . . . . My heart was heavy and I had tears in my eyes. Ever since July 17 my love for the students had disappeared. It was driven away by the cynicism with which they applauded the attempt of the clerk Adriano do Vale to murder the old Emperor . . . .

The vision of an ideal republic, which was promised to them, fascinated the country's young people. From every point on the Brazilian horizon the enchanted mirage was drawing nearer, appearing ever more substantial, and becoming ever more beautiful. Being real and tangible, the monarchy had certain undeniable defects which suffered strongly from the comparison. No one contributed more to that enthronement of a new deity than Ruy Barbosa. If it were possible to say that one man made the Republic, then no one would deserve that distinction more than Barbosa.

Ruy Barbosa, however, never declared himself to be a Republican. Possessing the tremendous authority which his talent gave him, he was merely the advocate of all liberal causes, great reforms, and administrative honesty. He skillfully made his principles shine, and vested them with beauty, but he never directly invoked the victorious myth which each day took on greater vigor and new strength through his powerful pen. The fascinating form of the Republic was to him only an alternative. His formula of "Federation or Republic," and his demand for necessary reforms with or without the monarchy, made converts in a much more dangerous manner than did the open preaching of the exalted revolutionaries. His newspaper, the *Diário de Notícias*, whose copies were fought over by the public, opened a constantly widening path to the Republic. The adversaries of the monarchy found their most brilliant arguments in it. A great body of thoughtful readers wavered with Barbosa between the two alternatives, and thus they accepted more readily the sudden blow of November 15.

Indications of the times also appeared in parliament. There the Republicans were few. It was in politics, in the two great parties, that the monarchy had its bulwarks. There it had a really unanimous support. One might allege that this was the most valuable kind of support, equivalent to all others in a country where the education of the masses was in no way an accomplished fact. Incontestably, politics brought together, in the Empire, the intellectual and social elite of the nation. Although the Republicans in the Chamber were very few, they were well respected, and the opposition tried to make use of them.

"When the Conservatives were in power," Nabuco related in the *Comércio de São Paulo* in January 1896, "the Liberal opposition thought it had an aid, or possible ally, in the Republican army of May 14 . . . . When the Viscount of Ouro Preto came to power, it was those on the Conservative bench who became sympathetic to the Republicans. Almost factiously, Sr. Lucena reached the point of organizing the last parliamentary session of the Empire by placing on the agenda speakers who promised to make professions of Republican faith."

In the session of September 6, 1888, the Republican deputy Monteiro Manso refused to take the obligatory oath because it was against his convictions, and withdrew from parliament. Deputy Gomes de Castro then presented the following resolution:

I suggest that the police commission propose with the greatest urgency the amendment of the oath established by Article 17 of the rules, so that it may be taken by an elected citizen regardless of what his beliefs and political opinions may be.

The commission immediately and diligently recommended that a paragraph be added to the article excusing an elected deputy from the oath upon his declaration to the committee that the oath was contrary to his beliefs. After animated discussion, the commission's recommendation was approved in the session of September 11, with an amendment suggested by Rodrigues Peixoto which added the words "political or religious" beliefs. The matter gave rise to various other amendments and speeches. Among the latter was a speech by Nabuco, who as a Monarchist was alarmed by the significance of the voting. "If perchance the Emperor regarded this matter as the Republican party regards it, there would be nothing else for him to do but to dissolve the Chamber. . . . . the monarchy is practicing the utmost tolerance." In another speech on November 5, Nabuco said:

. . . . It is proved that there are Republicans. Will it be proved that there are Monarchists?

Each day that proof is becoming more necessary. The spirit of perfidy against the present institutions has sought refuge not only in the army, but also in all the administrative departments, in the magistracy, in parliament, in the Council of State itself, and in the institutions to which appointment is a sign of royal confidence (applause as well as signs of disapproval). I say perfidy, because this behavior cannot be described as Republican spirit. . . . . In addition to the poor health of the Emperor, the revolution which the law of May 13 brought about in this country undeniably caused the two monarchical parties to become rotten. In the midst of this corruption, the government became the keeper of the throne, to which we owe the independence, the unification, and the redemption of our country from slavery. Consequently it is the duty of the ministry to see that the reaction against the law of May 13 and the revenge of the advocates of slavery who sought shelter under the shadow of the Republic do not triumph in their attacks on the throne!

. . . . I shall say only one more word, Mr. President. I cannot avoid seeing the undeniable origins of the present Republican movement. I consider it a good fortune for the monarchy, a fortune which is due to the high moral inspiration of the law of May 13, that the present Republican agitation was born out of class resentment against the greatest event in our land. This fact is enough to stigmatize the new Republic in the eyes of the civilized world, which applauds the progress of our country. It is enough to prevent that new Republic from taking root in the hearts of our people, who are identified with the dynasty in that great act! (Prolonged applause, the speaker is warmly congratulated.)

Deputy Pedro Luis Soares de Souza replied in the following session to "the worthy deputy from the first district of Pernambuco, who yesterday pretended to pass as the only Monarchist in the Chamber":

> No; the Liberals and Conservatives of the Chamber are as much Monarchists as the honorable member. However, they do not believe that they have as much responsibility as the honorable member for the Republican movement which developed after the law of May 13. The honorable member has heard his conscience, and it accuses him of having lured the government, carrying it in tow, into voting for the law to which he referred.
>
> It was the honorable member who summoned the government to . . . . decree immediate and unconditional abolition at once. Consequently, the attitude that the honorable member assumes, and his need to run to the defense of the monarchy, is explained. No one co-operated more than the honorable member, unless it be the ministry that was his instrument, to the passage of the law of May 13, and therefore to the development of the Republican party.

The welcome accorded the Emperor when he returned from Europe with his health restored in August of 1888 quieted the Monarchists' fears. He received an enthusiastic reception, Rebouças recorded in his diary, adding:

> I prevented Quintino Bocayuva from printing in *O País* the cruel article entitled "The Skiff" ("O Esquife"), written when Dom Pedro II, on the verge of death, was about to leave for Europe.

Abolition had joined with unbreakable ties the members of the Imperial Family and the leaders of the emancipation movement. On the 13th of May, when the Imperial Princess gave Joaquim Nabuco her hand to kiss, she asked him, smiling, "Are we reconciled?"

Her sacrifice of the throne, at the time that she made it, was appraised at its just value. It was strange to see how, even in 1888, the idea that the Republic would be a consequence of abolition, was taken as a natural thing. All of Nabuco's articles, in his last year on *O País*, discussed this possibility. On August 11, on the occasion of the meeting between Dona Isabel and the old Emperor after his return from Europe, Nabuco wrote: "What sadness there is in that embrace, for the person who thinks of the sacrifice that the Princess has made of her throne for her country and for humanity!"

Nabuco promised Princess Isabel, however, that she would not be a victim of revenge. In the Chamber he declared that the Imperial Princess, "on May 13 abdicated dictatorial monarchy. She abdicated traditional monarchy and invested it necessarily with the popular dictatorship which will last as long as she is loyal to the people." The abolitionists grouped themselves into a guard of honor about the Imperial Family. After the disrespectful acts of June, the Abolitionist Confederation held a special meeting in order to "take as its cause everything said with respect to the august persons who lent so much unselfish service to the emancipation of the captives and the redemption of national honor."

There was in the monarchism of all the abolitionists a good deal of both gratitude and remorse. A message from the abolitionists written by Nabuco and read to the exiled and dethroned Princess Isabel on the third anniversary of the law, said:

> Only for your Imperial Highness will this day retain the same shining brightness. For those who, up until November 15th, thought only of revenge, the day now recalls only the disillusionment of vengeance. For the slaves it has become a day of mourning, and for the abolitionists a day of expiation. The slaves feel a wound in their freedom, and the abolitionists a flaw in their gratitude.

When the Viscount of Ouro Preto came to power, everyone knew that the great problem of the government would be the repression of the Republican movement. On the very day of its presentation, Deputy Padre João Manoel received the ministry with an exalted speech which closed with a shout of "Long live the Republic!" Much applause, and naturally some protests, broke out in the galleries and on the floor. The President of the Council arose impetuously and energetically exclaimed: "Long live the Republic, No! No! No! It is under the monarchy that we have obtained the freedom for which other countries envy us."

His words were received with an applause even greater than that given to his insolent adversary, but the incident left a sense of uneasiness. The Republic was coming. "Skeptical parties cannot resist a new party that has a faith," said Nabuco in the Chamber.

A mind such as Nabuco's could not be deceived as to what was already inevitable. In a speech in Buenos Aires in 1889, he recognized that "some day we shall be a Republic." He thought it was too early, however, and he was opposed to "ideas before their time, to the Republic before the Brazilian people are prepared to govern themselves."

Finally on the morning of November 15, the forces commanded by General Deodoro da Fonseca and Lieutenant Colonel Benjamin Constant Botelho de Magalhães were posted in front of military headquarters, and the revolution was declared. Adjutant General Floriano Peixoto, who was the leader of the troops inside the headquarters, disobeyed the order of the President of the Council who had hastened there with his ministers, and refused to act against the troops outside. It was a conspiracy. The Viscount of Ouro Preto himself was made prisoner there. The generals called upon some of the most eminent figures of the Republican movement, Bocayuva, Ruy Barbosa, and Aristides Lobo, and with them made up a provisional government. The Imperial Family was notified of its deposition. The civil population, reduced to the role of spectator in a movement carried out by the army, hailed the new government. It is probable that the Republic represented, if not the ideal of the majority, at least the aspiration of a great part of the Brazilian people, who had neither been consulted nor allowed to declare themselves freely. The voices in favor were many and vociferous. Those who were discontent kept quiet. The people, lacking in education and happy with any novelty, willingly applauded the new order.

On the quarterdeck of the ship "Alagôas," the old Emperor, who had loved Brazil deeply, repeated to André Rebouças the words of the song of Simeon: "Now lettest Thou Thy servant depart in peace, according to Thy word."

Part Three

MEDITATION, 1889–99

CHAPTER XVII. A HOME. THE MONARCHIST. 1889–99

The year 1889, which so profoundly affected the public career of Joaquim Nabuco, was marked also by the most important act of his private life. On April 23, he married Evelina Torres Soares Ribeiro. She was the daughter of the Baron of Inohan, José António Soares Ribeiro, a Rio planter; she was also the maternal granddaughter of Cândido Torres, Baron of Itambi, the youngest brother of Itaboraí.

It was a most happy union. The groom, recalling that he was nearly forty years of age, wrote: "God will ensure that the difference in our ages, as so often happens, be one more source of happiness in our marriage, for I at least shall never again be foolish enough to think that any happiness in the world can compare with that which comes from a family." His home and children were to be from then on his constant concern and the source of all his happiness.

The newlyweds settled down at Paquetá on a small property which Nabuco described in *My Formative Years* in the chapter dedicated to his old teacher, the Baron of Tautphoeus, who had been a guest there.

During the latter part of Tautphoeus's life, we had a small retreat in Paquetá not far from the Castelo section of Rio de Janeiro, in a quiet spot in that beautiful landscape. It was an old one-story house to which one of its former owners, an Englishman, had added a veranda all around and in the center a small upper story with green shutters and a vine-covered balcony, which gave it the simple and yet picturesque aspect of a foreign residence. It faced the sea, and the low-lying coast behind formed a soft background. The house was on a slight elevation, and the slope to the beach was covered with a lawn, as carefully tended as any park. The island of Paquetá is a tropical jewel, without interest for the ordinary Brazilian, but of almost infinite variety for the foreign painter, photographer, or naturalist. It held a special attraction for me because it seemed to be a bit of northern Brazil set down in the bay of Rio. Whereas almost everywhere at the entrance to Rio de Janeiro one sees dark granite stones covered with dense jungles guarding the coast, on Paquetá the picture is different. There are palm-covered beaches, groves of cashew trees, and along the shore the flexible stalks of the wild cane, alternating with ancient mango trees and solitary tamarinds. At the same time, side by side with these miniatures from the north, in every cove of the sea one finds rocks covered with the vegetation characteristic of Rio.

Tautphoeus had always been in love with the Brazilian landscape. Since his arrival, he had been an explorer of its charms. Early in the morning or late at night, distance was no obstacle for him, when it was a question of seeing a beautiful sunrise, an effect of moonlight, a ribbon of water streaming down a cliff, or a rare tree hidden in the virgin forest.

He was very fond of our place on Paquetá. It offered him not only the silence and isolation of the library, but also the chance to choose at will among meadows, mountains, broad beaches, the near-by jungle, or the grassy plain if he wanted to take a walk. The quiet water of the bay lay in full view like a Swiss lake if he desired to take our boat and order Mudo, our lamented boatman, to sail to one of the tiny islands. From there, in one direction, can be seen in the distance the Organ Range of Teresópolis, and in the other direction the mountains of the capital. . . . . He always came on Saturdays and stayed for Sunday, and on his few brief vacations he would stay for several days. . . . . He often liked to sit on a bench by the seaside (or rather I should say the lakeside, from the impression it gave), and from there contemplate the evening. The variations in the air, the sky, the water, in the colors of the horizon, in the murmurings and the silences of the solitude were a gamut of which he missed not the least significant transition. . . . . How often by day, while walking through the woods by the house, as I opened a path for us through the thicket, he would ask me not to disturb nature, but to respect the intricacy and unexpected wildness of it all because its disorder was infinitely superior to anything that art might attempt. . . . . To him the poorest and most arid landscape was more beautiful than the gardens of Sallust or of Louis XIV. Ah! if he had been the discoverer and master of America, the axe would never have entered this land. And the torch? To him, clearing the land by fire was like burning someone at the stake! The fire licked up the precious resins, the sap, the life juices, the myriad designs made by artists each one insuperable in his field! These designs were models of color and sensitivity, and each was unique. The fire seemed to consume with a cruel pain all the tender bonds which linked Tautphoeus with nature and universal life, destroying all the nerves of his intellectual periphery.

It was at their home in Paquetá, which was hardly more than a stopping place for them between trips to the Rio de la Plata or Pernambuco, that the news of the proclamation of the Republic reached Nabuco and his wife. "What can it be? Someone is coming here," they said as they saw coming toward the landing a launch in which one of their friends was hurrying to tell them that Brazil was a republic.

The Republic found Nabuco completely happy, on the threshold of mature life, in the full flower of his activity, and with the glory of the triumph of abolition still fresh about him.

His friends and his constituents called for him. The provisional government convoked a constituent assembly for November 15, 1890. This assembly was later to be divided into a Senate and a Chamber and to hold the first legislative session. Nabuco's electors from Recife immediately urged him to attend. The voters of Nazareth, the fifth district, that once in a historic struggle had elected him just one month from the day the Chamber had annulled his credentials from Recife, used practically the same words as the people of Recife and sent him a similar request.

In his *Reply to the Messages from Recife and Nazareth*, later printed in a pamphlet, Nabuco refused these requests with the serenity of one who had not hesitated in the least. He would not attend the session, nor would he accept the mandate in a Republican congress.

> I cannot accept politically, because everything that I said in the Chamber, to you, in *O País*, and even last year in the Rio de la Plata area in favor of the monarchy as the proper trustee of the autonomy of the provinces and as the natural continuer of the labor of May 13, was dictated by the most profound and honest conviction that a sincere person can form about the vital problems of his country. I cannot accept morally, because of the humble part I had in the abolitionist movement, in that historic week in May, and in supporting the monarchy which liberated Brazil politically at Ipiranga and socially, with even more nobility and generosity, by emancipation.

He did not believe in the Republic; all his dreams of greatness for Brazil fell with the Monarchy.

"I do not know," he said later, "whether or not someday I shall have the faith of St. Thomas in the new Republic; however, I feel incapable of having the faith of St. Peter and of following the unknown master in a new apostolate."

In spite of such a definite refusal, he received many votes in the elections. In some sections his name was first on the list.

The news of this voting reached him in London, where he wrote another pamphlet, *My Gratitude to the Pernambucans.* He was glad to leave his strife-torn country and the events so displeasing to him.

In the peaceful atmosphere of old Europe he breathed more easily and found unchanged the pleasures of observation and travel. He saw the old Emperor again and felt a great emotion. "Good tears," Rebouças wrote to him, "were those he wept with you."

During his long foreign residence, from his association with great English statesmen he acquired the habit of viewing events in Brazil as they appeared from Europe. Distance, in time or space, clarifies one's view of political matters.

His pessimism was borrowed from the Old World, to which the beginnings of the Republic, with its intransigent despotism, its financial disasters, and its demoralization were bad omens. Europe looked upon the revolution of 1889 with a cold and hostile superiority because of the revolutionaries' lack of consideration for the universally respected figure of Pedro II, and because the revolution was carried out in the classic South American style by a group of officers who were unfaithful to their trust.

Encouraged by the success, among both friends and adversaries, of his words to the people of Pernambuco, Nabuco further developed his political ideas in still another pamphlet, *Why I Continue to Be a Monarchist.* In the course of a year, considerable opposition to the Republic had been built up, but Nabuco ignored this. In his lofty discussion of principles he did not look upon the excessive spending and the abuses of power as scandals to attack, but rather as symptoms which he noted in passing, in order to point out the impracticability of the Republic in Brazil. He said in *Why I Continue to Be a Monarchist*:

Do not let it be supposed that I intend to criticize the Republican administration. I am simply giving examples of the abandonment of republican aspirations by the Republican party itself in the day of its triumph, and I do it to demonstrate the lack of relationship between the institution which that party proclaimed and the state of the nation.

There could be no more serene, impersonal language than that of this pamphlet, which had already appeared in the *Diário do Comércio* in the form of a solicited letter to the editor, Fernando Mendes do Almeida:

I was a Monarchist because logic told me that it was not right for any national group to take advantage of the resentment that slavery had aroused; because I could foresee that the revolutionary successor of the parliamentary monarchy could only be military dictatorship, while its legitimate evolutionary successor was civil democracy; because I felt that the Republic in Brazil would be the same pseudo-republic to be found in all Latin America. I said that a republic would be unable to function as a free government. From the day of its proclamation we would lose that feeling of confidence that we have developed during the years of the monarchy. The confidence that our freedom within the law was inviolable would disappear. The source of our faith in the Emperor was the assurance that he could not abuse even the lowest citizen, just as the source of our pride in him was the certainty that, even in the most difficult circumstances, he would not want to.

No one who was that sort of a Monarchist, because of the idea he had of the Republic, could honestly become a Republican just because his foresight was being vindicated.

. . . .

As a matter of fact, morally speaking, the Republic has lost ground only since November 15. Not only was it shown that the country was not prepared for the Republic, but also, and this is even worse, it has been shown that the Republic was not yet prepared to govern. It is said that it did not have the men; that is completely false. It had at its service, besides a brilliant body of young men to back them up, ten times more men of high merit than it needed to become organized democratically in the whole country. What it did not have was principles.

I am the first to testify that the Republican party was initially a pure democratic movement; but the first great contingent it received, the slavocrats, caused it to lose sight of the people; the second contingent, the army, which gave it the victory without a battle, caused it to lose sight of the Republic itself.

These Monarchist pamphlets were an expression of a temperamental need. Since there was something of the apostle in everything Nabuco did, mere meditation and abstract conclusions by themselves were not enough to satisfy his zealous eagerness to proclaim, disseminate, and encourage. However, he was aware of the insufficiency of his leaflets as a means of propaganda, because the government, surrounded by many enemies in those first Republican days, severely repressed any manifestations of independent opinion.

But early in 1891, Rodolfo Dantas founded his Monarchist paper, the *Jornal do Brasil*, which was intended to be not a mere partisan sheet, an antipatriotic, opposition paper, but rather an active collaborator in the life of the country. In order best to aid the cause, its aim was to represent in Brazilian journalism so great a material and professional advance that it would attract and hold readers of all shades of opinion. The noble courtesy, gentleness, and tolerant spirit of its editor were the best guaranty of the lofty patriotism with which the *Jornal do Brasil* was to carry on its opposition to the government. The brilliant political career of Rodolfo Dantas was interrupted when he was still young by the coming of the Republic. The Empire, which had made him a minister at the age of twenty-six, had had the highest hopes for him, and he was a recognized authority on public questions. He had married into one of the richest agricultural families in the country, and the wealth at his disposal enabled him to gather the most notable group of collaborators ever seen in Brazilian journalism. Great names, both Brazilian and foreign, in every specialized field wrote for his newspaper.

He wrote at once to Nabuco in London that he was saving him a place on the staff. "We are going to distribute prospectuses of the paper with your name in bold type, and it will be announced that the first number will contain a letter from you." And on June 29, after the *Jornal do Brasil* had made its appearance: "You will read in our paper all the splendid articles you have sent me, including the last ones on the 'Chilean War' and 'Militarism in Brazil,' which made such a general and profound impression. Our paper is having a scandalous success."

Nabuco arrived in Rio soon after his first articles appeared, satisfied that he had found the permanent and far-reaching platform from which to express his ideas. The circulation of *O Jornal* increased steadily, and with it Nabuco's authority. On the staff he found old friends and kindred souls such as Rodolfo Dantas, Sancho de Barros Pimentel, Gusmão Lobo, and Ulisses Viana. The most complete unanimity of views existed among them and was the impelling force of the paper. Their monarchist propaganda was discreet, quiet, always careful not to push aside problems of general interest, in fact, eager to disguise itself completely. The high level of the paper was the first concern of its editors.

It was with careful impartiality that Nabuco dissected the "Republican Illusions" in his articles under that heading. Usually, but not always, his work was signed. Whether he spoke for himself or for the paper, it was as a Brazilian that he considered the acts of his political adversaries. He urged better education for the people, prematurely called upon to govern Brazil. He recalled that when the franchise was extended in England to include the working class, a great and noble voice had cried out in Parliament: "It is necessary to educate our masters." "That is what we must do in Brazil: educate our masters for the great national and impartial function we gave them on November 15."

Some see partisanship in his veneration for the Emperor, expressed at the time of his death in the *Jornal do Brasil*, or for example in the beautiful editorials which, under the title of "The Burial of the Emperor," Nabuco included later in his volume of *Literary Discourses and Writings*. It must be remembered, however, that the Republicans at that time were not sufficiently strong and sure of themselves to do justice to Pedro II calmly, as Nabuco did.

It is true that the Republican state of mind in the first few years did not tolerate any opposition whatsoever, no matter how diluted, and the *Jornal do Brasil*, as its influence increased, gathered along with that influence the hatred of the doctrinaire Republicans. Several months after its founding, the building which housed it was stoned. Threats of even greater violence against the paper and its staff reached Rodolfo Dantas. The Minister of Justice told its editors, as well as those of the other Monarchist paper, *O Brasil*, that the government could guarantee neither the lives of the writers, nor the safety of the printing plant. The fate of the Monarchist papers founded later justified the decision of Dantas to turn the paper over to other management. Its policy was changed and it continued to prosper. This step was a great disappointment to Nabuco, who left the staff when Dantas did. Shortly after, on December 19, 1891, they sailed together, with their families, for Europe, Dantas on a pleasure trip and Nabuco with the intention of settling in London. To the Baron of Penedo he wrote: "A militant, or rather, an outspoken Monarchist simply cannot live in Brazil at the present time, and even less under [Marshal] Floriano [Peixoto] than under [General] Deodoro [da Fonseca]."

Substantial reverses of fortune had wiped out the comfortable income with which the young couple had begun their married life, and it now became necessary for Nabuco to find employment. Encouraged by the memory of his experience in 1883 as a consultant on Brazilian law to large English companies, he attempted to renew this activity. This time, however, his practice did not yield the desired results, and Nabuco returned to Brazil, as he wrote to Rebouças:

. . . . never to leave again voluntarily. Thus I shall witness on the scene the progressive misfortunes of our country. I shall not have the material means to leave, nor perhaps the desire. Although travel still produces the same physical and moral renovation in me, the mainspring of locomotion is about broken at the center. In Brazil I shall withdraw from public affairs as if I were a foreigner. My worldly ambition can now be summed up in the hope that I may raise my children to live from their own labors. I myself, the rest of my life, must work in order to live, and that is the man they are going to know, if God grants me life to enjoy my children when they are old enough to choose among the various paths of life.

On another occasion he wrote:

Another great source of sadness to me is that I miss Sizenando—who has left us.[1] But I have my children, and I must above all prepare a future for them; I must give them roots, and outside of Brazil there are none. Some spirits may have roots in the cosmos, but mediocrity, which is the general rule, can have them only in the soil in which it germinated. . . . . My task is to verify whether or not our soil permits the development in it of the moral species that I legitimately aspire to produce. They surely cannot exist on the edge of a swamp, and in that case my duty would be to transplant them, because I should not like to see them grow up as parasites. I don't know whether you understand this enigma, but just suppose you had children, and then formulate your own moral and patriotic problem, given the conditions prevailing in twentieth-century Brazil.

Good-bye, my dear Rebouças. I have not yet given up hope of receiving a letter from you. Our friendship is not a Gordian knot that the sword of any Alexander can cut. It is the intermeshing of the tissue of two souls during a long period of social collaboration and moral reform. The links created in such tasks endure mysteriously in spite of separation and silence, and, if that were possible, even of forgetfulness.

And from Brazil, where life was not easy either, he wrote:

I have not yet found work. I am incompatible with anything that has to do with the government because of the moral struggle in which I was engaged from 1879 on. As for business, it is almost entirely in the hands of mercenaries.

[1] Sizenando Nabuco died in March 1892, leaving a great void in the affections of his brother. The paternal gifts, especially that of eloquence, were not restricted to the younger brother. Sizenando had, like Joaquim, of whom he was honestly proud, a brilliant and captivating personality. Just as handsome, though without the same even features, he had equal personal attraction and an even greater gift for familiarity with others, which Joaquim, more reserved and haughty, avoided. Without Joaquim's ambition and persistence, he preferred present joys to future glory. His talent as a criminal lawyer was well known, and his defenses were sensational. A series of fantastic anecdotes, lively and humorous, remained from his Bohemian life as a student. He left a vivid and beguiling impression upon all who knew him.

Therefore I am never sure about tomorrow. Until now, fortunately, God has given me my daily bread. My wife and children are well and form the magic circle within which I am untouchable. During these last few years a complete Catholic evolution has taken place in me, and I am writing about it, although not for the public. The best motto is still that of the old Alexandrine philosopher: "Live withdrawn."

Some time after his return to Rio de Janeiro, Nabuco became established as a lawyer with Councilor João Alfredo as partner. Times were still not very prosperous. Capital was leaving Brazil as rapidly as possible, and no clients, or very few, appeared. The lawyers' friends would gather around to converse, and at the end of a year the two partners closed the office, which not only brought no income, but was becoming a gathering place for Monarchists and a center of conspiracy. The violence of the government was equaled only by its vigilance. In the street any conversation that touched on politics was suspect. Monarchists could hardly speak to each other. "The expression on Brazilian faces is changing for fear of espionage," observed Nabuco in his diary. "The only permissible conversation is 'What time is it?' Anyone who said, 'What times these are!' would be taken prisoner." Nabuco's intimate circle of friends had remained almost entirely Monarchists, faithful to the many ties which bound them in general to imperial Brazil.

In Botafogo, where Nabuco lived on Marquess of Olinda Street, which was then shaded by huge old mango trees, his neighbors were Councilors João Alfredo and Soares Brandão, the latter also a former minister and senator during the Empire. Like the good friends they were, they met frequently, and with them many common friends from the old days. The past was recalled and the present criticized. Their three homes were a stronghold of the party, principally the home of Soares Brandão, where the lady of the house was the popular Dona Maroca, a member of the Paes Barreto family. A woman of rare gifts of intellect and hospitality, she enjoyed bringing together the innumerable friends whom she knew so well how to attract. Every vestige of the old regime, every tradition of Brazil, was kept alive. They argued heatedly, exchanging rumors, living in hopes of a restoration. These hopes, daily more fleeting, reached their high point with the Monarchist revolt of 1894, only to fall irrevocably with the death of Saldanha da Gama. "The Duke of Saldanha," his old friend, Nabuco, had already triumphantly called him. Drawn farther and farther away from the new Brazil, they saw the vacancies which death caused among them remain unfilled.

There was necessarily in such a group, where the feminine element had its influence, an atmosphere of conspiracy to which Nabuco did not easily adjust. The deliberate injustice of so many of those around him, the unpatriotic theory of: "the worse it gets, the better for us," which some of them maintained, the partisan intolerance, and the violent language were odious to his liberalism.

His own withdrawal had been spontaneous and generally deplored. It was not in any way caused by resentment as he wrote in *The Duty of the Monarchists*, 1895, because he owed nothing to the monarchy and knew his support to be coveted by the Republic. Yet he was unable to free himself from the pessimism natural to idle and biased spectators. This pessimism took on a more or less acid tone among Nabuco's circle of friends, according to the character of the individuals. Many of them were men of great worth, the best servants of the Empire, but now they found themselves placed by the force of circumstances in a position which prejudiced and isolated them from their country. To speak ill of the Republic and its leaders seemed justified to them, and the facts supported them, but their attitude was not a pleasant one. Their inactivity and their haste to criticize appeared to their adversaries as a lack of patriotism. There was in Nabuco's words none of the victorious warmth of his abolitionist speeches. When he spoke for the cause of the minority against the general opinion, his eloquence failed.

He wanted to see an independent, loyal, influential party grow up around the idea of restoration. He did not yet understand how dead the institutions which he defended were, how impossible was the task of setting fire to the ashes. He accepted through love of an ideal a position which involved sacrificing his own interests. His name evoked more Republican sympathy than that of any other Monarchist, as "Seutonio," the brilliant defender of the Republic, wrote in the *Jornal do Comércio*, and the Republicans frequently appealed to him. They tried to answer him in newspaper articles. They wrote him letters. His ally of the abolition days, José do Patrocínio, accused him in the *Cidade do Rio* of a lack of patriotism, "like those Monarchists who place the monarchy ahead of their country, and remain silent and cold like historians in the depths of their study, while the rights of their fellow citizens are trodden miserably under the feet of tyrants." To which Nabuco replied: "In general, no one examines scrupulously any but his own position, nor finds the best explanations for any deeds but his own." In a personal letter he spoke even more freely: "For my own part, I never aspired to anything in politics except to be sincere; that I have been, and I will die that way." It was more than a principle. It was an irresistible necessity.

Admiral Jaceguai, in an open letter, "The Duty of the Moment," printed first in September 1895 in the *Jornal do Comércio*, and later as a pamphlet, urged him to serve the Republic. Nabuco replied in the same way with a letter which he called "The Duty of the Monarchists."

The duty of sincere Monarchists, even though the monarchy were dead, would be to die politically with it. Do not think that the adhesion of a few more Monarchists to the Republic could serve as a brake on the train that is already rushing downhill at such great speed. What real influence in the guidance of the Republic has been wielded by the Monarchists who went over to it? None, it may be said. The influence that those who remain apart can exercise is different. It is all moral. It is to remain faithful to their principles and to their past. It is to demonstrate tolerance and benevolence, coherence and impartiality. It is not to accept the responsibility for crimes and mistakes. When Lacordaire was invited to preach again from the pulpit of Notre Dame during the Second Empire, he refused. "I realized," he said later, "that in my thinking, in my language, in my past, I also was a partisan of the Republic and that there was nothing left for me to do but to disappear like the others."

Meanwhile, conditions in the country improved. The military dictatorship, which represented the greatest danger and the greatest humiliation for the country, had turned over the government on November 15, 1894, to the first civilian president, Prudente de Moraes. The most difficult days were over. The attitude of the Monarchists became more and more artificial, their arguments more and more feeble.

Nabuco had been one of those most interested in the formation of a united party, engaged in an organized and fruitful activity. He was the direct agent in the reconciliation of those two adversaries, Ouro Preto and João Alfredo, who met in his home. The Monarchist party then was able to organize and present itself officially.

Their party manifest, "A Nação Brasileira," appeared as a paid advertisement in the *Jornal do Comércio*, January 12, 1896, soon after the reconciliation. It was signed by Ouro Preto, João Alfredo, Lafayette Rodrigues Pereira, Domingos de Andrade Figueira, and Carlos Afonso de Assis Figuereido, brother of the Viscount of Ouro Preto. It was they who formed the governing body of the directorate. Also on the directorate, in lesser positions, were Carlos de Laet, Afonso Celso, and Joaquim Nabuco, who, for the first time in his life was subjecting himself to the discipline of a political party—and a party full of hotheads, with few soldiers and many officers, composed mainly of former ministers, senators, and presidents of the Council—all of them men accustomed to wield power and authority.

Nabuco's affinity with the directorate was not complete, and the divergence became greater with the foundation of the Monarchist paper, which the party, fulfilling a prime and natural ambition, founded with capital secured by the Viscount of Ouro Preto. Nabuco was opposed, as he always had been, to violent attacks. He liked to treat his opponents with the same high consideration which he wanted to receive from them. On the other hand, the directorate felt that the Monarchists ought to fight for their cause using the customary methods of the Brazilian press. Nabuco felt that an aggressive attack showed a lack of liberalism. The Viscount of Ouro Preto, whose energies never waned with the years, was among those who felt that philosophical measures gained nothing.

Nabuco was invited to be editor in chief of *A Liberdade*, and to work with Carlos de Laet, a journalist who had no confidence in gentle measures, but he would accept no active part in the direction of the official organ.

In São Paulo there had already existed for several months another party organ more in accord with Nabuco's liberal ideas. It was the *Comércio de São Paulo*. Bought in 1895 by Eduardo Prado, it immediately adopted the Monarchist theme but avoided the lame theory that "the worse things get, the better for us," against which Nabuco never tired of speaking. "A paper with that theory," he wrote to Prado in 1896, "would be impossible for me." Prado's attitude toward patriotism was the same. Like Rodolfo Dantas, instigator of the worthy effort of the *Jornal do Brasil*, Prado was intelligent and progressive, and his culture had been broadened and polished by travel and leisure. Both Prado and Dantas were close friends of Nabuco and both were destined to die in their prime, just a few days apart. When Nabuco heard of this sad double blow, he noted in his diary:

> August 31, 1902. News of the death of Eduardo Prado. I have lost a comrade, one of my circle, my group of friends, one of the literary-political-social band to which I belonged.
>
> September 12. News of the death of Rodolfo Dantas. His friendship was a port on the shore of a sea full of shipwrecks; I could always reach it and find safety.

On the latter date he wrote to Caldas Viana about Dantas' death: "The blow wounded so many of us just as if we were members of his family. Shortly before, the news of Eduardo's death had shocked me greatly. Both were among the best men we had."

Eduardo Prado was an intellectual who was unable to resist the itch to write. He was curious about life and civilization in all their manifestations. His good friend Eça de Queiroz wrote in an article about him in the *Revista Moderna* that "the motive force of his thinking life and of his social expression was inquisitiveness." Prado served as the model for many of the fine qualities of the character, Jacinto, in *The City and the Mountains* (*A Cidade e as Serras*), by Eça de Queiroz. Prado was the personification of the typical Brazilian "dilettante," a word in great vogue during that generation when life seemed so easy in the stable, rich, and peaceful world of the time. Nabuco wrote in his diary:

> The novelties of the age, the facilities of the earth, travel were all his; loitering [*sic*] over the whole planet, he was a globe-rocket rather than a globe-trotter. We do not mourn the passing of such souls, for God made bubbles, the most ephemeral things, so beautiful. Let us try to understand this phenomenon. We witness the

uprooting of the past and as yet we have no roots in the future. In that state of fluctuation we are dilettantes, courtesans of our own pleasure.

Prado was away from Brazil a great deal. He divided his time among his apartment on the Rue de Rivoli in Paris—very similar to that in Eça's novel—his coffee groves on the Brejão plantation,[2] his trips to far places, recalled in his books, and a variety of other activities. Among these was his journalistic work with which he fought for his Monarchist ideas.

During the Empire, when his brother, António, took such an active role in politics, Eduardo was a mere spectator, but under the Republic he assumed, with aristocratic arrogance, the role of opposition journalist. Writing of this (*Revista Moderna*, July 1898), Eça de Queiroz felt that Prado's position as a Monarchist pamphleteer was particularly fitting:

Free from literary dilettantism and without professional necessity (rather, wrapped in a sort of contemplative indolence), he approaches his task purely as a duty, at the urgent solicitation of his conscience. Candidly and tenaciously he claims to have the truth, and since in intellectual matters he combines strict honesty with great temerity, he neither hides, nor limits, nor sweetens the truth, nor does he present only its pleasant side. Truth bursts forth from him in all its limpidity, naked, with the fearless nudity of a savage or a goddess. His ideas, too, are clear with the sharp clarity of finely cut crystal whose facets gleam with light. Confused in his desires, in his plans and in his methods, Eduardo Prado is lucid in his thinking. His is not a sparse lucidity which brightens far corners with a thin light, but compact and therefore richly intense, like a fiery dart that pierces horizons. With this clear vision he combines a rare power of deduction, of subtly unweaving and then joining tiny threads into a fine, tough web. In combat the web becomes the iron mesh with which the gladiators in the circus immobilize their opponents. At other times it is the gentle silk net recommended by the Holy Fathers for catching souls. . . . .

Added to all these superior powers was his great patience in scrutinizing texts, uncovering documents, accumulating examples, scanning all history and nature, gathering a fact here, a precedent or an analogy there. So it was that his logic, skillful and well armed, fought always with the heavy, formidable weapon of truth. In all this effort he was aided by a prodigious memory, which is the tenth Muse, or perhaps the mother of the Muses.

His manner of utilizing these gifts is excellent, his style the most appropriate to a publicist.

[2] From Brejão, Prado wrote to Nabuco on January 11, 1899: "You would find it very restful here. I live surrounded by trees and flowers, to which a background of garden and orchard gives a utilitarian savor that enchants me. I imagine that famous convent gardens must be somewhat the same. We have a French cook from Toulouse, who is moderately Meridional and not at all bad, and I have a library that is my greatest source of pride. And to place all this at your disposal there is a silent lady of the house and a master who respects the freedom of others and does not tyrannize his guests even when they deserve it, as you do for shunning me.

Nabuco wrote a column called "Political Notes" for the *Comércio de São Paulo.* Prado wanted to give him the editorship of the paper, and wrote him saying that it was progressing "with a tail wind. . . . . Will you come and take charge of the paper? I'll give you a capable assistant to handle the little local questions and you can have complete freedom of management. . . . . We can give you a salary of eighteen contos and an interest in the profits, which, I hope, will not be small. . . . . Come and try it for a month or two. If you like it, you can stay. Is that all right? I'll arrange everything, house, etc."

But even in that letter Prado spoke of the threats that he had received, and he soon sent another letter asking Nabuco to wait until things had settled down somewhat. "I am expecting an attack at any time. The anger of the Republicans against *O Comércio* is indescribable. . . . . The threats continue. We must surround ourselves with a thousand precautions in order to remain alive."

Nabuco's collaboration was prudently interrupted. In March 1896, in his "Political Notes," he said: "The readers of the *Comércio de São Paulo* must have foreseen in my recent writings the decision that I am announcing today, to close this column. In the despotic and dictatorial times in which we live . . . . " He stopped there. When he resumed his articles later, he emphasized literary matters.

O Comércio was able to continue its Monarchist resistance for another year, but early in March 1897, after the failure of the military expedition directed by Moreira Cesar against the dangerous fanatics who supported António Conselheiro in Canudos, the offices of the paper were wrecked by a mob of aroused Republicans. They were taking out their spite on the Monarchists of the city for the Republican defeat in the backlands. In the same irrational outburst of fury, the offices of the Monarchist papers of Rio de Janeiro were attacked and destroyed, including *A Liberdade,* the official party organ, whose offices were burned on March 7. Colonel Gentil José de Castro, manager and principal owner, was assassinated in the São Francisco Xavier station as he was taking the train for Petrópolis. The Viscount of Ouro Preto, who was at his side, barely escaped with his life. The Monarchists were called enemies of the Republic and were accused of connivance with the outlaws, whom the army could not suppress. They were victims of an unjust and partisan hatred, the most revolting manifestation of which was the murder of Gentil José de Castro. The government, at a moment when any false move might precipitate a civil war, preferred not to expose the bloody defenders of the Republic because it dared not punish them. In its accounts of the affair, the press showed cautious reserve with respect to the assassins.

CHAPTER XVIII. LITERATURE AND THE BRAZILIAN ACADEMY, 1889–99

That "silence enveloping the library," which Nabuco had mentioned as enchanting Tautphoeus at Paquetá, was no less enchanting to Nabuco himself and he took refuge in it. During the first ten years of the Republic, when his retirement from political life was complete, he lived entirely among his books—those he read and those he wrote. His whole literary production dates from this period. Besides his inclination for it, writing was always for him a possible means of gaining a livelihood. He resorted to it not only from necessity but pleasure as well. At Paquetá, in London, on Marquess of Olinda Street, with rare summers spent on his father-in-law's plantation or in Petrópolis, he lived an extremely busy and a purely intellectual life.

During these years of complete retirement, his spirit underwent a profound modification. The void which followed his political ventures together with the productive urge of his years of activity resulted in a concentration of effort for which Nabuco had always had a strong inclination but never enough time. The product was a new serenity, a richness much greater than sentiment or emotion. His conversion to Catholicism, his marriage, the life of meditation and relative isolation, wrought a definitive transformation and brought to a close what he called his period of "formation," the stage of life which he summed up in the closing words of *My Formative Years*:

> The last ten years have been the time when political interest has given way gradually to religious and literary interests, until nothing remains of political interest except what was bound up in the others. . . . . For years literary inclinations fought a winning battle within me against politics, until the abolition question arose and relegated them into the remote background with all other interests. After the extinction of that great focus of attention, no other interest ever had the same power to restrain my literary inclinations.
>
> When I speak of letters, I mean simply what they signify to me: the beautiful, sensitive, human side of things which are within my reach. I mean the resonance, the admiration, the spiritual state in which they leave me. It was the inner necessity to cultivate kindness which perhaps disposed me definitely to exchange politics for literature. I considered my public life at an end, I anticipated that for the rest of my days my intellectual vocation (politics was never anything else to me) would be polishing images, sentiments, memories that I might wish to carry in my heart. I looked at the different epochs of life through different lenses. First was the ardor of youth, pleasure, the intoxication of living, curiosity about the world; then, ambition, popularity, dramatic emotions, the effort and the reward in the struggle to make men free (all these were seen through a magnifying glass) . . . . Later,

in contrast, came the nostalgia for the past and the growing seductive power of nature, the withdrawal from the world into the sweetness of the home, the graves of my friends and the cradles of my children (all of this seen through emotional prisms).

Before I bid this life farewell, I hope yet to see life through the lenses of Epictetus, lenses of pure crystal and free from distortion: admiration and recognition . . . .

In the midst of an already immense literary activity, Nabuco was constantly working on the biography of his father. Patiently he leafed through vast archives in order to re-create a whole epoch in *A Statesman of the Empire*.

He published many things in the *Jornal do Comércio*, which, because of its importance and prosperity, paid well for solicited articles. Among these was a study of Queen Victoria in honor of her magnificent diamond jubilee in 1896, celebrating the sixty-year reign of the old sovereign. The study was later included in *Literary Discourses and Writings*.

Foreign Intervention During the Revolt was also published first in the *Jornal do Comércio*. The paper had commissioned Nabuco to make a study of the right of foreign powers to interfere in the Brazilian internal conflict of 1893–94. This was an extremely complicated case of international law, completely obscured by contradictory opinions. Nabuco solved it clearly and definitively in an enlightening exposition. In order to do so, it was necessary to recall the whole civil war of 1893 and that narration, taken principally from official documents, occupies the major portion of the book. Standing out clearly are the great figures of the moment with their mistakes and passions, and also the judgment with which he closes the book by comparing the two great adversaries, Floriano Peixoto and Saldanha da Gama.

"For three or four years," declared Nabuco in one of his infrequent discourses during that time, "I have been trying to habituate myself to apply to matters that relate to our country only that speculative interest shown by the historian in his library toward the figures and struggles of the past." [1]

After the coming of the Republic, it was as a historian that Nabuco was revealed to the public in the columns of the *Jornal do Comércio*. He reached his full vigor in the articles on the Chilean revolution of 1891. The name of the president of Chile, who was the central figure of the movement, gave these articles their general title of *Balmaceda*. As in the case of *Foreign Intervention*, the chapters of *Balmaceda* were published serially in *O Jornal* before appearing in book form.

From his extremely busy work desk he sent the following letter, which

[1] Speech at the Red Cross benefit fair for the wounded of the Civil War of Rio Grande do Sul in 1898.

portrays clearly Nabuco's new life, to Rebouças who was living in Funchal:

Rio, February 5, 1896

My dear Rebouças,

Best wishes for the New Year. I intended to write you on January 1, then I left it for the 13th, and now I see I have got far behind. You know, however, that I too live in Funchal, and that I visit you in my thoughts with the regularity of the sea breeze. A person who lives by his pen becomes tired of writing, especially since a letter full of recollections interrupts the mercenary work of the morning and frequently leaves one disgusted with that work.

We are all well. I now have a large family, which makes me feel much more strongly than you do my dependence on Him on whom *everything* depends.

I am sending you today a book of mine which has just come out, and a copy of *Balmaceda* on better paper than the one you have. Also a reprint of my letter to Jaceguai, in the form of a pamphlet. I have been working very hard, since all of that has been done without interfering with the work on the *Life* of my father . . . .

I am writing for the *Comércio de São Paulo.* There is talk of founding a Monarchist newspaper in Rio de Janeiro. I should like to be able not to write any more for the papers. What I already have to do is beyond my strength; you know what it is: the *Life* of my father, the history of our abolitionist campaign, and "my book." Greetings from all of us.

Joaquim Nabuco

The life story of his father progressed well, but of the proposed history of the abolitionist campaign he wrote only the two chapters which are contained in *My Formative Years.* What he called "my book" was a personal work in which he developed his Catholic philosophy, studying and recording the influence of religion on his spirit. He called it "The Desired Faith." Later he decided not to publish it and gradually he dismembered it in order to enrich other works. Most of the religious part of *Random Thoughts* is from "The Desired Faith," but stated in impersonal form. The first chapter is found in *My Formative Years.* It is the famous "Massangana." Another chapter, "The Influence of Renan," appears in his *Writings,* and both are included in their original French form in *Thoughts.*

The first few chapters of *A Statesman of the Empire* were appearing at that time in José Veríssimo's *Revista Brasileira.* Every afternoon a group of brilliant writers whose principal interest in life was letters, as was Nabuco's, gathered in the offices of the review. They would have tea and discuss literary matters. Graça Aranha describes those hours of pleasant companionship:

The review dated from 1895 when the country had barely returned to peace after the civil war. José Veríssimo, the founder, was not only a great man of letters, but also a shrewd organizer, energetic and devoted to his creations. Everyone was tired of politics. The experienced ones were disillusioned, the inexperienced, disgusted. An ominous absence of intelligence and culture from Brazilian politics was the result, and letters became the only refuge for talent. The *Revista Brasileira* was tolerant and harmonious. In its pages and its offices, a real spirit of fraternity was fostered among men of the most divergent opinions. It was a pleasure to find there militant Monarchists such as the Baron of Loreto, Taunay, Joaquim Nabuco, and Eduardo Prado; outspoken Republicans like Lucio de Mendonça; socialists such as Veríssimo himself, anarchists like . . . . the one-time follower of Kropotkin and Elisée Reclus. Politics did not cloud that quiet literary pool. Literature was the main interest there, and Machado de Assis gave it its most expressive form. There has probably never been in Brazil as intellectual a society as the group at the *Revista Brasileira.* It was a permanent reception every afternoon, and each one entered into the discussions to the full extent of his temperament. Never was there a greater joy for a young Brazilian than to hear Taunay tell, or rather, watch him act out a personal anecdote, listen to the hesitant lisp of Machado de Assis as he dissected voluptuously an episode from life, to fill oneself with the sonorous harmony of Joaquim Nabuco, follow the paradoxes of Araripe Junior, witness the pitiless criticism of José Veríssimo, to delight in the secret, exalted music of Raimundo Corrêa, in short, to live in that atmosphere of sentimental enthusiasm and to fuse one's faith in imperishable culture with the hope of glory.[2]

Another young man who was often present was João de Souza Bandeira. Speaking before the Academy of Letters in June 1912, he recalled:

The *Revista* soon became the center for all talent, a gathering place for intellectuals of all shades of thought. Men of culture who had occupied positions in the old regime and had been displaced by the Republic came to the *Revista* to discuss matters dear to them. They welcomed warmly the budding neophytes. There arose an atmosphere of good taste and civility that did more than is generally known to modify our primitive barbarity. The room on Ouvidor Street became the starting point of a movement that spread throughout the whole country. At teatime every day, almost everyone in Rio who was interested in cultural matters gathered there. It was a startling sight to see barons, viscounts, and councilors familiarly discussing politics with young Jacobins in broad-brimmed hats. Impenitent atheists discussed religion with fervent Catholics. Survivors of Romanticism, impassive Parnassians, and gloomy Symbolists fraternized harmoniously, moved by the same love for the poetry which each one understood in his own way. . . . .

"Machado de Assis presided over the group, although not through any desire of his own to hold a prominent place," wrote Antônio Sales regarding those afternoons which seemed to him, as to everyone else, "so serenely spiritual, so far above and beyond the passions and interests which dragged along down in the busy, restless street."

[2] Preface to *Correspondence Between Machado de Assis and Joaquim Nabuco.*

"I am sorry to see that the cordiality of the *Revista* is not present in our Academy. Those were good days which I recall with longing," wrote Nabuco years later.

The Academy of Letters grew out of the *Revista Brasileira.* Desiring to perpetuate these informal gatherings, Lucio de Mendonça initiated the idea and made it a reality. Machado de Assis, recognized for his supreme position in the field, was named president. Joaquim Nabuco was the first permanent secretary.

The founders were eager to make certain that no important living writer was omitted from the original forty members. In order that the group represent the whole literature of Brazil and that no great name from Brazil's brief literary past be left out, Nabuco suggested that each of the forty chairs should have a patron from among the great figures of Brazilian letters no longer living. Each was to be chosen by the first occupant of the chair, who would preserve the patron's glory. Nabuco chose as his patron Maciel Monteiro, and explained his choice in the inaugural meeting of the Academy.

> Maciel Monteiro was a mixture of physician-poet, orator-diplomat, and a dandy who finally died of love. I chose him because he was a Pernambucan. The list of our choices must be analyzed as a curious autobiographical document. The meaning of my choice lies in that.

Nabuco was always greatly interested in the Academy of Letters. Although he was away from Brazil for many years at a time, he always followed with great interest the election of new members. "The Academy appears to be established," he wrote in the last days of his life to Graça Aranha, "at least it rests upon the most solid of foundations—the love of personal glory."

He continued to concern himself with the Academy in his letters, not only to the survivors of the *Revista,* but to candidates for the Academy who wrote asking his vote. During the last month of his life, Nabuco wrote to one of these vote seekers, telling him that he had decided to vote for someone else. In order to console the man Nabuco added, "I would gladly give you my place, except that I am so fond of the Academy for Machado's sake."

This attachment to the Academy appeared to become even stronger after the death of Machado, whom Nabuco was to survive by only one year. José Veríssimo was present during the last moments of the great novelist's life. Nabuco admired Veríssimo and had written to him: "You were St. Peter and Mario de Alencar was St. John. You founded the church and he will write the gospel. Were we truly the twelve?" Veríssimo wrote to

Nabuco telling him of the death of Machado, who had more than reciprocated Nabuco's esteem.

On the morning of the day before, I was with him in the tiny room on the ground floor of the house where he suffered and died. The idea of death was always with him and he said to me: "Veríssimo, send word of my passing to my friends who are away," and he named you first of all.

One of his last pleasures was to hear Graça Aranha read your letter on the *Memorial de Aires*. He spoke of you with his usual affection, both on hearing your words and after.

His funeral was a great event. Never in Brazil has the death of a writer, a pure intellectual, so stirred the soul of the nation. I need not tell you that you were always present in our thoughts during these sorrowful moments. We all thought of the grief that Machado's death would cause you, and we all regretted your absence from our literary family at such a sad time and felt a great longing for you.

After the coming of the Republic, the political orator that was Nabuco died forever; but the literary orator still appeared from time to time and his eloquence was never more beautiful. Most of the speeches of this ten-year period of civic retirement are found in his *Literary Writings and Discourses*. The best known of these was the speech he gave at the inauguration of the Academy. He joined the Historical Institute on October 25, 1896, and in December of 1898 he delivered a eulogy of the deceased members. José Veríssimo wrote in the *Jornal do Comércio*: "I doubt that the Institute ever heard so beautiful and spiritual an oration." Eduardo Prado wrote to Nabuco: "Your discourse, in my opinion, marks a new era and will perhaps be sufficient to shock the Institute into action. I do not say resurrect it, because I doubt that it ever lived."

A number of speeches during this period were inspired by sorrow over the death of various friends. Such was the one he pronounced at the graveside of Taunay, when as Constancio Alves noted in the *Jornal do Brasil*: "he sculptured the bust of our friend with the affection of a brother and the inspiration of a great artist . . . . he expressed the emotions of all of us."

In 1896, Nabuco was called upon to close the brilliant series of lectures with which, on the initiative of Eduardo Prado, the third centennial of the Jesuit Father Anchieta was observed in São Paulo, the city which he founded. Nabuco offered to the Jesuits a tribute that is one of the most interesting portions of his *Writings*.

Take any object in nature. Whether it be a plant, a stone, or a form of life and movement, that which characterizes it is the perfection of its design and the finished quality of its execution. There are works of the human spirit, there are social creations which possess that perfection to such a degree that one may think that they too were part of the plan of creation; that the spirit which designed them and the multitude that develops and completes them, were, like any of the physical and chemical forces that compose and govern an organism, automatons of Nature. The Society of Jesus is one of those structures that bear the stamp of natural perfection, and in which one cannot fail to recognize a certain inspiration, a cohesion, a force of growth superior to the power of any isolated man or to the resources of any group of united men on the planet.

CHAPTER XIX. THE WRITER. THE HISTORIAN. THE THINKER.

"I should never be considered as anything but a literary man who never had time to be one," wrote Nabuco late in life. "The succession of tasks which life presented to me were all outside the sphere of pure literature, an art which must be pursued to the exclusion of almost everything else."

Another note on the same occasion said:

> Abolition took ten years away from me, the *Life* of my father another five years, the Guiana dispute five more. . . . . And my diplomatic work? It is as if I had been a judge or a lawyer. I often think of Ruy who never practiced a profession. In that sense the intellectual life we have had may be called a part of the "material life," because it is only the forced use of certain faculties necessary to the material life, and not the spontaneous use of other purely creative faculties.

Nabuco, however, would always have lacked time. In any case and in any circumstances of life, the man of action that Nabuco really was, would have dominated the artist that he felt existed within himself. None of his works had a purely literary aim. The novel, fiction in general, or purely lyric poetry did not tempt him. "All books," he once said, "should be campaigns."

Emile Faguet, the great French critic, made a brief study of the author of *Random Thoughts*, based on that book written in French. He was so certain that its author was not a foreigner that he called the name an "obvious pseudonym" and placed a perplexed "*sic*" by the Portuguese spelling of "Joaquim." Faguet recognized in him a philosopher who had "written less than he had read and had read less than he had reflected." [1] Nabuco de-

[1] Faguet's article in *Les Annales Politiques et Littéraires* for September 29, 1907, began as follows: "Joaquim (*sic*) Nabuco—obviously a pen name—is a man of about sixty with a good French-English education, who for some time was strongly moved by Chateaubriand, by Shelley, and by Renan, and at all times by the Bible; who in addition is familiar with German philosophy and with Auguste Comte; who has spent a part of his life, probably in the diplomatic service, in Brazil; who has written less than he has read and read less than he has reflected; who has achieved in this way a great intellectual originality, in which there is an element of strangeness, and who likes to write 'random thoughts' after the fashion of Nietzsche, rather than organized books. . . . . He is a most interesting philosopher . . . . who has a constant tendency to become a poet or a novelist. He says often: 'A novel to write . . . . a scene to write . . . . a short story to write.' However, of this novel, this story, or this scene, he gives us only a brief sketch and moves on. Life is too short and the occupations of practical life too absorbing, or the pursuit of ideas too fascinating, or perhaps laziness too strong for the philosopher to spend his time writing novels or stories."

nied some and confirmed others of Faguet's conjectures. He said in a letter: "I wrote a great deal before doing this book which pleased you, but in the language of my own country and for the causes I served. But in this also you may be right. Such books are nothing but action." He was thinking perhaps of *The Emancipation Movement*, a fine example of a book of action in which the writer is overshadowed by the apostle.

Even in the years of his retirement from public life, which the biography of his father did not entirely fill, he neglected the creative work which he felt capable of producing.

Isolation from politics meant a considerable financial sacrifice for him. Books, at that time, brought little profit in Brazil, but writing articles for newspapers was one means of earning a living. As a result, the majority of his books are collections of occasional speeches and of articles that had appeared in various papers. From the point of view of posterity, the writer suffered from the pressing realities of life.

The books by which we can judge his work, almost his whole literary production, including the works which did not appear until later, such as *Literary Writings and Discourses* and *Random Thoughts*, were written during this period of retirement just after the fall of the Empire. With the exception of *A Statesman of the Empire*, purely a labor of filial love without thought of gain, all his works either deal with matters in Nabuco's special field of competence but not always of permanent interest, or else they are fragmentary in nature, such as *My Formative Years* itself. By adding a few more intimate pages to some reminiscences already published in the *Comércio de São Paulo*, Nabuco composed an autobiography which departs from the usual chronological order, leaving "Massangana," for example, the chapter on his childhood, for the latter part of the book to which he gave the title, *My Formative Years*.

He was never concerned with popularity in the choice of subject matter. He had no desire to appeal to mediocrity. He dealt with matters that interested him even though they might appeal to only a few others. *Balmaceda* is an example. An episode from Chilean history, no matter how important it might be, could hardly be expected to attract many Brazilian readers. Even *Foreign Intervention*, a topic of momentary interest, was nothing more than a note on the margin of history.

Before he was twenty-five, the age at which he began to read more English, Nabuco's reading was almost exclusively in French, the language in which his generation absorbed the intellectual food that the native tongue could not supply. In this way they avoided mental stagnation, but neglect and carelessness in the use of the vernacular was common. Nabuco's early writings, like those of many of his contemporaries, are full of errors. His book about Camoens, written at the age of twenty-one, shows clearly that

Nabuco's great admiration for the poet did nothing to enlighten the author, who thought in French, on elementary points of Portuguese syntax. Later on, when this carelessness had disappeared, his form still revealed a lack of familiarity with the models of the Portuguese language. Even when his mastery of style was no longer in question, the critics made certain reservations. "His short, vivid, clear sentences do not have the proper roundness and finish," said José Veríssimo, but he recognized that this unconventional Portuguese usage did not detract from the appeal of the phrase. For the very sake of the language, which had been forced into the too-heavy granite-like classic molds, any effort toward making it more malleable, less harsh, more in tune with Brazilian speech and feelings, to give it variety, subtlety, motion, and light grace, was worthy of the applause of the younger writers. They sought to substitute new and perhaps more delicate tools for the instruments with which the Lusitanian masters engraved their masterpieces. They tried to paint with finer brushes and fresh colors.

From French, and especially from the works of Renan, came Nabuco's elegance of expression. The clearness which characterizes that most polished of living languages was natural to Nabuco; it reflected his temperament and his fundamentally lucid intelligence. It was most apparent in his logic of thought and precision of speech. Of course, his facility in handling intimately two foreign tongues with qualities and possibilities as diverse as those of English and French also contributed generously to his very personal style, so far from the vernacular cadence, yet always successful in clothing his thought in the most exact and fitting manner.

While the form of Nabuco's Portuguese acquired, through the frequent handling of other languages, the seduction of French expression and the conciseness of English thought, the reverse was also true. The Baron of Courcel, presenting Nabuco's *Random Thoughts* to the French Academy of Moral and Political Sciences in April 1907, said: "M. Nabuco's style is absolutely correct and the organization of his sentences is quite French. Yet the richness and at times the daring of his metaphors, as well as the colorfulness of his style, reveal the author's tropical background."

One of the great charms of Nabuco's style is in his use of images. He illustrates his arguments with them, colors his definitions, underlines his affirmations. Generally they are concrete images with a real visual appeal. Faguet says: "Nabuco excels at finding a new, strong and brilliant image to express a thought which might occur to anyone, but which very few could conceive in such an ingenious way."

To write a book about oneself is a delicate test which holds many dangers. Thanks to his sincerity and naturalness, Nabuco, in *My Formative Years*, succeeds in avoiding the choice between vanity and self-conscious modesty. He studied the influences he had undergone in his life and alternated them with reminiscences in which the writer is revealed with discretion and good faith.

In his historical works his style is necessarily different, it is merely an instrument. In *My Formative Years*, his most purely literary work, the style is the book. In that style, which later carried him to the highest level of his country's literature, there is no sign of that quality which was the hallmark of his public speaking. Eloquence, which resides in the strength of conviction and in the grandiosity of the phrase, is not a part of the characteristic charm of this book, which is so closely linked to the personality of the author.

My Formative Years was more than the consecration of the writer. It was also his supreme moment. By the time it was published, Nabuco had learned to be sparing of facile, dispensable words, to cut out everything it was possible to cut, never to permit the structure of his thought to disappear beneath a flood of rhetoric. He had overcome the exuberance of youth, but had not yet reached his last phase, that of *Random Thoughts*, where in the finished perfection of the style the cold breath of old age is sometimes felt, and the rarefied atmosphere of austere heights. In general the artist of sensations is not associated with the artist of thought, and the Nabuco of the later years was the pure philosopher, who had turned completely to contemplation, to religion. He wrote in his diary, after reading a modern poet: "I am a poor critic when it comes to verses. In the first place I am a stranger to the so-called plastic verse, and then too my reading now is contrary to the spirit of modern poetry. I am not fed from the same roots as the poet. . . . . Pleasure is to me now a completely idealistic concept. . . . ." In a letter to his beloved disciple, Graça Aranha, who was turning from the novel to philosophy, he said:

> There are many things, many arts, which dry up and destroy youth; but as the horizon of life broadens and one sees farther into the distance, the necessary begins to drive out the superfluous; the fundamental replaces the decorative in intellectual creation; and the poet gradually gives way to the thinker or the philosopher. But I must confess that I should like to see you go on for a long time producing flowers rather than become a shade tree and a large one, as you undoubtedly will be.

He followed literary movements without indulgence. He wrote: "We shall have been the age of the novel, which means for France and its literary satellites that their intellectual food was adultery as in Cervantes' time it was chivalry. And to think that the *Don Quixote* of this genre has not yet appeared, and that therefore it is a long way from its finish!" Concerning the tendencies of the moment, the *fin de siècle* expressions, to whose fleeting prestige his younger friends were succumbing, Nabuco wrote to Domicio da Gama:

If I were you, I would obliterate from my production all that you call *life*, the courtesans, Russian or not, the taverns, the feverishness, the adventurers. Your talent is too great, too elevated not to gain by emancipation from the so-called Parisian or modern literary and artistic atmosphere. The best resources of your spirit have not yet been channeled. How much poetry and tenderness of soul you waste on the filthiness of the world of morals! The word "lover" has a mysterious prestige with you. I should like to see you rise to your true level, which I place very high, and leave behind "literature for literature's sake," which is the cause of all this malady. Shake off feminism, worldliness, and cosmopolitanism (in the sense in which Bourget uses the term *Cosmopolis*, not in the human, universal sense). Then I would place you as one of the Brazilian evangelists in my gallery. You, Graça Aranha, and Magalhães de Azeredo should produce antiseptic literature in the twentieth century.

Nabuco himself, however, in his younger years, had suffered the same influences of the current vogues in literature. What the public clamored for then, and the novelist furnished, were other aspects of life: elegance, beauty beset with danger, aristocratic refinement, sensitive hearts, and titled heroes. In Nabuco's student days it was considered good taste to admire Octave Feuillet. His school friends found in *Monsieur de Camors*, which had just been published, the prototype of the ideal man. Nabuco later read everything by Jules Sandeau, and found a great charm in *Mademoiselle de la Seiglière* and in the other ladies that Sandeau seemed to lift bodily out of eighteenth-century pastel paintings and transport in the same suave tones to his literature.

At the same time, before the age of twenty-five, Nabuco was influenced even more strongly by Thackeray, the master of psychology, whose works he read to perfect his English. After these pleasant samples of fiction, the novel was never again able to capture him.

Nabuco's intellectual make-up impelled him toward history. "*A Statesman of the Empire*," wrote José Veríssimo, "is the living document of the productive duality of that fundamentally political and fundamentally literary spirit. That character led him naturally, when he turned to writing, into the field of history, of all literary forms the one which most closely approaches politics."

A statesman by birth and calling, Nabuco as a historian spoke with the authority of experience. His love of work, his interest in the past, gave him the patience necessary for the exacting task of research and documentation. Just so that nothing should be lacking, he possessed a serenity of judgment, the over-all view, expertness as a writer, and that eternal renovator, the gift of imagination.

It was only natural, too, that Nabuco should prefer political history, and go behind the scenes of the parliamentary parties in which his father took such a prominent part. *A Statesman of the Empire*, written about the jurist and statesman whose greatest glory is in the indelible stamp he left upon Brazilian laws, could not help being a specialized work as far as these laws are concerned. As a constitutional history of the reign of Dom Pedro II, it is the most complete work of its kind that has ever been undertaken, and has served as a basis for all later works. Many legal opinions by Senator Nabuco and many documents of interest only to the initiated break the thread of brilliant conclusions, rigorous syntheses, and portraits of well-known men of the time, sketches drawn with sure strokes which gain strength from their freedom from digressions. The author judges these men admirably and unhesitatingly. At times the portraits run parallel, as in the case of Rego Barros and Paes Barreto. At times he paints the characteristics of a whole class, like the aristocracy of the North with its reluctance to reveal its poverty, so proud that it would not think of restricting its hospitality. To economize with one's friends would be to destroy one's dignity, debt being a preferable alternative.

Different in this regard from *A Statesman of the Empire*, Nabuco's volume on the Chilean revolution, his study of Balmaceda's personality, was written without any new documentation, without his being personally familiar with the society he discussed. From documents and works already known, he wove the thread which permitted him to tell the story again, but seen as from a distance with free and penetrating eyes. His talent as a writer lends dramatic brilliance and classical elegance to the narration. At the time of the publication of *Balmaceda* in 1894, a divided Brazil was involved in a struggle between irreconcilable ideas. The political ideas set forth on nearly every page of the book, ideas about revolutions, government, about the constantly recurring rebellious movements in the Latin-American states, were not only notable, but of a burning timeliness for Brazil in the difficult moment through which it was passing. There are admirable passages in *Balmaceda*, such as the one concerning the fleet and its patriotism, inspired by the embarkation of the Chilean parliamentarians.

The possible defection of the Chilean navy had never occurred to Balmaceda, says Sr. Bañados Espinosa with regret. This is revealed in the fact that the fleet was ready for any emergency, instead of being practically disarmed, immobilized, or far from Chile, as it would have been if Balmaceda had imagined that opposition might begin there. The truth is that a naval uprising was a novelty for America, which had never had a Topete [Juan Topete y Carballo, Spanish admiral who led the 1868 revolution which expelled Isabel II]. Whenever the opposing parties count their assets, they always leave out the navy, which by its very nature is a neutral element in politics. The national character of the navy is everywhere more accentuated than that of the army, even though they be equally patriotic. The sailor is away from home, and, by the very character of the life he leads, he has to be much less regional than the soldier, bound to the barracks. The struggle of the seaman is mostly against the elements, or at least it was in the old sailing fleet from which he comes, and this leaves upon his character a mark of greatness that diminishes civil dissensions. For a cause to take possession of his soul, it must have something vast and unfathomable about it. The ocean is the mold in which his individuality is cast. The result is a broad extension of his interior horizon. The flag has an influence upon him that it can have for soldiers only if they have carried it into combat. For those who never saw the banners of the enemy waving in the distance, a challenge to their courage, the national flag cannot have the meaning it does for the sailors accustomed to carry it to the ends of the earth, as the distinctive ensign of their distant country. In the unfurling of the flag in the solitude of the ocean when ships pass, there is a suggestion of patriotism which penetrates to the bottom of one's heart. It is face to face with the foreigner that one's patriotic sentiment is educated, corrected, and purified, and the sailor is always face to face with the foreigner. From that comes his natural aversion to, and his incomprehension of anything that tends to divide his country, and his love for all that unites it. He thinks of his fatherland as united, national, impersonal; that is why the ancient traditions of a country remain alive aboard ship long after they begin to be extinguished on land. To this feeling is added the sailor's sympathy for the ideas and things that he knows to be universal because he has encountered them all around the world in every port of call.

In every country the navy has a unique popularity, a prestige all its own over the masses. The army is something else. Popular as it is becoming in our days, even so it is not possible for the people completely to disassociate the military uniform from the idea of oppression, a vestige of the use which governments have always made of armies in order to impose their will. A military revolution, no matter how liberal its inception might be, will always have to combat the popular prejudice against the authoritarian concept of armed force. But there can be no naval despotism. To the present time all sorts of tyrannies have existed, but there has never been a seagoing tyrant. The land has never yet been governed from the sea. The initiative of a movement may begin on board, as in Spain a signal from the "Zaragoza" started the revolution of September [1868]. But it was not Topete, it was Serrano [Francisco Serrano y Domíngues, regent of Spain after the downfall of Isabel II] and Prim [Juan Prim y Prats, Minister of War after the 1868 revolution] and the army that took over the government. The navy has no means of action on land. The bell-ringers of Santiago had no fear that the cannonading of all the fleets in the world could interrupt a single note of their carillon. From all this springs the certainty that a rebellion of the fleet cannot result in tyranny, and the presumption that it proceeds from an unselfish national impulse.

On January 6, 1891, Waldo Silva, vice-president of the Senate, and Barros Luca, president of the Chamber, went aboard the battleships. The Revolution was declared. It is a contradiction in terms to call it a congressional revolution; a national congress cannot be called rebels. When I call the members of Congress revolutionaries, I am simply using the term generally applied to armed movements, legal or not, against the *de facto* government. The opposition counted on the moral effect of the revolt of the fleet. They thought that the uprising on sea would be followed by one on land. The anti-Balmaceda candidate was to be General Baquedano, the conqueror of Peru, whose prestige was great in the army. But he did not move, and the army stood firm to the end.

When writing, Nabuco was first of all a thinker. "He who sees everything in terms of ideas never finds rest," he wrote in *Random Thoughts*, and truly his brain could never rest. Feeling, observation, and reasoning were incessantly active in him, producing without interruption. He liked to find formulas. He took pleasure in categorical affirmations and aphorisms. *Random Thoughts* is the most finished example of his art in this genre, but any of his books or even his briefer works would yield another series of maxims, genuine jewels of exactness, profundity, and conciseness. They form the vigorous structure upon which the sober beauty of his style flowered. It was always the thinker who inspired and nourished the writer. There is no banality in Nabuco. He is never lulled by mere words, nor by sonorous phrases which appeal only to the ear. Lyricism, to him, is always secondary. His whole effort is directed toward making thought more concise, description more concrete.

Thought was even more evident in his work as a politician than in that as a writer. It was not the cause of his popularity, which sprang largely from his oratory, and hence, in part, from rhetoric, from the sacred fire of his enthusiasm and from his personal magnetism. But it was the source of his greatness. His very eloquence, which he continued to refine until in his old age he confessed he no longer had the courage to make commonplace remarks, was broadened by his statesman's vision even in the most ardent and impetuous periods of his youth.

It is enough to see in his books the force of his political theories, his power of abstraction from the present case to the permanent conclusion, in order to imagine what his constructive action in the life of his country might have been when the opposition to slavery had passed, if it had not been for the coming of the Republic.

The maxims and impressions that formed the nucleus of *Random Thoughts* had satisfied him from the first. In his study in Villa Itambi in Petrópolis, where he wrote most of the *Thoughts*, he noted: "If I ever wrote anything that pleased me, it was certainly here. . . . . here I formed the habit of thinking alone, thus bringing about my intellectual independence. It was at this writing desk that the courage to be myself came to me. . . . ."

The book appeared many years later. As time passed, he became more and more fond of those notes, which were ever more numerous. They grew on the margins of his other works, on his newspapers, and on loose sheets of paper, like an overflow from his ever active mind. Once he had acquired the habit, he went on accumulating them until his death, planning to issue a second volume. *Random Thoughts* is a work of unequal quality, like any book of maxims. The courage to omit is rare among authors, and possibly Nabuco did not succeed in reducing his material simply to the most precious jewels. But in this book, where all his literary qualities appear, such as his niceness of expression, dramatic conciseness, translucent clarity, and richness of imagery, the most interesting study to be made is of the author's personality. Nabuco considered it his best work. He preferred it because it was the one in which he had put most of his soul, where he lived most, revealed most, where he best practiced the excellent literary advice of one of his own maxims: "Never let anything enter your language until it has passed through your emotions and has something of you in it."

This was what he had hoped to achieve in *My Formative Years*, but the focalization of the autobiography is false, and no matter how sincere the author tries to be, naturalness is lost in dramatization. His spontaneity is conscious, therefore artificial. The personality is revealed forcibly but often unwittingly, and not always as the author would have liked.

In *Random Thoughts* the process was just the opposite. Everything in its pages is in an impersonal formula, but anyone who knows the life of the author is constantly being reminded of some familiar episode, recognizes the determining factors of his whole conduct, and knows that the literary and political concepts have been tried by fire. Each of his maxims is a confession disguised in a generality, the crystallization of a past experience, the preservation of a thought or bit of advice that cost him dearly. The weight of his wisdom joins with the spark of his spirit and his keenness of observation. Some of the thoughts are hardly more than impressions, and it was not without some reluctance, as Nabuco said in his preface, "that I risk exposing to the light of day some of these intangible impressions which thought destroys as a flame destroys moths." It was probably some of these which inspired the only severe part of Faguet's criticism: "Some of these thoughts are not easy to understand; it appears to me that some of them are scarcely worth the trouble of being understood." Even the unprecise ones, however, the weak ones, those that have no value by themselves, join with the others in transmitting the personality of the author.

Random Thoughts could not achieve what modern publishers call success. It was a book for the elite. The general public does not frequent the heights which the author's spirit had reached at that point in his career. Serenity impregnates and softens everything, although a certain austerity is not lacking. There is coolness in his spiritual elevation and smiling aloofness.

Nabuco had created an intellectual atmosphere where he lived, especially in his later years, surrounded by his thoughts, his idealism, his gratitude toward God, his love, and all his dedications. This kind of noble isolation, which his deafness later accentuated, was the perennial source of his serenity. His *Thoughts* were largely born in those transcendental regions where most men do not breathe well or easily.

It is a book of old age. Faguet, curious about the personality of the author, quickly discerned that he was about sixty years old. A certain enthusiasm, however, a sort of youthfulness of spirit was always characteristic of Nabuco. Those who knew him could realize the absurdity of saying that age had lessened that enthusiasm. It became more spiritualized, but it could not, and did not, become extinguished. He preserved to the end some of that youthfulness whose definition was one of his most apt expressions: "Youth, fundamentally, is but a feeling of surprise at life; when one no longer feels it, one is no longer young; and one is still young as long as he feels it." Faguet, citing the sentence, said: "Very profound, and never before said, nor even, perhaps, thought of."

A study of Nabuco through his favorite book reveals his striking optimism which made him feel that sadness was a sin against the Creator; an optimism which had resisted all of life's wounds, creating courage to replace lost illusions; an optimism blended with resignation to form a complete philosophy of life. After he had cultivated and realized great ambitions, the years had taught Nabuco that happiness was the most simple and modest thing in the world. He portrays it as:

> . . . . the sweetest and most retiring of the fairies. The crowd of thurifers, the Pleasures, who cluster around Vanity, ridicule her [Happiness] because, although she is such a powerful fairy, she is accompanied by a single humble servant, Contentment. . . . . all that she has to give to those who seek her is a small talisman called Conformity, which makes its possessor happy with the lot that falls to him.

There is another thought, of an exaggerated modesty, which summarizes well his optimistic philosophy:

> I have studied no science, I possess no gift of language, nor the intricacies of an art; I am not, then, a writer. I am not to be classified for thought either among the Vertebrata or among the Articulata, but rather among the simple spongelike creatures of the great human ocean. Like the sponge, I can only soak in its undulation, not feeling the bitterness, but only the freshness.

The gentle goodness which those who knew Nabuco remember about him, especially in his later life, and which caused him to live surrounded by the reflection of his own kindness, can be seen in many of the thoughts in his book.

> It is the spleen of the fish that gives his sight back to the old man Tobit [a reference to the Book of Tobit, which Jews and Protestants reject as apocryphal, but which Catholics receive into the canon]. In life it is also by the spleen that certain cures are made, but it must never be our own spleen.

This is another, whose beautifully expressed theory Nabuco practiced in his life, by nature and by conviction:

> Keep devotion after having lost love, veneration after losing faith, gratitude after having paid the debt, generosity after having withdrawn esteem.

It is even more evident in the compassionate page, one of the most beautiful in the book, about Our Lady of Forgiveness:

> The most benevolent of the Madonnas is she who covers each day with her invisible cloak secret mistakes and misfortunes. She sees the terror of the weak, the criminals, and the victims, at the moment of weakness, of misconduct, or shame. She quickly turns wicked suspicion and insidious curiosity from their troubled faces, and their anxious looks. It is she who cures sweetly the wounds of conscience, of pride, or of love, until the scar is no longer visible to anyone. Around her fly vainly the harpies of slander, who far from her pounce on the tender flesh of reputations, as soon as a weak spot is exposed to broad daylight. The price she asks from those who want her protection is that they behave like her among themselves: to respect the shame of the conscience which is forced to hide the ulcer that gnaws it; to pretend to be ignorant of the faults that they have guessed or which have been accidentally revealed to them. The moment of her greatest tenderness, the one when her generous heart breaks into tears more compassionate than ours, is when she sees the one whom she has protected confess willingly and with overflowing sincerity, a secret never glimpsed by anyone. She holds the seals of the unknown, under which is kept the true story, that which has never been written. She always carries with her the book of secret amnesties, that Providence signs each day a thousand times. She takes delight in legends of virtue or of innocence that the least indiscretion would suffice to overthrow and which, thanks to her, adorn forever the tombs. She is the patron of those who have a high rank in the social, or even the religious, hierarchy, and who have not had the strength of character sufficient to resist the temptation placed in their way; of children who keep to themselves the mystery of their birth; of wives who blush before their children without knowing why. She prays for women more than for men, for the dead still more than for the living. When she covers over a mistake that would tarnish forever a name, she is remembering some ancient ancestor who bore that name in great honor, or else she is thinking of an innocent descendant, already inscribed in the book of life with the mark of God's approval. She runs ceaselessly after Fame in order to beseech him not to spread among the crowd news of the stiletto blows of calumny and hatred, the confessions that one would wish to have kept to oneself, the effusions of those who believed they loved each other eternally. Her wrath is against the coward who condemns others for the mistakes he himself has committed, for vices which are his. She has icy hands and a failing heart, when she sees in the assemblies of men or women the scapegoat that social morality claims and that human hypocrisy and weakness will deliver to it. She is not justice, nor equity; she is mercy. Her name is Our Lady of Forgiveness.

CHAPTER XX. THE CATHOLIC

Nabuco's religion was deep rooted. He wrote in *My Formative Years*:

I feel the idea of God in the most remote regions of my being; it is the most loving and cherished remembrance of several generations. . . . . There are souls who like to break all their chains, preferably those which others have created for them: I, however, was incapable of breaking even the smallest of the chains which bound me . . . . and, less than the others, one which I inherited. It was in the small chapel of Massangana that I became firmly bound by this chain.

The impressions which I retain from this period show well the profound depths of our formative processes. Ruskin wrote this version of the thoughts of Christ regarding childhood, "The child often holds within the grasp of his weak fingers a truth which mature age with all its strength cannot support, and which only old age shall again have the privilege of bearing." As a plaything of my youth, I had in my hands all the symbolism of the religious dream. Frequently, when reminiscing, I discover in my memory miniatures which, by their freshness and spontaneity, must be the first reflections of these impressions upon my soul. One can easily estimate the degree of the impression made by these indestructible images. This occurred to me when looking at the "Creation" of Michaelangelo in the Sistine Chapel, and that of Raphael in the Vatican galleries; for, in spite of all my ponderings, I could not attribute to any of these the internal relief which I felt when Paradise appeared before my eyes in one of the ancient popular Mystery plays.

I heard the last notes of the Angelus on the Roman Campagna, but more lastingly impressive was the family call to prayer, the small bell to which the slaves listened with lowered heads as they murmured "Praised be our Lord, Jesus Christ."

This inherited faith conserved itself intact until he was eighteen years old.

When I entered law school, I still had my virgin Catholic faith; I always shall remember the fright, displeasure, and shock that I felt when I first heard the Virgin Mary referred to in irreligious terms; nevertheless, within a short time little remained of that revered image but the gilded dust of memory.

It was the fate of most of his contemporaries to lose their faith when they went to the university. The new generation of intellectuals who were eager to grasp fresh ideas, did not find anyone among the older people who would guide them to Catholicism. The leading intellectuals of that period guided them along another path; imagination was finding new life in other sources; religious skepticism was an almost inseparable indication of intellectual superiority in the Latin world. Ever since the publication of *The Origin of Species*, the theory of evolution, with its faults yet undiscovered, had moved forward on a wave of prestige and novelty. It appeared to be the violent enemy of the Church, threatening *Genesis* with destruction. Thanks principally to Darwin, the word "science" shone with a new brilliance in the eyes of the world. The young intellectuals wanted rational proof of that which could not be proved; they expected to capture the intangible. The philosophical fashion was one which tended toward materialism and determinism, and was devoted to creating a universe which revolved mechanically according to strictly explicable laws.

In literature romanticism was dead. Further serving the new philosophic tendencies were the writers, especially those of France, which was the source of cultural nourishment, to the exclusion of all others, for that generation of Brazilians. They abandoned the "ideal" for the "concrete" and broke the last points of contact with religion. Naturalism, realism, and "the slice of life" soon became typical characteristics of the novel. Zola and the Goncourts headed the school. The art of criticism was transformed into determinism. Taine had led the school which taught the careful scrutiny, one by one, of the motivations of art, the impulses of inspiration, and the caging as often as possible of any ideas which had wings capable of flight. All efforts were directed toward a universal classification, scorning all forces which eluded analysis and comprehension by the human brain, and which, although thoroughly discredited by theory and eliminated by reasoning, continued to live by instinct in the irrepressible internal certainty of the freedom of man and the existence of God.

In law school, Nabuco felt, as did the others, that his faith "shrank day by day, leaving an ever widening field for new cultures." And he added: " . . . . the faith which I confessed to myself left me in such a manner that I hardly perceived it. . . . . I still believe firmly that I would not have become conscious of what happened so quickly had it not been for the intervention of a literary influence" ("The Desired Faith").

This influence, a decisive factor in his estrangement from the Church, was that of Renan. Joaquim Nabuco dedicated one of his most beautiful and polished literary criticisms to the writer who by the use of the only method possible, "the power of love," destroyed his belief in the divinity of Christ.

"If it were not for him, I would have continued along that same downward path, because it was intellectually fashionable, the mode of my times. Almost any other guide would have led me to greater depths, from which very few have ever returned. I saw so many of my best friends bound tightly to the earth. Their religious imagination was permanently atrophied" (*Writings and Literary Addresses*, p. 301).

Already returned to his faith, he wrote this lament in his diary: "My most intimate friends are all atheists." Taking all things into consideration, he decided that he really owed Renan a favor, for, had it been done by another, the damage might have been irreparable.

During my separation from the faith, I would not have felt the nostalgia which is felt by those for whom God has reserved a return to the faith.

It was Renan who caused in me the separation of imagination from reasoning when considering religious matters. As a result of Renan's influence, religion became for me a seductive literary form, a refined temptation of the spirit, and not, as before, a prison—an absolute moral impediment. Under such conditions, whatever poison his style could have hidden would have spilled into the darkest recesses of my reasoning. . . . . It was in this way that I passed from doubting whether Jesus Christ had been a man to the idea that he was nothing but a mere man. At the bottom of my heart I did not entirely renounce the sentiment and belief in His divinity, but my heart ceased being the basis of my belief. Reason became strong enough to imbue me, like the child that I was, with the doctrine that I should not inquire into things outside my reach. I would not confess to myself openly that I did not believe any more in the God to whom I had been praying all of my life. Prayer, really, was a most agreeable habit for which I had the sincerest affection; but after this I gradually became aware of the fact, which was like a secret guarded even from myself, that a considerable part of reasoning, that is the faculty or sense of probability and verisimilitude, had separated itself from faith.

Today, I understand better the manner in which this break occurred, and it was the only way possible with me. I have with me the notes which I used to take then and in them I see that it was only by the strength of love that the sentiment which I had for the divinity of Jesus was weakened. It was not by sarcastic statements or insults—what a difference is there between the pleasant jestings of Voltaire and those of the Jews in the Praetorium—that I renounced my most precious childhood friendship. It was, on the contrary, by directing to Him the outpourings of my love; it was by a new incarnation, which had for me the fascination of being literary; by a devotion beside which the apologetics paled for one who was incapable of appreciating them at that time. Thus was His divine quality soon extinguished. These things did not make Him seem to be less than before, but much greater . . . . His pedestal was no longer the sky, but the earth. He became for me the perpetual moral leader of humanity; instead of the Son of God, He was the first of His creatures. He was embalmed a second time for eternity with substances more precious than the aromatic drugs of Nicodemus. . . . . His descent from divinity in the nineteenth century was accompanied by the same piety manifested at His descent from the Cross. . . . . And He continued to be God; to Him was attributed only an ideal divinity, which each one could give Him according to the dictates of his heart. The change affected me little because I had not broken with Christ. It was just a simple exchange of concepts. I would continue to repeat daily the prayers which He had taught, but instead of directing them to God in Him, I would pray to God through Him and with Him. . . . . My heart continued to tremble in this manner in His hands. . . . . He remained always the Person whose sandals humanity could not touch. . . . .[1]

[1] *Writings and Literary Addresses*, pp. 290–92.

Once separated from the Catholic Church, the years widened the breach between Nabuco and his faith. He was present at the Masonic conferences of the Lavradio Valley. In the serious controversy between the bishops and the State, which injured the Church in Brazil and occurred a little after his graduation from law school, he frankly and openly sided against the clergy. At that time, he would write editorials in *A Reforma* which were filled with elevated liberalism, but not with Catholic submission. Afterward, in speeches, in newspaper articles, in every reference to matters of the Church—even to the images inspired by the Catholic culture—his departure from the ranks of the believers became increasingly obvious. His tolerance was not that of reverence, his impartiality, even when in admiration, was that of a critic. He spoke of the ceremonies, which even at that time impressed his imagination, as he would of any literary event. The article, "Natural Penance" in *O País*, June 1886, illustrated this well. "I wrote many things which I now regret and of which I am now ashamed," he admitted in a letter written in his later years.

In his mind doubt endured for many years. Never, however, did it amount to a negation of the existence of God. This clashed with his skepticism more than any affirmation of faith would have. The arguments against atheism which he used after his reversion most assuredly influenced him in many instances throughout his lifetime. Later in life he wrote to Graça Aranha:

"One could say, as you do, it is nature instead of God, but as soon as one ascribes intelligence and order to nature the idea of God emerges. The contrary hypothesis to the idea of God is merely that of a blind and unconscious nature, producing the most amazing patterns, organisms, and processes of life, without any previous planning, calculation, or combination, by a force inherent in every atom which is unknown to itself and all others. The principal defect of this alternative is that it reduces intelligence in the universe to a force which is almost nil, and which really appears only in man, while the belief in God supposes an intelligence in the universe, a force so unlimited that it becomes creative."

In his diary of June 28, 1909, he wrote:

"Our absolute incapacity to conceive of a being or a living form beyond our powers of recognition is transformed by the atheist into a rational negation, a synthesis of the universe. And he uses that incapacity in a singular manner. He asks, 'How can one imagine there is a God if we have that incapacity?' To be able to imagine the existence of God is to understand that incapacity."

And further:

"A preconceived notion when proved wrong dries up a fountain of love, and frequently permanently. Atheists are arid. . . . . Atheism may be a personal conviction, but it is a sin to propagate it."

Nabuco could not live without love, without ideals, without beliefs. His imagination demanded them and his mind, knowing that skepticism makes everything stagnant, praised them whenever they were indispensable, as means of action. It was his consciousness of this driving power of beliefs and ideals which made him write in *Random Thoughts* (chap. CXXXI, p. 49): "If it were finally decided that God did not exist, religion would have played an even more beautiful part, if that can be so, because it would have taken His place."

It is interesting to compare this cry of a man who *wants* God to exist, with this other regarding the immortality of the soul:

"Death is but a crevice across which we must jump with the courage of an antelope leaping over a chasm between lofty cliffs. Death is but a jump across the tomb, and we must make the jump with a shout of joy. Even if we were to die entirely, this cry of gratitude in the moment of agony would re-echo forever in the infinite spaces and would make God regret our disappearance" (*Random Thoughts*, chap. CCXXXIV, p. 169).

"I have the conviction that I shall meet God. Where, when?" So goes a note in his private diary. And another: "We do not have any of the senses by which God could be perceived. We just have that sense which makes us feel our need for Him."

It was necessary for him to believe in God. The sentiment surrounding the belief in the existence of a Creator, of a divine being, was for him as Faguet conjectured in discussing the *Random Thoughts*, "so to speak, permanent, which is after all the only way to have it. All creation and indeed the whole human soul, or at least what is best in it, sustain his Pascalian belief in 'God, who makes himself known through the heart and not through the mind.' "[2]

However, it did not seem to the great critic that the unknown thinker belonged to any special religion. After reading the article, Nabuco wrote to him stating his disagreement with "the exactness of his conjectures. Far from belonging to any sect, I consider myself to be a Catholic. I have probably brought with me some strange accent from the regions in which I traveled, only because I experienced all the sudden changes of fortune caused by having doubts, before turning onto my homeward path." The many maxims about God and religion had been taken from an unpublished work in French, "The Desired Faith," and placed in *Random Thoughts*. "The Desired Faith" was an intimate work in which personal memoirs were intermingled with philosophical considerations; the first chapter dealt

[2] *Annales Politiques et Littéraires*, September 29, 1907.

with Massangana; it was the product of a period of heavy concentration and of his conversion; a book, profound in thought, illuminated and intensified by the fervor of his first moments of grace. The work, which he did not submit to publication, except in chosen fragments, describes all of the phases of his return to the Church. In the Preface he sums it up:

"A few years ago, I saw before me in the field of my religious thinking, nothing but doubts without end, an ever moving sealike mass, which, however, for me was lacking in large waves or sudden surprises. Afterward, severe storms agitated that surface and stirred the bottom. I then felt that it was not very deep and decided to drive a first pile into it—that of God; then another—my human sentiment; lately a third—the collective character of the entire religion; and a last one—the absolute finality of Christianity. . . . . I could then construct a dam across the troubled waters."

The decisive factor, which vitally affected the lighting of his religious path, and which brought to him a confirmation of his convictions that restored him to the peaceful state of having a simple and secure faith, most assuredly was that of his marriage to an extremely devout Catholic. In his *Random Thoughts* he says: "The family brings about the religious conversion by concentrating the imagination on what is really worth while. Marriage does not extinguish light, it concentrates it."

In an unpublished note written in the same impersonal form, he completed the confession:

> With what patience and gentleness does God bring back to Himself the wandering and erring one. Sometimes it is by sickness, poverty, or separation, and other times by the mere companionship of a human being who is truly dedicated to God; the presence of a wife whose every act is the reflection of her ever present fear of God, and who creates out of the household, a school in which the children are not the sole students. Thanks to her, the faith which seemed extinguished in my heart, reappeared from its ashes and regained new life.

His marriage coincided with the proclamation of the Republic. His brusque removal from active life caused his hours of meditation to increase. He was just completing his fortieth year of life and already had discovered, as he said in "The Desired Faith," that "the downhill slope of life . . . . has a different horizon from that of childhood and it is from here that one can see his great aim and object of living."

During the first years of his married life he resided in London for some time. It was in that city, he tells us in *My Formative Years*, ". . . . thanks to forced concentration, which would not have been possible for me except in the London fog, my mind first began to puzzle about the great enigma of human destiny and of the solutions heretofore offered in attempts at its clarification, and little by little, in the hidden-away Jesuit church on Farm Street, the vibrant verbal whiplashings of Father Gallwey made me feel that my religious anesthesia was not complete; afterward, in the Brompton Oratory, where I breathed a pure and clear spiritual atmosphere impregnated with the exhalations of Faber and Newman, I was able to gather together again the broken fragments of the cross and with it once more renew the forgotten sentiments of my childhood. . . . . "

He became accustomed to frequenting the Jesuit church. He went to accompany his wife and to listen to the excellent music, the principal charm of which was the children's voices singing in chorus. The religious atmosphere prevalent there, so different from that found in Latin countries, gradually infiltrated his being. Little by little, he first became interested in the rites he attended, then he studied their origins and historical development, particularly those of the Mass, and deliberately permitted himself to be caught and seized by the external beauty of the divine services, by the antiquity and significance of the liturgical ceremonies, and by all the consecrated tradition of the Catholic Church.

In his *Random Thoughts* there are several references to the symbolism of the divine services which so impressed him in the chapel on Farm Street:

"The art of symbolism is one of the real treasures of humanity, for it conserves for us the pious memories of an era in a manner unequaled by any relics. Many of the traditions which were recorded in this way still remain lost to us, but, as with the riches hidden in the words, one can always depend upon science to bring to light those which endure in the symbols.

"If it be proven to me that one of the rites of the Church is but a transformation of a former pagan rite; that the incense was burned in Roman temples; that the priest in the Mass moves his hands in the same manner as the sacrificial priest of old; all of this, for me, would tend to add greater prestige to the ceremony which some seek to abolish. It is a curious fact that when people want to uproot a belief, they attempt to show the depth of its roots. There still are people for whom the most telling blow to destroy a long-established institution is to prove its antiquity."

In the manuscript of "The Desired Faith," the reader learns of Nabuco's first fascination with the religious services in the Jesuit church. There he began to attend regularly the High Mass which was sung at ten o'clock, as a private observer interested in the poetic qualities of the Mass. It was here that he permanently acquired the habit of preferring solemn High Mass on Sundays, the sacred sacrifice with the fullest extension of symbolical ceremony with which he became so well acquainted later:

The church had no decoration except the presence of those attending, the angelic chorus of children, and the marvelous execution of the liturgy. And for this very reason my attention more easily lent itself to the ceremonies and I tried to understand their significance. It was here that symbolism became for me the sovereign of the arts; for it employs all other artistic mediums for its use, or rather, for the service of God. As this new language became more and more comprehensible, so did the Mass appear more and more to me to be a masterpiece unequaled on earth. The detail of this miniature of the Last Supper of Jesus Christ has such a rich and condensed form that every paragraph, every gesture, every pause has a name and tradition behind it. At first, it is necessary slowly to isolate yourself from the moral effect of the ceremony in order to accompany its beautiful external aspects. Then, it begins to resemble a Byzantine mosaic, resplendent with gold, on which precious stones have been applied to depict angels, saints, prophets, martyrs, virgins, popes, and the signs of the Holy Zodiac in which there moves the great white Host, the inner sun of the souls. The "*Hoc est corpus meum*" glitters effectively in the center of this unequaled composition. The altar and the holy vases, the lamps and candles, the flowers and incense, the tabernacle and images, the ornaments and colors, the hymns and voices, the orisons and altar pieces, the celebrant and his deacon, each and every one has a separate story; it is all a great incrustation. The different parts of the Mass are the heroic rhapsodies of the persecutions, primitively recited from church to church by the confessors and martyrs, and unified by the Holy Ghost.

It was by the appeal to his imagination that he was brought back into the folds of the Roman Church. His great head naturally bowed in admiration before the majesty of an organization which was able to triumph for so many centuries, in spite of human vicissitudes and individual weaknesses. But the decisive factor was his attraction for the external elements of the services. Catholicism appealed not to his innate mysticism but to his poetic idealism. It also appealed to whatever respect there was in his temperament for accepted traditions and broad and general beliefs. For him, an ardent enemy of physical or intellectual solitude, doubt was a solitude and an isolation, both of which he abandoned with relief, for "in religion one either goes along with the multitude, or else at the slightest turning from the path of the pilgrims one finds himself in an echoless solitude."

He confesses in "The Desired Faith" that his return to the Catholic multitude was not "for mystical tendencies, but because of my horror of solitude, the feeling of having my life threatened. Death might occur during the course of the night, and I was afraid of continuing to live outside of the flock. . . . . " It seemed to him that in the field of religion, to isolate oneself was "to want to escape the general attracting force, which makes itself felt only in masses. God attracts humanity not by projections, regardless of how elevated they are, but by profoundness and depth."

It was only natural for Nabuco to seek God in Catholicism, the religion of his parents. One day, after having casually and unpremeditatedly entered into a confessional in Brompton Oratory in London, he walked out reconciled with the Roman Church. His personal diary records the ineffable impression he suffered on this day which became a notable one for him.

May 28, 1892. In the Oratory. With Father Gordon in the confessional. I told him of my spiritual development from childhood, and of the course of my ideas in the retreat to the old faith. I was the sheep which returns frightened to the sheepfold. Nine-tenths of me wants to believe, only one-tenth—all intellectual and without roots in my heart—opposes and doubts. With my will submissive, only a part of my intellect, a desirable part at that, rebels. I arose happy, contented, life seemed to be worth living, and the green of the foliage in the park was radiantly sympathetic toward me. The impression is a divine one, which, although extinguishable in me, will always be revitalized; while it lasts the soul seems to have wings. It was in the black, marble chapel of Our Lady of Sorrow that I received the courage to approach the confessor. That chapel shall be the Fountain of Tears for me because I had prayed there and cried.

Having returned to the road of Catholicism, the reconciliation was rapid and fervent. He discovered, the manuscript of "The Desired Faith" tells us, "that the innate Catholic structure in my soul was so imposing that all paled beside it."

Months after the first confession, in Rio de Janeiro, he returned to the confessional and the communion rail.

This passage is taken from his diary:

December 22, 1892. I confessed my sins today in the parish church of St. John the Baptist to Father MacNamara, the Irishman, who is a curate in the Lagôa area. . . . . Who knows but that perhaps the prayers of the slaves worked in such a way as to give me the courage to purify myself in this manner. Even during the period when I had lost the faith, I admired the greatness of the institution of confession. Father Gordon attributed his conversion to the prayers of his Catholic forebears. I want to believe that it was the slaves who offered some of their sorrows and afflictions to God for me.

On December 23 he wrote:

Today I took Holy Communion from Father Bos in the chapel of the Sisters of Charity. It was really for the first time, because the communions received at school were given at an age level in which I could not understand the significance of the act. Thanks to God, I was able to light the small candles in the ashes of my faith in honor of Christ. They will illuminate my death. I am grateful for the devotion and consolation gained from the receiving of the sacred heart of God, and I hope that it shall disseminate itself like a breath throughout my depressed body, like light spreading into the abyss which I carried in me. All of my doubts have grown pale, and flown like the owls from the bell tower at the break of day. . . . . The candles which I lighted today shall be religiously cared for, and all shall be forsaken for their benefit. I speak with respect to my own life, for I have not reached the state of fervor necessary to say that I would forsake my wife or children for it.

And with the happiness felt by someone visiting a dear and forgotten place, he went on reconstituting his faith:

> Day by day, the bending of my reason to permit the acceptance of the Catholic doctrine became more easy, while my feeling of personal liberty seemed to expand instead of contracting under the new discipline. The adjustment of my individual thinking to the thinking common to Catholics occurred by the simple phenomenon of affinity. I was grateful for being able to exchange the thousand insoluble questions which are the useless riches of the skeptic for the simple *omnia mea mecum porte* of the believer.

He abdicated his throne of independent thinking, as if it were a small thing in the religious sphere, and submitted himself to the truths of the Church. He recognized the fact that only in love is there any perception of the divine, and that intelligence misses it and errs, for with it he could not see the Creator waiting for him at the end of his life. He therefore treats the intellect from then on as an enemy.

Even the title which he chose for his book, "The Desired Faith," shows his constant appeal to his will to dominate the negative force of rationalization, that deep-rooted distrust of all which cannot be proved, argued, seen, or touched. Allying himself with his heart against reason, Nabuco reduced his intelligence, the dangerous adversary of faith, to the role of a servant, obliging it to serve him with arguments and images. In his case, what a rich gift! He was sustained by one side of his winged spirit, besides his avid imagination. The mysteries of faith served, as he says in the *Random Thoughts*, "not to narrow the horizon, but to broaden it."

His acceptance of the mysteries of faith was the Christian solution of his problems. He courageously accepted the prejudices, the irrational beliefs, and glorified the term " . . . . that beautiful term, 'prejudices,' which should be applied to all definite and assured loves. It precedes reason and defies analysis."

One prayer accompanied him throughout his entire life; it was the greatest of all prayers—which he had known since childhood and had not cast aside during his spiritual exile, because Renan respected it in his destructive works—"The Lord's Prayer." In his diary of 1897, he wrote:

> I would like to write a small book about "The Lord's Prayer." It is a little jewel, as a whole and in each of its individual parts. It is the summation of all impersonal prayers; it asks for nothing for itself, only in those parts in which it pleads for the mutual benefit of all. . . . . "Hallowed be Thy name!" is perhaps the only unnecessary part in the praise of the one created to his Creator. "The

Lord's Prayer" is in its simplicity the most sublime of all prayers, and as far as human perfection can be valued, it is worthy of God. The more I think of this marvelous treasure which Jesus has left us, the better I understand it and the more novel it becomes. It is extraordinary how such simple phrases and clear words can have such deep and profound meanings; it can easily be said that very few of the people who recite "The Lord's Prayer" truly realize the highly natural interpretations which Jesus joined together in these few words. Every letter of this poem is golden. "The Lord's Prayer" was improvised one morning before the multitude, and in comparison with it all other prayers seem importune and emphatic.

After returning to the faith, he added to "The Lord's Prayer" others which he had forgotten. He always carried his rosary in his pocket and while resting alone, or at times while riding in his carriage, he liked to recite the prayers of the rosary or others which he knew by heart, such as the "Salve Regina," and the "Act of Contrition," not as a routine exercise but as a repose for his spirit. In his prayer book, the page with the "Te Deum" was so worn that it tore with the touch of his fingers; he read it daily as a manifestation of his gratitude for the gift of life. Besides this hymn of divine praise, the poetry and beauty of the cantos and litanies of the Church, the pungent pain of "Stabat Mater," the sacred terror of "Dies Irae" penetrated to the depths of his soul. To him, prayer seemed indispensable to the believer. "If prayer has any reason for being, it is because it is the most serious and elevated of all acts; if it had no reason for being, then it would be the entire religion and not just the reading of the rosary which would crumble away."

Along with the ancient prayers of the Church, he also became deeply interested in sacred literature, particularly *The Imitation of Christ.* In his diary he says:

For days I have been rereading the *Imitation.* What a marvelous and truly divine book! But the main theme in the *Imitation* is to desire suffering, while to my way of thinking, life is not that. The *Imitation* is written for the ascetic, and asceticism is not my ideal of the spiritual life, of the communion of the created with his Creator. My Christianity is Platonism coupled with the death of God for mankind. In no way could I ever deny worship of the Beautiful, of Art, Aesthetics, Science, Progress or the Conquests of the Intellect for the contemplation of the death's head and the thoughts of suffering in Hell.

It was in his temperament to regard religion as a source of happiness. In spite of this, toward the end of his life, he moved toward asceticism, urged, as is natural, by his deafness. However, this asceticism served only to enrich even more the fountains of sweetness and gratitude which Nabuco bore in his soul.

"Religion should diffuse joy; it should be the cluster of flowers near the poor man's window; mortification and abstinence should be necessary only to repress sadness."

This joy of living, the appreciation of every moment of life granted him, became more intense toward the end of his life. In his diary on January 24, 1909, he wrote: "If gratitude were incense, I would offer my heart to be converted into a grain of it to be burned at the feet of the Creator."

And on September 27 of the same year, he wrote: "Praise the Lord for the fact that, whenever I look upon a beautiful scene or a beautiful day, the first string plucked in my spirit is that of appreciation and gratitude on the part of the created for the Creator who has offered him this great spectacle. And thus it is with all impressions of physical or moral beauty, and even every breath and joy of those who are dear to me."

"Old age and the presentiment of death only make me more curious regarding my future life," he says in one of his notes. "I seem to be on the eve of penetrating the infinite, exclaiming like Archimedes: 'Eureka! Eureka!' "

CHAPTER XXI. RECONCILIATION WITH THE REPUBLIC, 1899

During the ten-year period which he devoted to study and reading, the political situation in the country changed. Order was substituted for militarism. As each day went by, the Republic became more firmly established. The federation which had accomplished Nabuco's ideal now permitted Brazil to face its great destiny. A spirit like his could not be blind to the transformations which were occurring. The Republic, peaceful, organized, and successful, had, in Nabuco himself, a strong ally with which to defeat Nabuco's resistance: his lucid mind and innate sense of justice. Soon, his confidence in the Republic began to grow. "We had a long discussion at the home of D. Marocas," he wrote in his diary in January, 1898. They think that I have changed a great deal—when the actual truth is that the weather is changing and not the barometer."

Other notes indicate that the separation began to bother his sense of patriotism: "I want to be a Monarchist to the end, but I also want to die reconciled with the new aims and destinies of my country." In that same year, 1898, the *Estado de São Paulo* asked him if his opinion regarding the Republic had been modified. His reply was published in the *Estado de São Paulo* and reproduced in the *Jornal do Comércio* of September 26, 1898:

> You already know that I am an ardent follower of Chateaubriand. . . . . Look at this sentence: "I found myself between two centuries, as if I were at the confluence of two streams; I jumped into the agitated waters of both, and swam hopefully toward the unknown bank where the new generations land." I am pessimistic regarding our country in its present phase, and it is illogical for a pessimist to see good right away. . . . . all changes which have occurred in my thinking are the action of the fading of my monarchistic hopes and the natural subsequent desire that the Republic not ruin the country. We also are at the confluence of two epochs: contrary to Chateaubriand, I, who do not know how to swim, remain standing still on the shore where I was born, desperately hoping that the new generations, to which my children will belong, will not find a wild desert on the opposite shore. . . . . Furthermore, the problem which I wish to solve is not that of my generation, but that of the following generation, my children's.

The monarchist camp abandoned all hope in 1895, when Admiral Saldanha da Gama died. Nabuco in particular felt, after this loss, that "civil wars cannot be fought more than once." He later related in a speech given at a banquet at the Casino Fluminense in July 1906 that after this he sought "through the aid of God's judgment to busy myself in the isolation of books, and have almost nothing to do with the direction of the Monarchist party."

His problem was to pass from being an apostle in politics to a simple believer; an act, in the performance of which, as in the field of religion, one loses more than one had imagined. Out of the passiveness, in a gradual manner, grew doubt. Only after he had taken the decisive step in aligning himself with the Republic did he realize that he had always been heading in that direction, even when he was devoting himself to study, far from the political arena.

He wrote to Judge Domingos Alves Ribeiro on accepting service with the Republican government:

> For almost five years, while working on private projects, on the books I have written, for the *Revista Brasileira*, the Academy of Letters, the Historical Institute, and in correspondence with friends, I have concurrently and subconsciously been practicing the national and patriotic policies which have led to this act. This act was inspired by the thought of my tombstone. I never wanted to have the inscription "monarchical loyalty" placed upon it. . . . . I was and am a Monarchist, but that is a secondary and accidental characteristic as far as I am concerned; the basic and increasingly strong characteristic was another . . . . "liberal."

He never completely tore himself free from the past and most certainly never did he conform or agree to the unhappy exile in which Pedro II died. "I observed ten years of mourning for the monarchy, but I shall mourn the Emperor and the Princess eternally," he wrote later to Baron Homem de Mello.

Neither did he abandon his preference for constitutional monarchy as an ideal form of government. He upheld the ideas which had been instilled in him by the reading of Bagehot during early school days, ideas which the influence of England helped to strengthen in him. But he was later convinced, as he said in a speech given in the São Paulo law school on September 16, 1906, that "the great driving force of republicanism on the American continent would absorb successive restorations of the ancient regime." He saw that Brazil and the Republic were reconciling themselves perfectly. Defeated by these solid arguments, he gave way to other forces which he saw less clearly, "to a temperamental necessity, to an internal driving force, to an inevitable expansion of his individuality, and to the impulse of the destiny which had created him not just to write history with his pen, but also to make history. Thus wrote Ruy Barbosa in an article, "The Mission of Nabuco," which appeared in *A Imprensa* of March 13, 1899.

His activity when fully developed required a much vaster field; his patriotic spirit suffered greatly in following political events and not being able to participate in them. He accepted ten years' contemplative life without calculating the sacrifice. But the vigorous spark of his spirit rebelled against a tranquillity which was in utter contrast with the epochal years of the preceding abolitionist campaign. Campos Sales' invitation came at an opportune moment, and for that reason he obtained an answer different from that given others.

Immediately after the proclamation of the Republic, the provisional government unexpectedly offered him the post of minister to Great Britain. Every one of the governments which succeeded the provisional body could well have felt much more secure had it been able to announce Nabuco's participation and co-operation. The acquisition of Nabuco's services for the benefit of the Republic was one of the acts in which Campos Sales took the most pride during his presidency. Eduardo Prado wrote in the *Comércio de São Paulo* of April 6, 1899:

> More than three years ago, Carlos de Carvalho offered Joaquim Nabuco a permanent position as envoy extraordinary to some European court. Joaquim Nabuco turned him down because it was a position in which he could lend only secondary services to Brazil and also because he considered acceptance of such a position as being incompatible with monarchist feelings. He overlooked then, as he always had, his own personal advantage.

The first idea of President Campos Sales and of his Foreign Minister Olinto de Magalhães, in case Nabuco did not desire a seat in the Senate, was to offer him a legation. Offering Nabuco a senatorship was not a new idea, and he refused it immediately. He had thought more than once of returning to the parliament as a Monarchist, but since a negative task was repugnant to him, and since because of his convictions, he could not participate in the work of construction and consolidation of the new regime, his hesitations always terminated with a negative decision.

The transformation which was slowly effecting itself in Nabuco matured suddenly but not unreasonably because of the opportunity of serving Brazil in a purely patriotic manner as his country's representative in the dispute with Great Britain over the Guiana frontier. He hesitated a few more days, asking, before he gave his answer, that the government invite and consult Baron Rio Branco, who had already attained much fame in these questions, and who, at the time, was quite busy with the litigation over French Guiana. Only after the foreseen refusal arrived did Nabuco accept the government's invitation in a letter which declared openly his "known monarchist ideas."

Rio de Janeiro, March 5, 1899

Dr. Olinto de Magalhães:

I feel extremely obliged to you for your courteous letter, and the praiseworthy appeal which the President authorized you to make to my sentiments as a Brazilian for the acceptance of the task of preparing and defending the Brazilian cause in the boundary question, which is going to be arbitrated with British Guiana.

I confess to you that today there could be no sacrifice more painful than that of taking me away from this land of ours, where my heart cherishes its most sacred relics, and in whose vicissitudes I want to take part to the very end, both suffering and rejoicing with it. I already told you this when I urged you to excuse me from taking this appointment, principally because of the possibility of being able to postpone action and reserve this honor for Baron Rio Branco. At the present time he is busy with the Oyapock arbitration work, but he has produced notable results in diplomatic negotiations and has made a profound study of the problem in question.

Believe me, I spoke with the utmost sincerity during our most pleasant conference, when I suggested this and other alternatives, in order to avoid making the choice presented me, and still not break any moral obligations.

The new claim which we are going to dispute has a great importance, of which I certainly am aware. You have a legitimate desire to see the fate of the disputed Amazon territories decided favorably, and in a definite and permanent way. Since, after listening to my opinion, you still consider my participation to be necessary, my conscience permits me no other choice but acceptance. In order not to accept I could only have recourse to my known monarchical ideas. When dealing with a question solely national in character, such as the vindication of Brazilian territory against foreign designs, I would be failing the tradition of the past which I have been seeking to study and cultivate, if I were to get involved in political dissidences above which the Republican government itself has risen with noble detachment.

Under such conditions, nothing is left to me but to put myself entirely at your disposal, and to express my gratitude to you, as well as to the President of the Republic, for the confidence you have shown in my loyalty to my country. This acceptance, in principle, does not mean that I am not at liberty to reconsider it. If, after finishing the keenly interesting study which I am now making of the memorandum which you gave me, or after examining the documents which you promised to let me read, as well as the "Blue Book" dealing with the Venezuelan side of this question, I decide that in the national interest it would be better for me not to accept, I shall feel justified in refusing the appointment. If such a case were to arise—and I do not anticipate it, but feel it necessary to make a reservation—I would formulate my opinions with utter frankness; I am certain that in the event of such a renunciation, you would recognize the same obedience to patriotic scruples which accompanied my acceptance.

I remain your most humble servant,

JOAQUIM NABUCO

In order to avoid comments, the first meeting between Nabuco and the Foreign Minister took place at the home of a friend, José Carlos Rodrigues. As Tobias Monteiro explains in *O Jornal* of June 21, 1922:

All of these precautions were taken because, in spite of Nabuco's spiritual independence, loud protests might come from the press, because of pressure from the still active Monarchist elements intervening against his acquiescence.

The manner in which the surprising news of the nomination was received completely justified these precautions. It was only natural to expect that the conversion of one who had fought and spoken out so vigorously should attract attention. The opinions held by a cold, indifferent person are easily forgotten when he changes. On the other hand, it was difficult for the Monarchists, especially those who had been attracted to his side by his ardor and spirit, and united with him around the great hope of restoration, to see calmly and fairly his apparent abandonment of them. It was difficult for them, however gradual his development had been. It proceeded from the years in which their loyalty became worn and tired in the face of waning hopes for realization of their ambitions. It was further stimulated by the futility of internal divergencies and the growing strength of the definite reality of a republican government.

But the violence of the Monarchist reaction against Nabuco exceeded all expectations. "What I do not understand," he later wrote in a letter, "is that those who wanted me on the Monarchist side only until the day of restoration and then would execute me are the ones who appear to be so unhappy."

In 1899 there was still a party, prominent figures, and a press to defend the antirepublican cause. From all sides there was an upsurge of spite, insolence, hitherto repressed jealousies, and declarations that personal interest had inspired abandonment by a person who, as a Monarchist newspaper put it, "we all knew would be prime minister of the restoration when our anonymous sacrifices achieved it." The Monarchist party, a minority party aware of its weakness in the country, received the news of the loss of one of its greatest sources of strength with consternation and irritation. The entire party united itself against this "deserter"—who, in the words of the *Comércio de São Paulo*, "took with him the weapon of his dazzling intelligence." This absurd insult of being called "a deserter" and "a traitor" continued to be thrown at him even after his death.

The Republican press, the only one which exercised any influence, on the contrary, unanimously applauded the government which had overlooked partisan lines for the higher interests of the nation by regaining for it "a force in which the eyes of his colleagues, his friends, and compatriots always saw one of the finest hopes of our future." These are the words which Ruy Barbosa wrote in *A Imprensa* of March 16, 1899, at the time of Nabuco's acceptance of the mission.

A real sensation was caused everywhere. The *Jornal do Brasil*, to which Nabuco had granted an interview, had to print it for two days in succession in order to satisfy the public demand. "I well know," Nabuco said in the interview, "that because of our partisan education, acts like mine are always badly interpreted, but throughout my whole life I have never recognized that type of imprisonment or superstition." He remembered how he had always fought as "my own chief; for example, in the fight for abolition, I did not solely depend on any single party, and I assumed whatever attitudes my political instinct suggested. . . . . I have always been responsible for my own conscience and the judge of my moral obligations. My public life is the reflection of my own personal inspiration and culture, and not the result of outside pressures and influences."

"What I have just done," he wrote to a friend, "is what I have always practiced in politics: to ignore all prejudices and opinions."

In the meantime he was deeply hurt by the attitude of the Monarchist group, and the wound never healed. He saw himself deprived of friends whose affection he had supposed transcended all political differences, of companions with whom he had lived for ten years, taking part in their schemes and unsuccessful dreams, and who now left him as if the past had never existed. When later he returned to Brazil, anxious to forget these unpleasantnesses, the Monarchists circulated verbal instructions: "Do not have anything to do with him." There were exceptions, of course, as Nabuco stated in a letter which he wrote to one of these Monarchists who had understood and accompanied him: "There are still many friends who will apply the soothing balm of tenderness to the wound which the heart is not ashamed to acknowledge, for it is a loyal heart."

The former Imperial Princess sent him a note of sympathy: "I want Mr. Nabuco to know that I approve of his act of patriotism, as my father would if he were now alive." Eduardo Prado defended him valiantly in the press. "For a time," Nabuco gratefully wrote, "only his voice was raised in my behalf from the Monarchist camp."

Prado applauded him in the *Comércio de São Paulo* of April 6, 1899, as:

> . . . . the great man who always sacrificed himself for his generous ideas. Without being confronted with hatred from the victorious Republicans, he interrupted his glorious career purely from a love of justice. Although he was in the prime of his popularity, he submitted himself to ten long years as an exile within his own country.

Tobias Monteiro, under the pen name of José Estevão, wrote in the *Jornal do Comércio* on April 2, 1900:

> While the other Monarchists rejoiced over the misfortunes of the Republican government and gave full vent to their spleen in that formula of destruction—"the worse it is, the better"—Nabuco followed sympathetically the victories of the law, the consolidation of order, and the progressive steps made by the administration. He preferred the revival of his country to the turmoil of a new cataclysm . . . . with the Republic now fully established in its organizational stage, and with all

signs of disorder fast disappearing, ... what barrier was there left to separate the noble liberal spirit of Nabuco from us?

On March 21, Nabuco wrote to a friend:

Truly, only the individual can know himself, know his own motives, and the honesty and sincerity of his intentions. If they wish to judge me, it is a futile mental effort, for they know nothing of my psychological characteristics. If I wished to judge them, I would have the same difficulty. It was for this reason that in the *Life* of my father, I always tried to explain the acts and attitudes of numerous people by using the most elevated of standards, for in that way, if I were mistaken, I would still be erring on the side of benevolence and charity. The simple truth is that they and I never see political problems from the same point of view, and never were we the same type of Monarchists. Someday we shall have a reconciliation after the cloud of forgetfulness covers us all. Today I am trying to face my personal problems objectively, as it were from a point one hundred to two hundred years away.

And in a letter to his mother, after he was in Europe:

Ever since the Monarchists labeled me a renegade, an apostate, and I do not know what else, because I accepted the commission to support our boundary dispute out of purely patriotic and certainly not political reasons, they have made it impossible for me ever to co-operate with them again on terms of equality. The truth is, as you wisely observed, that for years I have been drawing further and further away from them, and that neither morally nor intellectually, could I breathe in the old atmosphere which they had created around themselves. I realized then something they had never wanted to face: the plans for restoration, if they were to be feasible, had to be the product of totally new inspirational elements, which had nothing to do with the past.

Nabuco left without delay, for it was the wish of his government that he take part in the negotiations for the treaty of arbitration which the minister was trying to conclude in London. On May 3, 1899, he sorrowfully embarked with his family. In writing to Ruy Barbosa, he said:

It was for me indeed a painful sacrifice and a grave commitment to bury myself intellectually in the Tacutú and the Rupununi, and above all, to separate myself from my mother who had just recently achieved the perfect age of the Greeks, eighty-one years, and whose happiness is today my greatest joy and obligation. Therefore, with regard to my political beliefs, I do not hear the reproach "Thou hast forgotten thy people and the house of thy father" resounding in my ears as did Newman on leaving Oxford and the Anglican religion. The monarchy could only return and benefit the country if Monarchists were to show greater patriotism than the Republicans. Only in a duel of patriotism would I like to see this noble cause decided.

Believe me, I am sincerely convinced that I did right at the cost of the greatest of sacrifices, that of exposing myself to the judgment of the Pharisees and Publicans. Instead of finding myself now in the meditative refuge of religion and letters, if I should die tomorrow, I can envision taking to my tomb not only the spirit of monarchism and liberalism, but also the heart of a Brazilian.

Although Nabuco had accepted this task as a temporary assignment independent of politics or party, it was the first step; the second step, that of actually joining the main body of servants of the Republic, was easy. That was the thought which struck everyone in March of 1900 upon the death of Nabuco's old friend, the Brazilian Minister in London. Nabuco's reactions to the minister's death are recorded in his diary:

March 24, 1900: Yesterday I was informed of Corrêa's sudden death in London, and today the newspapers say he was found dead in his bed. Since yesterday I have been under the influence of this great loss. . . . . Without prejudice to the Christian point of view regarding sudden death . . . . the minister's sudden demise, while enjoying the position he had always sought, as well as prosperity, was probably the most merciful thing fate could have done for him. . . . . For me, the opening of the void caused by his death in London, where even Penedo was not to be found, was a great blow; his death for me was more like the digging out and removal of the bottom supporting layer of a large and insecure mass on the verge of toppling. . . . . The secret of his success, and it was outstanding (for he became one of the intimate friends . . . . of the Prince of Wales . . . . and of the Court of St. James's), lay in the kindliness of his manner, his personal affability and willingness to please, the facility with which he adapted himself to the English social graces and customs, such as whist, horseracing, the constant and tireless daily "dining out," . . . . but above all was the neutrality of his spirit which caused no social disturbances. . . . . Poor Corrêa! . . . . he did not aspire to glory . . . . For a long time now, I have been watching the departure into the unknown of my comrades and friends as if they were the advance guard for my departure. . . . . I feel I have received my marching orders. . . . . during our youth we always look forward and never backward, we are among the tumultuous crowd, in the fray of the battle in which we step upon our fallen comrades without qualms; while in our declining years we are among those wounded and abandoned on the battlefield, listening to the groans of those beyond the reach of aid, and awaiting our turn to rest.

The legation in London had always enjoyed high prestige, from the time it was occupied by the Baron of Penedo, who lent to it an air of regal hospitality, to the occupancy of the deceased minister, Arthur de Souza Corrêa, with his enviable material situation and his modest yet noble personality. He was filled with affable simplicity and familiar conviviality. He appreciated life in country houses, and was a guest, friend, and whist partner of the heir to the throne, the future Edward VII.

The office of minister in London was of special interest to the Brazilian public, which was very sensitive to European thought, and well informed as to what happened in the Old World. The Brazilian public drew life from the life of Europe, and keenly regretted the fact that Brazil was so little known abroad. Brazilian public opinion unanimously turned to the support of Nabuco after Corrêa's death. All groups along the Rua do Ouvidor, which prided itself on being the center of civilized Brazil, indicated their full-fledged support; these groups circulated the witty remark of a well-traveled and ironical writer, "Nabuco is the ideal man for giving a false impression of Brazil abroad. He is tall, fair, and handsome."

The people with whom Nabuco corresponded at this time reflected this atmosphere in their letters from Rio de Janeiro. Tobias Monteiro wrote:

> Perhaps the fact that we have always had personages of wide fame as diplomatic representatives in London during the past years is responsible for the special interest which the present generation has in the office of minister in that capital. . . . . You cannot imagine the discussions which went on for days regarding the filling of that post. . . . . Your name was suggested unanimously by Greeks and Trojans. I have never seen such unanimity over the filling of a public post. . . . . I asked the President if he were weighing the difficulties involved in making the appointment, and added that I thought you would be a good choice. The President added in saying good-bye: "He was the first person I thought of for the appointment. . . . . "

José Carlos Rodrigues wrote:

> When I read of the death of our friend, Corrêa, I immediately thought of you as the logical choice for his successor, as did everyone else. I am authorized by Campos Sales to ask you to accept. . . . . You should realize that you now are virtually minister in London by acclamation; there has been a unanimous clamor for the designation of your name to fill that post since Corrêa's death.

Caldas Viana wrote:

> One can easily say that the past two weeks have been devoted to your name, which has been on everyone's lips . . . . since the news of the death of Corrêa reached us here. It became a watchword. The spontaneity and sincerity of such an acclamation deeply stirred all of your friends. Dr. Olinto sent me an urgent call to come to the secretariat. . . . . There he told me that, upon hearing of the vacancy in London, only one thought struck the government regarding the choice for it.

There was only one difficulty. Nabuco, who had loudly alleged the patriotic and special character of his mission, did not have any intention of being subtly pushed toward outright service to the Republic. But the responsibility which he had assumed obliged him not to abandon negotiations on a treaty defining the limits of the contested zone; these negotiations were in the hands of the legation in London. England, having agreed to arbitration, was in no hurry to sign the accord, and at that time was attempting to reach a direct understanding. In the middle of these negotiations Corrêa died. Nabuco, naturally, was forced to continue alone the discussion of the question which until then had been under their joint supervision. The government immediately saw the disadvantage of placing another person in charge of the legation; and Nabuco, having been invited to assume the post, confessed to the President of the Republic that even with Corrêa, "my intimate friend, I had verified the fact that it would be impractical for two to handle the delicate question which brought me to Europe, and since I had an interest in the final settlement, I could not refuse, having been invited, as I was, to assume responsibility for the negotiations." [1] Still influenced by a residue of Monarchist scruples, he did not officially accept the ministership, but agreed to his nomination as minister plenipotentiary on a special mission, that of handling the boundary question; the legation was placed in the hands of a chargé d'affaires, whose authority would stem from Nabuco; Nabuco, with the knowledge and approval of the British Government, was therefore virtually in charge of both missions, the extraordinary and the ordinary.

In a letter to Caldas Viana, who, along with Graça Aranha, was one of the first assistants in the mission, Nabuco attempted to explain what still remained of his Monarchist party beliefs.

In the strictest confidence I wish to tell you that, if my health permits, and if what I am going to experience gives me the hope that whatever sacrifice I make shall be amply rewarded by the results I achieve, I shall feel obliged not to refuse the invitation which was made to me in such a gentlemanly manner. I have no reason for adhering to the republican faith, burning what I adored, and reciting a new *Credo*. I have, however, many reasons for further disassociating myself openly from all movements or agitation against the present form of government.

Believe me, I do not suppose that I have changed in the slightest, nor do I wish to contradict a single line of anything I have written; what I wish to do, on the contrary, is firmly to grasp the literal text. The articles, for example, which I wrote in the *Jornal do Brasil*, at the time of Rodolfo, the *Answers to the Messages of Recife and Nazareth*, my letters in the *Comércio de São Paulo* which so scandalized the chiefs of the party, all of these attest to the logic of my present attitude of separating myself from the Monarchist current.

When I accepted the first invitation of the government, making the reservations which you know, I believed I had assumed a position which was completely

[1] Letter to Campos Sales of May 12, 1900.

irreproachable; the Monarchist party, that is, its principal members, chiefs, and nearly all its followers, in statements made regarding my person, have made it impossible for me to co-operate with them again.

I must add, to be entirely frank, that even without this unfortunate display, I would be separated from them now. . . . . There was much about which we differed. How else could it be? I was living alone, among my books, writing history, and attaining that period in life when impartiality begins to appear, and when the spirit, having lost some of its ardor, becomes more acutely aware of what is happening. Burning passions can no longer live in it. Then comes the period of ideas which still cannot settle down because of the inflamed spirit. Water, in order to be deposited on the land, must be placed upon a surface which has cooled, otherwise, the internal heat will transform it immediately into vapor. This is also true with ideas, for they cannot enter a person's thinking until it has reached a degree of maturation at which they will not immediately be transformed into burning passions.

The fact is that I have entered a phase of life which is free from politics, and better yet free from party influence, which unfortunately is the same thing, for in the politics of today there is room only for party members; not only there in Brazil, but also in France and England, the political field is openly divided into battling camps; there is no tolerance of anyone who is not a partisan of either one side or the other, of anyone who is not thoroughly intransigent, who sees the mistakes of both sides, and the evil to be found in the spirit of obstinacy, regardless of which flag it waves. What else can result from this new credo of force which the civilized nations now seem to be professing but the evolution in the field of international relations of a spirit of intransigence and the proscription of all natural mediatory and cohesive forces? The only result of this terrible attitude of "the worse it is, the better" among us can be to exasperate and arouse the Republicans. Men such as Figueira can arouse the Monarchists and revive the Monarchist faith within a small circle of people. However, they should not exasperate the other side, and in case all faith is dead on their side, not arouse a feeling of irresponsibility among the Republicans to whom the resources and defenses of society have been entrusted, as well as its blood and capital. To scandalize the Republicans, in my opinion, indicates an extreme lack of familiarity with the means at the disposal of the Republic.

Therefore, I have no political impediment which would give me reason to refuse it, and I cannot use the nonpolitical excuse (the only one left me), for the government asks only for my patriotic participation, looking upon me only as a Brazilian, as I look upon it as Brazil. My hesitation is derived from other sources, and will depend upon the examination of my conscience which I shall make when in actual diplomatic service. . . . . How horrible! do you not think so? The diplomatic life with its innumerable gastronomical and ceremonial obligations appears to me to be a replica, but only worse, of the torment of Tantalus. There is no consolation in the fact that the atmosphere of Tartarus was as bad as the fog here. I believe that my mind is like yours, requiring wave after wave of light to cause it to move and expand.

In August of 1900, Nabuco, who had just enjoyed a year of almost complete freedom—working where he desired, enjoying excursions to watering places, the seashore, France, Switzerland, Spain—established himself in London with his family. The trial period lasted a few months. In December, the government wired Nabuco advising him of the intention to fill the post at that time and requesting his answer as to acceptance. Nabuco did not hesitate this time. His reconciliation with the Republic was firmly cemented. Now a functionary of the new regime, he combined his love for the Brazilian Empire of the past with that for the Brazilian Republic of the future. When he returned to his homeland in 1906 after a longer absence than he had expected, the evolution of his political thinking had completed its final cycle, and he took advantage of the first opportunity offered to divulge his thoughts. No one asked him to do it, but he felt a necessity for doing so. During the period in which he thought Brazil would be better off under the monarchy, he supported it ardently and in his usual frank way. His innate repugnance for any show of insincerity forced him to make a belated public confession of faith within a week after his arrival, at a banquet given by leading government representatives in Rio de Janeiro.

> This is the first time that I speak in public to a Brazilian audience as an ambassador of the Republic, as its servant, linked to its destiny, sincerely desiring that it overcome all its hardships, disprove all of my past prognostications, and make impossible the success of new revolutionary disturbances which during short periods may interrupt the incontestable finality of the republican form of government on the American continent.

These declarations, interrupted by the ovations of the audience, hurt his former friends even more, and served to separate him more openly from the august lady, to whom he felt such immense gratitude for the abolitionary decree, a sentiment of veneration which he mentioned even in his discourse. This speech, which was widely discussed by everyone, and violently attacked by what little there was left of Monarchist opinion, necessitated supplementary explanations in other speeches. He could not idly ignore without protest the title which various newspapers had given to his speech, that of "adhesion to the Republic." He said in a speech to the São Paulo law school on September 14, 1906:

> I did not adhere to the Republic, for no one has the right to say that he shall or shall not adhere to the institutions of his country. Foolish is the man who uses the expression, adherence, with regard to his relationship with the various forms his government takes with the passing of years. What I have done is to stop making objections in the shadow of this great institution which since its beginning I have accepted as the model form of government. . . . . It was an act of placing my faith in the new destiny of my country, an expression of a hope that the better

elements, and the highest and purest qualities shall be exercised more and more in the forward march of our institutions; an act, which I can say was one of love for that great American ideal, the republican ideal, which is not only American but that of every Greco-Latin who has always preserved it on the altar of Pericles as his political religion.

I, therefore, did not perform an act of contrition, for I did not have to. My intentions were always of the purest, and never for a single instant did I attempt to stir up strife between the dynasty and my country.

No one could continue to have any doubt as to his way of thinking. They could accuse him of inconsistency; but that is not an accusation which would be made by someone seeking after the truth. He was not an obstinate person, as he told the university students of São Paulo:

When I became convinced that the road on which I was traveling was blocked, and since I had not resolved to die a Monarchist, I sought to reconcile myself with the new destinies of my country. . . . . Renan, the great magician of language, once wrote this sentence: "Faith should never become a chain about our necks; we can become free of it by enveloping it carefully among the shrouds in which the dead gods rest."

I am released from my monarchical faith because I have religiously wrapped it among the purple shrouds in which rest the great founding dynasties of the past.

Part Four

THE LAST PHASE, 1899–1910

CHAPTER XXII. DIPLOMATIC MISSIONS, 1900–1904

In July of 1900, Nabuco took over his new post in London, the city which seemed so friendly to him. His first impressions relive in the letters which he wrote to his wife, who had remained for a few days in Paris.

July 26

We had a good trip, thank heavens. Graça Aranha is well. Today I have time to drop you only a few lines. I am engaged in a round of activities. I have already gone to the Foreign Office, and tonight I am to see the Prince of Wales at the home of my friend, Baron Alfred de Rothschild, who wants to introduce me to him. I have taken rooms in Fleming's Hotel, Half-Moon Street, Piccadilly. I passed the church today and my thought was that God may permit me to return there unconditionally.

July 27

I cannot tell you how tired I am after my first social day here in London, which was my first full day in London besides. Graça had dinner here with me today, and after dinner he slept even more soundly than I did. It had been a work-filled day: the arrival, the search on foot for rooms in hotels and in homes, lunch in a restaurant with Oliveira Lima, after having seen Alfred, then to the Foreign Office to be introduced, and to speak to the various sections, on to the Legation which is at the other end of West End, back to Piccadilly, shopping, ordering, etc., etc. By nighttime I was dead. However, by eleven I felt refreshed from the nap I had taken, the nap of a beginner who after years of seclusion is thrown out into the wide world. I then went to the concert at Alfred's, where he immediately introduced me to the Prince. . . . . Thus I spoke to the Prince before speaking to Lord Salisbury. Happily, however, the formalities of protocol were not observed, for all were highly unconventional, all disliked formalities, curtsies, visiting cards, and etiquette in general. Carl Meyer, who today is a South African millionaire and who was the Rothschilds' man, told me that my definite appointment was very popular, not only in social but also in financial spheres. They admire my command of English . . . . and since my English is my own and cultivated by myself, they consider it to be quite choice. . . . . They say in the Foreign Office that the Queen is to receive me at Osborne. With things going the way they are, only after the audience is arranged shall I know when I am going to Paris.

July 28

Yesterday morning José Carlos Rodrigues was here. Afterward, I went out to sign officially at Marlborough House, then to the Brazilian Treasury Delegation . . . . later I walked about showing a little of Piccadilly to Graça. . . . . I exchanged my chain for another, and thus was bereft of the last external sign which I had of being a foreigner.

July 31

Today I shall be received by Lord Salisbury at 3:15. I do not know whether the Queen will receive me at Osborne; on this depends my attendance at the Anti-Slavery Congress on August 6, 7, and 8, at which one of my works is being used. It is entitled by them *La Lutte anti-esclavagiste au Brésil*. . . . . It does not seem to me to be purely an accident, having gone to Loyola on purpose, to be received by Lord Salisbury, that is, to start my mission on the day of St. Ignatius. May this be a good omen! Great diplomats St. Ignatius trained and inspired!"

August 1

Yesterday I went to the Farm Street Church, to say my rosary at the altar of St. Ignatius, before starting my diplomatic work on his day, for which I thanked him. I had lunch with Rodrigues at the Carlton, and afterward we went to the Foreign Office, where I saw Lord Salisbury. He is really the last great man of this nation. What a handsome face ennobled by the fact that the years, the events, and the spirit of a generation which ends with him have lent to it a spirit of augustness, typical of an ancient Greek statue. Because of this same august expression, I feel that the most handsome male faces which I have seen are those of Gladstone and Lord Salisbury. . . . .

Graça has dinner with me every day. Yesterday after dinner we visited Rodrigues, who lives but a few steps away. Tonight he is having dinner here with Oliveira Lima. We shall have dinner with him tomorrow, and on Friday I shall have dinner with Alfred, who has invited me so that I can meet the Duke of Devonshire, who is, thanks to his wife, the great man of Alfred's circle, which follows the Prince of Wales. This circle does and controls everything, from wars to ties and waistcoats.

I still do not know whether I shall be able to attend the Congress. Because of the death of her son, the Queen will not receive me until later, but I do not know whether I have to be here for the funeral rites or some other reason. What is really bad here is the expense. Two houses, one here and one there—in a short time we should have to dip into our own little capital. I have already asked an agent to give me a list of houses in the city and in the country, so that we can fit our lives into a single home. Nevertheless, even the prospect of sharing expenses does not bode too well here in England.

The new Brazilian Minister was the last diplomat to be received by old and ailing Queen Victoria. He presented his credentials to her at Windsor in December, and on February 2, followed her majestic funeral. It was the first of those scenes which English tradition has inalterably preserved, and about which Nabuco wrote to his friend:

The opening of Parliament was a great spectacle, and the procession from Windsor breathtaking. We have now a series of scenes, for, in reality, a picture of great splendor is composed for each ceremony. Those of the House of Lords and also of the funeral, one might say, were painted beforehand. Imagine what the coronation is like!

He observed these resurrections of the past with interest. In the House of Lords, with its walls of carved wood, the stained glass windows gave the proper brilliance to the wives of the peers. He noted in his diary on February 14, 1901, that their presence "well indicated their preoccupation with decorative effects. Their diamonds, pearls, and necks set off the effect of the blackness of their dresses, while below there were the red uniforms of the peers. We were in our gold uniforms. This will give you an idea of the color of the scene."

However, he found the participants "clumsy, awkward, and fully aware of the emptiness of the spectacle they were presenting!" He missed the spirit of faith which gives such life to Catholic ceremonies, for example, the jubilee of Leo XIII, which he attended the following year in Rome, and about which he wrote to Dona Evelina Nabuco: "What we saw in Westminster does not even compare with this."

To be Minister of Brazil in London, according to the tradition established during the Empire, was the highest step one could attain in the Brazilian diplomatic corps—the axis of Brazil's foreign policies had not yet been oriented toward Washington. However, he was but the chief of one of the missions of minor importance in an immense diplomatic body, in which he felt lost among the many classes which the British recognized with pride—her statesmen, and great landed nobility.

The South American republics, about whose existence Europe had not yet begun to think, were remembered only as faraway centers of eternal and often quite grotesque revolutions. The life of the representatives from Brazil was not always free from annoyances. An incident—which did not occur at the beginning of Nabuco's tenure in office, and which may seem insignificant because it involves a banquet—illustrates well the lack of prestige which the Latin-American countries, whose hour for world attention had not yet sounded, enjoyed in Europe. While Nabuco was away from London delivering the memoranda to the arbiter in Rome, he received this letter from his chargé d'affaires:

> The Minister of Chile just left, having come here feeling quite disgusted. He wanted to talk to me about a subject which must be quite familiar to you: it is the humiliating exclusion of Latin-American diplomats by the King. It is a fact that this has happened many times, but it was flagrantly repeated again just recently, when the King gave two official dinners only two days apart, inviting all of the ministers from Europe and Asia (including the officials who arrived recently from Siam, Korea, etc.), and completely excluding South America.

Nabuco, being absent at the time, could take no action on the matter. After returning the following year and seeing the same humiliating act repeated, he wrote to the Foreign Secretary. Lord Lansdowne attempted to explain the exclusion, which did not happen again, at least not so pointedly. The correspondence regarding this case was quite delicate and conducted expertly by Nabuco in his usual dignified and gracious manner. The last letter, written at the request of his Argentine and Chilean colleagues, asked the British government to give them proper satisfaction. In private Nabuco handled the case humorously. He noted down a few verses which escaped the wastebasket:

> Au Palais Buckingham, dîner diplomatique.
> On n'attend que le Roi. Sir Thomas, liste em main,
> S'approche ... du Lord Chamberlain.
> Et lui dit: "Vouz avez oublié l'Amérique."
> L'Amérique? ... on pâlit, on va se trouver mal.
> On cesse de manger ...
> Mais Sir Thomas, continuant sa phrase:
> "Du Sud ... " Eclats de rire, appétit général.

Baron de Penedo, the most illustrious of Nabuco's successors, lent much more brilliance to his post than he received from it, and spent a large amount of money in so doing. Nabuco, poorly remunerated, and with a large family, could not think of following the example set by the leader who had introduced him to the grand style of English life. The inability to put on an adequate display was to be an initial obstacle for Nabuco. However, it was not an important obstacle, in view of the obvious fact that Nabuco's personal qualities would permit him to overcome hindrances of this type, as others had done; but, in view of the slight appropriation granted him, he gave up all ambitions for material splendor. This was responsible for his decision—in a place where the location of one's residence is of capital importance—to establish a comfortable residence in a spacious home at Cornwall Gardens in South Kensington, at the other extremity of West End, and not in fashionable Mayfair.

His hospitality was limited to dinners now and then, and infrequent receptions for outstanding Brazilians. After his glorious airplane flight around the Eiffel Tower, Santos Dumont received a warm reception in London, and during the same year, the Brazilian warship "Floriano" anchored for a few days at Portsmouth. Nabuco conceived the idea of having the crew pay tribute to the tomb of the great Admiral of Brazilian independence, Thomas John Cochrane, the tenth Count of Dundonald. In ancient Westminster Abbey, where he reposes in glory, Brazilian sailors, in full dress and arms, placed a wreath upon his tomb. It was the first time in history that foreign troops had marched through these Gothic naves. For the first time, the great organ filled the venerable vaults with the echoes of the Brazilian national anthem. The heir of the Cochrane title, the Admiral's grandson, received the officers at a lunch, and played an important part in planning a full program for them during the few days when they were in London.

Although already organized, work at the legation was pressing; so much so that the second secretary, Domicio da Gama, in a letter to a friend, complained of the lack of time he had for the literature in which he was interested; "I have just left the special missions in which work is concentrated and hard, and now I enter a legation where there are daily shifts of from four to six hours."

Nabuco preferred the absorbing study of the boundary question, for which he was Brazil's counselor, to the monotonous task of diplomatic bureaucracy. In November of 1901, having finally signed the treaty of delineation of the arbitral zone with the Marquis of Lansdowne, and having agreed to the choice of King Victor Emmanuel III of Italy as arbiter for the case, he was able to begin the life of intense work which was almost indispensable to him by now.

In his diary for January 18, 1902, he says:

> I now work every day until lunch, from lunch until dinner, and from dinner until midnight. I consider every invitation to go out to be an encroachment upon my time, which I feel is very scarce.

The year 1902 was one of incessant labor. With a date set for the presentation of the first memorandum in defense of Brazil's rights to the disputed territory, Nabuco labored for months on end without leaving his desk; during the summer he spent a few snatched week ends at the seashore with his family. On August 19, his birthday, he wrote, "with a pain in my heart," excusing himself: "I am, therefore, bound, almost crushed by the time limit, which seems so short—and which gets shorter day by day—for turning in my memorandum. . . . . from now until the completion of this affair, I shall not get a moment's rest."

Two painful occurrences stand out in his life in the month of September of that year. One, the death of Dona Anna Nabuco, who was eighty-four years old, still vigorous and lucid. Joaquim Nabuco, her favorite son, whose absence was the last grief in her life, wrote in response to a letter of condolence:

> I probably would have grieved less for her during the period of my passions and my independence. Now that I see and consider myself to be fully in the past, and my children in the future, this loss, although partly softened by the shades of dusk which are beginning to envelop me, is the subject for meditation for both them and me. I desire for them the same happiness over an equal length of time.

A few days before, unexpectedly, a heavy cross fell upon his shoulders, and he was to bear it until death. In September, when he had finally got ahead in his work, he went to the Scotch lakes, Loch Lomond, and Loch Katrine, for a few days of rest. "What beauty," he wrote from there, "what calm, what delightful and sweet solitude! . . . . I could easily stay at these places for a month."

While taking a boat ride on the lake he suddenly found himself in the midst of a great silence. The murmur of the water and the wind ceased; the voices of his companions were silent. Then he noticed that they still spoke, but the natural tones of their conversation did not reach his ears. He was deaf.

Throughout his entire life he had depended upon only one ear and it now had suddenly failed him. The doctors said that it was probably caused by the rupture of a small vessel or a local congestion—a diagnosis which his state of health, his incipient arteriosclerosis, and excessive mental strain tended to verify. But there might possibly be some other direct cause for the deafness, so with this in mind he immediately consulted a specialist in London, and then left for Paris, and from there to The Hague to see other leading specialists.

His letters written during this trip have a note of despondency quite alien to him. Soon, however, resignation triumphed over disappointment. "I hope it is not a permanent affliction," he wrote his wife from The Hague, but already on the following day he added: "Perhaps if this period of trial does come, it will ultimately be of benefit to me." His optimism was of the type which assaults conquerable obstacles but does not vainly waste itself against insuperable odds. He then found succor in Christian submission. On September 23, in spite of the doctor's assurances, he felt quite downcast. "I am indeed now listening through my bad old ear." From The Hague on September 24, he wrote: "I expect to make the best of my deafness, but it pains me that it should have come upon me while I am in this post." On the 25th, he wrote: "May God give you courage to withstand the blow which has struck me, and from which you, as my constant and obliging observer, will suffer more than I. The deaf person has a tendency to withdraw into himself, just as others tend to stay away from him. I have, therefore, much solitude ahead of me, but I am depending upon you with the same faith that I have in the company and solace of my books. As you can see, I am not happy."

In another letter he wrote:

Deafness is a bad thing, I am convinced; it is morally bad, because it disposes one toward unsociability and fear, even though one realizes that very fact, as I do. In a way, it is the closing of one of the windows of the human spirit. I do not doubt that when the windows of the eyes and ears are closed, the internal illumination becomes more brilliant and thinking more elevated . . . . but I thank God for waiting until after my fiftieth year before condemning me to deafness. . . . . How different my life would have been had it come sooner!

From Vienna, where he went the following year seeking still another specialist, he wrote:

Today I met my old colleague, the Serbian Minister in Rome, on the stairway leading to the office of the ear specialist, Urbanschilsch. Such is fame! . . . . he came to the great oracle to seek help for his daughter; he is even more unfortunate than I.

From Rome, March 1, 1903, he wrote:

Of my own accord, I offer this small token [his deafness] to God, with the fervent wish that he keep my children from the paths of temptation, above all from those which morally dishonor and disfigure life. This is worse than deafness, blindness, or paralysis.

"I no longer hear the sweet murmurs and whispers which are the most intimate of sounds," he lamented in another letter. His deafness turned out to be partial, and his condition became slightly better afterward. With time he was freed from the fear of "losing what little hearing was left, the small skylight through which enter the few outside noises that I hear, for the inner noises are quite constant and are for me like sitting on the brink of a waterfall." These loud sounds, which filled him with consternation, gradually disappeared and the partial deafness which remained did not transform his life as he had expected.

Although it was impossible for him to engage in general conversation, to the very end one of his greatest joys was to converse with another person or group which would address him directly. He constantly utilized the already indispensable hearing aid and continued to enjoy, if sitting close enough, lectures and music.

Of course, he could no longer enjoy the theater. If he did go—as he wrote to a Roman lady when refusing her invitation—he would have to pretend to hear: "I should have to make a pretense of hearing, and I have never been guilty of pretense. It is so sad."

And to Dona Evelina Nabuco he wrote:

Perhaps the most painful thing for the deaf person is the straining and the careful attention he must pay to every spoken word. For that reason the tendency of all deaf people is to give up listening.

But Nabuco was not and could not be of the type who gives up. He had infinite patience. His temperament made isolation distasteful, saved him from indifference to the things that went on about him which he could not perceive, and greatly helped him in his efforts. The gesture which became habitual in his last years of cupping his ear with his right hand to facilitate hearing also subconsciously accentuated his interest in what was being said. His friend Count Prozor wrote in the *Revue Hebdomadaire* of July 20, 1912: "His ailment had become an additional attraction. He strained his ear with a pleasant attentiveness which inspired in all complete trust."

When the ladies about him would lower the tone of their voice, he would jestingly complain that he could no longer take part in conspiracies. At dinners he conversed easily with the person sitting at his right, but not so with the person sitting at his left. As for the rest of the guests at table, they were for him, as he noted in *Random Thoughts* (chap. CLXXVI, p. 241), but a large spectacle of faces and gestures: "After turning deaf, the man about town can still enjoy the pantomime but not the comedy of society."

Rodrigues Alves was about to assume the presidency of the Republic. Having been invited to be Minister of Foreign Affairs, Baron Rio Branco, before accepting the post which he was destined to occupy so brilliantly, hesitated and became fearful, distrusting himself and the job. He begged the advice of his old friend, Nabuco, who urged him "not to become a dead weight at a time when the nation wanted to urge him forward." Rio Branco telegraphed him:

> Only to you and Hilário de Gouvêa do I speak openly. I am letting you know an absolute secret. Do not repeat it to anyone. Having been invited, I should reply soon. How can I place myself and the Acre controversy in the political fires of Rio, among people who are all new to me. And what about my health, getting there in the middle of summer? Financially, it would be a disaster for me. I would happily sacrifice two years for it if I could do it in April, but now it would be an enormous sacrifice. . . . . Give me your answer as a close friend. Urgent.

This was on August 7; on the 9th he wired again:

> You may tell Raul [his son, Raul Paranhos do Rio Branco, secretary of the special mission in Rome] about what is bothering me, but keep it secret. I am hesitant . . . . In the long run I shall gain something and be able to work on the projected books. . . . . But, right now, I stand to lose. Many will be unhappy, in spite of my plan not to become involved in politics.

On the 13th he wrote:

> I very much fear doing it, accepting a sterile sacrifice, losing what I could gain in the long run for immediate benefits.

On the 16th he wrote:

> Very downcast, indecisive, almost certain I can do nothing useful. I see . . . . the Acre dispute becoming more and more involved.

On August 30, he finally decided to accept, and wrote to Nabuco asking him not to stop encouraging him:

> I have just given my answer: "I shall make the sacrifice which Your Excellency deems necessary, happy to do so for all I owe to our country and Your Excellency." Keep this secret and divulge it only to Raul with the same reservation.
>
> Rest assured that we shall clear away the obstacles which have been placed in your path, so that you can devote yourself more fully to the problem at hand.
>
> It is resolved, then, that in 1904 I shall try to hand you my staff of office in Rio; if you want nothing of this, then return to London, but understand that you should go into the Ministry, and from there find a way of entering into and influencing our internal politics—something which I do not want to hear of for myself—and perhaps reaching the presidency. I shall occupy myself with the Foreign Ministry only until you are freed by a victory in Rome. The sacrifice which I shall make—with my great family burden, and without any political ambitions at all—is truly enormous. . . . . Great political reforms cannot be made overnight. Loving political life, you can attempt to bring about these reforms opportunely when you return to Brazil, doing your utmost so that we will have a better republic. . . . .
>
> I am not a volunteer; I am a recruit. I expect to get my discharge when you, who were born for politics, finish your task in Rome in 1904.

Before the end of the year, the first memorandum was completed. The doctors, taking his deafness as a symptom of excessive mental strain, prescribed a rest cure for Nabuco. They ordered him to spend three weeks at Cambo in the Pyrenees, as far as possible from the English climate.

In the letters which he wrote to Dona Evelina Nabuco from Cambo, we become acquainted with the picturesque figure of his volunteer travel companion.

November 16: "In Bayonne he decided to come with me to Cambo, and once here he decided to remain until tomorrow. He was wearing a top hat, but last night I had to lend him a pair of pajamas."

November 18: "Today I experienced a slight twinge of sadness during lunch and thought of how really sad it is for me to live here in this complete isolation so far away from you, doing nothing. I even thought of leaving immediately for London. The cause of this attack of melancholia was my companion, a very lovable soul who came here to Cambo and remains so as not to leave me alone, but whose company is much more empty than the depths of solitude. He suffers from profound melancholia, has contemplated suicide, speaks of nothing but his illnesses, and now is taking my Carlsbad water, wearing my shirts, and using my cap which I shall never be able to wear again. He came with only a top hat and overcoat, as I told you. At the table he makes me quite upset, by serving ribs of meat to me with his hands, eating large chicken bones with his hands, and by constantly placing things on my plate with the fork which he has just put in his mouth. Really! He is my companion, but I cannot endure him much longer; if I had St. Anthony, I would pray to him to take this person away as soon as possible. Please pray for him to go. . . . ."

November 19: "How extraordinary! And though it would take but a few hours, it never occurs to him to send for his clothing, nor to his wife to send it to him, so he continues to use mine! It is impertinance carried to the extreme. Really I do not know what to do. The poor man is sick, visibly so, but what a singular illness."

November 20: "My companion is still here. We took a two-hour car ride today without exchanging a single word. He does not speak. Really, it is stretching the bonds of friendship quite far to do the things he does with my clothing. Why does he not send for his own? That is what I cannot understand. If it were not for his excessive spitting along the promenade of the hotel and serving food with his fork, I would say nothing."

November 21: "Today he left. He was a very fine person, very kind to me. But he was not the type of companion I would like at this time. . . . . Now I am alone. Today I fully enjoyed my two-hour ride through these beautiful roads. . . . . I do not want to complain about these lovely people; it is my nerves that keep me from devoting all my time to them."

From Cambo, at the end of his rest, Nabuco wrote to Dona Evelina Nabuco in London:

> Tomorrow I begin my trip home. Thank heavens. I shall be in Paris, closer to you, only a few hours from now. If I still had the energy and did not fear damaging the engine by opening the throttle too much, I would go from here to London nonstop (in train talk). However, I cannot do it. My life is now not only a national trust, but yours and our children's, and while the latter involves love, the former involves honor. Thus it shall be throughout this entire year of work. Then I shall recover, and may God grant, successfully.

Upon returning to London, he finished the written presentation of his case, which filled a large volume in folio entitled *The Rights of Brazil*, and the preparation of additional documentary proofs. Early in 1903 he went to Paris to direct the printing and editing of his work. There he observed a rigorous schedule from eight-thirty in the morning to midnight, his work being interrupted only by meals, the masseur, and an hour's walk after lunch. In his diary, after a month of revising proofs, he noted:

"During this period I conversed with others and received visitors only during the lunch and dinner hours."

The legation in London remained under the care of the chargé d'affaires for over a year and a half. Nabuco spent most of this time working where his memorandum was printed and in Rome, where it was presented. He wrote the second one, the counterplea, in the summer of 1903 in the mountains of Savoy, and the third in the winter of the same year in Nice. These changes did not disturb him much, but rather gave him great pleasure, in spite of the difficulties caused by his large family, his six assistants who always accompanied him, and the transportation of many cases of important documents.

In February of 1903, he arrived in Rome to begin his special mission. He presented his credentials as minister plenipotentiary and delivered officially into the hands of the King of Italy the first memoir outlining the case. The reading of the English memoir, which likewise was presented to the arbiter at this time, caused a great feeling of relief to come over him. He wrote to Dona Evelina Nabuco:

> Today was a great day. I received the English memoir today, and was a hundred times more satisfied with my work, our investigations, and with the distribution and method of presenting my proof. Praise the Lord.
>
> . . . . We still have two more rounds, but the advantage in the first round was ours, quite definitely ours. I feel happy and rested now. I can continue my march forward without stopping to repair the damages caused by the adversary's attack. I came through uninjured. . . . . All that I built up remains intact. It was indeed a solid job.

On the following day he added:

> In spite of everything, the second memoir, in order to be worthy of the first, needs a great deal of revision, and if I do not begin immediately the preparation of the third, the time limit for it will be too short for any serious work.

Having delivered the memoirs, he delayed leaving until the official presentation was made, which he felt obliged to attend because his group had now taken on "the glitter of an embassy."[1] He spent the greater part of that winter and the following in the Eternal City, receiving and gathering together the various reports at various dinners at which he always gave an off-the-record talk. These meetings were, he was once told, beautifully organized. Every moment of this life is described in the letter which he wrote daily to his wife. Because of the difficulties involved in moving the caravan (as Nabuco used to say) to Rome for a short time, and in in-

[1] From a letter to Dona Evelina Nabuco, May 25, 1904.

terrupting the children's schooling, Dona Evelina remained at Pau in southern France. Nabuco left there on February 20.

He wrote to her from Monte Carlo:

It is 5:30 and I have already retired. My hotel room is quite high above the sea, so that when seated at the closed window, I have the waves and the yachts, which are just now lighting up, for companions. After writing the first sentence, I watched the sunset for twenty minutes.

I came from Marseilles to Monte Carlo alone in my compartment; the views of the sea are so beautiful that I was inspired to repeat more than one "Te Deum" out of sheer reverence and contentment. Tomorrow afternoon I am going to continue on to Genoa.

I went to the Casino for a few minutes. What a mass of people, and what a crowd! This game must have a tremendous attraction for these people, if it causes them to spend so much time in this hothouse atmosphere, acting as if they were breathing the balmy air of an open garden. Lourdes and Monte Carlo—these are the two Meccas. After seeing Delos, I had to see Corinth and I must admit that the nausea was worth it. This place is beautiful, the buildings, landscapes, and the ever radiant Mediterranean, but the crowd of mere pleasure seekers is abhorrent to me. How different the two religions are, the two ideals, the two lives! The atmosphere here is saturated with vice and the lust for profit. This idiotic lust for profit hopes to enrich itself under the protection of luck; it is even more sordid than usury, which deprives itself of everything to attain the end it seeks. And what painted women! Yet there should be many beautiful women here, for this is a select cosmopolitan group seeking a fortune. The various nations of the world compete to send these beauties here. What I saw were wasted and painted women. The men are also an unattractive mixture of enthusiasts of all ages and types from all over the world. It all reminds me of a world's fair, a side show of such a fair. This roulette is shameful and so is this prince [of Monaco] who derives his income from it.

February 23

I am writing to you from Genoa where I spent the night. I came by carriage yesterday from Monte Carlo to Menton. I had lunch in Menton, and from there took the train to Genoa. The sky was overcast; when the color of the sky is missing, the Riviera landscape loses its enchantment, because the barren harshness and nude sterility of the soil, mountains, and hills are overpowering. When the blue disappears, as it did yesterday, I prefer the landscapes of the Pyrenees.

February 24

I am writing to you from Rome, where I arrived safely after having a much more comfortable train ride than the other night. . . . .

Here I was met by everyone at the station. The King will receive me informally on the 26th, and on the 27th he will receive me in his role of arbiter. Everything has arrived, thank heavens. Although I have not actually met any of them yet, these people please me very much; in spite of the noticeable contrast in appearance between the visible riches of Paris and London and the relaxed familiarity of everyone and everything here, I find the atmosphere of the Italian cities to be much more pleasant than that of the modern "millionaire" civilization of the great capitals. The clear atmosphere and the abundant sunshine also are important factors.

February 26

Today the King is to receive my mission at 11:00. In the meantime I continue to pray in the oratory, for I have not yet received the official notification of the granting of an audience. Yesterday, Graça, Dantas, and I visited the Forum. They both had dinner here, and Barros Moreira had lunch with me; he is an excellent person, one of the best I could have met here. The excavations at the Forum interested me very much, as they most certainly would have interested you, for where formerly there had been an immense earthwork surmounted by a church, today the first floor of Caligula's palace lies exposed; in the center of this exposed area stands a small church or chapel which still exudes the spirit of early Christianity. To find a bit of Christian Rome in the middle of the pagan Forum was truly a surprising experience; I was made much more cogently aware of the coexistence of paganism and Christianity by this experience than if I had read several books on the subject. The frescoes are very interesting. There is the first known picture of St. Ann, which made me think of the pleasure Mother would have derived from hearing me tell about it. The large fresco depicting the martyrs of Sebaste [the city in Anatolia where the incident described took place] portrays well their fanatical devotion; this is the type of devotion which now typifies our religion. There were forty Christians, condemned to die in chilled water while standing next to a tepidarium or warm bath, which served as an enticement for those who wanted to save themselves by renouncing Christ. In the fresco the martyrs (as far as I could see) are depicted standing in the water up to their knees, while one of their group, beaten, tired, and exhausted from the severe punishment, is stepping out toward the tepidarium. The story goes that life left his body when he entered the water; one of the Roman soldiers was so deeply impressed by this miracle that he took the place of the fallen one among the martyrs. You would greatly enjoy seeing these ancient Christian relics; whatever I see, I see in your behalf, while I constantly think of you; that should serve as a consolation for you in the prison which the five young ones have made for you.

February 27

Yesterday, the day rushed by successfully. In the morning I was received by the King and was enchanted by his genuine sincerity and simplicity. In such an exalted position, there could be no one more unpretentious. As far as popularity at home is concerned, I believe that if he remains unchanged to the end of his life he will become one of the most popular monarchs in Europe. I had lunch in the Quirinal Hotel with Barros Moreira. Afterward I returned to the Forum, this time with Graça, Dantas, and Hermano Ramos, who had just arrived in Rome. We walked for an hour and a half. As you can see, I have been doing much more walking since I left Pau. Costa [José Augusto Ferreira da Costa, Brazilian Minister to Switzerland] dined with me in the evening. He had just arrived in Rome, so I took him to visit the very charming Dona Emma Barros Moreira. I returned afoot, taking still another walk. As far as my hearing is concerned, there is no news of any improvement. However, I thank God every day for not letting it get worse.

Today I am to hand in the memoranda! Raul has not yet arrived. After reading the English memoranda, I shall be better informed as to what we shall do this summer. It is an awful pity that you cannot be here; the sky is so lovely, and the happiness and spontaneity of these people is so infectious that it would be a great relief and a source of pleasure for you to get away from the stifling atmosphere of the northern peoples, such as the English, and, in spite of everything they say to the contrary, the French also. My soul is still split, trying to reach out and attach itself to something which is not here. Nevertheless I am interested in the past, and experience the same old feelings when I am among the ruins. These old feelings are really new to me, since so many new excavations have been made since I was last here.

February 27

You would love this divine city so much! My heart is full of it now! Today was a great day. I received the English memoranda . . . .

March 1

Rome enchants me! I am not sure, but it may be that my hearing is even better. It does not seem so to others, but I want to believe that at times my hearing seems to have changed. Yesterday I had lunch at Barros Moreira's home; he has been an ideal companion for me; we always lunch and dine together. Today I am going to give a small luncheon, and later on in the week, I am planning a small party at the Tivoli for twenty or so people . . . . I am delighted. I do not know whether I shall have the courage to leave Rome in a month's time. If that is the case, I shall look for a place where we can live until next winter, and I hope we shall spend the winter in Rome. In spite of the many small informal gatherings I attend (always with the same friends, and certainly not in the whirl of society life), this one month's rest may do me a great deal of good. Today, while I was taking a drive over Janiculum, a happy and lively young girl about twelve years old ran after my carriage, begging for alms. When Barros Moreira tossed her a copper, I asked the coachman to stop so that I could ask her why such an angel of a child was begging in that way. She, however, could not speak. She was a deaf-mute. That is life. It is best not to go too deeply into things.

March 2

I do not believe that most of those who are here working with me will remain after the month of March. It means much to sacrifice a whole month, particularly when the English have remained in London without any disorganization in service or personnel, and are all ready to begin work again as soon as the bearer of my memorandum arrives. I expect to be back at my office desk in April. Where will it be? That is the question, for I want you and our young ones at my side . . . .

I am quite fearful that I may be forced by my work to go to Paris. I do not want to miss the hearing for the witnesses which is scheduled to take place here in Rome, especially as the Italian climate is good for me. Yet, with my translators and publishers in Paris, and Zagury leaving in May for London, how can I take care of everything in so short a period of time and then go so far away from everything? However, I have enough time to decide what is best to do.

March 3

Today is the great day. I awoke at 6:30, had breakfast at 7:30, and at 8:00 Barros Moreira and I left for St. Peter's. I was in the gallery under the nave behind locked doors from 8:30 until 1:30. After hurrying through lunch at 2:00, I had an audience with the French Ambassador, who showed me the Farnese Palace; yesterday the Austrian Ambassador took me through the Chigi Palace. After seeing the French Ambassador, I returned to the legation, and from there I went visiting; I paid a long visit to Bruno Chaves, the Brazilian Minister to the Holy See. Now, before lunch, I am writing you, with no other care or worry except that caused by a cold! . . . . Now let us talk about Pope Leo XIII's jubilee. It was an incomparable spectacle. Anyone who saw this and the Forum could truly say that he had attended a Roman triumph. It was a deification. God permitted me to hear the silver trumpets and even the "Te Deum." The Pope's entrance into the basilica is beyond description. I can only say that I carefully gathered all the blessings which the Pope was dispensing, and am saving them for you, our children, our relatives, and friends . . . .

The delirious acclamation, the applause, and the waving of handkerchiefs by thousands of Catholics when the Pope was borne through the basilica on his processional sedan chair was an exceptionally impressive sight. The applause was repeated when he suddenly arose from his chair to pronounce a blessing. The Mass in itself was a great event; in this act of human consecration, in spite of its being the divine sacrifice, the Pope, upon entering, disappears in the overwhelming greatness of the nave and the vastness of the building, as does the individual in a multitude. It is an ancient spectacle; the blending of the glorious entry of the emperor with the splendor and tradition of the Christian idea sets one to serious thinking. The effect of this mixture or superposition of historical epochs as symbolized in the ritual and ceremonies is truly extraordinary.

March 4

Barros Moreira, Navenne, and I had lunch together. Navenne told me some very pleasant things about what I read to him in French thirty years ago! Afterward I visited three more ambassadors, in other words, three more palaces. What places of splendor! These embassies are typical of the glory which is Rome. In April and May, there will be many festivities for the arrival of Czar Nicholas II of Russia and Kaiser Wilhelm. I plan on seeing them with you as a mental companion from far away. They also say that if King Edward comes to Naples there will be a naval review. I shall send you a description of yesterday's ceremonies. Graça said he was so impressed that tears came to his eyes. Your friends here all thought about you. I hope that later on you will see something even better, such as the complete ceremony with the Pope himself saying the Mass . . . .

Leo XIII himself has sung the Mass during some of the jubilees; now, however, his age and debility do not permit it. Yesterday's spectacle was simply amazing! I shall never forget the ovation the Pope received when he passed over the milling multitude seated on his "sedia gestatoria," pronouncing blessings on all who were near. I believe that it would have been even more impressive for me had I been able to hear well; nevertheless my heart was filled with emotion, and it overflowed in the form of tears when I thought of you and the children and fervently desired that His Holiness' blessings be bestowed upon you and the young ones.

I am still unsure as to what I shall do, where we shall be reunited, but I feel much better now that I have decided not to stay in Rome after the month of March. I shall spend the months which follow the second and third memoranda with you and then return later to Rome. . . . . I do not know on which day in April we shall meet, but it will be before José's birthday! If my hearing improves, I shall be afraid to leave Rome and go to a place such as Pau, which has a colder climate. If that be the case, you may meet me either in northern Italy or southern France.

March 5

This morning I had an audience with the Russian Ambassador. Unlike his French, Austrian, and Spanish colleagues, he does not live in an old palace. His official place of residence is a museum in which he keeps his huge collection of antique art objects—medallions, rings, bracelets, and gold necklaces; the most precious and outstanding object, a real work of art, is a bronze statue—a copy of Alexander of Lysippo. I had lunch at the Hotel de Russie with my constant companion, Barros Moreira. At 3:00 I visited the German Ambassador, who had not forgotten me since the time when he had been embassy secretary in Brazil. We conversed for over an hour. Then Dantas and I went to the hot baths of Caracalla, which I had seen before; as far as the actual structure of the place was concerned, I was as impressed with it as I was with the Colosseum. We spent another hour among the ruins. After returning home, Count Gubernatis visited me. He is an old erudite scholar who specializes in oriental literature and comparative mythology.

March 8

An hour ago I was received by the Queen [Elena of Montenegro], who is simplicity and sincerity personified. She told me that the King was quite interested in the memoranda which we had presented to him, and that she herself had seen my beautiful atlas. Afterward I took a walk with Barros Moreira; we visited the church of St. Agnes, because yesterday I had paid homage to St. Cecilia at her tomb. Since it was Sunday, the catacombs were closed to the public. . . . . Now I am going out to dinner. . . . . This life is getting to be too much of a social whirl for me. I prefer a ten-hour workday a thousand times more than I do this type of life. Nothing tires me more than this active social life. I am now anxiously awaiting my "letters of emancipation" which will set me free from this life. . . . . The martyrs whose tombs I visit daily should sympathize with me. My anxiety to return to work among my papers has almost reached the fever pitch. I yearn to return to your side and resume work on the great diplomatic contest in which we are engaged.

This coming week will be a terrible series of dinners, and so will the following one, but I have hopes that God will make it the last. Afterward, regardless of what happens, I can lock myself up with my documents.

March 10

Yesterday, after writing to you, I went to look at some furniture for the legation on the Corso. We are quite well established here. We also visited a bathhouse which is considered to be one of the best in the world. One would not think that Rome could support such medicinal luxuries. There were all types of electric baths, pools, old Roman baths, and a large room, similar to those in Paris, which contained all types of apparatus for exercise and massage. There was a saddle which simulated the movement of a camel; according to the attendant, it was good for the kidneys! It was certainly a curious sight to see all of these people engaged in their own particular exercises—on horseback, on bicycles, on the camel, swimming, rowing, etc. That evening I had dinner at the home of the Portuguese Ambassador to the Holy See, Mathias de Carvalho.

I attend all of these dinners, etc., as an offering for the quick recovery of our son, José. It is not that I am ungrateful to my hosts in Rome, or that I do not appreciate their hospitality, but it is too much of an effort for me and does not really lie within the scope of my present interests. This evening I am going to have dinner with the English chargé d'affaires. By the end of next week I expect to have made my way safely through this crisis of daily dinners.

March 11

Yesterday I had lunch at the English Legation; tomorrow I plan to attend a luncheon at the Austrian Embassy; Saturday I have lunch with Bruno Chaves; Sunday several friends are having lunch with me, and on the 14th the Rudinis are having lunch here, while on the first I have lunch with them; and that is all. Is this not enough? I do not know whether I shall live through these festivities. They make me feel so tired—you should really feel sorry for your husband. I shall not stay in Rome after the 23d or 24th. Then I shall go wherever I so desire. Weather permitting, I shall cross the Alps. I want to do the bulk of my work as near to Paris as possible. Already, before leaving, I am tired of so much moving around. May God accompany me wherever I go. When I look at all the papers which I brought with me and at how many I have to take back with me, and at how many I have to leave behind or pack away several times on several more different trips back and forth, I become quite discouraged and feel like going to sleep for a month and completely forgetting all of this.

As you can well see, I am leading a pitiful life now. I am like one who has been forced out of the normal path of his daily life and placed in a position whereby he has to play two incompatible roles on a stage of life. I have been transformed into an actor who has no faith in himself. In other words, I am painfully counting the days, and there are not more than seven in the week and only two more weeks.

. . . . The religious atmosphere is the most pleasant and the most sensible. I, however, cannot turn to it now out of preference; the work and obligations of the mission have made me a slave to society; that is what I am paid for, as the expression goes. Physically I feel much better, but morally this social life would hasten my downfall. I am beginning to feel like a fool listening to some of the conversations which go on in these circles.

March 12

I have just returned from a dinner given at the Austrian Embassy; although it was a splendid banquet laid against a wonderful background, I feel now as if I had just finished a long, arduous, and seemingly unending task. I was friendly and gracious to everyone there, but since I like and really appreciate only the family life, the tired feeling which this life among outsiders and strangers causes in me is almost indescribable. During these occasions, I always picture myself as being an actor in a comedy, always acting in the same indifferent way, obliged to appear to be interested because the impresario is watching and the profession demands it. What quantities of dissatisfaction, reluctance, and lack of conviction would be discovered by anyone who delved into my innermost thoughts!

March 14

. . . . There is really nothing that can compare with the Roman Campagna. The beauty of the light and coloring which transform everything is without equal in the world. I never like to discuss or analyze my emotions; but Rome has made a unique impression upon me. How different my impression of Rome is from those which have delighted me throughout Europe, such as the *landes* [the sandy wooded flatlands south of Bordeaux] where you are, the Basque provinces, the wheat fields of England which lie near the coast, remember?—and all the other places. It is a varied impression, sweet and yet solemn at the same time; it seems as if the outer colors, which transform everything in front of our eyes, had also touched and illuminated us internally. . . . .

March 17

Today I was most cordially received by Queen Margaret. She is always smiling; her manner is much different from that of the present queen, who is a very simple person and still possesses her preregal traits, but both are extremely considerate people. Afterward I went to the legation, took a long walk, and in the evening enjoyed a splendid dinner at Costa's home, at which there were sixteen guests. We were all Brazilians, except MacSwinney.

March 19

. . . . The dinner which I gave yesterday in honor of the Rudinis, who were dining out for the first time since they had gone into mourning, was held in the main salon of the Grand Hotel; everyone here prefers to have dinner in the main dining room with all the other guests; they do not like reserved dining rooms. The daughter of the Marquis of Rudini gave a party near our table. After dinner, the two groups mixed in the "Winter Room" of the hotel, so that the Marchioness actually seemed to be holding court. She is the leader of the social set of Rome. "There she is," is what everyone says when she enters, and immediately all know who it is. I just cannot understand how anyone can seriously and conscientiously choose to follow this type of life; however, since we all should do everything to the best of our ability, I am at least trying hard.

March 20

I have just returned from visiting Priscilla's catacombs, where the body of St. Philomena was found. The tomb in which she was found is no longer there; the tradition is gradually dying out, but there is hope of finding the tomb someday because its measurements exist and no two tombs have exactly the same measurements. Dom Francisco do Rego Maia, the bishop of Pará, went with us. We were also accompanied by our guide, a priest who specializes in studies regarding these particular catacombs. The first-century paintings were very interesting, but the object of most extraordinary beauty was the statue of the Virgin with the Child. It is the oldest statue of Our Blessed Lady in existence, yet in spite of this, one might say it was a Renaissance fresco. It left an indelible mark in my memory . . . .

March 21

Today was a wonderful day. I awoke at 6:30 to hear the Bishop of Pará say Mass in St. Peter's Crypt, just above St. Peter's tomb. Afterward we visited all of the crypts and the basilica. Then I took a ride by carriage with Costa. At 1:00 I gave a lunch for the bishop. . . . . It was a very successful and happy luncheon, with excellent service besides. Everyone was quite pleased with the way the morning had been spent. After that I went to the legation, and then for another carriage ride. I returned with a slight cold and a sore throat. After a ten-minute nap, I went to the private dinner which the Marquis of Rudini gave. I can say that the Marquis and Marchioness of Rudini are my friends now. The dinner was a confirmation of our newly established friendship. We all toasted the success of our cause. This is between you and me. After all, what do you think others would say if they knew? After 10:30, Barros Moreira, the wife of the Brazilian Minister to Austria, Dona Amelia Regis de Oliveira, and I went to the Austrian Embassy where I met many people. . . . .

The most pleasant thing I did today was sending you a telegram. I have as gifts for you part of the cross on which Christ was crucified and a gold reliquary which the bishop gave you.

March 25

. . . . I attended a High Mass of the Greek rite for the first time; it was sung by the monks of St. Basil's. What a tremendous saint he was! I am going to send you a statue and a picture of a beautiful fresco which is in the abbey. . . . . We had lunch with the monks in their refectory, with communal prayers and readings during the meal. I sat next to a bishop from Pennsylvania; we spoke English all through the meal. The Greek Mass was most interesting; they use bread and wine in the distribution of Holy Communion. I very much enjoyed the lunch in the monastery, the visit to the abbey, then the fair at Grotta Ferrata, and the return trip at sunset, watching the sun sink in the west, framed by the arches of the aqueducts and other ruins. In some places the fields seemed to be covered with frost; the individual white flowers in these blankets of white were almost indistinguishable from a distance. The light and coloring of this sky at dusk is a unique sight. Even the smallest bushes and flowers are transformed into pictures of beauty like the pines and cypresses! . . . . How wonderful!

March 29

. . . . In the afternoon, at Mathias' reception I became well acquainted with Princess Pallavicini, of whom I have already spoken; she is an elderly matron who would fit perfectly into the court of Louis XV; a rarity among her species.

I took advantage of Barros Moreira's lunch to have a long conversation with the geographer who is going to have a conference with the King . . . . .

April 1

Yesterday, after lunch, I went to the Russian Embassy, where we made new plans for a lunch next Monday. It is a farewell luncheon which at the same time is designed to make me remember Roman society and feel like returning soon. . . . . Since I shall be here only a few more days, I have to do many things in a short period of time.

April 9

Today, in spite of the general strike, I visited the seven churches. There were no carriages on the streets; even though people do not like to walk long distances, all of the carriages are locked up. Costa, however, used his coach, so for a few hours we enjoyed the luxury of driving about Rome, something which, of course, attracted much attention, for we were in an open carriage. There were no demonstrations, however, not even a whistle. The owners do not permit the carriages to be used because they fear the coachmen, and any malicious damage which might be done to the carriage or the horses. The masses appeared to be as quiet and peaceful as it is possible for them to look. I imagine that most people consider this strike to be a perfect comedy, an inoffensive and ingenuous bluff. I hope things do not get worse.

. . . . I am getting ready to leave Rome as soon as the strike is over.

After spending two months in Rome, Nabuco met his family in Cannes, where they made plans to look for a quiet place in which he could seclude himself while doing research for the second memorandum. He set up his workshop in a peaceful mountain retreat, called Challes-les-Eaux. His residence was an old hotel which formerly had been a castle. He called for his assistants and returned to his old schedule, working from early in the morning until the late hours of the night. In his anxiety to complete the reply within the specified time and still turn in a good job, the only leisure which he permitted himself was to take his daily constitutional.

In a letter to his brother-in-law, Hilário de Gouvêa, he said: "If I lose this case, I cannot ever say again 'Labor omnia vincit.' " In September, the memorandum was finished, and one of the secretaries took it to the arbiter. Nabuco then slipped away to Vienna where he consulted another ear specialist, who subjected him to a long and painful treatment, which completely demoralized him.

Surrounded by his assistants, he worked feverishly for three months in Genoa and Nice, where he finished his work on the third memorandum. It was all over—the end. In February, he went to the Corniche, near Marseilles, to revise and check over the work and to relax.

The first secretary of the mission, Graça Aranha, who was in Paris supervising the printing of the last pages, sent Nabuco a brief two-word telegram: "Good-night." Nabuco saved the telegram, adding a note in pencil to it: "It has been years since I have had the right to sleep. I have now regained that right!"

He returned to Rome once more, to turn in the last plea for Brazil's case and to await the decision of the arbiter. What would it be? "I am in Rome," he wrote to his wife, "and therefore I am equally prepared to go up to the Capitol or to be thrown from the Tarpeian Rock."[2]

[2] Tarpeia, the daughter of Spanish Tarpeius, the governor of the Roman citadel on the Saturnian hill, afterward called the Capitoline Hill, was tempted by the gold on the Sabine bracelets and collars to open a gate of the fortress to T. Tatius and the Sabines. As they entered they threw their shields upon her, and thus crushed her to death. The Tarpeian Rock, a part of the Capitoline Hill, was named after her. From it, in later times, criminals were thrown to their death. Nabuco's expression simply means that he is prepared for glorious triumph or ignominious failure.

CHAPTER XXIII. LIFE IN ROME. THE TRIP TO SICILY. 1904

In his letters to Dona Evelina Nabuco, Joaquim Nabuco wrote:

ROME, March 11

I arrived safely but slightly upset. I took an apartment across the street from the hotel so that I could feel more at home. This is a better arrangement. . . . . I had to rent furniture to convert the master bedroom into a library.

. . . . If you can solve the problem of what to do with the children, come and spend two months with me, and afterward we can go to London together.

March 15

. . . . I am anxious to move into my apartment . . . . Once I have paid some necessary calls—fulfilled some of my obligations, and when the approximate date of the arbitration announcement, which the King said he would set ahead, is decided upon, my only remaining problem will be how and where we can be reunited as soon as possible.

March 17

. . . . On Sunday, I move into my house; that evening I shall give a dinner for Rodrigues . . . . I do not want to move in on Saturday, the 19th, because it is the anniversary of my father's death; true, it is the great feast of St. Joseph, and I should consider his death on this day as being a manifestation of divine intercession. The house is mine then from today, the 17th, for three months. If, in spite of all this, the arrangements which I have made with you fail, then I shall not be able to spend the month of May with you. Everything depends on the decision of the arbiter; if the King wants to speed it up, then you will have to come here so that we can return together. We have many things to discuss and confirm by mail and telegram before that happens.

March 20

. . . . I have . . . . a bad cold, and would very much like to stay in bed, but I do not have the right to be ill, that is not a privilege reserved for me right now. Today I have a heavy schedule, I have to go to a charity matinee this afternoon and to a dinner for sixteen in the evening. The automaton, the diplomat, is the one who undertakes these jobs, while the man, the thinking human being, capable of having feelings, sets himself aside and apart from his other self.

March 21

I slept in my new home, and am quite happy here making plans to see you as soon as possible and then have you come later here to Rome. You will be all right here if the children are in proper hands there. Yesterday I gave the first dinner here. . . .

March 25

. . . . How sad it is to be in these brightly lighted rooms, entertaining people and yet not to have you with me! It seems a mockery to me, a social lie; in the middle of these affairs I often feel like retiring to my bedroom; many times I have walked through the crowded rooms with my distracted thoughts miles away from here; when the guests leave, a great feeling of relief comes over me, relief from this unnatural life, this unreal pleasure, which is devoid of soul and heart. How much better it would be, if, instead of this life, I could return to the old routine of ten to twelve hours of work per day! Often I would forget myself, and I found comfort in the pleasure of feeling that I had completed the task assigned me and fulfilled my obligations in a spirit of perseverance and dedication. However, I must overcome these tendencies and not let myself be downcast . . . .

I shall probably end up by spending much more money on the apartment to make it more comfortable. I dislike, however, one melancholy event, ... and that is moving into a house. I certainly do not enjoy being away from home, but enjoy it even less when I am in a house elsewhere. In a hotel one is fooled by that spirit of being en route, of being on a trip, of thinking that he will return home soon, while in a home, the absence of the family is sensed more. However, God will help me. A curious thing has just happened! I suddenly feel much happier. . . . . perhaps it is that perennial fountain of joy which I have in my soul.

Good Friday

Today I have attended the various devotional services. I engaged in my own form of abstinence on this great day. I went up the "Holy Stairs" [the church of Scala Santa has a long stairway which the penitent climb on their knees], and to the Church of the Holy Cross of Jerusalem. I did not climb the stairway on my knees; I merely attended the devotional services, which you should see, particularly on this day. Since the stairway is crowded, the penitent take much longer in making the ascent. Truly it is the most beautiful devotion to the divine passion that exists in the world: climbing on one's knees up the stairway used by our Lord!

April 7

Yesterday I attended an auction of the sculptor d'Epinay's great collection. I purchased a big beautiful alabaster Virgin, holding the child, Jesus, in her arms. It now presides quite well over my work in the office . . . .

April 8

Yesterday I had a most enjoyable lunch with Mathias de Carvalho. . . . . I am terribly anxious to see this separation of ours come to an end and return to our normal life. There is not much point in my writing to you about people who do not interest you, and who are only casual social acquaintances. They are the type of acquaintances one makes at the various spas and watering places.

April 9

Yesterday I gave a dinner here, a small one, but more expensive than if it had been given in the Grand Hotel. Everyone enjoyed it very much, except myself.

I could not get you and the children out of my mind. I could not listen to the conversation which was going on about me and did not feel like taking part in it, so I abandoned myself to longing for you and the children. . . . .

April 12

Yesterday, after a lengthy conference with the subsecretary, Fusinato, I took a long two-hour walk with Navenne, and attended a banquet given by the Marchioness Gonzaga at the Grand Hotel. (I am so confused and homesick for you and the family that I took a letter from Carolina out of my wallet and read a part of it to the Marchioness!) This morning I attended an auction; this evening I am giving a dinner in honor of the Marchioness of Rudini, and since it is to be her party I have invited about forty people to come over after dinner. The dinner is at 8:30 and it is now 8:00. . . .

April 12

I am so tired today! What an effort it is to keep the members of Roman society satisfied! They are so pleasant and yet so unrestrained. The dinner yesterday was quite a success. I was obliged to say a few words which were warmly applauded. . . . . I feel that I was a success, at least among those in my small circle of friends, for deafness keeps me from mixing in with too large a group. Judging from the manner in which I was received here, I can say almost certainly that my book, *Random Thoughts*, will be successful, but in a limited sense, for it is a carefully prepared and serious work. Everything is now for me a means to an end: the welfare of you and the children. Fortune, fame, high positions, I desire them only in so far as they relate to you and to the youngsters. . . . .

Yesterday, as I have already said, eight of us had dinner together: the Marquis and Marchioness of Rudini, Mme Maria Mazzoleni, the Barros Moreiras, the Italian Foreign Minister, Senator Malvano, Count Keller from the Russian Embassy, and myself. After dinner, the following people arrived: the Marquis and Marchioness Guerrieri-Gonzaga, the Marquis and Marchioness Carlo de Rudini, Count Piella, the Prince of Belmont, Count Witten, the Pachecos, Bruno Chaves and his wife, Raul Regis, Dantas, and Veloso. There were about twenty of us, and since I had hired a pianist, we danced in the salon. By midnight everyone had gone home. It was a small intimate party given in honor of the Marchioness, who was celebrating her birthday on that day. Since I had made preparations for forty people, there was much food left over. I am dividing the food among the families of the doormen of this building, the mission, and the building in which the mission is located. The doorman of the mission building has a five-year-old daughter in whom I am much interested; she is subject to frequent convulsions and suffers from hydrocephalia [an illness caused by a hydrencephalocele, a hernial protrusion through a cranial defect of the meninges containing cerebrospinal fluid]; she is always happy and smiling in spite of having a paralyzed arm. I am going to do my utmost to see that she always receives the proper care.

April 13

Today my servant, Alfred, awoke late, and I told him that we were not taking him to London. I do not want to take him, and forgive me, but I would not even "try to keep myself" if I felt that, by so doing, any harm were suffered by someone, whether he deserved it or not, particularly someone who had been close to me for years. My main concern is that he find a job which suits him. Do not think that I want him at the legation. It is enough that you find him unpleasant . . . . But I also do not want him to be unhappy later because of some action on my part or his. He just is not doing a good job and that is all there is to it. . . . .

Today, the 13th, I attended a dinner at the home of a Dr. Dupuy, at which there were thirteen guests in attendance. Afterward I was obliged to go to a charity ball; I stayed but a minute. I am all agog; after I have completed my sacrifice to Roman society, I shall be with my family sooner than you think, a family which means more to me than anything else on earth, and which is the source of my life-blood, even here where I can think only about them.

April 15

. . . . On Sunday I am giving a dinner at the Grand Hotel for thirty-six people, and another for forty-two on Saturday, the 23d (remember?). Afterward, I shall go to Sicily for fifteen days. By the middle of May the social set begins to leave Rome. Then I shall arrange to go and see you. The meeting date will depend on the time when the King announces his decision. . . . .

April 17

Today I am giving a big dinner. Next Sunday I have dinner with Princess Pallavicini. On the second I shall pack, and on the third I leave for Sicily. I have to rest after this first engagement with worldly forces, and gather my strength for the next encounter in May. In June we shall talk about it and by July 1, I expect to be free and ready to embark upon a trip to the various watering places with my entire troop. What a great day that will be! Especially if we are victorious! Soon the only thing on my mind will be the King's decision. . . . .

April 18

Today one of my major struggles begins, and from now until next Monday your husband is to be pitied. I shall awake tired from the party and be faced . . . . with another which is to be given on Saturday, and for which I have already invited sixty people! I do not even want to talk about it; these monstrous dinner parties make me feel ashamed, but since I have very little time, I have to do in two parties what others do in ten. But . . . . the work, excitement, movement, and yet the futility of it all!

April 20

I am almost crazy with longing to get to Sicily and be able to rest for a fifteen-day period and be freed from this constant round of dinner parties.

Yesterday I recited A. Marquet's poem about Granada to Countess Colleoni:

> Be warned against the siren songs you hear down here
> Oh traveler! Because of them you may not hear
> The sweet and tender voice back home which says to you
> "The ones whom you forget may well forget you too!"

I then added: "Now you can see what Providence really is! She took my hearing away because I was coming to Rome so that I would be unable to hear the song of the mermaids." The mermaids here are not women, nor the socially elite, but the sky, the colors, the gentleness of the climate, and the *dolce far niente* spirit which dominates everyone and envelopes everything. All of the people here forget and are forgotten by the rest of the world. Our compatriots no longer want to leave; they dedicate themselves completely to listening to the song of the mermaids who live in the fountain of Trevi. The men are quite gallant . . . . Mme X has been seen with apparently habitual women-chasers, and she is already fearful of not being properly seated at the banquet table. When Mr. Z is far away from his wife, he indulges in the pleasure of being charming to other women. The other day when they were together, she more or less placed a damper upon his activities of this type. While he was talking to the Countess of ———, his wife, our very happy part-Brazilian compatriot, sneaked up behind him seductively and temptingly covered his mouth with her hands. Mr. B, who is all protocol and extremely reserved, was horrified by this Brazilian display of conjugal love in a society in which such indiscretions are tolerated only during the honeymoon period, as now with the newly married couple, the N's. The same is true of the young Marchioness. She is a living picture of Teresa Estrella, in the manner in which she speaks out of the side of her mouth, in the constant animation expressed in her facial movements, and in the rapidity of her speech. She is always surrounded by a swarm of professional seducers who are accompanying and encouraging the growth of this lovely butterfly. In a word, it is the life which has always typified Rome, eternal Rome, eternal in the arts of seduction and the cult of love.

Deafness keeps me from catching all the details regarding the life of these people; my courting here is confined to old ladies such as the Princess Pallavicini. When and if I do show an interest in any others younger than she, such as the Marchioness of ———, it is only for the sake of politics, friendship, and the affection they have shown me, as they do to all others, for this social group is most friendly and affectionate. . . . .

Look at all the time I have wasted. But Rome is like that. I could never settle down here because the only thing that one can do here is "live" (enjoy life, leisure, and *dolce far niente*). My heart is full already and I am preoccupied with matters of a different type. I am today, as they said of Gladstone near the end of his life, "an old man in a hurry." His was an anxiety to finish a political mission of considerable import in the few remaining years of his life. Mine is to assure my children of having a less precarious life than that which they would have if I were to die now. The solution of this problem will be the chief cause for my cogitations and deliberations, after I have left this Roman delirium behind me, this fever of doing nothing, in which I have lived for a month, and which I shall have to endure for another month, after returning from Sicily. What an extraordinary struggle this is! The things I have to do to gain the Rupununi for us—this has been one of the most futile experiences imaginable, especially for me, who am, as I said, an "old man in a hurry," anxious to finish his work and tasks, and who has devoted twelve hours daily to hard work and research for years!

April 21

Your husband is quite tired of this worldly and culinary company! Yesterday, Hermano and his daughters and the Barros Moreiras had dinner here; the Pachecos and Veloso came over for tea. All I did was talk about you. A dream come true would be to spend a month with you at Cap Martin, but that would be too late and too expensive. I need this trip to Sicily as much as someone who is asphixiated needs air. After my return we will plan everything. By then I shall have paid my final tribute to Roman society. What a day yesterday was, and today and tomorrow with dinner and a "lake" to worry about! I am planning to have a "lake" set among the twelve tables, in which there will be placed an illuminated Venetian gondola! We have spent days making and remaking lists of guests so that they will be properly distributed. Your poor husband! But God will help me because He is aware of my intentions. I shall be quite tired during the next few days. Afterward, I shall recompense you by sending you a daily account of my impressions of the Sicilian journey.

April 22

Yesterday I dined at the home of the Marchioness of Rudini. The Marquis drank to the success of our mission. He had already done this a year ago. I consider this to be a good sign; do not breathe this to a soul. After dinner we all went to Countess Taverna's dance. Today the Rudinis had lunch here. Tomorrow is the day for my grand banquet. May God spare me from its being an immense fiasco!

. . . . I do not leave for Sicily until Tuesday. In all I shall have about fifteen days of rest. In Rome I have had no rest—I work for the mission in the manner for which I am most poorly suited: dining, giving dinners, living a life of constant agitation, going from one place to another, visiting, making new one-day acquaintances . . . . things which are not worth the effort expended. "Martha, you occupy yourself with many things, but only one is worth while." In this world I consider only one thing to be worth while and that is my family; but the diplomatic life has embroiled me in all kinds of things, just exactly like Martha—that of being hospitable and sociable.

April 24

Praise the Lord! My struggle is over. Today I have dinner with the Princess Pallavicini, then I escape to Sicily to avoid the returning of my invitation by all of those whom I invited and who feel obliged to do so. Since there were sixty-seven of them, some twenty would be enough, and I could not face another ordeal like those of the past month.

Yesterday's party was wonderful. Everyone told me that they had never attended such a beautifully decorated dinner. Only God knows why I did it! The tables were presided over by the outstanding women of Roman society. Afterward they danced, and this required the use of the three main salons of the hotel. Imagine what the bill is going to be! I hope they have a conscience, but it will probably be very high.

I do not want to think about it any more. This is another reason why I am going away to Sicily. I want to get away and place time and space between this lavish party and myself. I did not enjoy the party because of your absence. During the evening, Graça heard many hopeful things said about our side in the arbitration. And that is my main object and goal. . . . .

The feminine beauty of Brazil was amply represented by MacSwinney, Hermano's daughter, and Nazareth. The most beautiful of the Italian women was the Princess de Teano, although the most gracious and elegant one was the lady who sat at my left during dinner. I told her that I was sitting between beauty and genius. My dinner partner on the right was Ristori . . . .

The lake was placed in the center and surrounded by twelve tables. The tables were occupied only on one side so that the guests could look at the decoration without turning around. The shores of the lake were lighted, and in the middle there was a Venetian gondola flooded with light. This little scenic centerpiece was further enhanced by rocks, rushes, and various types of greenery. Along the shores of the lake, the beauty of the women, their perfumes, and jewels, and the gaiety and animation of this huge living picture charmed not only the guests but also those who were watching through the doorways. I received an ovation from the Marchioness of Rudini, followed by a virtual shower of flowers from her side of the room. . . . .

April 26

This is a crucial day for me. I had a big quarrel with Alfred yesterday. . . . . I was quite angry, that is if one can describe as anger a feeling of utter indignation, but still not devoid of charity. This emotion is however bad for me, my heart, and my hearing. Last night the two things for which I have been reprimanding him for years (his lack of zeal and his abuse of my patience) were carried to such an extreme that I finally was forced to take drastic steps. I told him that his account would be settled this morning, and that his services were no longer required. This morning I dismissed him irrevocably.

My trip to Sicily has been delayed by this mishap (the loss of a servant); I feel now, even more than before, and it is probably because of this unseasonable occurrence that I shall not replace him definitely until I can find a man who can stay with you and the children when I am away, something which was not true of Alfred, whom you had always wanted to dismiss and rightly so.

April 27

Yesterday I had dinner with Barros Moreira; Hermano and his daughters, and Veloso were there. Afterward we went to see the fireworks.

I am completely up in the air, now that Alfred is gone; it will be a long time before I can find someone who knows where all my things are, the way Alfred did. He knew too much and took advantage of the fact that I was unfamiliar with the whereabouts of my clothing. I shall miss him for a long time. I wrote him a note of dismissal but was not actually there when he left. Barros Moreira told me that Alfred was sobbing. Only God can see into our souls. Perhaps, in spite of all his defects of character, Alfred was devoted to me. But what is done is done.

MESSINA, April 30

Yesterday evening at 7:20, Raul Rio Branco and I left Rome and at 9:20 today we arrived at Messina. From this lovely Sicilian countryside I want to express the great longing for you which I feel in my heart, the great sadness I suffer because you are not here at my side, enjoying these new vistas, and also I want to express my gratitude to God for enabling me to see His spectacular creations. From Reggio to Messina is an hour's trip by ship; it is similar to the trip from Rio to Niterói—the two shores are so close. Calabria is more beautiful and colorful and fresher than the Riviera. It is summer here—a most agreeable summer. The sea is blue like ours and the climate reminds me of home. Sicily's mountainous coast, in spite of being arid and volcanic, somewhat like the coast of the Riviera, has in it charm and gentle beauty, a quality which reminds me of our granite cliffs at home. The entrance to the fortress of Messina, and the turn which the ship has to make in order to enter, as well as the line of crowded houses along the wharf, all remind me of Recife. The city has a lovely freshness; the paving of the streets with large stones lends an air of neatness and cleanliness like that of a city square or an ancient forum, which indeed it probably was. There are many original and picturesque details to observe which are quite beautiful—for example, the paintings on the wagons and carts. However, we still have not gone very far into the interior of Sicily. Tonight we shall sleep in beautiful Taormina. Raul is an excellent traveling companion, chiefly because he is an enthusiastic tourist. Today he arose at 5:00 to watch the colors of the early morning sun—I shall do the same thing tomorrow, for they say it is the most beautiful time of day in Taormina. We shall travel in the meantime by ship. The main altar in the cathedral is the richest mosaic work I have ever seen. In it is kept a letter which the Most Holy Virgin is said to have written to the city of Messina! When I entered, Mass was being sung and I received a blessing for my trip. . . . .

TAORMINA, May 1

Yesterday, after we had visited Messina, which aside from its location, its Sicilian character, and the altar of the cathedral, offered nothing novel or interesting to me, we left for Taormina along the wonderful road which follows the coast. I recalled a similar ride we had enjoyed together along the Riviera, although looking out upon the Ionian Sea and the distant Italian mainland was a new sensation. On approaching Taormina, the first glimpse of Mt. Etna was spectacular. It was an incomparable sensation. Both the grandeur of its massiveness and the tranquillity of the sight of the terrible volcano's shoulders, covered by a mantle of snow, are more impressive than any volcanic eruption which might occur. Taormina is a paradise. Taking the various differences into consideration, it is a sight comparable to the Corcovado [a mountain which dominates the city of Rio de Janeiro], but Etna has the added depth and significance lent to it by the Greek myths and history which we lack in Brazil. It is simply marvelous. This morning I awoke at five o'clock to see the effects of the light upon the snow, but the sun was not up yet; nevertheless, it was deeply moving to watch the sun dissolve the gray mist which enveloped the volcano, and to see the outline of the huge form slowly appear. At eight o'clock we visited the ruins of the Greek theater, from which one looks out upon a beautiful panorama—like looking down at our beaches from our mountains. This will be a full week for me. Today during Mass in the cathedral, I suddenly felt as if I were in the church of Maricá. The people are similar to ours, with the same poverty, the same happy simplicity and grateful sincerity. . . . .

SYRACUSE, May 2

What a long and wonderful day, and how good God is to spare me the strength to still feel such emotion! At seven o'clock we left Catania, and, remaining always within sight of Etna, we arrived in Syracuse at ten o'clock. Yesterday in Catania I was in the city dedicated to St. Agatha; today I am in one dedicated to St. Lucy; you already know that these saints are two of my special patronesses. It was St. Agatha who saved Catania from the torment of lava from Etna, and St. Lucy is the guardian saint of Syracuse. The five hours from two o'clock until seven were most fascinating. We went from the fountain of Arethusa[1] to the museum, where I saw the beautiful Venus of Anadiomene and where I admired the Syracuse medallions and the rare coins; from there we went to the large stone quarries, where thousands of defeated and enslaved Greeks suffered, and where one can still see "Dionysius' ear"—a big cut in the wall which resembles the human ear and possesses strange acoustical qualities; it is said that Dionysius could hear even the slightest noise made in the prison by listening at this spot. Then we saw the Roman amphitheater, the Greek theater, the supposed tomb of Archimedes, the road of the tombs, and many other places. I was impressed most of all by the stone quarries. All of this impresses me immensely, and fills me with a sense of life and admiration. In these moments I am seeing not only for myself but for you and our little children. After five hours of sightseeing, I still had to take a long walk after dinner in order to buy postcards for you.

Now I am going to retire, for tomorrow will be an equally arduous day. We are going on two three-hour excursions. Here we are in a world of mythology and Greek history! What numerous recollections! In the Capuchin quarry I seemed to hear the cries of the prisoners, and the image of Alcibiades[2] has been before me ever since I first came upon the site of his ill-fated expedition, which probably because of the persecution against him was so fatal to Greece. And the myths? The Cyclopes,[3] Galatea,[4] Arethusa, Proserpina.[5] We are in the land where the genius of Greece is always being evoked. I cannot describe to you the inexpressible and ineffable fascination which this place holds for me!

[1] Arethusa, one of the Nereids (fifty daughters of Nereus and Doris), was a nymph who was changed into a fountain on the island of Ortygia near Syracuse.

[2] Alcibiades, son of Clīnias and Dinomache, was brought up by his relative, Pericles; in 415 B.C. he was appointed, along with Nicias and Lamachus, as commander of the expedition to Sicily. There occurred the mysterious mutilation of the busts of the Hermae, for which he was accused and asked to stand trial. He deserted, but later returned to Athens as a hero after being victorious in battle.

[3] The Cyclopes were associated with the east coast of Sicily, and particularly with Mt. Etna, where, according to Virgil, they were servants in Vulcan's forge.

[4] Galatea, sea nymph, daughter of Nereus and Doris, was the lover of the Cyclop, Polyphemus; they both lived in Sicily.

[5] Proserpina (Persephone)—goddess, daughter of Zeus and Demeter. Sicily was the scene of her rape by Pluto.

May 3

. . . . Today I walked to the Ciani stream, which has wild papyrus, imported from Egypt centuries ago, growing on its banks. The clear waters of this river or rivulet come from a beautiful blue spring in which Cyane, the nymph, was transformed by Pluto because she was opposed to the rape of Proserpina. Yesterday I mentioned to you the fountain of Arethusa, another Greek metamorphosis. This Ionic countryside abounds in phenomena of this sort. I find myself surrounded by the most beautiful works of poetry, which humanity in its youth gave to us. Today, now that it is old and tired, humanity has turned to science, for it has lost all imaginative powers.

Upon returning to Syracuse, I visited the cathedral, which is built upon the site of the temple of Minerva. St. Lucy's tomb is in the cathedral. . . . .

At 6:30 I returned from a visit to the fort of Euryalos[6] in Syracuse. What an amazing view one has from there—what an immense historical stage setting unfolds itself! Mt. Etna and Calabria were obscured, but the Ionian Sea in all the glory of its broad expanse was enough to arouse my deepest admiration. The fort—a Greek fort—was a worthy enough object in itself for a pilgrimage! But the view was even more awe-inspiring than the ruins. Before me I had the entire stage on which the Sicilian expedition took place; one can say that I had the grave of the power of Athens before me—Athens did not have faith in its great man, so it succumbed here. In contrast to the recollections I have of the Carthaginians, the Romans, and even of the great Archimedes, this one stands out, obscuring all others. Nothing can compare with this afternoon's experiences which will live in my memory till my dying day. As I told you before, this is a consolation for not being able to see Athens.

GIRGENTI, May 4

Today I do not have much to relate to you. I awoke early at eight o'clock, something to which I have now become accustomed, and took a short carriage ride. Then I visited the Convent of St. Lucy, where I saw an unusual arrangement for conversations between the nuns and visitors, something which made the worldly life of the old Portuguese convents more understandable to me. At 10:20 I left Syracuse, which I shall never forget, but not until I had searched for the works of Thucydides, Plutarch, Titus, Livy, and Ovid in order to read about Alcibiades' expedition, the Roman capture of Syracuse, the metamorphoses of Cyane and Arethusa, and the mythology about Mt. Etna. We were aboard the train from 10:00 A.M. until 9:00 P.M., eating both lunch and dinner on the train. I have just arrived at this hotel and can now write to you. It is 9:30.

As you can see, I now go out in the morning, which is really something for me. Furthermore, I am traveling without a servant. There is not the slightest possibility of my rehiring Alfred, who would not work and did not like his work; however, the servant problem is going to become quite serious for me. I did not keep the one I had in Rome. He could not see well, and he moved about with difficulty, always fearful of further complicating his various ailments; he would have the hair dresser

[6] Euryalos—a fort on the western outskirts of Syracuse, now known as Monghibellisi.

and dyer come over to dye his hair . . . . Night has already fallen; I was unable to see anything on my way into town. Tomorrow the beauty of the Girgenti temple will be unfolded before me. It should be a new experience for me, because never before have I seen a Greek temple still standing and intact.

Palermo, May 6

. . . . We took a long walk in order to see all of Palermo. It is a big and beautiful city, with a sea front like a terrace overlooking the sea. It reminds me of Nice. It lies in a mountain amphitheater, and thus reminds me of St. Sebastian. There is nothing new here for those of us who already know the Riviera and Italy. It is said that the climate here is delightful in winter, and I wholeheartedly agree; the southern part of the island, however, should be even more pleasant.

May 7

. . . . Today we saw two marvels, the Palatine Chapel and the Cathedral of Monreale. Both of them possess endless mosaic works of a beauty worthy of St. Mark's, with even more brilliance and gold, or at least more lustrous gold. Palermo is really a spectacular city. We have gone all through it carefully, and, of all there is to see in the city, nothing is more beautiful than Monreale. From there, one can look down upon a sea of orange trees rolling down between hills to the curve of the beach. It is the way St. Sebastian would look if it possessed this fertility and this open ground.

Tomorrow we shall probably return to Naples by sea. Now all that is left for me to see are Paestum, which is near Naples, the new excavations at Pompeii, and perhaps Capri . . . .

May 8

Today we shall probably leave the enchanted isle of Sicily and go directly from Palermo to Naples—nothing is definite, however, for my correspondence has not yet arrived. For eight days now, ten days to be more exact, I have not received any mail from you.

This morning I attended Mass, took a walk, and now I am going to have lunch; afterward I shall pack my bags in order to leave, if we go at seven-thirty. I have managed quite well without a servant, but I must confess that I can get along without a servant for a matter of only a few more days while traveling in Europe. . . . .

Naples, May 10

. . . . Yesterday I awoke early, attended Mass, ate in a hurry, and caught the noon train. Since then I have been traveling until eight this evening. I traveled from Palermo to Messina by train along a beautiful coast, but there were so many tunnels! Together with the fifty tunnels we went through along the Calabrian coast, they add up to an amazing total—but they are so dark, and so full of fumes and heat! This morning at five-thirty we were ready. We traveled from Agrópoli to Paestum in a carriage which could hardly move. The poor horse! If you could only see the inn where we had coffee and milk! The coffee was served in a container almost as large as a hand basin. I used a cup and utensils which I carried with me. They offered me a room in which I could shave—it was the bedroom for the family, with five filthy beds; I ran out in horror. Fortunately we had better luck in the small restaurant of the little inn where we had lunch. The temples are wonderful. I did not visit Paestum thirty years ago and have been regretting it until today. I have finally been freed from this remorseful feeling. Here are the most beautiful Greek temples in existence outside of Athens. This is a consolation to me for not being able to see the Parthenon. We were in Paestum from eight until two —there is nothing else to see except the temples. At two we embarked upon a six-hour train trip to Naples. I have become a traveler as you can well see. I was not very fatigued when I arrived. At nine we had dinner. Now I am beginning to feel the effect of this day—so I shall retire. Naples has changed very much since I last saw it in 1874—there are new buildings in all parts of the city; but I shall have to wait until tomorrow to see the new city. From the huge terrace of the hotel I have a superb view of the lights of the city, but whoever has enjoyed the views from Santa Teresa and Nova Cintra [mountains in the city of Rio de Janeiro] can never find another comparable sight. Tomorrow morning I shall be able to view the sea; it should be wonderful. How Etna puts Vesuvius to shame! Still, at sunset the view is lovely.

In Palermo there are images set up for public devotion at every street corner; every night they are ablaze with candles lit by worshipers. Twice last Sunday I happened upon an immense bier on which the people were carrying the crucifix. I believe this to be a good omen. St. Rosalia is the patron saint of Palermo. . . . .

May 11

It is nine o'clock in the morning. My next letter will be from Rome. I am leaving for there in the evening by sleeping car today. We are going to visit Pompeii and afterward Naples itself, which will appear so different to me after all these years. Nothing makes us realize how much we have changed as does a visit to a place about which we have formed a childhood impression. Life is divided into periods, or seasons, each of which has its own way of thinking. . . . .

. . . . tomorrow . . . . Tittoni's lunch. Attending these luncheons and dinners which typify Rome's materialistic life makes me more weary than did all of the Greek temples or even a trip to the Tacutú and Rupununi rivers in the Guianas, from which I have strayed a long way. However, I shall now return to them . . . .

May 11, 7:30 P.M.

I still have a few minutes during which I can send this farewell note to you. Not taking into account the two hours involved in getting there and returning, we were in Pompeii from one o'clock until three. Pompeii was not disillusioning to me at all; on the contrary, I appreciated it even more than I did thirty years ago—especially the Vetti house, which is for us the life of ancient Rome. It helps us to achieve a better understanding of the rest of the city, because of what can be deduced from the wall frescoes and the marble bas-reliefs which have been so well preserved. I purchased a large collection of postcards, but it is a pity to send these by mail. I am saving them, as I have so many other things, for the time when we are happily reunited. Naples, on the other hand, is a different story. It no longer means anything to me. It is a large city like so many others, full of new apartment buildings for the middle classes, and even the lower classes, but without the local color of yesteryear. Their appearance is always the same. These immense beehives have been built everywhere in Genoa, Rome, and in Paris. They hide the beauty of the ancient lines of the cities; they have engulfed the picturesque retreats such as the Graziella in Naples. I do not know what has happened to Sorrento; I hope it has not lost its poetic quality. Either the city has lost its quaint old Neapolitan character, or else I am the one who has changed.

Now I am going to have dinner; at midnight I shall return to Rome. God has been with me throughout this entire trip. I have moved about from one enchanted spot to another.

ROME, May 12

I am now writing to you again from Rome, thank heavens! My arrival here on Ascension Day is quite a coincidence. I have already gone to Mass, had lunch with the Foreign Minister, and attended the horse races; now it is raining, so I have come indoors to warm up with a cup of tea.

A new servant was waiting for me. He is twenty-two years old and called Spartacus, a good name for a former abolitionist's servant; I call him by his family name, Lapo. We shall wait and see how he turns out. . . . .

May 13

Today I am beginning to live my normal life again. I have a world of things to do to put everything in order.

The three-month rental period for this house expires on June 17. Then I shall join you. That is the problem which I have to solve next. You are so far away! . . . .

May 19

. . . . The hot weather has already begun here—a burning sun. Yesterday I had dinner in a restaurant which is frequented by Roman society in the summertime. It is not, however, first class, for it has only one decent view and one dines in the open air. It was a farewell dinner given by the Marquis and Marchioness of Gonzaga. I am clearing up my work so that I can be at the beck and call of the King and of you. Soon I shall have finished; this heat makes any type of work seem arduous.

May 25

Today I am having my dinner on the Pincio, in the moonlight, with a view of Rome at my feet. The Pincio closes at eight, so that we shall be left alone, and there will be a mandolin concert. . . . .

May 26

Yesterday's dinner was quite successful. The Pincio was wonderful in the moonlight, especially since the garden was exclusively ours. . . . . Today the King's Councilors meet, and today also is the day of Rome's patron saint, St. Philip Neri! I told the general that I was anxious to know the hour, so that I could light a candle at the altar of Our Lady of Perpetual Help. Although I was not serious about it, Barros Moreira ordered a candle. It is a symbolic homage to our need of divine protection.

May 28

Today I am giving a dinner at the Pincio, and on Monday, a small dinner at home for the new bishop of Pará. After that, there will be nothing else to do until the decision is announced, except to wait. May God guide us! Forgetting all longings and yearnings, what I am most thankful for is the fact that the children are getting strong at the seashore. . . . .

May 29

Yesterday, I gave another dinner at the Pincio. It was deeply appreciated, but, being the usual automaton who prepares and plans the affair, I found myself saying: "How happy I would be if all of this were to fade away like a useless dream, and I were to awaken at home, the only real thing that there is in life!" However, all of this is coming to an end . . . .

CHAPTER XXIV. THE ANGLO-BRAZILIAN DISPUTE AND THE 1904 DECISION

A vast area was under dispute. More than 30,000 square kilometers were being submitted to arbitration. Admittedly, the territory was uninhabited; the English Foreign Minister, Lord Salisbury, when discussing the dispute with Nabuco, referred to it as "a region in which there is not even a single cow." It was also equatorial and torrid. But it was of primary importance because of its location, for it opened the Amazon basin to England, and the Essequibo basin to Brazil. Both countries desired the territory because of its immensity, and its unexplored potentialities—rich land, endless jungles, savannas, and great rivers with many tributaries. One of these rivers, the Rupununi, which is the principal affluent of the Essequibo, is now entirely within British territory, in spite of the fact that the first British explorers did not cross it except with the permission of the Portuguese. The other river, the Tacutú, since the announcement of the Italian king's decision, has served as the boundary between Brazil and British Guiana. At the mouth of the Tacutú is an old Portuguese fort, abandoned, unfortunately, by the Brazilians. Its sphere of jurisdiction could not be proved by either party to the dispute; however, it attests to the former Lusitanian supremacy in the lands traversed by the Tacutú. The river is one of the main feeders of the Rio Branco, which has its source at the confluence of the Tacutú and Uraricoera rivers. The Rio Branco flows into the Amazon, as does the Rio Negro, and these constitute the principal Brazilian river system. One of its tributaries brings the waters of the Pirara River to the Tacutú; the Pirara played an important part in the dispute because it is the key to the Amazon Valley. The Pirara River serves as the only communication link between the basins of the Essequibo and the Amazon, which are separated from each other by high mountain ranges and desert plateaus.

The first person who thought of claiming this territory for England, a territory which previously had been recognized as being Portuguese even on British maps, was a German who had been naturalized as a British subject, Sir Robert Schomburgk; he had been sent to this area by the Royal Geographic Society "to study the physical geography and astronomy of the interior regions of British Guiana." "The purpose of his trip," as Lord Palmerston explained when requesting a passport for Schomburgk from the Brazilian Minister, "was simply to make discoveries along the unexplored frontier areas," and the passport was necessary "because while exploring the mountain range which divides the watersheds of the Amazon and Essequibo basins, he might possibly cross into Brazilian territory several times."

In his first reports to the Royal Geographic Society, he recognized the frontiers claimed by Brazil. He spoke of his arrival by way of the Repununi at a spot called Mt. Anai, "which is a place generally considered to be the southwestern extremity of the British colony." Afterward, he was fascinated by the beautiful little town of Pirara, which was inhabited by the Macuxi Indians, and "had thirty-one thatched huts . . . . and a population of two hundred souls," and was situated on the banks of Lake Amucú, the supposed site of "El Dorado," where the Spaniards from the Orinoco hoped to discover the "land gilt in gold in the interior of the Guianas." This fascination aroused in Schomburgk territorial aspirations on behalf of Great Britain.

An Anglican missionary, Youd, whom Schomburgk had met, became quite enthusiastic about Schomburgk's plans. On August 25, 1838, Schomburgk wrote to Thomas F. Buxton, one of the more illustrious members of the Royal Geographic Society:

> The dividing line for the watersheds of the Essequibo tributaries on one side and the Amazon tributaries on the other would, without a doubt, form a more natural frontier. . . . . But everyone is completely ignorant of the fact that the Portuguese and later the Brazilians have extended their jurisdiction east of Fort St. Joaquim. The fact is that the British flag flew over Pirara before the Brazilian flag did. We shall raise the British flag in the village and render all possible honors on the occasion of the anniversary of our King.

But Pirara was quite strictly considered to be Brazilian territory, and in response to Schomburgk's attempt, the President of Pará sent an army captain and a detachment of soldiers to effect a permanent occupation of the village. However, while diplomatic notes were being exchanged regarding this matter, British troops occupied Pirara by force. At that time, the Brazilian official, Captain Leal, had only one soldier at his disposal and a Catholic missionary. Schomburgk, on the other hand, continued his explorations, however, no longer as an explorer for the Royal Geographic Society, but as one who had been commissioned by the English government, which had been misled by his promises.

He explored the entire territory, defining all of the boundaries. His claims for England had grown, for he claimed the entire courses of the Tacutú River and the Cotingo River. It was perfectly obvious that greed was the only basis for his claims. "In this manner," he declared in his report, "Great Britain shall confirm her sovereignty over these vast savannas, to which Portugal, when she possessed Brazil, attached such great importance. By confirming our control over the savannas located between the Tacutú River and the Cotingo River, all internal navigation will be under the control of the colony. . . . ."

The Brazilian government lodged a protest with the English government regarding this arbitrary demarcation, and all was settled satisfactorily. The British troops were ordered to return to Demerara; Lord Aberdeen wrote to the Brazilian Minister in London informing him that "positive orders had been issued to Schomburgk to remove immediately the boundary markings which he had set." But doubts arose over the actual boundaries, and in time, the agreement fell to pieces. In 1842, a plan for neutralization of the zone was accepted by the two governments.

Sixty years later, in a friendly expression of the rights of each country, and with the arbitration of a party chosen by both nations, namely King Victor Emmanuel III of Italy, Brazil and England found themselves defending their own individual rights and debating opposing claims in an honorable dispute. To Joaquim Nabuco, who was his country's spokesman, fell the task of clearly stating and presenting Brazil's rights to the territory and the bases for its claims. Portugal, the discoverer of the Amazon, long before Brazil became an independent country, had openly considered herself to be the sole master of this basin. Earlier maps recognized her sovereignty and treaties had confirmed it. The first nation to question Portugal's sovereignty over this area was not Holland, who had had sovereignty over the Essequibo basin for a long period of time until it was definitely ceded to England under the London Convention of August 13, 1814. Rather it was Spain who had challenged Portugal's claim since the period of the early conquests. The northern boundaries of Brazil were not disputed. It was the western frontiers which caused a controversy from which Holland disassociated itself. This dispute was settled in Portugal's favor by the treaties of 1750 and 1777.

As discoverer of the Amazon, and even more, of its tributaries, the Rio Negro and the Rio Branco, Portugal used her sovereign title over this rich fluvial network to assert her claim over the Tacutú-Maú, the branch immediately below the Rio Branco. To prove this claim, Nabuco appealed to the doctrine of the division of watersheds, which was accepted international law and which had been used by the majority of English jurists. As a matter of fact, England herself, in her dispute with Venezuela, based her claims to the tributaries of the Essequibo, Marzaruni, and Caiuni rivers on the "watershed line" doctrine. In this dispute England won an almost complete victory in the Paris courts.

Nabuco took advantage of another doctrine to assert the rights of Brazil, a doctrine which previously had been used by England on various occasions to substantiate successfully her claims. This doctrine, to which Brazil owes her extensive expansion into unexplored and unprotected lands, is known as "inchoate title." It is the right to property based upon explorations not followed by effective occupation; occupation in this case consists merely of the act of discovery and the declaration and publication of the intention to take possession of the land.

But Brazil, although strengthening its case by relying upon this legal principle, also claimed that its titles to the contested areas were not just based on noneffective occupation. Brazil offered numerous proofs of complete and continuous control over the regions touching the Rupununi. On several occasions, this area had been overrun by troops liberating Brazilians from Indian tribes and also by missionaries. It had always been subject to the jurisdiction of the sovereign police of Fort St. Joaquim. Nabuco went on to point out further the lack of legal validity of the acts of sovereignty exercised by England over the Indians, and the contradiction between her present claims upon the Amazon basin, and her attitude toward the basin when present-day British Guiana was a Dutch possession.

"In the seventeenth century, England rendered Portugal noteworthy assistance in its struggle against Spain and Holland to maintain its national existence on the Iberian Peninsula and its empire in South America. . . . . England . . . . did this by saving the Amazon Valley for Portugal in the Congress of Utrecht. On February 17, 1713, the Secretary of State, Bolingbroke, wrote a letter to the British Ambassador in France, in which he declared: '. . . . In short, My Lord, what I wish to say is that it is necessary that the source of the river belong to the Spaniards and the mouth to the Portuguese; neither France, England, nor any other nation should have a free entrance into this country (Brazil).' " (*The Rights of Brazil*, pp. 359–60.)

The Brazilian mediator, in the closing paragraphs of his voluminous work, recalled to mind the cordial relations which existed between England and Brazil. They were not, nor would they be affected by this dispute.

Nothing in this memorandum which we are submitting to our worthy arbiter should be construed as a lack of deference to the nation with whom we are disputing the territory. The author and signatory of this memorandum has always felt the most sincere and deepest admiration for England, and its role in the history of civilization, and nothing ever could possibly alter this admiration and respect. Special bonds have always linked Brazil to England, even before the proclamation of Brazilian independence, and it may be noted that even today in our present litigation, we have turned to old English traditions to implement and strengthen our case. Aureliano Coutinho, in his note of March 24, 1841, was already referring to England's guaranty of the integrity of the Portuguese domination over the Amazon regions: "The Imperial Government could never have expected for a single moment that the power which would guarantee the territorial integrity of possessions at one time would attempt to alter it later." Our attitude is the same as that which Portugal adopted at the Congress of Utrecht, when Lord Bolingbroke, in referring to the Amazon regions, declared: "Neither the French nor the English, nor any other nation (except Portugal and Spain), should have a free entrance into this country."

Because Brazil, prior to the proclamation of its independence, was already a conscious and homogeneous nation, it was able to maintain its mighty physical mass intact when independence came, while the unity of Spain's crumbled. In defense of the titles which Brazil received intact from Portugal, Brazil has in the last few years submitted itself to three arbitrations: the first was with Argentina regarding the Misiones territory, under the arbitration of the United States; the second was with France regarding the Guiana coasts and also the Amazonian frontiers, and the third is this one with England which concerns the territories west of the Rupununi. I have the firm conviction that Brazil was successful in the first two arbitrations because of the moderation it exercised in asking only for those territories to which Portugal previously had held incontestable title.

In this dispute Brazil has continued to follow the same line of conduct. Before entering the dispute, Brazil had to sacrifice all doubtful titles, in order to defend only those which were effective and long standing. As a matter of fact, up until the time when the dispute began to take form, England had respected these rights in the colony of Essequibo during its occupation of more than fifty years [fifty years' occupation of the colony up to the time when the dispute commenced in the 1830's].

Brazil maintains that England has no right to cross the Rupununi and establish itself in the Amazon basin.

Presented in Rome on February 25, 1904.

For Brazil:

JOAQUIM NABUCO

England based her claims solely upon actual occupation and possession. Admittedly she exercised effective sovereignty and had real commercial influence, according to the testimony of the Indians who inhabited that region and recognized England's sovereignty. England offered herself to arbitration as the *de facto* owner of the territory. She claimed to have held and developed the land ever since it was ceded by Holland. But most of these proofs of actual development of the area were later than 1842, when the territory was neutralized by joint agreement. The Brazilian mediator, in his reply, said that these proofs should not be considered because, after the neutralization agreement was signed, no new titles could be created.

The defense offered on behalf of the English cause was a work by several authors. It had been carefully worked on by many experts in the Colonial Office and had not been signed, as had that of Brazil, by a single mediator. Although they were much less voluminous, the English memoranda represented a great effort. This, however, made Nabuco's accomplishment seem all the more outstanding.

In a year's space of time, he presented to the arbiter eighteen large volumes made up of texts, maps, and documents, all of which had been carefully scrutinized by him, and two thousand pages which he wrote himself in his clear, thoughtful, and eloquent style.

He had only one doubt as to the value of the defense which he presented, and which had permanently shaken him in health and shortened his life: whether or not he could have made it shorter. Besides the essential clarity, he gave to it certain superfluous qualities, which being the person that he was, he could not refrain from attaching to everything that he touched—touches of imagination, and the well-rounded harmony of form which is the mark of an artist.

In writing to a friend he said:

> Even when defending a sure cause, the arbitration of a secular dispute, such as this one, is still a very dangerous and ticklish matter. When argument after argument accumulates, they form a puzzling confusion about which it can easily be said that "one cannot see the forest for the trees."
>
> My main difficulty is to find a means of arranging over a thousand confused and contradictory statements in such a manner that the arbiter can at a glance see the truth, and also to present these facts in a sensible order of importance. . . . .

He solved this problem to his own satisfaction. The thread of his argument is completely lost at times in the mass of details when he is expounding a many-sided question dealing with areas which are almost uninhabited. It is further complicated by various points of international law and the problem of using old documents. Yet the principal points tend to reappear again and again, re-emphasizing the various rights and facts.

After its completion, his defense memorandum seemed to him to be an armed fortress immune against all enemy blows. But the element of chance also enters into an arbitration. Brazil, with so much confidence in its case, should have had all the more reason for being extremely careful and watchful. In the preceding few years, Brazil had gained everything it claimed in the disputes with Argentina and French Guiana. Baron Rio Branco, the victorious author of the defense memoranda for these two arbitrations, had not only been decorated and idolized by his country; besides receiving the lasting gratitude of his nation, he received a generous financial bounty from the national legislature. Brazil, a new nation, proud of its immensity, was overjoyed to see its boundaries fixed and enlarged.

To Nabuco and Rio Branco, Brazil's rights to the territory being disputed with England were no less valid than those involved in the two previous arbitrations. Perhaps in the French Guiana case there was a slight advantage because it was based on a point of geographical uncertainty. Moreover, the respective position of two rivers constituted a more material if not stronger proof than did the application of various principles of law.

Nabuco's anxiety increased as the time for the announcement of the decision approached. This is clearly shown in his letters to Dona Evelina:

June 1

I have just found out that the King's decision will be announced within the next three or four days; I am both anxious and at the same time extremely overjoyed at the thought of finally ending my period of exile.

June 2

I am now awaiting the announcement of the decision which, it seems, will be made within the next three days. I suspect that the line decided upon will be different from those which have been discussed; however, I am quite hopeful that it will be most satisfactory. I am prepared for almost anything—nothing will really disturb me too much, for in my conscience and in my heart I feel I have done the best and the most that I could. We must neither wish for the impossible nor believe that we can enjoy all the happiness in the world. I shall leave the house on the 16th or 17th; once the decision is announced, I shall embark upon my return trip. However, I shall need about twenty to thirty days' time to prepare my departure, chiefly because my two secretaries will have to clear up a lot of matters pending between the various governments.

June 3

You will probably receive this letter on the eve of the announcement of the decision, that is Tuesday, June 7. I still know nothing about it and do not even venture to hazard a guess. However, I am sure that I have done my best. J. C. Rodrigues wrote me these few lines: "I can readily imagine how you must be counting the days, for even a person with an extremely calm disposition could not remain unperturbed by the ramifications of a contrary decision in a dispute such as this one. But, regardless of what the decision may be, your work will remain as evidence that you did all that was humanly possible, and much more than any other defender of our claim could do."

Now all that there is left to do is to wait and that is what I am doing.

My thoughts are no longer here—they are with you.

For you and for the children, I want this to be a resounding and clear-cut victory, so that there will be no discussion regarding the decision and involving us. I cannot envision the King handing down a decision which would not give us a satisfactory and ample victory.

If, perchance, the decision is almost entirely unfavorable for us—it could never be completely unfavorable—do not for a moment believe that I would be utterly disheartened. I know how strong my desire to live is, and for me the primary concern in life is to be of good cheer and in high spirits.

But, then, why talk about these things? When awaiting combat one should only envisage victory, and for this victory I embrace you and the children.

June 8

The decision has not yet been announced. How I can feel your anxiety! We are all in readiness awaiting the King's word. I expect it tomorrow. I telegraphed you today so that you would not remain at home awaiting my telegram, as Rodrigues, the poor soul, did yesterday in London.

What will happen? It is useless to conjecture here regarding it, for when you receive this letter you will already know everything.

Once the decision is announced and telegrams are exchanged with Rio de Janeiro, and four days have elapsed allowing for the calming of emotions, whether aroused by victory or defeat, I shall begin to prepare myself for my departure. You should do the same thing. This time we shall meet to rest, and not for me to work day and night at your side. Where will it be? It is still too soon to know, what with all of the problems which are likely to arise—our problems, those caused by others, and even those brought on by the government. I would like to try the mountains this summer, but little by little and slowly.

. . . . from your anxious and praying J.

June 10

I am now devoting myself to completing plans for closing down the mission and for our meeting. The announcement of the decision is so close at hand.

I do not know whether it would be worth while for you to come with the children so that we could leave together. I do not know what Gouvêa will say about me and Mauricio, but my wish is that you come here if I decide that we shall spend July and August in Switzerland. Soon I shall be able to tell you everything, for I am sending Rio Branco a telegram.

Yesterday four candles burned on the altar of Our Lady of Perpetual Help, where the miraculous statue is kept. Barros Moreira arranged to have it done. I do not apologize for this. On the contrary, at such times I usually invoke Our Lady of Good Counsel.

Go right ahead preparing everything for our meeting either late in June or early in July. This is my greatest consolation and causes me the most anxiety. I have also been thinking that the children are probably missing me very much. I had their group picture enlarged and it turned out splendidly. But it was last year's; I would like a new one every year. . . . .

When I think that I was condemned to stay here until the end of August and that I shall be free on the 12th or 13th (I hope), I do not know how to thank the King.

June 11

This afternoon I shall really know whether it is going to be announced tomorrow and shall telegraph you. . . .

God is great and kind, and will not permit me to be made unhappy at this time when I am expecting victory, not because I deserve anything, but because of your saintliness and the God-fearing children which you are rearing.

June 12

Yesterday I was quite upset over the postponement of the audience which had been set for eleven o'clock today. The reason for it was the absence of the British Ambassador who was still in Naples. I really do think that the notice given was too brief, although that is one of the privileges of being a King. However, they should have set the audience for tomorrow, St. Anthony's day, the patron saint for the discovery and restitution of lost articles.

Yesterday I had dinner at the MacSwinney home. Two cardinals were there—Agliardi and Matthieu. Agliardi has the grand manner, while Matthieu is completely unsophisticated in comparison; he does, however, possess the spirit and culture of France—superior qualities. The robes of the cardinals matched the silk of the large chairs very well. Afterward I visited the Belgian Minister. I had not done any visiting for many days.

Perhaps it will be tomorrow?

Your father's letter moved me deeply. What a wonderful soul! I shall send him a wire if we are victorious. Yesterday I spoke to Cardinal Matthieu about Father Perreyve. Astonished, he said to me: "There are very few diplomats who can speak about Perreyve." We then talked about bridge. I think he told some very humorous stories, but my hearing is quite bad.

Nazareth was quite attractive, all dressed in black.

Today I shall have lunch with Gubernatis. He reminds me of Tautphoeus, who always begins his letters: "My dear friend and distinguished Minister—."

June 13

Tomorrow the announcement will be made. I am tired, upset, and fearful that all of my work will have been in vain. Will I look with sorrow upon my eighteen volumes? I do not believe so, for if we obtain only a half or a third of the territory, with the effort we have made, it should be an indication of the fact that without this effort we would have salvaged nothing.

When you receive this letter you will already know everything. All that remains for me to do now is to get ready for our meeting, the tenderness of which will not be affected in the slightest by any eventuality in the dispute.

On June 14, King Victor Emmanuel III read his arbitration award (dated June 6) to the British Ambassador, to the Quirinal, and to Brazil's special mission.

It started out with this affirmation invalidating Portugal's historical claim: "Discovery by itself does not constitute a sufficient title; possession can only be considered effective after uninterrupted and permanent occupation in the name of the State; and furthermore, effective possession does not constitute sovereignty when it is exercised in only a part of the region and when that part because of its physical configuration does not form in reality an organic unit."

It was a repudiation of the doctrine of "inchoate title." In one of Nabuco's letters, he states: "I was quite shaken by the application of principles which if suddenly applied to the rest of Brazil by ambitious foreign forces would cause us to lose two-thirds or one-half of our country—the Amazon basin, that of Paraguay, and all of our unexplored and uninhabited hinterland."

The arbiter decided that neither Portugal nor Brazil had exercised complete and effective possession of all of the territory. After examining first the Brazilian claims and then the English, the arbiter decided the following: Holland had exercised her sovereign authority over certain parts of the disputed area; the governor of the colony controlled the commerce of the region and partial recognition of the governor's authority was made by the natives. When England became master of the Dutch colony, she continued to enforce the same acts of authority and jurisdiction. These rights were developed gradually and accepted little by little by the independent native Indian tribes; Holland and England, by the successive development of this scope of jurisdiction, established their sovereignty over a part of the contested area.

Having debated the claims of both sides, the arbiter then decided to cast them aside, because the documents exhibited as evidences of proof by both sides offered no historical or legal proof of sovereignty except in isolated areas in the contested territory; the arbiter declared that the boundaries of these aforementioned areas could not be precisely determined, nor could a definite decision be made as to which side had the preponderance of evidence, Brazil or Great Britain.

He finally decided that, since it is impossible to divide the territory into two parts, equal in area and value, because of the lack of geographical data regarding the region, it should be divided according to the lines made by nature, giving preference to the line which is most definite throughout the entire extent of the disputed zone, and which more equitably divides the area, that is, the dividing line of the watershed, from Mt. Iacontipú to the headwaters of the Ireng (Maú), and after that along the course of this river and the Tacutú until the established boundaries are reached.

For Brazil, this apparently equal division was much more than a half-defeat. In the first place, when Brazil signed the treaty delineating the zone to be placed under arbitration, it made all the sacrifices consistent with its rights, while England at that same time was adamant in maintaining her maximum claims, those based on the Schomburgk line. Brazil then decided to strengthen its claim over the disputed area by abandoning the d'Anville line.[1] Nabuco, in the first few pages of *The Rights of Brazil* (pp. 5–7), appeals to the arbiter by explaining this renunciation:

> . . . . It was a large area to the east of the Rupununi, between the treaty line and the d'Anville line (about 45,900 square kilometers), to which Brazil always

[1] The map of the Frenchman, d'Anville, was one of the first maps of the Guianas; it was dated 1748, and constituted a title for Brazil because it was recommended by the Governor of the colony of Essequibo in 1758 to the Navigation Company of the Indies as containing exact information regarding the boundaries of the colony; he stated that "the delineation of our boundaries shows us that the compiler was well informed." *The Rights of Brazil*, p. 347.

claimed to have better titles than Great Britain had to the territories which she now claims west of this river and west of the Maú. . . . . Brazil enters the dispute without being able to lose anything except at the expense of its old territory. She has already made all the compromises she could by accepting the line of the present treaty. She had already sacrificed those titles which were at all doubtful. What Brazil now submits to the judgment of the arbiter is an area which has been considered and accepted by all as Portuguese territory since the middle of the eighteenth century. England, on the contrary, submits herself to the arbiter, without having relaxed or altered its maximum claims; England, in making this demand, claims territory which she desires to acquire and not an old possession which she might possibly lose; in other words, in this litigation, she is only disputing territory which lies outside the boundaries of the former Dutch colony of Essequibo, in spite of the fact that the only rights accruing to England were those which belonged exclusively to Holland.

In the second place, England had the advantage, because the line which seemed to be better suited as a natural frontier favored England in the amount of land awarded to her. She received three-fifths of the disputed area and gained an opening into the Amazon basin. Finally, the terms of the decision were much closer to the proposals which England had made early in the dispute than to anything suggested by Brazil.

As a matter of fact, it was exactly the same line which a high functionary of Foreign Office had verbally proposed to Nabuco on August 23, 1900. The line proposed at this time gave Brazil a frontier on the Rupununi, satisfying its maximum claim regarding this one point. At that time Brazil was quite certain of the validity of its claim to the entire area, so it did not accept the proposal. Nabuco did not discuss the proposal in his memoranda because it had been a verbal proposal without any official character. Furthermore, Brazil had turned down the proposal, and Nabuco did not deem it proper to mention it in the arbitration, since for this reason it had already been withdrawn from the discussion. Because of his overscrupulousness, Nabuco did not let the King of Italy know about this proposal either directly or indirectly, in spite of the fact that it might have influenced the decision by clarifying the matter.

Nabuco was profoundly disillusioned by the King's award. He always regarded it as an English victory. He was the one who congratulated the British Ambassador, Sir Francis Bertie, after the official reading of the King's arbitral award. That same evening, unsuccessfully trying to control his grief, which was equal in intensity to the enthusiasm he displayed when working, and seeing before him what seemed to be the destruction of all of his work, with heavy heart he wrote to Dona Evelina Nabuco:

June 14

I did not write to you earlier in the day, but I cannot go to bed without doing it; I have been thinking about you and the children all day long, and about the disillusionment which my failure today must have caused you. Listening to the King read his arbitral award, which was a victory for England, was probably the most terrible quarter of an hour I have ever endured—and most pleasant for the British Ambassador who also was there. I never once expected that the King would give the English a frontier along the Tacutú. . . . .

Everyone today was most kind and understanding. Today I had dinner with the entire mission, the Regis, Barros Moreira, the Bishop of Pará, and the Bishop of Goiaz. The only problem remaining now is that of hastening the day of our meeting. In my conscience I feel that I have done all that was humanly possible. . . . . this made me feel a supreme disdain when I heard the decision; however, the disdain which the loss of our incontestable territory left in my mind was balanced by my heart's lament. I was so overcome by what happened that my hands were shaking when I signed the receipt for the award.

June 17

I did all that was possible for me to do, devoting my whole life, love, and energy to my work; I am sure that if our cause was lost, it was not because of ineptitude on my part. I am not going to commit suicide because we lost. On future maps of Brazil, the aperture through which England penetrated the Amazon basin, after having prevented France from so doing, will always call my name to mind, but it will also call to mind the presentation of a great defense, a work of dedication and thoroughness far beyond the nation's expectations. Having fulfilled my obligations to the best of my ability, I have an easy conscience, but my heart bleeds with sorrow. I feel as if I am the mutilated one and not Brazil. My spirits rise and fall as my thoughts drift from one point of view to another . . . . I am distressed by the thought that I was Brazil's representative in the dispute in which the right bank of Tacutú was lost. But then, what could I have done when the arbiter attached no worth to the notes of Aureliano Coutinho, Rio Branco's memorandum, and seventeenth-century Portuguese maps?

On June 16, he sent the following telegram to Baron Rio Branco: "Only Your Excellency can imagine how I felt during the lengthy reading of the arbitral award." Later, in a friendly letter, he wrote to him: "By the measure of joy which you experienced in winning arbitration judgments, you can easily calculate my unhappiness."

But even at the moment when Brazil's representative was suffering the full brunt of this blow, voices of help and sympathy were heard. Affectionate messages came from all sides. From far and near he received notes which were deeply moving, words of appreciation and praise for the completion of his colossal task, and silent sentiments of admiration which sought expression in order to console him. The unanimous manner in which they did him justice was tinged with an affectionate feeling of condolence, which caused him to acknowledge the kindness and love of compatriots, friends, and even strangers, with a heart overflowing with emotion.

The confidence which his name inspired in Brazil remained firm and unshaken. The Chamber of Deputies passed a resolution proposed by James Darcy, indicating its "keen gratitude . . . . for his noble efforts which have been consecrated with exceptional brilliance and unsurpassable devotion to the national cause." His friend, João Ribeiro, wrote him these encouraging words: "Everywhere—on the street, in trolleys, in the schools, and among all the groups of people I know, frequent, or ever hear, I have seen, heard, and felt applause for you and praise of you as a great patriot and a great Brazilian." Oliveira Lima wrote: "There was greater sadness over the disappointment it meant to you than over the loss of the territory." Tobias Monteiro said: "Yesterday an article in *A Notícia* mentioned that rarely among us does one ever see such a unanimous attempt to console someone who has not succeeded in spite of his tremendous efforts and bravery."

The *Jornal do Comércio* expressed the general feeling of solidarity behind Nabuco in these noble words:

> In the dispute which terminated recently, Brazil's case was pleaded by a man whose intellectual abilities, originality of thought, and capacity for work is unsurpassed in the present generation. There is not a single line among these numerous pages which was not written by Nabuco himself; there is not a single item in the eighteen large volumes or in the atlas which was not chosen or examined by him. He planned and conceived the entire thing without ever abandoning his artistic love of form. During the last two years of such intense concentration on this one subject, he has given us further proof of his astonishing intellectual energy, to which our race should rightfully point with pride. Unexpectedly called to serve his country, and thrown into studies which had never been his specialty, he was confronted by difficulties which only the exceptional brilliance of his talent and his tremendous capacity for work could surmount. He had great hopes for the complete success of our cause, which he had illuminated so amply and clearly. The fact that his hopes did not all come to fruition should in no way detract from the full recognition and appreciation which the nation owes him, the nation for which so much of his life's energy was consumed.

And his old friend, Count Prozor, who had by then become Russian Minister to Brazil, where he formerly had been secretary, wrote him the following:

> I do not think that the loss which Brazil suffered in the arbitral award will be a fact of considerable importance. On the contrary, I can see clearly how much Brazil is gaining morally from the homage which it is rendering to the most valorous of its defenders, without attaching any significance to a legal accident for which he was not responsible. I only wish that other countries would follow such an example!

Immediately following the announcement, manifestations of sympathy began to arrive by telegraph and Nabuco was soon enveloped in this comforting and consoling atmosphere. He wrote to Dona Evelina Nabuco on the day following the announcement of the sentence:

June 15

That which the destruction of all of my work did not do to me yesterday has been done today by your sweetness and the generosity which is being showered upon me; these have completely overcome me. I feel most grateful to you and to all the others. Rio Branco's telegram was most sincere—I am sending you my reply to him. Yesterday I slept quite well in spite of being exhausted from the emotional strain and anxiety that I have been subjected to during the last several days. . . . .

The Bishop of Pará does not leave my side; Regis is here now . . . . there are always many people around.

I have received many proofs of affection.

June 16

During these days, do not expect detailed letters from me. We have a great deal to do. Consider one telegram to be the equal of ten letters, and go on preparing yourself for our next meeting, which will probably be during the first days of July.

. . . . And then there are all of these telegrams which I am still receiving. The generosity which has been bestowed upon me because of my ill fortune is the most beautiful recompense for which I could ever have wished. May God be praised for this generosity! God moves in a mysterious way.

June 21

Here are some more telegrams to comfort you also. I can imagine how full the mail bag from Brazil will be, for telegrams are rather expensive.

Now the main thing on the program is to get everything in order for the departure, yours as well as mine. Once everything is set in order, we shall meet en route to wherever we are going.

St. John's Day

. . . . My progress in setting everything in order is amazing. Tomorrow I shall wire Gouvêa to find out what will be best for my health. I can leave next week and so can you. I cannot describe to you how much of a consolation for me our meeting will be. I am hoping that this reunion will cure my bleeding wounds, for I am sure that if I were alone in this world my wounds would be six times less serious . . . . that is because my love for you and the children is responsible for my profuse bleeding.

June 27

The house is in a state of confusion, with everyone packing and getting ready for the departure. Gouvêa advised me to go to Aulus in the Pyrenees. I have just written him a letter pointing out the difficulties in going there with such a large entourage. However, the main thing is that Saturday I leave here to go and meet you. You will know then where we are going and which route I shall take to meet you; if you are ready, we can shorten the distance by meeting at a halfway point. I hope to receive when I am with you the diplomatic pouch from Brazil.

I do not have a minute to myself . . . .

I am getting ready, and do not even have time to write . . . .

Today I am giving a dinner to the segment of Roman society which has not been driven out by the heat of summer. I shall have to give an appearance of being above feeling unhappy about the unfavorable arbitral award. Tonight I shall be as happy as possible, but what sadness I shall feel deep within me!

The award, which had been awaited with great interest in Brazil, was received with amazing restraint and presence of mind by the Brazilians. It was almost impossible for the layman to make an authoritative criticism of the questions involved in the arbitral award because of their complexity. The Brazilian people did not at this time of defeat, or at any later time indicate any loss of the confidence which they had placed in the arbitral judge. Nabuco, in the first public address he made after the announcement of the award, said on July 23, 1906, in the Casino Fluminense [a Rio club]:

I was not as fortunate as Baron Rio Branco; I did not bring back the rights to our disputed national territory unscarred and untouched. However, it is only with the deepest respect that I look upon the arbitral award made in the British Guiana dispute. I shall never cease to admire the nobility and fairness of the arbiter in his efforts to obtain true justice. . . . . He admitted to me that an impasse had been reached because the proofs and rights canceled each other out. He therefore had to divide the disputed territory between the two contenders.

At first, Nabuco was quite disappointed, for he had expected that the true course of justice would have brought nothing but complete victory. Afterward he consoled himself to a certain point with the half-victory which Brazil had won in gaining the beautiful piece of territory between the Cotingo and the Maú rivers. This area was incorporated into the state of Amazonas by the King of Italy's award. Nor was this strip of territory all that remained from Nabuco's heroic effort. There were also the volumes which he presented to the arbiter, which were worthy of being placed among his greatest works. José Veríssimo described them thus in the *Jornal do Comércio* of April 7, 1910:

In spite of the fact that this was a dry, technical subject made up of dull and intricate controversial details . . . . Joaquim Nabuco still managed to add to them the form and brilliance of his literary genius, treating them . . . . from the point of view of an inexhaustible scholar and a polished artist. . . . . In this monumental work . . . . he drew upon the entire scope of his multiple and varied capacities, which were always heightened in quality by his extraordinary literary talents.

The tremendous size of this work has protected it against readers. Even Ruy Barbosa, who was not usually dismayed by long tiresome works, permitted it to sit in his library for four years before looking at it. When later he perused the volumes, he wrote to Nabuco:

> Recently in pursuance of my investigations on the Acre case, for which I am the Amazonas delegate, I decided to read your memoranda regarding the British Guiana question, and from the onset I was extremely interested and impressed; I read the entire work. Such superior skill of writing and organization can only be the result of sorcery! Please permit me to say that I finished the book in wondrous admiration. You have displayed to us in this work qualities of criticism, argumentation, logic, good sense, clarity, adroitness, amenity, elegance, brilliance, and lucidity, yet unaccompanied, despite the inordinate length of the work and the dryness of the subject, by tediousness or lack of continuity. These qualities make it probably the outstanding expression of your great talent. That is what I have told many people here, when I have had the occasion to discuss the subject. It would be worth while to extract a sample of a precious mineral from this granitic mass to attract the attention of the curious and recall to the studious this rather discouraging episode in the iniquities of international justice.

Ruy Barbosa repeated this opinion in public on several other occasions. No one else, with the exception of Rio Branco, had more authority and capacity with which to judge the quality of this work. There could be no more respected opinion than that of Ruy Barbosa, who wrote in his *Rights of the State of Amazonas to the Northern Portion of Acre* [*Direito do Amazonas ao Acre Septentrional*]:

> The defense of our claims made by Joaquim Nabuco is a marvelous work of colossal patience, criticism, argumentation, and genius. This one work would have been enough to earn him fame and honor.

Even within the last few days of Nabuco's life, Ruy Barbosa, in a speech delivered on December 18, 1909, to the School of Law in São Paulo, repeated this opinion in the following words which the last mail from Brazil scarcely had time to bring to Nabuco's eyes before he died:

> The work of our representative in the arbitration was gigantic. I have read it all, and find it to be without comparison in its field. Our rights shine out with the brilliance of the sun. Although we did not convince the arbiter, we have convinced the specialists of Europe. It is only necessary to read the opinions and admirable studies made by outstanding international scholars in the *General Review of International Public Law* to be convinced of this fact.

Glory comes only to the successful. Yet, after tasting the bitterness of defeat, Nabuco could see by the actions and words of his compatriots that he had won new honor and esteem. "Your name," Machado de Assis wrote him after the announcement of the award, "is twice yours, first from the brilliance which your father gave to it years ago, and second from the greatness which you yourself are lending to it. You have written the biography of one (Nabuco), someday the biography of the other will be written, and included in it will be the chapter which you have brought so nobly to a close."

CHAPTER XXV. BRAZIL'S FIRST EMBASSY, 1905

A few days after the announcement of the King's award, Nabuco wrote to his wife from Rome: "This morning an earthquake took place. It was a telegram from Rio Branco offering me Washington. I shall think it over carefully before answering. Think, pray, and rest assured that no obligation will remain unfulfilled. There, perhaps, is our children's future. I always wanted to have them educated there . . . ."

Rio Branco's telegram said:

> Continue finishing up the work of the mission peacefully; take months if necessary. As you know, Washington is our most important post. We need a good man there. If you can accept, tell me as soon as possible, so that I can set the proper machinery in motion. We shall ask for an increase in salary. Before deciding, talk to Aranha. I believe that you will agree with me, but if not, it is understood that, if you prefer London, I shall withdraw this request.

On June 21, Nabuco replied:

> I plan to leave Rome at the end of the month. My files are in London, where I shall arrive in August. I am perplexed as to what to do about such a vital matter, since I am ignorant of conditions surrounding this proposed change. I answer by making you my proxy. If you have some plan in mind for which you think my presence is best suited, do not take my ordinary preferences for London into consideration. Granted the well-known importance of the new post, transfer would not appear to anyone as a demotion. I thank you for your kindness.

This well-known "importance" which Nabuco required before accepting a transfer outside of the normal bounds was not the elevation of the legation to the status of an embassy, but some frank act of friendship toward the United States, some attempt on the part of the Brazilian government to establish a specific foreign policy for its relations with this hemisphere, or indeed some official sign of the fact that the relative importance of the two posts, London and Washington, had been shifted. Foreign policy had undergone a transformation from what it had been when the imperial constitution had been in force. Then it was a reflection of the parliamentary organization and political customs of England. Then also the entire material development was based upon English capital.

To Nabuco the creation of an embassy in Washington seemed to be a hasty action which could well have been delayed. He feared that Brazil would gain nothing and would probably lose by it, perhaps attaining premature and uncertain fame, far out of proportion to its place in the concert of nations. The rank of ambassador was still a privileged one zealously guarded by six or seven of the major powers, which gave to its diplomatic agents a right to all precedences and priorities as personal representatives of their monarchs. It was not surrounded by a numerous confraternity of equals as it is today, but carried within its exclusiveness the atmosphere of a small royal court, presided over by the bearers of noble and illustrious names from the respective countries. The United States vulgarized the rank from the very beginning of its use by American diplomats. Because of its basic democratic tradition and its powerful international position, the United States had been indifferent to the various prerogatives attached to the title of ambassador ever since the days when the phrase was current in London that "the first of the ambassadors to the Court of St. James's was the minister from the United States." The United States had already agreed to the elevation to the status of embassy of Mexico's diplomatic mission in Washington, and had likewise raised its own mission in Mexico. Extending this same courtesy to Brazil would be a natural continuation of the same policy. The plan for doing this was forming in Rio Branco's mind.

While the matter was pending, Nabuco returned to London. The creation of the new embassy was set for the end of the year. On January 20, 1905, the new ambassador wrote to Rio Branco:

> I repeat again the best wishes I sent you for the new year. You opened my new year for me in a memorable manner—whether it is for better or for worse is still doubtful. This move which attracts attention beyond the boundaries of our country, will have greater repercussions than anything else which you have done. All types of rumors are being spread about it.

Nabuco, in thanking his colleague Costa Mota for sending him congratulations when he was appointed, wrote the following:

> In doing this, Rio Branco distinguished himself more than at any other time, certainly not because of my appointment, naturally, but by the declaration he made in so doing. At first I objected to the rank, but now I must confess that the rank lends itself to the policy. The worst thing for him is that, assuming certain suppositions to be true, he has virtually obligated himself to go to Washington.

To Graça Aranha he wrote:

> At first, as I said in a previous letter, I thought that the title was useless, but now I see that the promotion in itself was a stroke of audacity and inspiration which opened new and larger horizons for our country and for all of Latin America. . . . .
>
> . . . . I realize that the title of ambassador is in itself just an announcement—one which has the great advantage of saying everything and requiring nothing. I

can see that it is an opening measure. Obviously we are facing the dawn of a new era . . . .

The Monroe Doctrine lays down a definite foreign policy for the United States which is now beginning to take shape, and it lays down a similar policy for us. Under such conditions, our diplomacy should receive its principal impetus from Washington. Such a policy would be better than the largest army or navy . . . .

For me, the Monroe Doctrine . . . . signifies that politically we have broken away from Europe as completely and clearly as the moon has from the earth. In that sense I am a Monroist.

For many years he had desired a foreign policy for Brazil based on friendship with the United States. He had been advocating friendship with the United States since the beginning of his political activity under the imperial government, when he launched his program of "Abolition, Federation, and Peace." When the idea of organizing the first meeting of a Pan American Congress in 1889 was proposed, Nabuco, in an article in *O País*, was outspoken in his support of the idea and of any plan of confraternization which would be capable of guaranteeing peace on the American continent.

He was constantly preoccupied by the problems involving Brazil's activities in international affairs. Even at the time when his monarchical sympathies kept him from participating in the internal politics of the nation, when interviewed in 1898 by the *Estado de São Paulo*, Nabuco said:

Today we are one of the many unknown quantities of a vast problem, namely the American problem. Europe, Africa, and Asia now form a single political unit. Confronted by this colossal mass, which should be called the European mass, what is Latin America's destiny?

The obvious solution lay in the Monroe Doctrine, in the indestructible union of American states. In a letter to Tobias Monteiro from London, Nabuco said: "Tell the President that there is no Monroist more enthusiastic than myself." To Campos Sales himself, he wrote:

My impression is that the importance of the problem of foreign relations in all European and American countries is gradually tending to surpass that of internal affairs, and that we are heading toward a time when the fate of all of these countries without exception will have to be decided by the adjustments and agreements developing from the conflict of influences and interests between the present power blocs, such as the Double Alliance, the Triple Alliance, the British Empire, the Monroe Doctrine, etc.

When in September 1902, after much hesitation, Rio Branco notified him that he had accepted Rodrigues Alves' offer of the Foreign Relations post, Nabuco answered:

As I have told you, I am an ardent "Monroist," and for that reason a partisan of the ever increasing harmony between Brazil and the United States. Instead of considering me as your successor two years hence, perhaps you should consider making me your collaborator in carrying out this policy of uniting the two legations in London and Washington. . . . .

Although written in jest, it was a certainty that the legation in London did not suffice as an arena for his activities. He wished to institute a truly creative international policy with which to face the uncertainties of the future. In this sense his London assignment was disillusioning. A short time after presenting his credentials in London, he wrote the following in his diary:

The legation here is of minor importance politically, but of greater importance financially. The political significance of the Washington post is greater than all of those in Europe, and the American post is steadily becoming more important financially.

In January 1905, Nabuco, who had already been appointed to the Washington post, went to Rome to hand in personally the documents terminating the special mission. It was really a pretext for escaping a month of London's miserable winter. He enjoyed seeing Rome's blue skies again, but felt remorseful at having spent only a few months in the Eternal City out of the two years during which he was accredited to the Quirinal. Christ's Vicar no longer was Leo XIII, who had never forgotten the eloquent apostle of Brazil's abolitionist movement, and who would always ask the Brazilians he received about Nabuco. Many times throughout the years, Nabuco's friends had informed him of this papal interest. He would always reply: "It is a blessing."

From Rome, during these days of leave-taking, he wrote this letter to his wife:

February 10

I have just returned from a visit to the Pope, Cardinal Merry del Val, and Cardinal Rampolla. He is the third pope I have seen. Pius X, in appearance and manner, is the personification of kindness, although he lacks the majestic air of Pius IX, and this is one of the fundamental characteristics of this high office. Perhaps it is a quality which is developed after years in office, especially for those like the present pope who did not live in the Vatican prior to their elevation. I believe

Cardinal Rampolla would have possessed this quality from the very start. Pius X's kindness is visible in every gesture, work, or look. His kindness is sincere and makes him beloved of the people. Pius IX truly had a smile of consummate bliss.

I was completely taken with Cardinal Rampolla's deep and genuine affability; a bond of enduring friendship has been established between us . . . .

February 11

Yesterday Tittoni offered me the Grand Cross of St. Maurice and St. Lazarus, which was the highest honor that could be bestowed upon me; I had to refuse it because of the inalterable precepts set down in our constitution. . . . .

February 12

. . . . Yesterday I visited the place which according to one source was the tomb of St. Anastasia and according to another was her place of prayer and devotion. Of my seven patronesses[1] only two are missing: St. Felicitas and St. Perpetua. These are in Carthage. I have venerated all of the other saints where they left evidence of their sacred deeds.

My longing for you is changing now to expectation, like night changing to dawn. Wednesday or Thursday will find me in the daytime fog of London. . . . .

In May 1905, he left for the United States to occupy his new post, intent upon strengthening the ties between the two countries, not with the skepticism of an old diplomat decaying in the service, but with enthusiasm unabated by his white hairs, with the fervor of someone who saw things in the light of an imagination which was eternally young, and which transformed all that came into contact with it.

He worked toward achieving greater harmony between the United States and Brazil with the same enthusiasm he had devoted to his efforts in resolving various internal problems when he was active in politics. His desire to strengthen the bonds of friendship between the two nations was not a routine act of amenity by a diplomat attached to a friendly country. Such acts are usually made hesitatingly and with reservations. His active faith in the ultimate good to be derived from bettering Brazilian-American relations added a very necessary sparkle and interest to a career which after the attainment of old age is usually uncomfortable and dull. Nabuco was quite aware of this fact, as can be adjudged from this letter:

The life of a diplomat is the least suited of all for the pursuit of definite ends; the only exception is when one is furthering a clear policy. . . . . normally, occupying a diplomatic post provides a life of boring routine; the predominating characteristic of which is the futility of the numerous social obligations, dinners,

[1] The seven martyrs which are invoked in the canon of the Mass and which were Nabuco's particular patronesses, were: Felicitas, Perpetua, Agatha, Lucy, Agnes, Cecilia, and Anastasia.

and balls. These social obligations and festivities make it the wrong career for anyone seeking to widen his intellectual horizons.

I am nearly sixty years old and at that age one does not enjoy an artificial existence such as that of the diplomat.

He was glad, however, to return to a post about which he had very fond recollections. He enjoyed the sensation of disembarking, the arrival in New York, and his stay, as before, at the Buckingham Hotel on Fifth Avenue. After the passage of thirty years, the Buckingham Hotel was no longer the last word in American comfort. Across the street was the Gothic cathedral whose construction he had watched. Once again it was the first thing he saw in the morning when he opened the windows before being served the same breakfast of kidney omelette and milk rolls, which he still remembered. He was coming into contact with a country in which he again found the same hospitality of friends who were still there and of new acquaintances; in one house he found a picture of himself when young in the same place where he had left it.

But, as he said to a reporter, he felt like a Rip Van Winkle. Everything, although familiar, seemed new to him, and every friendly spot which he revisited called to mind his former impressions. For example, he wrote the following to his old friend, the jurist Oliver Wendell Holmes, about Niagara Falls which he had not seen since the spring of 1877: "I had seen Niagara in its summer dress . . . . when I myself was young; now I saw it crippled by the winter ice, rheumatic and old, in a state of hibernation, again like myself."

After spending two days in New York, he went to Washington where he arrived on May 22, 1905. On May 25 he presented his ambassador's credentials to a man who interested him very much and who was arousing world-wide interest.

Theodore Roosevelt, still a young man, was just beginning his second term in office as President; he was attacking at one and the same time all of the problems which his keen eyes could discern; he was attempting widespread basic reforms; he was discovering and utilizing all the able men he could find, denouncing private and national vices with a frankness which could not be intimidated or silenced by anyone, and unmasking powerful vested interests.

He jealously guarded the dignity of his office, but thoroughly divested it of all moderate attitudes and diplomatic expressions. He was prudently violent; his acts were surprising but discreet, and his authoritarian manner was benevolent. Although involved in hard work and struggles, he appeared to derive a precocious child's pleasure from life. He was rapidly becoming a national symbol, for he was the living personification of the expression which at that time more aptly characterized his country, and which was incarnated in him more than anyone else: the strenuous life.

His countrymen had already begun a cult of him. Roosevelt, whose physical intrepidity was equal to his intellectual courage, was tireless. He rested from his hours of intense work at his desk and of receiving callers by spending an equal number of hours engaging in exhausting exercises—sprinting through Washington's parks, climbing hills, wandering afoot far off the beaten path, winning races either running, on horseback, swimming, with an energy that left his younger companions far behind. He took advantage of a short vacation to write the biography of Cromwell. Roosevelt, who had the culture of a great scholar, enjoyed the robust health of a cowboy. He was proud of the spirit of toughness which inspired him to cry out to the audience from the rostrum: "It takes more than that to kill a bull moose," when a traitor's bullet penetrated his chest while he was delivering a speech. Roosevelt was already becoming more than a popular candidate; he was a national hero.

The President, wearing the stiff formal clothes appropriate to the solemn occasion of receiving the new ambassador's credentials, was the man whom Nabuco had long waited to meet. He was struck by the penetrating gaze through a pince-nez; the expansive charm; the smiling affability; the energetic and engaging handshake; the natural dignity of a wellborn citizen who rose to world fame but not unexpectedly; the famous excess of energy which overflowed in Roosevelt's every gesture, in his emphatic manner of speaking in which every word was stressed by striking his open hand with a closed fist many times; his universal inquisitiveness; his radiant and democratic spirit of good-fellowship; his prompt appreciation and recognition of men and deeds, an appreciation expressed in a simple compliment, richer in sincerity than in political implication; his positive plain-spoken words unadorned by rhetoric and excessive motions, indicative of practical, clear, and direct thinking.

Nabuco delivered a short speech in English, uttering the remarks which are customarily repeated when credentials are presented. He expressed his government's and his own desire to see the strengthening of the bonds of friendship between the two countries, and a wish for the continued happiness of the chief of such a friendly state.

Afterward, President Roosevelt read the official reply which naturally had been prepared by the State Department, reiterating desires for greater ties of friendship, repaying courtesies, and congratulating the Brazilian government for having chosen such a capable diplomatic representative. When the President reached the end of his discourse, he folded the prepared speech, and without pausing, said with his characteristic and captivating spontaneity:

"I am now going to do something to which I am unaccustomed! I am going to enlarge upon what I have read." He again expressed his pleasure at the creation of the embassy and stressed the mutual desire for greater friendship between the two nations. He further indicated his burning wish for an effective collaboration, in the sense of forming what Nabuco referred to as a "neutral zone," his faith in the greatness of Brazil's future accomplishments in the twentieth century, and his confidence in Brazil's becoming another guardian of the Monroe Doctrine. He concluded by declaring that he would retain a fond recollection of this first meeting, which had far exceeded his expectations.

In his official dispatch to Rio Branco, Nabuco said:

> The determination with which he expressed his confidence in us, his desire that we should join forces and work toward the same goal, and also what he said to me regarding my appointment, caused me to express to him my immense satisfaction for having permitted me to inaugurate our first and only embassy under such happy auspices. . . . .
>
> . . . .
>
> My discourse did not contain any sentiments which were not either expressed or implicit in the one which our President pronounced when he received the American Ambassador and spoke of the creation of this embassy and my appointment to it. You are acquainted with these sentiments already; I explain my nomination to this post through them. I do not doubt for an instant that the attitude which I expressed in the White House on May 24, 1905, will have your approval and that of the President of the Republic. I would like to add that I was referring to our President as much as to President Roosevelt when I made this statement recalling Washington, Monroe, and Lincoln: "In the course of your duties, there are also hours that become epochs, gestures that remain immutable national attitudes . . . ."

One of the first official functions attended by Nabuco was the funeral of Secretary of State John Hay. His successor was to be Elihu Root, who was then the Secretary of War. Both Hay and his auspicious successor, Root, belonged to the minute intellectual aristocracy of a country of businessmen.

From the very beginning, Nabuco always considered Elihu Root to be a great man, and with this in mind he was never able to understand why the Americans never thought of making him President. He once expressed his surprise at this fact to President Roosevelt. "He would be a wonderful President but a very bad candidate," promptly answered Roosevelt. His own popularity had been won in the vigorous years of outdoor life spent in the West, and was reflected in his dynamic vitality, his crusades, and his violent idealistic attacks couched in words which could be understood by all classes of people. He could well evaluate the insufficient powers of attraction which an extremely intelligent man such as Root, scholarly, reserved, and retiring, would have for the millions of ordinary citizens, common workers, and electors of limited culture who are uniformly scattered from east to west and north to south throughout the United States. They desire and choose a candidate with a temperament and background similar to theirs, one whom they can admire and understand. Root was a noted lawyer from distant New York, and among his clients were some of the most powerful trusts. For that reason he was vulnerable to malice and political attack. He could not be the candidate of the masses, the candidate who would inspire their support.

From the very beginning of their relationship, when both assumed office at the same time, they had a complete unanimity of views and purpose. Each immediately recognized and appreciated the other's qualities; soon the working relationship became a sincere friendship. Root said that Nabuco fulfilled the role of ambassador better than anyone else he had known, and Nabuco noted in his diary that Root "is a friend whose esteem is for me one of the greatest satisfactions of my career."

With Nabuco's constant collaboration, Root made Pan-Americanism one of the principal ideas of his program. They rivaled each other in the immense efforts which they devoted to this cause. After delivering a speech, Root wrote to him: "I am so glad that you like what I said to the Central Americans. It was a bit of the gospel of common sense, of which you and I are both missionaries."

"He is unique among his species in his interest in Latin America," wrote Nabuco to Rio Branco. He was however not unique in the sense that there was any divergence of opinion as to the necessity of such a policy of greater concerted action, nor that there was even the slightest opposition. When at the Pan American Exposition in Buffalo, on May 20, 1901, Roosevelt said: "I believe in the Monroe Doctrine with all my heart," he undoubtedly expressed the thinking of the majority of his countrymen. The only obstacle to the establishment of bonds of friendship between the various peoples was indifference in the United States. This indifference, however, contrary to its European counterpart, was not colored by disdain, but was easily transformed into a friendly fraternal spirit when sufficiently aroused.

Root's actions which brought about this awakening, and his deeds on behalf of the cause of democracy were appreciated by Nabuco more than by anyone else. Nabuco had been instrumental in defining Brazil's part in the formation of Root's policy. When, at the end of four years, Elihu Root was removed from the State Department by a change of administration, Nabuco wrote to Graça Aranha:

> Root in the Senate will not be the leading figure of this administration. His heart is in Latin America today as Taft's is in the Philippines.

The atmosphere which Nabuco found in Washington was far different from that of England. In London, a foreign ambassador, especially one from South America, was not offered much of an opportunity to distinguish himself or stand out in any way; only with difficulty could he attract the attention of the indifferent population of Europe's largest city. In the United States, on the contrary, even without their figuring on the national scene, the local importance of ambassadors was considerable, both in Washington and wherever they were taken by their desire to know the country better, or by the necessity of attending ceremonies. The press always emphasized, in its coverage of the news, the prestige enjoyed by foreigners and by diplomats, a much greater prestige than they enjoyed in Europe.

Reflected also in the press was a general interest in the Latin countries and life in Brazil in particular, an interest which is quite meager in Europe. The newspapers showed their interest by giving complete coverage to Nabuco's arrival, together with detailed background stories.

Wherever an ambassador went, the reporters followed to obtain the inevitable interviews. From the very start, Nabuco traveled a great deal and gave many speeches at large and small meetings and at political banquets attended by hundreds of people, not counting those in the galleries. Newspaper interviews with Nabuco were always preceded by some commentary regarding the "splendid personality" of the ambassador and his imposing stature, which in the vocabulary of the reporters was aristocratic and military.

Often the surprised newspapermen revealed their ignorance with expressions such as this one, which was intended as praise: "But he seems more like a New York clubman than a South American."

In comparison with the rather inadequate observations of the lesser papers, the remarks of the great journals, which weigh their words carefully, are well worth recalling: "He is ranked with the great constructive statesmen of the world," said the *Literary Digest*. And the veteran *Boston Transcript*, in an editorial about Brazil's prosperity, remarked:

> Not least to her credit in our eyes should be the fact that she sent as her ambassador to this country one of the ablest diplomats and most accomplished gentlemen to be found at any court or capital in Europe.

The fame which Nabuco's varied abilities had already achieved for him in his country gave him a great deal of prestige on his arrival, which was later increased by his personal charm and further confirmed by his prudent statements. The United States is a country where oratory is of primary importance; where almost everything offers a pretext for speeches; where speeches are one of the principal methods of action for any type of propaganda; where speeches are frequently instrumental in conducting political candidates to the highest positions; where even presidential candidates, traveling vast distances to reach new audiences, address their fellow countrymen from the rear platforms of trains, always convincing people with the spoken word, and the direct contact; in such a country, Nabuco could not avoid having a clear advantage over most of his colleagues.

He took advantage of his oratorical gift for propaganda purposes on behalf of Brazil. Thus a second oratorical phase emerges in his life.

He realized that the spoken word was one of the necessities of his post. Either because of their difficulties with the language or their aversion to public speaking, in general most of his colleagues in the diplomatic corps slipped away or gave excuses when the numerous occasions for giving speeches at ceremonies arose. The principal exceptions which stood out were the British Ambassador, Bryce, and the French Ambassador, Jusserand, both eminent men. The *Boston Herald*, at the time of the replacement of the German Ambassador, who had just died, insisted upon the appointment of a man "who could participate in American life as an orator at academic functions and as a source of enlightenment."

American audiences were not demanding. While the Latin audiences of other lands, in order to listen patiently, demanded exceptional qualities of thought and expression, the American audiences only asked for good humor and conciseness; a speech which was to the point, practical, logical, convincing, and brightened with an occasional joke. If any speaker possessed qualities in excess of these minimum expectations, naturally, he would be noticed and favorably discussed; and thus it was from the very first with the speeches of the Brazilian Ambassador, who was oratorically so gifted. His words immediately attracted attention because of their intimate personal quality.

A short time after Nabuco's arrival, a Brazilian warship visited the United States. At the first banquet given in the new embassy in honor of the naval officers, his intellectual superiority already proved to be impossible to disguise or imitate. The *New York Times*, on July 18, 1905, did not let it pass without comment:

> The speech given by the Brazilian Ambassador was as significant as it was interesting. No more pleasant remarks were made than those of the host, who proposed a toast to the President's health, which was a great personal homage as well as a national tribute. It is perfectly true that, as Nabuco said, "a toast to the President is as impersonal as a salute to the flag." And the observations which follow this one are no less accurate and noteworthy:
>
> "The American presidency is an eminency which can be seen rising day by day. You do not notice the change because you are rising with it and because the relationship between the nation and the President remains fixed. But in the eyes of the world, every successive American President is seen at a higher level than that of his predecessors. This historical progression will be as applicable to President

Roosevelt's successors as it is to him, but it is during his administration that the period of American ascendancy above all the other nations of the world has begun. This could not have been the result of the work of one man or one party; it is a rising surge made up of millions of your population."

The editor immediately utilized this opportunity to spread some propaganda for Monroism. That was exactly what Nabuco wanted: to arouse an interest in Brazil, about which almost nothing was known in the United States. He accepted invitations to speak at all types of celebrations. He never refused an opportunity to make his country better known, even though it might have meant, as did his trip to Chicago to deliver a convocation address to the university, a journey of twenty hours. Moreover, because of his lack of time, he was forced to make the return trip without stopping for rest. "How these people enjoy my talks; they like nothing better than to listen to speeches; I could deliver many more, but I am so tired!" he said in writing to Graça Aranha. ". . . . See if my talk was well translated there in Brazil. You know that at American dinners, like at English dinners, jokes are obligatory in a way, and for that reason I had to accommodate myself. Overlook it."

His particular manner of seeing and saying things became apparent during his first days in the embassy. The press noticed it, when, after the termination of the Russo-Japanese War, Nabuco congratulated Roosevelt, who had been the peace intermediary, by sending him this telegram:

I beg Your Excellency kindly to accept the expression of our gratification and our common American pride at the noble page you have written in the history of civilization. The whole world will undoubtedly read it as the preface to a new age of peace. The use which you have now made of the untouched prestige of your country to bring about the end of the war in the East will be taken everywhere as a pledge that you would not hesitate to draw again upon that incalculable source of strength to prevent national feuds in other parts of the world from breaking into war, if that could be avoided by the earnest and friendly remonstrance of this great nation in the interest of mankind. In that way you have created for the American presidency a function that will win for it the moral hegemony of the world, the only leadership it can accept. I can imagine how deeply thankful Your Excellency must feel for the inspiration that allowed you to invest your nation at the proper time of her history with that mightiest and noblest of powers.

CHAPTER XXVI. THE PAN AMERICAN CONFERENCE OF RIO DE JANEIRO, 1906

The outstanding event of the year was going to be the Third Pan American Conference in Rio de Janeiro in July. Most of Nabuco's efforts during his first year at the embassy were directed toward making preparations for the conference, re-emphasizing its importance, and adding the finishing touches to vital resolutions. The preliminary discussions took place in Washington among the twenty-one diplomatic representatives of the American republics, presided over by the Secretary of State of the United States.

Root's desire to lend as much importance as possible to the occasion was responsible for his decision to attend in person the inaugural session. He planned to go to Rio de Janeiro aboard the warship "Charleston." Afterward, in order to strengthen the fraternal spirit in the manner which he desired, he hoped to visit the principal republics of South America. It was an unexpected decision which was most pleasing to the Brazilian government. It was the first time that an American Secretary of State left the United States on an official visit.

To no one was this news more gratifying than to Nabuco, who wrote the following to Rio Branco, attempting to destroy the impression that it had been done on his advice:

> My part in all of this was only to create the proper situation and background from which that impulse spontaneously took form. That was all I did.

In his diary he wrote on January 29:

> I had dinner with the President . . . . he told me that had I not come to Washington, Mr. Root would not be going to Brazil, because his decision to go was caused by the impression which I made upon him.

On June 11 he wrote:

> I had a farewell visit with the President. He repeated the flattering remarks which he had made to me before. His words were to the effect that the choice of me as Brazilian Ambassador marks an epoch in the relations between our two countries . . . . not only in the relations between Brazil and the United States, but also between the United States and all of the nations of the continent. By that he meant that I had done much toward changing the attitude of Latin America with regard to the United States. Brazil's example was decisive. It not only forced them, it convinced them.

The example which he set was further strengthened by the advice he gave to his colleagues. After a conversation with a friend who was the minister of a foreign country, he entered the following in his diary on March 2: "I am trying to modify the anti-American sentiments which I found in Mr. X."

If in the United States the great impediment to greater friendship between the two countries was indifference, the impediment in Brazil and the other nations was suspicion, the refusal to trust the good intentions professed by the stronger power. That is the gist of Nabuco's letter to Lloyd Griscom, who was about to assume office as American Ambassador to Brazil. Nabuco hoped that in assuming his new post he was

> . . . . aware of the determination behind our policy and the great strength of the currents of opposition over which an extremely solid bridge must be built. "Time does not respect that which is done without it." So goes one of the wiser proverbs. We cannot produce time to suit our needs. Your tasks, as well as mine, are not exactly introductory in nature, but primary and basic. In this land I have to fight the indifference caused by the vastness and self-sufficiency of your population. In my country you will have to fight against mistrust, born of the antithetical difference between our races and nurtured and cultivated by foreign mercantilism. . . . .

In both countries there was the natural apathy of the people for all long-range policies and slow fundamental projects. On both sides there was a mutual lack of comprehension of each other, born of the differences between the races and the almost complete ignorance of each other. Before the era of the motion picture and of export industries, the internal development and expansion of the United States absorbed all of its energies and strength. Brazil, exclusively under European influences, loved France like a second motherland, and absorbed her literature and her ideas. These molded like wax the national mentality of Brazil, which was still in the formative stages. Brazil received its inspiration from Latin ideals, preferring spiritual victories over material triumphs. It was indifferent to commercial struggles and defended itself against American influences with all its conscious and unconscious strength.

Rio Branco established bravely the foundations of the "American policy," and supported the creative measures which Nabuco took in Washington. Yet, in spite of the proved worth of the "American policy" and the breadth of Rio Branco's great statesmanship, he did these things against his personal sympathies, which were as European and aristocratic as possible.

Nabuco left for the Pan American Conference filled with apprehensions regarding the cause which was so close to his heart. Certain articles which appeared in the Brazilian press were quite unfavorable to the United States and expressed doubt as to its sincerity and disinterestedness. Although these articles were isolated exceptions, Nabuco exaggerated their importance and was apprehensive as to the possible repercussions. He feared that the delegates to the conference, Root above all, would not find the friendly and receptive atmosphere which he had tried so hard to prepare for them.

These apprehensions were quickly dispelled as if by magic when they arrived. The delegates experienced relief after the arduous voyage to Brazil by way of Europe; the ships which followed the direct route left much to be desired as far as comfort was concerned. With such a large family, and for such a short duration of time, Nabuco decided to travel alone, in spite of the sacrifice involved. To his wife he wrote:

> I am too old now for these separations, even if just for a period of months; however, you must not leave the children . . . . I am too tired to live far away from you . . . . Yet what cannot be avoided must be accepted with resignation and forbearance, for true submission is forbearance. It is for the good of all of us, and certainly what benefits you and the children is far more important than anything benefiting me alone. . . . . I know that this trip to Rio will bring me greater vexation than pleasure . . . . but that is one of the less attractive features of the work in which I am engaged. As far as my liberty of action is concerned, everything would be worse if you went, and we would have to delay much longer before returning. . . . . I shall try to make my father-in-law understand this. I shall console him and try to put him in good spirits . . . . to make such a large-scale move for such a short period of time would be unfeasible.

The year 1906 was full of travel for Nabuco. Before crossing the ocean four times, not counting various excursions, Nabuco traveled continuously over nine thousand miles on a one-month trip by railroad across the United States from New York to San Francisco and from there to Canada. Nabuco had immediately accepted the invitation of his old friend, Richard Cutts Shannon, to cross the continent in all the comfort of a private car, accompanied by whatever guests he chose to invite, and making stops according to the fancy of the guests, delaying as long as they wished. His ardent love of traveling, something which had always fascinated him, and a compulsion to be always on the move made it impossible for him to refuse the invitation. He accepted with pleasure the hardships of the journey which certainly were aggravated by his old age and failing health, and also the longing and sadness of another separation from home, feelings which were becoming stronger with each successive separation.

The trip across the United States lasted an entire month. Five friends were aboard the private car, "Commonwealth": Nabuco; the Portuguese Minister, Viscount d'Alte; Lieutenant Colonel Achilles Pederneiras, the military attaché of the embassy; and Colonel Shannon and his secretary.

Some of the impressions of the trip are to be found in his letters to Dona Evelina Nabuco:

"COMMONWEALTH," NEAR CHICAGO, April 26, 1906

. . . . It is really comfortable, a real bed of gilded bronze in a steel train. There is so little vibration that I can write with my pen as we travel along.

KANSAS CITY, April 27

. . . . The weather has been perfect so far; I have complete freedom, either with company or in isolation, and the food is excellent. When is the chef going to tire or when will we tire of him? That is the question!

COLORADO SPRINGS, April 29

. . . . The Cave of the Winds . . . . is a marvel which must be seen slowly and leisurely. We simply entered and left in a hurry. The natural works of sculpture seem to have been made by human hands. Some are of old marble and others of alabaster. The interior reminded me of the catacombs. Everything was illuminated by portable kerosene lamps and burning sticks of magnesium, while in Rome just a bit of twisted wax or matches were used. The most amazing thing was the road. For the first time in my life I realized what was meant here by the word "canyon." It is a narrow gorge between two high mountain walls whose massive formation reminds one of the ruins of old fortifications, castles, Roman temples, and ancient walls. The red coloration of the rocks and clay gives it a very dramatic appearance. In some sections of it I felt as if I were in the quarries of Syracuse. I climbed up the road just a short distance, but after I had reached the hotel to have lunch, I was quite proud of my feat, as I said in the letter which I wrote to you from there. After lunch we went to the Garden of the Gods. This extraordinary place is a strip of arid land like the rest of these mountains, with huge red rocks in the most fantastic formations. They seem like a colossal work produced by human efforts and look Egyptian. This unexpected fantasy has a singular beauty. The beauty of the whole thing is obviously the color, for, at least in my opinion, without any color the desolate sadness of the landscape would be more intense, while with color, it has life and freshness. It was quite cool when we returned, cold in fact . . . . We ate in the private car. The cook, as I told you, is excellent and is introducing us to the dishes of the French Antilles. It is quite a specialty. Today I took a ride and afterward attended High Mass. . . . .

GRAND CANYON, ARIZONA, May 2

. . . . This is a unique and incomparable sight! Imagine a deep chasm in which have been gathered all of the temples of India, the walls of ancient cities, the Colosseum, and the Castle of St. Angelo, but all in colossal proportions, in marbles of all colors, some entirely in terra cotta! At the bottom are deep excavations, forming the bed of the many branches of the Colorado. All this is fantastic, amazing, and awe-inspiring. There is a hotel next to it. However, I would prefer to spend my life looking at our small estate on Paquetá Island in Guanabara Bay, or on the banks of the Tagus. There is no vegetation in the canyon, just color and sculpture. It is simply marvelous. The pyramids of Egypt placed at the base of the canyon would seem like ants on the Minas Gerais plateau. Do you remember?

PASADENA, CALIFORNIA, May 4

We crossed a great rocky and sterile desert before arriving in California from the Grand Canyon (or is it Cañon?), which we left yesterday. However, we awoke in a garden. Pasadena is a garden, all green, and filled with flowers like Cannes. Its streets are lined with trees from India.

The pepper trees are fine and delicate; I say fine because the leaves are light and fall easily. The country is a vast orange orchard; the orange trees here are small but loaded with fruit, and the leaves are a much clearer and neater green than that of our trees on the Maricá road.

SAN FRANCISCO, May 11

. . . . We found San Francisco to be a shamble of ruins, a huge Roman Forum, with buildings standing erect and untouched here and there among the ruins. It is a phantom city. In many places the walls remain standing, but the interiors have been entirely burned out. Everywhere one sees tents, shacks, women cooking in the open air, wagons attempting to carry off debris, which it seems it will cost millions to clear away. There are encampments scattered about the city, of which parts are intact and other parts seem so when viewed from the outside. That is my impression. The city will rise and flourish again. What an endless number of domestic tragedies were caused by the earthquake! However, the great fire was chiefly responsible for most of the damage, which occurred over a period of several days. The people here do not even want to know about this damage; they do not have the time. Masses are being said outdoors on portable altars. Despite the destruction, order prevails. There are many carriages for hire as well as automobiles. Many people from San Francisco have crossed the Bay and established temporary residence in Oakland; this interim period is a boon for Oakland. Ruins, however, do not fit into the American scene; whosoever desires to see ruins in the United States should hurry along.

WINNIPEG, May 20

. . . . In spite of the fact that this is the worst hotel of the entire trip, it is the one in which I slept the best. The air here is ideal. Even in the warm sunshine one can feel the purity and crispness from the glaciers and ice sheets of the pole whence the air comes without being spoiled by anything. The air which we breathe is the air from Hudson Bay, tempered by direct rays of the sun. It is delightful . . . .

The trip to Brazil followed almost immediately. On July 13, Nabuco once again set foot on Brazilian soil at Recife and was received with the same affection that this city had shown him in the past; he described this pleasant hospitality in a letter to a fellow Pernambucan: "This is the happiest recollection which I shall have of this life or of this world. I expect it will be recalled to my children by the name which I gave to my first son in memory of our beloved Mauricéa" [name given to Recife or Pernambuco during the Dutch occupation under Prince Maurice of Nassau; Nabuco's oldest child, Mauricio, is at present Brazilian Ambassador to the United States].

In Recife, and later in Bahia, he was welcomed enthusiastically. There were demonstrations on the wharves and in the streets. All shops were closed and banquets were held in government palaces. In both cities moving ceremonies had been prepared. In Bahia they awaited his arrivel so that he could attend the unveiling of a commemorative plaque in the house where his father was born. In Recife, trying to re-create the scene of the glorious days of the abolitionist movement, they took him to the Santa Isabel Theater and packed it with a capacity crowd to listen to him speak.

At this scene of his former triumphs, recalling Mont' Alverne, he cried: "It is late! It is too late!" Nabuco spoke about the Pan American Conference which was to be held soon. He introduced the delegates, who were his travel companions, and transferred the applause to them, asking them to speak also.

"The historical truth is this: the abolitionist movement was won by us here." In this manner Nabuco spoke to the audience which filled the theater on that day, to the young people who listened with the respect due to tradition. They were naturally not the same young people who had helped him achieve the triumphs of 1884. But, then again, he was not really the same speaker. The poet Olavo Bilac, after hearing him in Rio, wrote the following in the *Gazeta de Notícias* of July 22, 1906:

> He is not the same speaker, he is better. His style is a model of concision and clarity; and his great talent, now fully matured in the abundance of autumn, is bearing its best fruits—rich fruits of political wisdom and cautious and prudent diplomacy, which the fatherland gathers gratefully and affectionately. His appearance and voice are the same—and the former, perhaps a little more majestic because of the new dignity lent by his white hair. His voice retains the same musical and singing resonance of his youth. He is still a master at emphasizing and stressing all of the beauties of the language.

"Never before have I had such a unanimously favorable reception," he wrote to Dona Evelina Nabuco.

It was the first time, as a matter of fact, that he had been acclaimed by the Brazilian nation, without having his name, now a part of the national patrimony, serve as a blazing torch for the purposes of some political party. To Dona Evelina Nabuco, he wrote: "I am aware of my personal popularity as I am of that of others, and in the same manner that I was aware of earlier unpopularity and public indifference. It is due to one fact. But it is a fact which is a symptom. It reveals the hope and resolve of the country. It is my 'American policy' which is being acclaimed."

He wanted to believe in the existence of such enthusiasm for his cause, but the reception which he received in Rio de Janeiro was quite personal. He was fascinated by the new beauty of the modernized Rio. The avenue, today called "Avenida Rio Branco," which had just been completed and was normally almost deserted, was filled with people. The mosaic sidewalks and store windows were teeming with people, eagerly watching and applauding a Nabuco different from the one who had departed seven years before, and who had disappeared from public view since the fall of the Empire. In the words of the well-known journalist from Bahia, Constancio Alves, he was a Nabuco who united,

. . . . in his appearance that which one rarely sees: the beauty and majesty of old age . . . . , that ineffable hour of dusk when the violent colors of sunset begin to fade into a dark melancholia. Then everything seems to prepare for the august and mysterious moment of concentration and piety, when, as the birds fly away, over the silent earth, the attention of the heavens is called by the reverberations of the bells tolling the "Ave Maria."

He is the Nabuco of this twilight hour, crowned with snow and with a soul of resplendent Alpine whiteness.[1]

His soul was indeed shining, but he was seriously shaken in health; he never recuperated. Nabuco saw his robust body racked by arteriosclerosis, and minor disturbances increasing in number day by day. He calculated rightly, that, with extreme care, he could perhaps live for another five years. When his eyes were absorbed in space, a profound sadness was revealed in his expression, almost a sharp sadness, especially at the times when he could not succeed in overcoming the enforced isolation of his deafness. But his smile melted everything.

His ability to sway others did not disappear with old age; on the contrary, the years brought an enhancement of this attribute. His kindliness was always apparent in his beautiful yet ever dominating eyes, in his eager desire to please others, which, in view of his great prestige, was even more touching. For all who knew him, he had a spontaneous charm and sincerity, and was always ready with a nice remark for the ladies. The serenity of his spirit did not dampen his enthusiasm, nor diminish his interest in keeping informed about happenings, the doings of individuals, especially of his friends, or politics in general. In physical appearance he remained unchanged. He had preserved his vigorous and erect mien, which had been enhanced by the dignity of age. Even the redness of his face, which gave him the appearance of a foreigner and which was a visible sign of his failing health, only served to heighten the effect of his silver locks. Throughout his life people commented on his fine masculine appearance. In the United States, where there is a tendency toward exaggeration, the conductor of a

[1] Inaugural address given in the Brazilian Academy of Letters, August 1922.

sightseeing bus once shouted to the tourists through his megaphone while passing the Brazilian Embassy: "The Brazilian Ambassador is the most handsome man in Washington!"

When Joaquim Nabuco, almost a sexagenarian, returned to Rio de Janeiro in 1906, "the beaming expression of the victor seemed veiled by a thin dark cloud of sadness, skepticism, or disillusionment." These were the words of Levi Carneiro, one of the many who welcomed Nabuco at the pier, although he was not acquainted with him. He further stated:

> . . . . All of those of us who knew him only by reputation immediately fell captive to his charm. An uncontrollable impulse made us accompany him afoot through the city to the Praça José de Alencar. There his cab stopped at the entrance to the Hotel dos Estrangeiros; standing on the footboard, Joaquim Nabuco cast his noble and lofty eyes over the crowd of admirers. He then spoke a few simple words of gratitude. To my eyes, his figure appeared to be revitalized by a touch of magic. He was the same Nabuco whom I had seen in the great campaign in which he triumphed, and who was directly responsible for my immediate and active support of the abolitionist movement. His voice of rare tonality, resounding like a victorious trumpet call without any effort or use of oratorical tricks, was clear, resonant, and full. His well-chosen words, which revealed his great imagination, still resound deep within me. He himself wrote the following, almost belittling his past oratorical triumphs: "How different it would be today. I could no longer derive any spiritual pleasure from any of that!" But all of us could recall his words of 1888 in everything he said in 1906. We could all feel the emotional resurgence. I could picture him, I could hear his eloquence vibrant for the great causes of emancipation and federation, burning, hot with passion, brilliant, and avenging. I felt as if I were in the crowd which had listened to him twenty years before. I was convinced, won over, and attracted to the cause.
>
> A few days later I saw Joaquim Nabuco again and heard him speak at a great banquet of extreme political significance given in the old Casino Fluminense. I shall always retain in my mind's eye the picture of him standing there with the elegance of a man of society, and the serene, harmonious, and enchanting beauty of the speech in which he expressed his thanks. I never saw or heard him speak again. However, these impressions made swiftly during my adolescence were enough to allow me to imagine the impression that would have been made in speeches advocating federal reform.[2]

After the public demonstrations, the most illustrious names in Brazilian politics, finance, and letters, and his personal friends celebrated his arrival with a banquet at the Casino Fluminense.

As the honored guest, Nabuco's speech was one of elaboration upon his happiness at being home again. He began by expressing his gratitude for the kind affection which Brazil had showered upon him since he landed in

[2] "Joaquim Nabuco e a Monarquia Federativa," *Jornal do Comércio*, December 25, 1926.

his native province. Then in giving a rapid account as a traveler who has returned to his resting place, he explained and harkened back to the long years of separation, declared his faith in the future of the Republic, in which he had not believed when he left, and finally with the tone of intimacy used by someone who was speaking at home, he began to speak in favor of Pan-Americanism to ears which were easy to convince; to engage in propaganda on behalf of Pan-Americanism was something which seemed indispensable to him.

When the Baron of Rio Branco was named Minister of Foreign Affairs, I told him that if someday he desired to have a true "American policy" he should send me to Washington. Our policy of friendship toward the United States is highly advantageous. It has the greatest advantage which any policy can have, that of having no alternatives, of being irreplaceable, because isolationism is not an alternative policy. Isolationism would not be adequate for handling the immense problems which the future holds in store for us.

A few days later, the Pan American Conference was held, and he was elected its president. Like Root's visit, the conference was a success; there were no hitches. President Afonso Penna opened the conference:

The International American Conference in Rio de Janeiro and the visit by the eminent American statesman, Mr. Elihu Root . . . . which have distinguished our nation and others of Latin America, are factors of extremely important political significance, marking a new era in the relations between the peoples of the New World.

Nabuco wrote these comments to his wife regarding the opening of the conference:

Yesterday was a memorable day in my life. I presided over the session of the conference honoring Mr. Root. I was successful in having Rio Branco propose to the President that the name, Monroe, be given to the building in which the conference was holding its deliberations. This the President did and the result was announced that evening. Everyone feels that it was a historical session, a mark in our national life. [Today the Palácio Monroe, a conspicuous landmark at the end of the Avenida Rio Branco, houses the Brazilian Senate.]

A concise report of what occurred that happy night was noted down by a newspaperman stationed at the door of the Palácio Monroe. Describing the movement and the color, Oliveira Viana wrote:

We, the students, marched past, excitedly forming a torchlight parade in honor of the American statesman. At the head of the central stairway the diplomatic corps, the ambassadors from the American countries, and ranking civilian and military officials were arrayed. Below them thousands of paper lanterns on the ends of long canes oscillated to and fro, causing the multicolored lights to create fantastic patterns over the noisy milling mass of onlookers.

At the moment when an array of brilliant fireworks were set off over the stairs, the silhouette of Nabuco in his topcoat could be clearly seen above everyone in the sudden bluish glare of the illuminated night; he stood out majestically, towering proudly above Root and Rio Branco.

He was leaning a bit to the right as if he were resting. He was calm and serene. Standing between those two men of normal stature, one thin, the other heavy, his elegant figure dominated all. All eyes were concentrated upon him. Nabuco seemed to be aware of the admiration which he had inspired; he relaxed even more and assumed an insouciant air of Olympian serenity—as if he had been placed at that moment before the objectivity of history and wanted to leave the ideal model for his statue as a legacy to posterity.[3]

The Third Pan American Conference was peaceful and profitable. At the last session Nabuco reviewed the accomplishments of the conference:

. . . . Your meeting here has not been a sterile and fruitless one. The political observer who interprets these events in the same light which the future will cast upon them, will see in your accomplishments a great implanting of creative ideas. Above all, he will see the inception of a new spirit, on the formation of which the real worth of these conferences depends, as well as the creation of American solidarity.

The general impression which we shall take with us is that of the harmony and unanimity of thought prevalent throughout the deliberations. The few apprehensions we had prior to holding the conference were dispelled as if by magic when the sessions began, and thus we could see that they had merely been misunderstandings. Our discussions were confined to the various means of attaining the desired end. The final objective was agreed on unanimously from the very start. The only differences concerned procedure. With this in mind, it can be said that the general atmosphere and spirit of this conference promise well for the success of subsequent conferences, for it produced no hints of mistrust or skepticism regarding the roles which these countries should play in the unification and progress of our continent. The merits of this policy of co-operation are now unquestioned. The Pan American Union came of age in this Third Congress. Its reason for being has now been approved by the nations of this continent. No one asks for more than that which he can give, and all of the nations look with favor upon the Union. Gentlemen, I want to congratulate you for being the first to set and fix the course which should be traced by future periodic meetings of this body, that is to formulate only those policies about which there is general accord. In this manner you eliminated all problems which could be a source of discord. Thus each succeeding meeting will receive more and more applause from all of America. They will not be perpetual focuses of discord and competition; on the contrary, they will be centers of co-operation and harmony.

[3] Oliveira Viana, *Pequenos estudos de Psicologia social*, p. 205.

It is most gratifying to me to review your work. You began by praising the happy results of the mediation of President Roosevelt and the President of Mexico in re-establishing peaceful relations between the republics of Guatemala, Honduras, and El Salvador. We had the good fortune of meeting just after peace had returned to Central America. You ratified the adhesion of the American republics to the principle of arbitration, and you made an appeal to the coming Hague Conference to perpetuate this principle in a treaty worthy of the approbation of the entire civilized world. In effect, if this great principle is not to be sacrificed in attempts and schemes which will make it useless, all of the enlightened powers of the civilized world should agree to the one aim of giving it the form and sanctions best suited to it. It would be a serious responsibility to use it in the case of every disturbance which arose. You recognized the Bureau of American Republics in Washington by giving it a ten-year term and converting it into an institution capable of fulfilling its lofty purposes. It is now a permanent center of action, common to all of the republics of this continent, for all activities concerning their relations and their progress. The manner in which you gave life to that secretariat and the auxiliary organs which you established in the respective states would be enough to justify the holding of this conference. You signed a convention regulating the effects which the renewal of residence for more than two years in a naturalized citizen's native land would have upon his naturalization. This action was not aimed against cases of necessity or good faith. For nations in which naturalization is a relatively simple process, this agreement will discourage or reform the acquisition of citizenship for non-patriotic ends. You extended until 1912 the treaty regarding pecuniary claims signed in Mexico in 1902, which subjected these claims to arbitration when recourse to diplomacy was justifiable. You created a dependency of the International Secretariat of American Republics for the purpose of studying the tariff legislation of the continent, to compile and clarify it in order to facilitate greater uniformity and also to attain more uniform commercial statistics. You created a union of the nations of America for the purpose of protecting literary and industrial property by means of an appropriate international registry, with two centers, one in Havana and the other in Rio de Janeiro.

You created a legal commission, having its first seat in Rio de Janeiro, entrusted with the preparation of a code of international public law and another code of international private law, to regulate relations between the American nations. This will be the American continent's contribution to the progress of international law, which tends to be only one, but whose variants authorize and make possible so many rules of procedure, all differing from nation to nation. It is a contribution which can be important, so considerable is the influence of international law upon this continent, thanks to the forward-looking initiative which the United States has taken in this field. Even if this were not so, everything which stimulates the interest of our publicists in law and international questions lends a great service to the culture of our countries.

You paid serious attention to devising means for broadening the activities of the International Sanitary Bureau in Washington. Among other things, you gave it an auxiliary center of information for South America, to be established in Montevideo. You allied the Pan American Bureau with the International Sanitary Bureau in Paris.

You recommended that our governments consider the advisability of asking the Hague Conference to study the question of the collection of public debts by force and more generally to investigate methods for diminishing the possibility of conflicts exclusively pecuniary in origin. Thus you permitted our governments liberty of action in a matter which, although not controversial in principle, is quite delicate as far as the manner of its presentation to the nations of the world and its incorporation into international law are concerned.

You confirmed the treaty dealing with the practice of the liberal professions which was signed at the Second Conference.

You indicated an interest in seeing the continuance of the Pan-American railroad project, the development of commerce, rapid communications, the establishment of a postal and parcel service between the various nations, and duty exemptions for merchandise in transit.

You indicated an interest in gathering all of the available data regarding the monetary system of the American republics and the exchange fluctuations during the last twenty years. These exchange oscillations are actually the major cause of disturbances in all types of commercial intercourse, especially international commercial relations; they also are the main obstacle to the afflux of foreign capital.

In the interest of introducing foreign capital into these American nations, aside from what I have already mentioned, you made other important recommendations regarding concessions of lands, mines, forests, and public works.

You recommended the calling of an international American conference in the city of São Paulo to help the coffee-producing nations. São Paulo will be greatly honored by this choice.

You solemnly received the Secretary of State of the United States of America during the June 31 session. The manner in which you acclaimed his words and applauded the Foreign Minister of Brazil when he declared that, in honor of Secretary Root's visit, this building would be named the Monroe Palace, indicated that there no longer remain any remnants of political antagonism between Latin America and the United States. The general aspiration of the entire continent is to form one sole community in all matters of international law and for all the common interests of our civilization.

Although we confirmed thus the existence of an American political system, yet by reserving to The Hague the solution of two important questions, we have shown that we do not recognize the existence of a private system of international law for ourselves and that we do not form a separate community from world civilization.

Toward the end of our conference, when the deliberations were evolving in a most auspicious manner, we were shocked by one of these catastrophes which leave a lasting mark in history—the Valparaiso earthquake. The nations here fought among themselves for the honor of rendering the first homage to Chile in the name of all of them; by unanimous vote, the flags of the nations were placed at half-mast and will remain so until the adjournment of our conference. The conference also expressed the wish that the inauguration of the Fourth Pan American Conference will find the Chilean nation enjoying happier days.

Finally, you approved giving the power to fix the time and place of the next conference to the representatives of the American states in Washington; this was done because of the constant necessity for placing the power to call these meetings in the hands of some body; but you went on record with a clear indication of your unanimous desire to have the meeting held in Buenos Aires.

Throughout the entire period of acclimatization, the principal function of these conferences for a long time will continue to be simply that of meeting periodically, and the most favorable symptom of this acclimatization is the good will and harmony which I have mentioned. In this sense, the Third Conference is already indicative of a healthy growth. However, it is necessary to allow time for the tree to grow, for it has to live for centuries. We must not expect the tree to give shade before it has roots. At this moment it depends upon each one of us; the time will come when we all will depend upon it.

Gentlemen, aside from the honor which you gave to Brazil by designating it as the seat for three of your creations, you also honored Brazil by naming the Baron of Rio Branco as honorary president of this conference and the president of the Brazilian delegation as its effective president. The representatives of the American states in Washington had already conceded to you the privilege of nominating your secretary-general. For all of this attention and all of these courtesies we are especially grateful.

Having merited your confidence will be for me one of the fondest recollections of my life. My hope and desire is that the Fourth Conference will mark an even more definite step forward in the history of this great institution.

"The conference," he wrote to his wife, "was a huge success; I was overjoyed when I left it. I am, however, terribly tired; the worse, if not the more intense, fatigue of trips still awaits me, for I have to visit São Paulo, Belo Horizonte, and Pilar."

A very changed and ever progressing São Paulo celebrated his arrival on September 13. Nabuco received an ovation on the fourteenth at a special session held in his honor at the law school, where he had been a student. On the fifteenth, he was honored by a torchlight parade organized by the students. They forced him to get up from the dinner table and address them from the terrace of the "Chácara do Carvalho," the country home of António Prado, who was his host.

On the eighteenth he noted in his diary: "For my departure, the railroad station was jammed with students acclaiming me. They accompanied the train along the track for a few seconds. The platform was filled with such enthusiasm that I feel I am going to die a young man."

Afterward there was the trip to Belo Horizonte as the guest of his old friend Afonso Penna, who was soon going to take his oath of office as President of the Republic. One of the first bits of news which Nabuco received upon arriving in Brazil was that he would be invited to take over the Ministry of Foreign Affairs. There were two decisive factors preventing his acceptance of this high post. One was the conviction that his health would not withstand the intense work which he would impose upon himself in carrying out the duties of his office. "But if I am offered the post," he wrote his wife, "my refusal must be explicable in terms of my previous activities."

On August 5, he again wrote to her: "The task of refusing to collaborate is not a pleasant one. However, people should not be obliged to sacrifice their lives, and I feel that I could not withstand the strain of the ministry. Moreover, I still would not be giving as much to my job as I could if I were to take a rest for a while."

The second reason why he did not want to accept was his characteristic devotion to the post which he had recently taken up in Washington. He saw no one who could possibly replace him there: "If Rio Branco were not occupying the foreign office, I would be in a difficult position, but with Rio Branco desirous of continuing in office, I will not be caught this time." He continued in his letter to his wife: ". . . . my main desire now is to settle down for a few more years there in Washington. . . . . I have thought up this fitting formula: If I were Minister of Foreign Affairs, my first act would be to appoint myself to the Washington post."

In this way he answered his friends who were sounding him out on the subject. By retaining Rio Branco, his predecessor's foreign minister, Afonso Penna created a precedent of reappointing Rio Branco which was deservingly received with applause. Rio Branco remained Foreign Minister of Brazil until his death. On August 30, Afonso Penna wrote the following to Nabuco:

> For no possible reason could I ever dispense with your co-operation during my term of office in the post in which you felt best suited to serve Brazil.

Nabuco spent his last days in Brazil on a beautiful plantation which was falling into decay. It was located at Maricá in the state of Rio de Janeiro. There he witnessed the last painful days of his father-in-law, the Baron of Inohan. From Maricá he wrote to his wife:

> October 3
>
> My departure is as sad as my arrival here was joyous. Your father is stricken at Pilar, where there are no facilities for treating him. . . . .
>
> . . . . I have always had a foreboding that this stay in Brazil would have a sad end, since I enjoyed such ovations and had so much success. God, however, will not let me bring you mourning and a saddened soul.

October 4

. . . . In this world we never get something for nothing. We pay for everything. God's will be done! What receptions upon my arrival and what sadness for my departure! . . . .

The rapid advance of his infection is discouraging.

October 7

. . . . I found the old carriage awaiting us in Maricá, with Evausto as footman, we then came here. . . . . How sad was this trip which I made so many times and still expected to make someday under different conditions, as part of a family celebration. Along the road I met some of the tenants who spoke to me with disconsolate countenances. Among them was "Racha pé" ("Foot-splitter"). How run-down Pilar is! The fields are now forests; the buildings are turning to ruins, everywhere one sees misery and neglect . . . . The Baron is surrounded by the old personnel of the plantation, blind Mr. Candinho, and the tenants who help. He has had over five hundred visits from poor people. When he dies, he wants to be buried in the Chapel of Health. The funeral will be an immense demonstration by the poverty-stricken of Maricá to their benefactor. What a beautiful death! What a consecration! It gives me unspeakable sadness to be a witness to Pilar's last days, but I am here as your representative and I shall drink the cup of sorrow to the dregs. Besides, it is a great consolation for your father to have me here and to have Beatrice at his bedside. The worst thing will be the resettlement of these people whom he supported by running himself into debt. . . . .

As a consolation for this, his room is always filled with people, a continual stream of visitors whom he is pleased to see; their devotion is amazing! What a beautiful reward! It is impossible to imagine a more touching end; even in death he feels the sweetness of this reward. He is with those whom he loved so much that he never wanted to be separated from them. Poor people! For them the blow is tremendous; throughout the entire day, during this crucial hour, all of them have forgotten themselves completely and thought only of him! As I said in my letter to you, in watching him during his fading hours, I am recalling a scene which impressed me so much during my childhood. The death and disappearance of my godmother robbed me of a source of strength, which had served as the center toward which so many others had oriented their existence. Moreover, your father's tomb in the Chapel of Health is a faithful copy of my godmother's tomb in the little chapel of St. Matthew in Massangana. The same end! It is all so similar: the love of the former slaves, of the old servants, of the poor people whom he tried to help . . . . In a way it is comforting that I happened to be here at this time. . . . . It was God who kept me here in Brazil . . . .

What days these are in Pilar! You can well imagine how violently my heart has throbbed and how many images and pictures have flashed through my mind, how many recollections have been evoked.

October 8

. . . . All of the people in Pilar are disconsolate, relieving each other in shifts day and night at his bedside, wanting only to be with him, thinking only of him to the exclusion of everything else, on the eve of the day when they would lose their protector . . . .

October 9

. . . . The end should come soon. Here in Pilar, besides us three—Mme Beatrice, myself, and Chermont—are the following: Margaret and her daughter; blind Mr. "Candinho"; the physician, Dr. Baptista; the vicar at night; Juca Mendonça during the day; and numerous tenants and servants—among them are: "Carrapicho" [little horn of the young ox], who is extremely devoted to my father-in-law, never leaving his side; Quinquina, who is beyond consolation because she cannot leave Pilar and go to you; Oscar, Belisario's brother; in the kitchen is Carlos, who I believe was formerly the coachman, and many old ladies; Isabel, who has a little boy and prepares my rice soup. In the dilapidated slave quarters are the old men of another era and those who have aged since our last stay here . . . .

October 10

At two o'clock in the morning he received Extreme Unction; at five o'clock in the afternoon, the supplicatory litanies.

We sat up with him through the night. Beatrice prayed. At five o'clock in the morning (on the eleventh), in the presence of Carrapicho, myself, and Margaret, who placed a candle in his hand, he passed away . . . .

October 11

At nine o'clock, Mass was celebrated in the presence of the body . . . .

At three o'clock the body was borne away by hand. The principal figure was Juca Mendonça, solemn and dignified. With your eyes I watched the funeral procession descend the hill of Pilar, go around the sugar mill, out onto the pasture. It was most impressive. I cannot describe it. Afterward we followed by carriage and attended the funeral. That night we returned to Rio by express train . . . .

On October 18, Nabuco trod on the soil of his country for the last time. His last three years were to be spent abroad, always dreaming of a last trip home. When the ship on which he was returning to the United States passed through Recife and he was unable to land because of lack of time, he entered this final impression of his native land into his diary:

We followed the coast; at a distance there was Maceió, then hours later Cape St. Augustine, the familiar Pernambucan landscape—the white border of beach, the coconut trees, the green hills; in the afternoon we were opposite Recife. After my friends and the students left, I remained standing there, looking at the sunset in the west blazing like a Turner over Olinda. At night the moon seems like a ship, a golden caravel floating on a black cloud. In this way I take leave of Recife, perhaps forever.

CHAPTER XXVII. SPEECHES AND ACTIVITIES IN WASHINGTON, 1907–8

One of the most useful results of the Third Pan American Conference and the first article in its resolutions concerned a reorganization involving principally the creation of a permanent secretariat in Washington. The future Pan American Union was born in the First International Conference of American States, held in Washington in 1890. It was confirmed by the Second Conference, which took place in Mexico City in 1902. It underwent a change during the Third Conference, which gave it permanence and notably enlarged its functions and ends. Having begun as a simple agency for information and propaganda, precarious in existence and solely for commercial ends, it soon became a consultative assembly for international deliberations, a permanent factor for good will among nations, a basis for peace.

Nabuco held that the development of this organ for greater concerted action was one of the strongest aids to the program of Pan-Americanism, and of continental peace. As far as Brazil was concerned, this program did not limit itself exclusively to friendship with the United States. In a speech to the Liberal Club of Buffalo, Nabuco dealt with the "Lessons and Prophecies of the Third Pan American Conference":

> The repeated meetings of our countries will force them to exchange ideas, iron out mutual difficulties, and become more vividly aware of their natural relationship. The creation of the organ actually preceded the formation of the policy and principles it was destined to espouse, but now the principles have completely enveloped it. Mr. Root completed Mr. Blaine's work; he converted the dream into a reality. In the creation and formation of anything, many things, of necessity, remain hidden. The founders were hardly beginners. The statesmen who conceived it could hardly have imagined that the small Bureau, originally intended to be a simple disseminator of information about the American republics, would become a political bond of great force uniting them. In the meantime, the representatives of the American nations could not meet regularly every month in the Department of State with the Secretary of State presiding, without feeling themselves, or giving to the entire world, the impression of a united America, deliberating jointly. This impression would tend to grow, especially now with Mr. Carnegie's magnificent gift, which will permit us to build a worthy home in Washington for the Permanent Council of American Nations.

All aspects of the secretariat were transformed. "The Bureau of American Republics," Nabuco wrote to J. C. Rodrigues, "which at the time of my arrival seemed to be the focal point of conspiracies and manifestations of ill will against the United States, following Brazil's example, soon became a busy arena in which the combatants vied with each other to gain the favor, friendship, and confidence of the United States."

The initial informative functions of the agency were extraordinarily increased by the indefatigable zeal and the ability as a promoter of the new director, John Barrett. Mr. Root, seeing that the institution which was the basis of his policies, was functioning in a modest rented house, pointed out to Andrew Carnegie the necessity for a more worthy and dignified Pan American building. This public-spirited Maecenas of the world's institutions for peace had just given the Hague Court a palace in which to carry on its deliberations. Immediately he gladly gave several million dollars for the construction of the Pan American Union building in Washington. The council in charge of directing the construction began forthwith to discuss the choice of architects and plans. Nabuco, who was consulted, wrote the following to Barrett:

> There is no such thing as Spanish-American architecture, at least worthy of the name of an art. I think it would be better to make a building beautiful in itself, like so many in the United States and leave the historical or political allusions for the decoration of the rooms. I am sending you a copy of my speech in Buffalo with a suggestion for naming our building and selecting its two patrons. We cannot have more patrons than those two, as they alone represent a great fact common to all the continent. Columbus is its father and Washington its political godfather, as our institutions were all received from him. . . . .

On May 11, 1908, the cornerstone was laid during a beautiful and solemn ceremony. Cardinal Gibbons and the Episcopal Bishop of Washington invoked God's blessing upon it. Speeches were delivered by Roosevelt, Root, Carnegie, and Nabuco, as dean of the American diplomats. An immense crowd filled the large bleachers which had been set up in the open air. It was a beautiful day. Not even Nabuco's voice succeeded in carrying the words of his speech to the most distant listener. Perhaps of all the speeches which he gave in the United States, this one gained for him more applause from friends and the admiration of more strangers than any other. It was a very fortunate speech, not only because of his choice of words but also because of the inspiration which Nabuco seemed to feel for an ideal that was still new, and which now has been universally accepted. It was a successful speech because of its august dignity and conviction:

> Mr. President, you spoke about the other nations on this continent in a manner which gave them much satisfaction and won you their gratitude. You can easily see that along with their admiration for your powerful race and its heretofore unequaled degree of progress, they also offer to the Union their pride in their Latin heritage, of which there is no greater proof than the English language itself. The

world will be able to measure the greatness of Columbus' domain only when the future permits the Latin-American countries to develop their share of that which was given to each one of them in his cradle, as this country already has done. I hope that your happy prophecies are as auspicious as usual. In addition to your generous greetings, your talk betrayed the soul of a nation which could never permit any differences between nations, whether they be weak or strong.

We were thrilled to applaud the high tribute which you paid to the present Secretary of State when you conferred a high distinction upon him on this, his day of triumph. His visit to Central and South America was one of those acts which typify a great statesman and which will make him live forever in the hearts of many people. He won over the hearts of our peoples and was able to send you one of the most brilliant *Vini, vidi, vici's* in the history of diplomacy, because of his high ideals, his sense of justice, his great charm and his ability to understand the feelings of other countries. They, on the other hand, won his soul and will cherish his image as a friendly pledge of peace and good will by this great Republic.

Mr. President, you can well be noble-minded. No other American president will leave a more indelible mark in the history of Pan-Americanism. You are now cutting a route from one ocean to the other, altering the world's sea lanes and bringing the people and cities of the opposite shores of our continent closer together. [The Panama Canal, opened by Woodrow Wilson, was a project of the Roosevelt administration.]

To you Mr. Carnegie, we express our gratitude for your munificent donation. By choosing this city as the permanent seat of our Union, the Latin republics have most fittingly shown that they are proud of the nation which has been the leader of our continent and which has placed our continent in the vanguard of civilization. You remembered that your country, as well as being our associate, was also the host, and that being chosen as host was the highest tribute ever paid to your American democracy, which your book has endeared to the present generations. You were also moved by the idea which has inspired so many of your books, that of striving in the future for the triumph of world peace. You rightly believe that peace is universal charity. Our alliance is, in effect, a completely peaceful one, which shines outside of the American orbit only to let the rest of the world know that it can be called the hemisphere of peace.

Gentlemen, never has there been a parallel to the scene being portrayed here today, in this ceremony in which twenty nations speaking diverse languages are constructing a home for their joint deliberations. Even more impressive is the fact that these countries, in spite of their great differences in size and population, have established their Union upon a basis of the most absolute equality. Here the vote of the smallest member counterbalances that of the largest member. So many sovereign states could not have been mutually attracted to each other so spontaneously, as if drawn together by an irresistible force, were it not for the existence in each of the individual national consciences of a feeling of having a common American destiny. Indeed, it seems as if in the dusk of history Divine Providence decreed that the western coast of the Atlantic should rise as the chosen land for the resurgence of humanity. Ever since the first days of the period of colonization, there has always been a feeling in the hearts of its sons that this is truly the New World. This is a feeling which unites us all on this auspicious day. We all feel that we are sons of Washington. The new seat for the Union of American Republics, rising above the plains of the Potomac in sight of the capitol, will be another monument to the founder of modern liberty. There we see his national memorial; this will be his continental memorial.

Gentlemen, with the voice of His Eminence, Cardinal Gibbons, still echoing in my ears, our only prayer is for the strengthening of the vows which we have mutually taken, so that we can all be thoroughly inspired by the indissoluble association of the two Americas.

Another very successful speech was the one which he gave that same year at the Corcoran Gallery of Art on December 15, during the commemoration ceremonies for one of the outstanding figures in American art, the sculptor Augustus Saint-Gaudens. Roosevelt and Root also spoke on that occasion. The French Ambassador Jusserand spoke as did Bryce from England, who was introduced on that day by Root as "today, ... the Ambassador from Ireland" recalling Saint-Gaudens' native land.

Nabuco spoke only a few words but they were profound:

Ladies and Gentlemen:

I can well understand that no American genius could dream of any other type of immortality than that which his own country can give to his name. But art, like science, is a unity, and a name, in order to retain immortality, must necessarily conquer the world. I believe that Saint-Gaudens' name will live forever, and that it has already begun its conquest. It is not difficult to recognize immortality at the first glance. From Plato to Phidias and from Emerson to Saint-Gaudens, the impression of immortal intelligence was immediately made. I remember my first contact with Saint-Gaudens. It was on the day I disembarked in New York and saw his *Sherman*. I did not know whose statue it was, but I immediately realized that there before me was one of the most inspiring symbols ever conceived of the triumph of art. I again felt the sensation experienced by one when unexpectedly confronted by a great work of art, when I found myself standing in front of the Wayne MacVeagh plaque in a salon in this city. It was so simple yet so unforgettable. Later, when I went to the Rock Creek Cemetery, I was prepared to find an immortal work of art; but how could I have expected to see that magnificent spectacle? There was no more possible doubt. Only a genius could thus portray eternity. Of all modern creative works, this one alone can be compared with Michelangelo's *Night*. Very different in form, they are both reflections of the same obscure ray of mystery which embellishes and darkens for the spirit all of the glitter of creation. In the case of Saint-Gaudens' last-mentioned work, the idea might have been suggested by Michelangelo. The two earlier works were direct inspirations.

Do not believe that glory is dispensed by critics. It existed long before they did. It emanates from its own fountain. Glory most frequently comes from the rivalry and desperation of men in the same field who are struggling to achieve the degree of perfection already achieved by another. Vasari, in his *Lives of the Painters*, relates that fame is attained in that profession sometimes as a result of friendly rivalries, often because of envy, and even as a result of bitter hatred. The artists among themselves are unable to immortalize a work of genius; it is necessary that their recognition be supplemented by the emotion of the masses whose heart pulsates in the work. We are all but drops in the ocean. Yet we all want to have the consciousness of the ocean and not just of a drop. In each one of us present here today this consciousness reflects the image of the great American sculptor. This is glory; this is immortality.

Afterward, President Roosevelt wrote him the following:

MY DEAR MR. AMBASSADOR:

I want to send you a few words of personal gratitude and to congratulate you for the speech which you gave about Saint-Gaudens the other night. Many people have spoken to me about it. It was a magnificent discourse, profound in thought, rich in wording, and well delivered. Believe, my dear Ambassador, that among the many people who admire you as a philosopher, a politician of broad vision, and an accomplished man of letters, none admires you more than your sincere friend,

THEODORE ROOSEVELT

Among the many and varied settings for these speeches which Nabuco as ambassador was obliged to deliver, none was more pleasing to him than that of the universities. In speaking to America's youth, he found consolation for not being able to address the youth of Brazil in the twilight of his life. Expansive in nature, he was even more so with students. The apostle's spirit in him inspired him with a desire to join the academic profession, and a supreme eagerness to speak at length to his young countrymen before his death. In one of his letters written in 1909 he said: "My ambition in this final phase of my life is to speak to youth, to spread the sentiments and ideas which I shall take away with me when I depart and thereby carry with me into eternity. I believe that I could leave a political testament which would be a chart showing the reefs ahead and the route we should follow to avoid them. The greatest glory of all is to train disciples, in other words, to relive politically another generation, still serving the fatherland. I am afraid that I am too ambitious for my age and the present state of my health."

It was also in these universities that certain of his literary and spiritual qualities stood out more and were better understood; his vast fund of knowledge and culture, for which he received the epithet "scholarly"; the subtleness of his critical judgment; and, in a utilitarian country, his ardent love of the beautiful.

After two of these successful visits, he wrote the following to his old friend, J. C. Rodrigues:

I returned fascinated by Vassar and Cornell. At Cornell I was the guest of President Schurmann, one of the outstanding scholars in the country, with whom I am proud to have formed a spiritual and political friendship, in the Aristotelian sense of the word. He told me that my visits to universities and the friendships which I form with those who model the enlightened opinion of the nation are the best way of tightening the bonds of friendship between the United States and Brazil.

Most of these lectures were given during his last two years in Washington. As time went by, the invitations he received indicated more and more respect; the universities reserved their most important dates for him. The extremely interesting study published by the *American Historical Review* on "The Contribution of America to Civilization" was the Baccalaureate Address at the University of Wisconsin in 1909. His lecture on "Strengthening the Bonds of Friendship Between the Two Americas" was the Convocation Address in 1908 at the University of Chicago. From Chicago he wrote to Rio Branco: "This is written on the evening following the reception given in my honor. President Judson introduced me to eight hundred guests, half of whom were men; I shook hands with all of them."

Columbia and Yale bestowed honorary degrees upon him. Other similar distinctions had been planned for him, but he died before receiving them.

For these lectures he had one favorite subject, the great Portuguese poet Camoens. At Vassar he spoke about "Camoens, the Lyric Poet," at Yale about "Camoens' Place in Literature," and at Cornell about "The *Lusiads*, Epic of Love." He left, in the state of near completion, a fourth lecture on Camoens which he had promised to deliver at Harvard.

Placing Camoens before the American people was good propaganda for the Portuguese language, and it permitted him to talk about a subject which delighted him. Throughout his life he cherished a love for Camoens, a love which had inspired his first book at the age of twenty, *Camoens and the Lusiads*. At the age of sixty, he composed several sonnets in honor of the poet, which he left unpublished. He noted the following in his diary:

> I am reading the *Lusiads*—this book is truly my companion as it always was. I am sorry that I have not memorized any more of it, but I must rememorize the Isle of Love and Venus' supplication to Jupiter, so that I can recite them along with the sections on Adamastor and Inez de Castro, which I have never forgotten.

His colleague from Great Britain, James Bryce, wrote to him about the three lectures on Camoens:

> I have never read literary criticisms which were more polished, more delicate, or more suggestive. You have a mastery of our tongue which arouses my envy, if the feeling of envy could possibly be reconciled with such a fascinating subject.

The preparation of these lectures was more of a rest than a cure for him. It satisfied his need for literary activity, which also caused him to put together his *Random Thoughts*, in which he gathered the notes and lost thoughts from his manuscripts and added new ones.

He also removed from his drawer a work written in his youth, and fondly re-examined it. Written in French, it was a classic tragedy in Alexandrine verse. However, he never thought of having it published. It was written under the emotional stress of the war of 1870. It vibrated with enthusiasm for France and pity for the misfortune which had befallen it. The political subject of *The Option* prevented his publishing it. Furthermore, he realized the unequal worth of the drama and his inexperience in theater technique; the style on which he had based the play in his youth had become antiquated, deterring from its quality. The writing of the play gave him many fascinating hours of work. Many times afterward, when Nabuco gave dinner parties at the embassy for small groups, usually of diplomats, who were familiar with French, there would be readings of one act or even the entire play. When the guests showed signs of being touched emotionally by the eloquence of the lyrics and the sorrowful dignity of his verse as read by the smooth-voiced counselor of the embassy, Silvino Gurgel do Amaral, who always served as the talented interpreter, and when tears appeared in the ladies' eyes, Nabuco felt consoled for not having been able to submit *The Option* to a wider audience, and to give it more than the success it had achieved among his intimate friends.

The play begins on the eve of the war of 1870 in a Franco-German household, that of Prince von Fehrbellin and Hélène, his French wife. During twenty years of married life, their happiness had concealed the secret tragedy of a union in defiance of racial hatreds, and this union of enemies was just on the verge of being repeated in another generation, in the life of Clothilde, the daughter, who is engaged to a Frenchman at the outbreak of the war. While the German general is gaining fame and glory on the battlefield, he sees his home broken up and the happiness of his family vanish. Clothilde's dreams of love fade rapidly after the wedding feast. Robert, the son, who could never reconcile his love for France with his Prussian lieutenant's uniform, returned home to his parents on the historic day of The Option, when the inhabitants of Alsace-Lorraine had to choose between France and Germany. The tragedy of his fate is completed in the last scene of the drama.

Apart from his efforts on behalf of Brazil, in supporting and fighting for its interests in various disputes, Nabuco felt obligated by a self-imposed duty to strive without ostentation to gain greater distinction for Brazil and himself. This he did by paying due attention to purely temporal duties and obligations.

The social influence of the embassies could be very great. In a desire to take advantage of every kind of action, he gave the embassy all of the worldly brilliance which his resources would permit. He always maintained open house; for him, through preference and habit, it had become a necessity.

As far as Nabuco was concerned, entertaining someone was synonymous with inviting him to dinner. He always had some pretext for not offering any other type of hospitality. He did not enjoy large receptions. He did not like to entertain by watching others dance, and it bothered him to have his work interrupted at teatime. For him, a dinner with friends was the most pleasant way to end the day. It created a favorable atmosphere for conversation. A small dinner was very useful for straightening out tangled relations; a large dinner added a personal touch to the official homage which inspired it.

Thus, dining alone with his family was a rare event for Nabuco. Many times, it is true, the guests were the secretaries who had always been treated by Nabuco as an extension of his family. In general, they became devoted friends of their benevolent chief, whose confidence they enjoyed. After winning their affection, he returned it in full. He wrote the following to one of them:

> I am always true to those who show me friendship and affection, and also, because of my innate disposition which I myself could not alter, I give unto others that which is theirs. Therefore, you may consider my sense of justice to be something which you deserve and which you can count on.

Most of Nabuco's political activities were carried on in public. In order to be worth while, they required a large amount of publicity. On the other hand, many cases arose which received no publicity, either because they were invisible basic activities, or because they were confidential diplomatic activities, the record of which was to be placed in government archives.

Among the many opinions paying tribute to his work as ambassador, it should not seem strange to choose one of the most modest, that of the young stenographer, Emma Smith, who, during the entire period that he spent in Washington, was constantly at his side while he worked. Since it is easier to be brilliant in the eyes of admiring spectators when appearing before the public than in the unclouded eyes of those who watch from the sidelines, this letter which was discreetly and spontaneously left on his desk deserves a place in his biography:

> To me it seems to be a great pity that all of your compatriots cannot be made aware of the tremendous amount of work which you do every day in the pursuit of the duties of your high office, so that they can better appreciate them. No one,

except those who work with you, can be made to realize the amazing amount of energy which you expend in completing these arduous tasks and the firm perseverance which you maintain in accomplishing even the most difficult tasks.

It may be a bit forward of me to write you such a letter as this, when there is such a gap between our ages, our intellectual achievements, and the dignity of our positions. I beg you not to consider this to be an attempt on my part to meddle, or to exceed the bounds of my modest position, but, on the contrary, a sincere tribute from someone who feels great admiration for a truly noble character and a great intellect.

In the satisfactory solution of one case, which was divulged to the public only in general terms, the Brazilian press attributed great importance to the part played by Nabuco.

The newspapers noted with unhappy surprise that the German sailors were sent ashore from the German gunboat, "Panther," in the state of Santa Catarina, arrested a German citizen, and placed him in the ship's prison. Pessimists were of the opinion that little else could be expected as a result of the imperialistic designs which the German Empire was reputed to have on southern Brazil. The absence of immediate explanations caused a feeling of anxiety to sweep through the entire nation. Later complete reparations for the affront were forthcoming. It was finally announced that the "Panther" had given the Brazilian colors a twenty-one-gun salute and that the captain of the ship had lost his commission.

This case was not in Nabuco's sphere of activity, but a well-founded report reached the Chamber of Deputies stating that the Brazilian Embassy in Washington had asked for the intervention of the United States in the misunderstanding with the Imperial German government, and that it was only because of the avowed intention of the United States to enforce the Monroe Doctrine that the German government changed its attitude. The Brazilian government loudly denied the report that any foreign pressure had been required to obtain the apology owed to its national honor; a doubtful silence settled over the case.

Nabuco's work, along with adding interest to his life, also brought its share of inevitable disappointments. His friend, Rio Branco, frequently busy with other matters, did not always have an enthusiasm for Pan-Americanism as great as his own. In order to be content at his post, he desired liberty of action and the unanimous support of his government in carrying out his policy of greater friendship with the United States. Without this the position would have become perfunctory in nature. This was something which he did not feel disposed to tolerate. It was regarding this matter that during his first year in Washington he wrote to Afonso Penna, who everyone knew would be the next President of the Republic:

You will find me in this post and I do not know whether to ask you to retain me. This will depend on your policies. If they be definitely pro-American, in the sense of having a thoroughgoing understanding with this country, I shall take great pleasure in collaborating with you. If, however, you do not decide upon such policies, perhaps it would be better not to have here a Monroist of such pronounced leanings as mine, for it is not wise to delude the Americans. You could then send me to a place where my work would not be useless.

In his diary he wrote:

Negotiations between two countries should be conducted in the plain view of the stronger of the two by a capable agent and not just a "messenger boy." Rio Branco's practice is to reduce diplomatic agents to the role of a messenger, sending them instructions as to what they should say and reply—all prepared in advance, without any semblance of diplomacy, completely inflexible and intransigent. This is no way of accomplishing anything . . . . I would never get anything done if I observed the instructions which he has sent to me and did not seek to achieve the desired end by using other means. . . . . He associates himself so closely with various causes that he is unchanging and immovable in everything. He does not make requests, he imposes his will. He discusses matters like a lawyer in his telegrams. But what admirable zeal and what amazing vigilance he displays when protecting the key points of his diplomacy!

To Baron Rio Branco, Nabuco wrote:

I am dedicating the remainder of my active life to strengthening the bonds of friendship which unite our two nations. This is an end which one agent alone cannot achieve, or one minister, or even two administrations in agreement, one here and the other there; it can be achieved only with the assistance of many statesmen and diplomats on both sides over a period of years.

. . . . You already know quite well that I cannot do anything without conviction or enthusiasm; please think about finding a substitute for me if our foreign policy is changing the orientation of its security axis.

These, however, were all just temporary fears and anxieties which paralyzed his activities in Washington. He was most vexed by the needlessly incurred delays surrounding the signing of the arbitration treaty, which Root had signed with various other American nations. He was as anxious as was Nabuco to conclude it with Brazil before he left the office of Secretary of State. Official difficulties, small irritating obstacles, and unnecessary delays were all bothersome, but eventually cleared away. The difficulties which hampered the signing of the treaty faded in time.

Nabuco was invited to head the Brazilian delegation to the Hague Conference before Ruy Barbosa was, and he had accepted the mission when, before his acceptance had been made public, a newspaper campaign was launched in Rio proposing Ruy Barbosa's name as chief of the delegation. Rio Branco, always mindful of public opinion as manifested in journalistic outbursts, and knowing quite well that neither Ruy Barbosa nor Nabuco would accept any position except the chairmanship of the delegation, was faced with the delicate task of withdrawing his first invitation. He therefore telegraphed Nabuco, inviting him to serve at the Hague Conference under Ruy Barbosa: "We have already had 'a ministry of eagles,' we could send to The Hague a 'delegation of eagles,' if you wished." Nabuco refused for the reasons which he enumerates in the following letter to Graça Aranha: "As much as I would like to offer Ruy this proof of my friendship and confidence, and regardless of how strong my desire is to be with him in Europe . . . . I cannot go to The Hague as second delegate and he can go only as chief. . . . . No nation which attended the First Conference sent an ambassador as second delegate. Moreover, to send the President of the Pan American Conference of Rio as Brazil's second delegate to the Hague Conference would be a reflection upon the Rio Conference. . . . . were it not for this reason, I would be proud to serve in the delegation which necessarily will be led by Ruy Barbosa." To Ruy Barbosa he sent the following telegram: "My health obliges me to decline your offer, but I shall be with you in spirit. I take pride in seeing Brazil represented in this way among the nations of the world. Many, many congratulations."

Nabuco felt disillusioned at seeing Brazil in disagreement with the United States at the Hague Conference in 1907, with Ruy Barbosa and Choate assuming opposite positions. His worry was partially assuaged by the reports of the effect produced on the rest of the world by the eloquence and wisdom of Ruy Barbosa, and finally vanished completely. Root was the one who consoled him, as is attested by Nabuco in this letter to his brother-in-law and faithful confidant, Hilário de Gouvêa:

> Several days ago Root told me the following in confidence: "I did not propose anything at The Hague. I just wanted to see our delegation on the side of Right in all questions which were discussed. If I had had anything to propose or any issue in mind, I would have asked for your assistance."

On the whole, Nabuco's pro-American policy was operating so well that he was becoming more and more attached to his post. On August 3, 1909, he wrote to J. C. Rodrigues:

> At the same time that the thinking part of me wants to retire from the struggle, the Brazilian in me insists on staying to the end, perhaps even to die here, because I do not know who would succeed me in this embassy, or whether it would be a person with the same vision as I have of the future of America.

His many duties kept his mind off the sad side of his life, which was accentuated by his absence from Brazil, and his steady loss of health. "I live among strangers," he wrote to José Veríssimo, "and speak a strange tongue: For this reason I am spiritually isolated. Everything which comes to me from Brazil has a deep effect upon me."

CHAPTER XXVIII. THE EVENING AND NIGHTFALL, 1909–10

His health continued to get worse. The semblance of his former strength and vigor which he regained after taking a cure at one of the French watering places in 1907 soon vanished. His discouragement at seeing himself so old and ill was clearly reflected in his letters and diary: "I was tired and exhausted when I reached the pinnacle of my life," he wrote to Magalhães de Azeredo, "I was not intended to be an old man."

His arteriosclerosis was visibly becoming more serious. He had always had a ruddy complexion. Toward the end of his life his skin became redder, as is frequent in elderly people. With medical books always at hand, he accompanied the progress of his illness step by step. He was well informed about his malady. He saw the terrible condition of his arteries, and feared that a fatal coronary thrombosis would occur sooner or later. He was well aware of the possibility of this development in an elderly man suffering from arteriosclerosis.

His spirits, however, began to rise. In his diary of March 1, 1909, he wrote:

> In my last hours, I do not want to feel only the decline and passing of my body. As my friend Taunay used to say: "How terrible it is to waste away!" I would also like to feel the flight of the spirit, and see the light of the final solution. . . . .

For every sign or note of disillusionment and discouragement, three of optimism are to be found; this optimism was always evident when he took active advantage of what he thought were his last days, for which he was most grateful. In a letter to Machado de Assis he said: "Do not for a minute feel ingratitude toward life, in other words, sadness." He was the living example of these words. In his diary he wrote:

> I never expected to attain old age, and in the meantime it is becoming the most beautiful part of my life. . . . . every day now is fraught with importance and intensity for me. I have to take full advantage of each one. I enter upon this last phase with the greatest optimism regarding the Creation. The pessimist is an atheist. . . . . I never imagined that I would become an old man. I have always felt the fires of youth burning within me; I still do.
>
> . . . . In my inner horizon there are now many gray and foggy days. No longer are there days of bright sunshine—the appanage of youth. But in compensation for this, I now see starlit nights more beautiful than any I have ever seen in the past.

I am now embarking upon my sixtieth year. The last decade is not going to dim the happy impression of life which I have had up to this time, because of the freshness and lucidity of mind which God has permitted me to keep since childhood.

On August 19, his birthday, he wrote: "At dinner there was a cake with fifty-nine candles. I shall have to live until I am sixty so that I can have a cake with many lights on my birthday! This was a perfect day, for which I have thanked God innumerable times, and I shall never forget it. . . . ." And the following year, on the same date, at the end of the day which was to be his last birthday, as he was to prophesy several times during the course of that year, he wrote with his usual serenity: "It was a perfect day filled with calm, happiness, and gratitude, and spent with my family. Praised be the Lord! Any time granted me beyond today is a special gift."

To Professor Bassett Moore, he wrote in English, following the medical beliefs of his time:

Your remark that my letter led you to think that I was in perfect health cheered me. I was then better than I thought! While the colored complexion proper of my disease, too much red blood, makes me appear healthy in body, my mental optimism makes me appear happy and cheerful in depression. I am really not at all well, in fact; and I am seriously considering if I will remain longer at my post. But that does not interfere with my pleasure, often real joy, as a spectator at God's plays.

He believed that the year 1909, like all of the years ending in nine had done since his birth, would leave an indelible mark, a radical transformation in his life. His entire life was divided into definite decades. He was born in 1849, went away to boarding school in 1859. In 1869, he made his first acquaintances in Pernambuco, which from then on was to play an important role in his life and where he was to enter public life for the first time. In 1879, he entered parliament, and began the abolitionist campaign—the period of most action. In 1889, the change was twofold in nature: his marriage and family life on the one hand, and on the other, his abandonment of public life, his period of mourning for the monarchy, and absorption in writing. In 1899, his reconciliation with the Republic, and a new career in diplomacy. The years which ended in nine modified everything.

A shadow of superstition made him believe that the precedent would be confirmed in 1909. The state of his health left him little doubt as to what form it would take, in spite of his moments of hope; it would probably be death, the closing of the final cycle. "If it be not death," he wrote in his diary, "then what will it be? . . . . Will it be the decadence of an invalid's life, with the illness finally reaching my mind? . . . . God save me from such an end, such a final phase." On March 1, he wrote, after a melancholy reference to his ill health: "During this month, my father died, and so did many other of my relatives and Evelina's also."

In January 1909, he left for Havana to attend, as Brazil's special ambassador, the ceremonies being held to celebrate the restoration of the national Cuban government. From there, in the midst of a full program of official ceremonies, he wrote this letter to Dona Evelina Nabuco from the American Legation:

This garden is a paradise. . . . . It is a palace, with many high doors, patios filled with tropical plants, marble walks. It is like a basilica of ancient Rome, and in it are the most beautiful things which Mr. Morgan brought from Korea and the Orient. It is difficult to take leave of this princely hospitality, but it is completely outside of Havana.

MIAMI, FLORIDA, February 3

Here I am in the United States again after spending a week in Havana. . . . . The short two-day trip was most enjoyable, and the little stopover in St. Augustine gave me enough time to see this city which was quite pleasant, but not as nice as Pasadena and other cities in California. At St. Augustine I rejoined the diplomatic caravan which was led by the Cruz's. The crossing from Knight's Key to Havana was interesting and comfortable, except for the service aboard; I could only get soft-boiled eggs, and even for that I had to complain to the captain. The sea, however, was beautiful, and at dusk I felt as if I were in Brazil—the same landscape as that of northern Brazil, the same breeze, the same warm air, and the same sky. Havana delighted me. Here is an hourly and daily account of my activities.

25. Arrival; Mr. Morgan came aboard to welcome me, and I was received by the chief of protocol. The Secretary of State and his brother were on the pier. It is said that his brother will be made minister here in the near future. We went with Mr. Morgan by automobile from the embassy to Marianao. We had tea, and dinner with Mr. Morgan an hour and a half later. We chatted until ten-thirty. He lives the opulent life of a Lucullus, always entertaining many guests.

26. In the morning I visited Governor Magoon in his palace. Afterward we had lunch with the McVeaghs at the Miramar. The President's brother, Mr. Taft, and his wife and daughter were also there. After that I visited the Secretary of State.

27. Mr. Morgan gave a lunch for me today in the Miramar. In attendance were various American and Cuban officials. In the afternoon we returned to Marianao and in the evening we attended a dinner given by Governor Magoon in his palace. (Mauricio [Joaquim Nabuco's son, at present ambassador in Washington] is always with us and invited to these affairs as if he were part of the mission.) Afterward we attended a dance held in honor of the governor. It was a beautiful spectacle. I returned at midnight to the Quinta Hidalgo.

28. I came to the palace today by automobile, dressed in uniform for the inauguration. I stood for a terribly long time in the midst of a huge throng. From there we rode in uniform through the streets down to the pier, where the entire diplomatic corps bade Governor Magoon farewell. We then returned to the

palace, where I had to wait for over half an hour for my automobile. Afterward we went for another trip . . . . which lasted half an hour. We had lunch and returned to the city. In the afternoon we returned to Marianao. Then two more half-hour trips by automobile. In the evening, Morgan gave a small dinner in the Quinta . . . . Today we moved to the Hotel Sevilla. My colleagues leave on Monday, and I leave Tuesday. I shall spend very little time in Florida . . . . I have accepted an invitation to attend a banquet in honor of Mr. Root in New York on February 26. Since leaving home I have not felt the slightest discomfort.

29. I have moved to the Hotel Sevilla. Tonight for dinner I have invited the Quesadas and our consul, Dr. Aróstegui; afterward we shall attend a ball being given in the same hotel by a Cuban lady.

30. I am giving a luncheon for Mr. Morgan, which will be attended by the McVeaghs and the Tafts—I have many visits to make today. This evening we are having dinner with all of the special delegates at the State Department. Mauricio and Amaral are going to a German dance, but I am going to bed at eleven.

31. I went to the palace to take leave of the President. This caused Mauricio and me to miss ten o'clock Mass . . . . We had lunch at our consul's residence. It was a family party attended by the Quesadas and Dr. Montoro, our minister in London, who was my companion during the Third Conference. The cuisine, from what I saw and from its aroma, is equal to the best in Brazil and more attractive. It was a very cordial gathering. Afterward we had group pictures taken and visited various interesting spots. In the evening I gave a banquet for forty guests, the only one given specifically for the special guests, in whose behalf I said a few words.

February 1. We were supposed to leave today, but because of Mme Cruz we feared the sea trip. The sea was quite rough. We had lunch, that is Mauricio, the McVeaghs, and I; I invited Dr. Aróstegui to dinner. After walking about the city looking at the shops, I retired early, quite tired.

February 2. The same people saw us leave today from Havana that welcomed us when we arrived, except for Mr. Morgan who had left earlier with the McVeaghs to visit a sugar mill . . . .

February 3. I am at the Royal Palm Hotel in Miami. What a paradise . . . . !

PALM BEACH, February 5

. . . . I am staying until Sunday . . . . We should arrive in St. Augustine on Monday, and in Washington on Tuesday morning. Do not worry about us. We shall catch a taxi at the station and drive home. Do not tell anyone at the embassy when we are arriving . . . .

It is very windy here, making this hotel quite uncomfortable, with its wide open windows facing the sea. If it were a beautiful day, the cold which has been bothering me would have gone away. You cannot imagine how uncomfortable it is to spend an entire twenty-four hours waiting in one place anticipating leaving the next day, as I have today. Tomorrow will not be as bad, for I leave Sunday evening. I have nothing to do; I feel that I am robbing you if I stay away from home another day. As far as resting is concerned, I do not believe that one can rest in enforced idleness.

On one side of my suite there is a large terrace overlooking the sea, with a sweeping view of a beach as beautiful as any in northern Brazil, and, had it not been for the wind, the hour I spent there would have been a perfect one. We enjoyed ourselves for two hours on a large wheel chair which was propelled by a Negro who pedaled it with his feet like a huge velocipede. It is a delightful mode of transport. We then saw an alligator and crocodile farm. There were about thirty crocodiles together. A female living by itself was about four hundred years old according to the caretaker, and its fecundity was always the same; he also said that it developed a new set of teeth every year as did the rest of its species. Our good grandfather would have said, "I cannot swallow that." However, I did . . . .

I paid an interesting visit to Mr. Flagler, an old associate of Rockefeller. He is now a millionaire. He has developed and built these places here in Florida, and is now constructing an overseas railway to Key West over immense viaducts. He lives in a palace whose entrance hall, with all of its marble work and columns, reminds me of Hadrian's Villa. He is eighty years old. He will leave his name written on the world's map with the railroad extension which he is building to Key West. He said that the only damage which could affect his project would be that caused by an earthquake or a bombardment by an enemy squadron. [In point of fact, a hurricane destroyed the railroad a few years ago; it has been replaced by a highway.] It will place Havana much closer to the United States . . . . He is a man who really knows how to use his millions.

After returning to Washington, in spite of being shaken in health, he continued his full, vigorous schedule. He was active in social, intellectual, and diplomatic matters. This victory of mind over body carried on to the very end, much to the surprise of the doctor whom he had in attendance. In his last season in Washington, he managed apparently to maintain his usual social and diplomatic calendar. In January he went to Cuba. In February he delivered an address in New York at the banquet which the Peace Society gave for Elihu Root. In April he made the last of his pilgrimages to the universities as "rhapsodist for Camoens," visiting Cornell and Vassar this time. In Washington he continued to follow the same schedule of dinners, both giving his own and attending those of others. His political activity was even intensified by his efforts to get an arbitration treaty signed and to find a satisfactory solution to the problem which threatened to cause so much trouble for the Brazilian coffee industry.

On the day of his departure for Cuba, January 23, he wrote in a letter that he was "overjoyed, because on that same morning Mr. Root had signed the treaty." Upon returning he was confronted with an American Congressional amendment which threatened economic disaster for Brazil—a tariff on the importation of coffee into the United States.

It was one of the most serious problems which arose during his stay in the embassy. The American point of view, which was clearly stated by

Congressman Payne, was that the high export tariff charged by the Brazilian states which produced the coffee, unjustly favored the Brazilian treasury and worked a hardship on the consumer nation. The tariff had as its object the re-establishment of equilibrium, forcing the reduction of the export tariff.

"Senator Root and Secretary of State Knox have had several conferences since the tariff on coffee was proposed, and it was Senator Root who furnished the Finance Committee with the confidential data bearing upon the effect which the countervailing duty would have" (*New York Herald*, March 31, 1909).

The measure, which was deemed necessary by many, was received with great interest. "In every direction today, the House is divided in little groups discussing the tariff bill and laying plans for effecting changes . . . . Coffee and the plan of American valuation seem to be the chief subjects of conversation" (*New York Times*, March 19, 1909).

Pressures from overt interests, such as the Puerto Rican planters, and from undercover groups, such as the speculators, created an atmosphere unfavorable to Brazil. Suspicious capitalists scurried about trying to get as much coffee into the country as possible before the imposition of the new tariff. The newspapers took notice of the fact that millions of dollars were being cast into this venture.

"All of these are weary days in the great campaign against the coffee tariff . . . . ," Nabuco wrote in his diary on March 31. "Today the newspapers are saying that the tariff amendment will be withdrawn because of my efforts." However, alarmed by evil presentiments, he threw himself into the fray, utilizing all available forces at the same time. He appealed to friends. In a letter to one of them he said:

> I would be held responsible by the public opinion of my country if I did not prevent the creation of a tax which did not exist when I came here, a tax which would force our coffee states to give up their only possible source of revenue.

His friends did not fail him. An influential Senator from West Virginia declared that he would do nothing which would be contrary to the wishes of Nabuco. On March 31, the *New York Herald* said: "When the tariff bill came in, therefore, with a countervailing duty on coffee on the list, Ambassador Nabuco went to the State Department and mildly, but firmly, intimated that if the contemplated program were carried out, Brazil would be obliged to cancel the concessions granted American exporters."

He unmasked the chief of the speculators, who had millions of dollars' worth of coffee stored in warehouses, and was trying to make some of the Senators believe that the federal government of Brazil was not opposed to the tariff, and that, in fact, it favored it.

After a long conversation at a dinner party given by a friend, he received a promise from a powerful Rhode Island Senator that the tariff would be passed only if there were a dire need for revenue. As the problem was being ironed out, Root declared in an address given to the Senate, that it was his hope that relations between Brazil and the United States had not changed in the slightest. The amendment of Senator Daniel of Virginia removing the tariff from the bill was unanimously approved. Congressman Douglas gave a speech in the House based on information furnished by Nabuco. It convinced the Congressmen of the evil of the tariff. Douglas wrote the following to Nabuco:

> . . . . The proposed countervailing duty on coffee is now happily disposed of. As you know, it was on account of the suggestions you were kind enough to make to me when I met you at the home of Mr. and Mrs. Jennings that I obtained the facts and presented them to the House.

His deep longing for Brazil became greater as days went by. Fear of dying in a foreign land is a recurring note in the letters of his last years. "I do not want to die among foreigners; I want to give my sons roots in our land." In another letter Nabuco said:

> But God is very great. The day will come when I rest under mango trees without fearing mosquitoes . . . . Every day, I regret more and more having to end my life outside of Brazil, but it is necessary to fight to the very end, and God willing, to die standing up.

To the same person, in another letter, he said:

> Suddenly, even during one of these happy convalescences and smiling moments, some treacherous illness or accident may occur and I shall have died away from home. To insure against such an eventuality, I shall plead dispensability and ask for retirement . . . . but the illusion of life is a strong one, and I am lulled by it.

In August 1908, he wrote to Machado de Assis:

> It is a great privation to live abroad in a strange land and away from one's friends—above all, to die this way. But I hope to return before darkness overtakes me. Then my future sixties shall try to accompany your future seventies. May God grant this wish!

For the first time, in June of 1909, Nabuco was forced to cancel an important engagement because of ill health. The doctors forbade his appearance at one of the leading universities where he was going to deliver the Commencement address and receive another honorary degree.

A little later he was bedridden for weeks by an acute heart disturbance;

his family was quite worried. He was severely weakened by the illness, which he called "an abrupt attack of old age." His high blood pressure caused him so much pain that at times it frightened him: "My memory's telephone . . . . sometimes does not function with its usual clarity," he noted once in his diary.

His anxiety and on the other hand the enforced absolute rest enfeebled him even more: "Here in Manchester, Massachusetts [where he fell ill], I have come to the conclusion that I must keep working all of the time." And on October 2, he wrote:

> Formerly I could never find within my soul any diseased plants or weeds, but now I find grubs and thorns everywhere. I no longer see flowers everywhere in the fields. However, I am sure that this will all pass away when I return to my normal busy life.

And as a matter of fact, it almost did disappear. His diary records several "ideal" days in this very same village.

Back in Washington for the last time, he reduced his public activities because of his declining health; he continued, however, to attend important functions. He was becoming old in appearance, and looking very tired; but he always managed to stand firm and erect, with his usual smiling amiability. On Thursday, November 25, he spoke for the last time in public at a Thanksgiving celebration. In January, he wore his uniform at a formal reception in the White House for the last time. He remained at home more than before, among his friends—his books. Plato was the last of his literary friendships. Exactly a month before his death he wrote the following to his brother-in-law: "I am now entirely taken with Plato. I do not know whether at the age of sixty it is too late to enter the Platonic academy, but it is the most convenient preparation for the hereafter."

In his diary he wrote:

> Plato is now a bright resplendent sun for me! How my Chateaubriand seems pale and small when compared to Plato. . . . . In 1871 I had four philosophical lectures on Platonism published in *A Reforma.*

During the last days of November, Nabuco won a notable diplomatic victory in the solution of the Chilean-American dispute over the Alsop question. It was an old dispute which had been partially forgotten and which few people thought would lead again to strained relations between the two nations. "Some time ago," Nabuco wrote in an official message to the ministry, "I mentioned this subject to the Chilean Minister, but he replied that there was no longer a dispute, that he considered the issue to be as dead as an old extinct volcano." "It was as deplorable as it was absurd," wrote Senator Root to Nabuco, "that the old Alsop question should still produce such results."

The trouble began when the territory in which the American Alsop firm had mining concessions was transferred from Bolivia to Chile; Chilean laws did not grant them the rights which they thought should be theirs. When matters began to appear to become serious, the Chilean Legation and the Department of State commenced discussions regarding a possible arbitration.

The American government refused to submit the matter to arbitration unless the Chilean government would exclude from discussion a point which it believed should not be brought before any arbiter: that is, the right of the American government to make claims for debts owed to American citizens.

Chile had alleged from the very start that the United States had no right to intervene in a private and juridical case of this type, and it made this objection one of the principal bases for its defense. For this reason, Chile refused to make any reservations in presenting its case before an arbitration tribunal.

The two principals in the case were irreconcilable and adamant in their stands. On November 17, the Secretary of State, Philander Chase Knox, had an ultimatum delivered to the Chilean Legation in which Chile was given two alternatives: breaking diplomatic relations, or accepting within a ten-day period set by the United States one of the proposals made by the American government regarding the payment of the Alsop claims. The Chilean Legation sent a counterproposal which the United States refused to consider; Chile suggested in this note that a mediator for the case be chosen.

Nabuco was closely following the progress of the dispute from the first-hand information given to him by the Chilean Minister, Aníbal Cruz, who was one of his intimate friends. He was pained to see the time limit set by the ultimatum rapidly coming to an end. On November 21, when Elihu Root stopped in Washington between trains, he received an urgent appeal from Nabuco, explaining the problem to him and asking for his intervention in the case.

Root received the appeal just as he was leaving his home. However, he fortunately had time enough to see his successor before the train left and to convince him, as much as it was possible, that nothing should be done which would threaten the continental peace which he had tried so hard to establish and protect.

His influence was a happy one. When two days later Nabuco, acting on instructions received from Rio de Janeiro, offered Brazil's good offices in effecting a reconciliation, he found the Secretary much more inclined to reach an agreement.

"Before receiving orders to see the Secretary of State," he wrote to Graça Aranha, "I had appealed to Mr. Root, the father of the cause of Pan-Americanism, to save that for which he had fought, by saying to him:

> Oh haste and come, because if you delay
> There may be no one left alive today!
> [*Lusiads*, III, 105]

He heard my appeal, which he called, 'your cry from Macedonia' and like St. Paul he ran to save the nascent Church."

In his diary on November 23, he wrote:

> I found Mr. Knox not disposed to break relations except in extreme circumstances, and I also brought about a *détente*; I told him about what a possible break would mean to the success of the Pan-American policies of the United States, which he had professed the desire to continue after Mr. Root left office. This calmed him very much, and when I pointed out to him the difference between the Hague proposal and the mediator proposal, which he had not understood too well, he immediately saw that the latter was the solution. In this manner I brought about a *détente* but left the solution to him. Root must have worked hard in an attempt to bring about a solution; I had the good fortune of placing the problem in focus.

In an official communiqué to his government, which was published later, Nabuco gives an account of his meeting with the Secretary of State:

> From my telegrams, you know by now the minutes and the results of the meeting which I had the pleasure of holding with the Secretary of State at his residence on the afternoon of the twenty-third. I went to the meeting from the Chilean Legation, where they did not have the slightest hope of an agreement. It was not until the thirtieth that I found out that Mr. Root had been with Mr. Knox. The Cruz family was making preparations for a hasty departure, in accordance with the barbaric custom (which I deplored before Secretary Knox), which obliges the personnel of legations to uproot themselves suddenly, abandoning all of their interests and private belongings, even though there be no prospect of war or any animosity extant. My meeting with him lasted three hours and was most cordial. From the very beginning, Mr. Knox was desirous of finding a solution. He told me that telegrams which he had received that morning from Santiago had renewed his hope of an agreement, and that he was going to investigate the matter again with the greatest interest. He repeated that he would never submit to arbitration the United States' right to claim debts owed to its citizens. It was at that time that I called the Chilean proposal to his attention; this was the proposal which avoided the aforementioned preliminary reservation, and called for the nomination of a friendly party to resolve the differences. I explained the significance of the proposal to him. He had not understood it fully before then, and had believed it to

be another delaying measure. Since the mediator proposed had been Brazil, in order not to appear as if I were going to dispute that honor, I told him in passing that it would be difficult for us to choose between our two principal political friends, the United States and Chile. In that way, without refusing in advance that which was not in my realm anyway, I left him free to choose another nation, without hurting our feelings, if our friendship with Chile seemed to be prejudicial in the eyes of the interested parties. Furthermore, Brazil then would not stand as an obstruction to the only acceptable solution. As I explained in a wire to you, the Secretary of State immediately went to work on the proposal. "When the Brazilian Ambassador explained the Chilean viewpoint to me," he later told the Chilean Minister after all was settled, "I said to myself, if I have any intelligence at all, I certainly should be able to find a solution now."

When I returned to the Chilean Legation, it was to let them know that all danger of a rupture seemed past. I had brought about a *détente*, thanks, I am sure, to Mr. Root's efforts, and had pointed the way to the solution. You can imagine the surprise and joy with which the news I brought was received in the Chilean Legation. On that same night it was cabled to Santiago, where all hope had also been lost.

The Chilean press expressed great satisfaction at the happy turn of events. The bonds of friendship which linked Chile and Brazil were tightened even further. The Brazilian Embassy received official notifications of gratitude for Brazil's good offices from the two interested governments.

The author wrote the following letter to her brother, Mauricio, who was studying in Germany at the time:

"Relations here have been bad between the United States and Chile, ever since Chile refused an ultimatum sent by Secretary Knox. The two nations were on the verge of breaking diplomatic relations, but Mr. Root and Papa, one at a time, conferred with Mr. Knox and he withdrew the ultimatum, so that now everything has been settled. Papa was the one who bore the glad tidings to the Cruzes, for he went to see them right after he had discussed the matter with Mr. Knox. Mama went with him and told him later, after they had returned home, that she had detected disillusionment in Sr. Cruz's face for not having had a personal part in the making of Mr. Knox's decision. This idea had not even entered into Papa's mind (you already know that envy is something completely foreign to Father), but he immediately telephoned the Chilean Legation to explain to Sr. Cruz that it was his note to Mr. Knox which had really resolved the case, for Mr. Knox had not understood it until Papa explained it to him. Thus Sr. Cruz must have been made much happier, that is, if Mama had been right in her conjecture and observation."

During the last season in Washington, Nabuco's health did not permit much social activity. After returning to Washington, he had adopted the rule that he would not dine out. He intended to make exceptions only for official invitations which could not be refused, such as diplomatic dinners at the White House, but giving in to the affectionate insistence of his friends from Chile, after the settlement of the Alsop case, he accepted an invitation to attend a dinner given in his honor at the Chilean Legation, the date of which, January 5, he was permitted to set himself.

On that day, however, he was laid prostrate by one of the terrible migraine attacks which had been tormenting him during the past years. "During one of those attacks he will pass away," the doctors used to say to themselves. At the last minute, he was unable to attend this dinner given in his honor. On the following day, disconsolate because of the disturbance which he had caused by not being able to attend the banquet, he resolved, after seeing this proof of his bad state of health, to excuse himself in advance from the presidential dinner. He wrote this note to the hostess, disguising with a pleasantry a melancholy forecast:

> Since I was unable to attend your dinner, I shall not attend any other! Alas! I shall not see your white formal dress in the White House, where I imagine you will wear it again, according to Carolina, after yesterday's rehearsal. However, I have to resign myself to the laws of sickness and old age.

His headache never left him. Death was near and he could feel it approaching. A few days before his death, he wrote a recommendation "to be given to the first secretary in the event of my death." It was addressed to E. L. Chermont, who was to leave the post in less than a month.

The last note to be found in his diary is that written on the eleventh: "A little better . . . . I am cautiously resuming my normal life. I still have my headache and my drowsiness."

On January 17, 1910, he passed away, without suffering, without passing through a long period of coma, and still in full possession of all his wonderful senses. It was a kind death, sparing him the mental decline which was his last fear: "My hope," he wrote in his diary in January 1909, "my fervent prayer is that, when the sickness of old age overtakes me, it be not in that part of me which God created in His image. The body may be destroyed, but never the mind, and if it has to be the mind, let me suffer from a mystical mania, and not die having forgotten the Lord."

CHAPTER XXIX. THE TOMB, 1910

When the young Danish Minister, Count Carl Moltke, returned from Nabuco's funeral, he wrote some profoundly expressive remarks, which he did not remove from his desk drawer until fifteen years later, while engaged in a chance conversation with two Brazilians. One of these Brazilians, Lucilo Bueno, Brazilian Minister in Copenhagen, translated Count Moltke's remarks and had them published in the *Jornal do Comércio* at the time when Count Moltke as leader of the Danish Socialist party was President of the Council, and Minister of Foreign Affairs. In the preface Bueno said: "Count Moltke could not contain himself upon hearing us talk about Nabuco. He said that meeting him had been the greatest emotional experience of his life. Thanks to the conversation I had with him, I obtained the notes in which he wrote about the painful grief he felt at the loss of his friend."

WASHINGTON, January 20, 1910

Poor Nabuco passed away on the seventeenth of this month; with the widow and children of the beloved deceased, I am mourning the loss which they have just suffered. Death, the great gravedigger, however, did not come as a surprise. Nabuco had been expecting to leave us. Already last November, he wrote me these lines filled with resignation: "Thank you for your letter. I am going to save it as I did Bryce's, as a remembrance of Washington. I shall have to prepare myself during the remainder of this summer, in order to be able to face the oncoming winter, which does not wait for those of us who are sexagenarian sons of the tropics." A few weeks before, he had shown more hope, for he wrote that he would be able to render his country another year's service. Undermined in spirit and body by an illness with which he had been afflicted for years, he was snatched away from us before he could realize this hope. Yet when he passed on, he left us a legacy of abundant treasures of deep thought, filled with the nobility of his great soul, enveloped with his moving religious faith, based upon his vast knowledge, and replete with a patriotism capable of the greatest sacrifices.

Joaquim Nabuco did not serve merely Brazil. Sure of its ultimate success, he ardently embraced the cause of Pan-Americanism. He possessed a quality, rare among Latins, which helped him in his desire to accomplish this delicate task: that of correctly understanding the American people. They, unfortunately, did not possess the gift of appreciating those two extraordinary elements which contributed so much to Nabuco's efforts toward the betterment of Pan-American relations: Christian generosity and greatness of soul. He was truly a "grand seigneur."

I say generosity, because in his everyday life he never received anything in exchange for what he did. The deafness with which he had been afflicted for some time helped to accentuate the isolation into which he was driven by his pious meditations, his scholarly activities, and the complete absence of any affinity of tastes and likes with those around him. The moral suffering which such a situation must have caused him was borne in silence. He never complained about the nation to which he was ambassador; on the contrary, he always spoke benevolently about it, was always ready to absolve it, and never engaged in discussions of its defects. During the last portion of his stay in the United States, he devoted himself primarily to the preparation of various lectures which he was frequently invited to deliver at universities. Young American students have imaginations unaccustomed to elevated thoughts and talents, and a mentality averse to being influenced by the Latin soul. Yet they must have felt strange and sudden emotions well up within them when the lightning of Nabuco's genius flashed before them as he spoke about the great poet, Camoens, or when he attempted to explain, with his breadth of vision and skillful powers of expression, the civilizing role played by the variegated mass of humanity which now inhabits the United States.

Officialdom paid to the Brazilian Ambassador a final tribute which was as impressive for its pomp and solemnity as it was for the feeling of individual mourning manifested on this occasion. Beneath the cupola of St. Matthew's Church, the grieving hearts were throbbing together under the embroidered frills and decorations of formal dress. Many tears were secretly shed, and thousands of prayers were offered for the repose of his soul; his memory will ever remain sacred to those who had the good fortune to bathe in his eternal fountain of wisdom.

This vivid testimony by Count Moltke is just one of the many offered by his colleagues. The other messages did not have as interesting a history prior to publication. They are the official communiqués in which the British and French ambassadors informed their home governments of Nabuco's death, in terms which made the Brazilian government most grateful and appreciative. They were delivered by the respective governments to the Brazilian government and subsequently were released to the Brazilian press.

James Bryce said:

Sir, I beg to report, and I do so with very deep regret, that Senhor Joaquim Nabuco, the Brazilian Ambassador, died here suddenly on the 17th ult. Senhor Nabuco was one of the most distinguished of South American statesmen and diplomatists, and it will be remembered that he was Brazilian Minister in London from 1900 to 1905 and was agent in the numerous arbitration cases in which his country was involved, more especially in the recent Anglo-Brazilian arbitration regarding the Guiana boundary.

He was also a most accomplished man of letters, having written several philosophical works in French, while both his poetical tastes and his admirable mastery of English were attested by the addresses which he delivered at three American universities on the *Lusiads* of Camoens. They were masterpieces, both of refined thought and of felicitous expression. No one was more popular among his colleagues and with society of Washington, and he held a position in it which probably no diplomatic representative of any South American state ever before attained. The elevation as well as the simplicity and geniality of his character made him generally respected and beloved; and I have seldom known any departure from this world more sincerely mourned. . . . .

And the French Ambassador, Jusserand, wrote:

On the seventeenth of this month, the Brazilian Ambassador, Joaquim Nabuco, died in this city. He and Mr. Bryce were the most illustrious members of the diplomatic corps accredited to the United States.

Long a faithful servant of his country, which he honored with all of the nobility of his distinguished person, on account of his high sense of justice and his lofty and unselfish attitude toward life, which no personal considerations could ever alter, he was highly esteemed in Washington circles and I can even say, universally admired. "Our country does not produce men of his caliber very often," the first secretary of the Brazilian Embassy told me in tears at the funeral. With the utmost sincerity I responded: "No country produces many like him."

He spoke our language perfectly, although he received all of his education in Brazil. Aside from many important works in Portuguese, he has left us a volume of thoughts and recollections in French, which Mr. Faguet, in a critical article, declared could not have been written by a foreigner, and he further stated in this article that the name on the cover must have been a pen name. Mr. Nabuco has also left us the manuscript of a tragedy in French, about which it can be said without exaggeration that certain sections are Corneillian in breadth. In 1870, he was as stunned as any good Frenchman by the catastrophe in France, which in the eyes of our Latin-American friends is the standard-bearer of world civilization; in this work he expressed the anguish which this blow aroused in him during his youth. This play, which he had retouched many times, was ever in his thoughts. He planned to publish it some day, but death overtook him before he completed this project.

A picture of an Alsatian, reminding him of that terrible year, was always before his eyes and was hanging on the wall of the room in which he died.

President Taft, members of the administration, and a large group of mourners attended the Ambassador's funeral; Nabuco's support of Mr. Root's policies brought the two countries even closer together. The body will be conveyed to Rio de Janeiro on an American warship. His kindly widow and five children will precede him to Brazil. I want to place in this message a genuine testimonial of admiration for Joaquim Nabuco's noble qualities of heart, wisdom, and personal charm, which have inspired me as the representative of the nation which his heart embraced when we suffered our great national disaster.

The opinion of the American press was well expressed in this editorial from the *Washington Post*, on the day following his death:

For his courtly kindliness, his conciliatory diplomacy, his grasp of world affairs, his splendid literary ability, but most of all for his warm and attractive personality, Joaquim Nabuco, ambassador from Brazil to the United States, and dean of the Pan-American diplomatic corps, will be sadly missed. He was a strong man, yet gentle; firm in diplomacy, yet kind and generous; a man of letters, yet close to humanity. And he was the kind of man whose loss will be felt as deeply here in

Washington as in his own country, where his strength and ability had made his political position firm.

A man of wide culture, a linguist of marked ability, the Brazilian Embassy under Mr. Nabuco's regime became the center of attraction for many distinguished men. It was but natural that he should become a warm personal friend of Mr. Roosevelt and later of Mr. Taft. In fact, the friendship of all the statesmen in Washington came to him as naturally as steel to the magnet. Death came suddenly to him, for he had been ill but a week, and in his passing the capital where he served for five years suffers a deep, personal loss.

The entire press paid tribute to him in eloquent terms, stressing his important actions in favor of Pan-Americanism. Here are a few quotations:

"The development of the Pan-American idea into practical form was due in large measure to his vision and talents" (*Washington Herald*, January 18). "Americans entertained for him the warmest admiration because of his steadfast friendship for the United States and his unceasing efforts to aid in bringing about relations of the closest friendship among the nations of the Western Hemisphere" (*The Times*, Troy, New York, January 18). "Thanks to his splendidly balanced mind and his belief in the unselfishness of the United States, he resolutely refused to entertain suspicions of our alleged designs upon southern territory. He labored for the Brazilian nation, but he labored as well for the world . . . . and the American people may mourn with those of Brazil in his loss" (*Chicago Tribune*, January 18). " . . . . his influence toward the spread of Pan-Americanism in general, and to a good understanding between North and South America in particular has been second only to Mr. Root's" (*The Outlook*, New York, January 29). "Mr. Nabuco's usefulness at the capital can hardly be overestimated, for he made Brazil and the Brazilians known to Americans, he established sympathy and understanding between his own country and the country to which he was accredited" (*Evening Transcript*, Boston, January 18). "Mr. Nabuco's lifework was the strengthening of the ties between his country and the United States; and not only between Brazil and the Union, but between all the South American republics and this government. Great statesman as he was—he saw the unlimited influence and power and mutual benefit to be derived from a close affiliation between North and South America. He worked shoulder to shoulder with Mr. Root, then Secretary of State, in furthering the Pan-American policy to which he gave new life" (*The Northwestern Chronicle*, Milwaukee, January 29). " . . . . His efforts were directed strongly and sympathetically toward maintaining the closest and most friendly relations between South America and North America. In the truest sense he was an ambassador of good will and international friendship" (*The Courier*, Buffalo, January 19).

Throughout the entire nation the newspapers printed the official tribute of John Barrett, the Director of the Pan American Union:

> Along with Elihu Root he labored with all the strength of his great statesmanship and his brilliant mental attainments to develop the spirit of comity, good will and solidarity among the American nations. . . . . His name will go down in history as one of the most notable men of Pan-American progress and relationship, and he will always be known as one of the foremost statesmen of Brazil and Latin America.

The loss of a conspicuous helper and friend was solemnly lamented by his companions in the various bodies which were continuing their work for the common cause of Pan-Americanism. Wherever they gathered to work, his memory stimulated renewed enthusiasm to follow the victorious path in spite of international derision and indifference. His parting was lamented in various speeches. In the meeting of the Pan American Union's Board of Directors, which was held to mourn Nabuco's passing, the Chilean Minister's tribute perhaps best symbolized the continent in mourning: ". . . . the Brazilian government has suffered an irreparable loss; the Board of Directors of the International Bureau of American Republics has lost its most illustrious member, and Pan-Americanism has lost one of its most enthusiastic supporters. As for myself, all I can say is that I loved him very much, for I knew him well."

Speakers turned to his memory again and again, with words of praise and tribute, in the legislatures of the various American nations, at the Pan American Conference in Buenos Aires, where he would have led the Brazilian delegation, and finally in a day of triumph for the cause at the opening of the Pan American building in Washington.

Joaquim Nabuco's body was entering his home waters when, amidst great pomp and circumstance, the opening of the building took place in Washington. Elihu Root terminated his speech with these moving words:

> One voice that should have spoken here today is silent, but many of us cannot forget or cease to mourn and to honor our dear and noble friend, Joaquim Nabuco. Ambassador from Brazil, dean of the American diplomatic corps, respected, admired, trusted, loved, and followed by all of us, he was a commanding figure in the international movement of which the creation of this building is a part. The breadth of his political philosophy, the nobility of his idealism, the prophetic vision of his poetic imagination were joined to the wisdom and practical sagacity of statesmanship, to a sympathetic knowledge of men, and to a heart as sensitive and as tender as a woman's. He followed the design and construction of this building with the deepest interest. His beneficent influence impressed itself upon all of our actions. No benison can be pronounced upon this great institution so rich in promise for its future as the wish that his ennobling memory may endure and his civilizing

spirit may prevail in the councils of the International Bureau of American Republics.

His veneration in Brazil began at the moment of his death, but these demonstrations of public opinion no longer belong in the annals of his life. They are the beginning of that immense collection of national expressions of appreciation, from which judgment of him will slowly take form, commentaries made when his death was announced, and Brazilians were still confused by the shock and surprise of this news. Brazilian newspapers, likewise, published cables describing in detail the tributes and honors bestowed upon him in the United States.

President Taft offered to have Dona Evelina Nabuco and her children conveyed to Brazil on the presidential yacht, "The Mayflower," with an escort of warships. In the invitation, he stated that his desire was to have the Nabuco family return to Brazil in the greatest possible comfort and with full honors from the American government. Nabuco's widow thanked him but declined the offer.

Nabuco was embarking upon a long voyage with many stops when American soldiers escorted the artillery caisson which carried his body, wrapped in the Brazilian national colors, through the tranquil streets of Washington, from the Embassy to St. Matthew's Church, for the first Solemn Requiem Mass.

"The only way in which I do not want to cross the ocean is in a coffin"; thus Nabuco wrote to his sister a few days before his death. He was anxious to return to his fatherland before death overtook him. Feeling death approaching, knowing that his remains would not be permitted to rest on foreign soil, he had protestingly foretold the manner of his last voyage home. His embalmed body, lying in state on the deck, guarded night and day by United States Marines, crossed the desolate expanses of the ocean aboard the cruiser, "North Carolina," which was escorted by another warship. The latter, however, flying the Brazilian standard, was the battleship, "Minas Gerais" [then recently completed at Elswick].

In Rio, glorious last rites were solemnly held under the auspices of the government, and the old torn standards of the abolitionist associations were removed from the museums and symbolically paraded through the streets.

Afterward, before finding his final resting place in Pernambuco, he had to take another ocean voyage. The sailors of the Brazilian warship "Carlos Gomes" had less stateliness in their presentation of arms than the Marines of the "North Carolina" whom they replaced, yet nearly all bore in their dark-skinned faces a remembrance of May 13 [1888, date of the emancipation bill].

Nabuco had foreseen that his tomb would be in Recife. Many times he had said to his wife: "If Pernambuco asks for my remains, do not deny that wish." Since the citizens of Pernambuco, immediately upon hearing the news of his death, held a public meeting and asked for his body, the mortal remains of Joaquim Nabuco returned to his native soil after the federal ceremonies.

Thus came to an end the final cycle of a happy life, about which he had said in retrospect, when delivering an informal speech in the Casino Fluminense during his last visit to Brazil:

> Within the sphere of activity which I had prescribed for it, my life is concluded. . . . . To me, my life, when viewed in this happy light, seems to be a beautiful dream which Divine Providence as a special favor permitted to come true.

BIBLIOGRAPHICAL NOTE

It was planned to publish as an Appendix to this volume a bibliography of the works of Joaquim Nabuco, as well as of the principal studies about him. This task has now become unnecessary, since such a study has just been published by the Brazilian Ministry of Foreign Affairs, commonly known as the Itamaratí. The book is *Bibliografia de Joaquim Nabuco* by Armando Brito de Souza and Armando Ortega Fontes (1949, pp. 93). Those wishing for a detailed bibliography should consult this work. The complete works of Joaquim Nabuco have been published (1941–1950) by the Companhia Editora Nacional of São Paulo. We list here simply the principal works of Nabuco, with the English translation of the titles, used in this book.

Amour et Dieu (Paris, 1874), *Love and God*
Camões e os Lusiadas (Rio de Janeiro, 1872), *Camoens and the Lusiads*
Escritos e Discursos Literários (Rio de Janeiro, 1901), *Writings and Literary Addresses*
"Foi Voulue," "The Desired Faith"
L'Option (Paris, 1910), *The Option*
Minha Formação (Rio de Janeiro, 1900), *My Formative Years*
O Abolicionismo (London, 1883), *The Emancipationist Movement*
O Eclipse do Abolicionismo (Rio de Janeiro, 1886), *The Eclipse of Abolitionism*
Pensées Détachées et Souvenirs (Paris, 1906), *Random Thoughts*
O Direito do Brasil (São Paulo, 1941), *The Rights of Brazil*
Un Estadista do Império (Rio de Janeiro, 1888–89), *A Statesman of the Empire*

INDEX

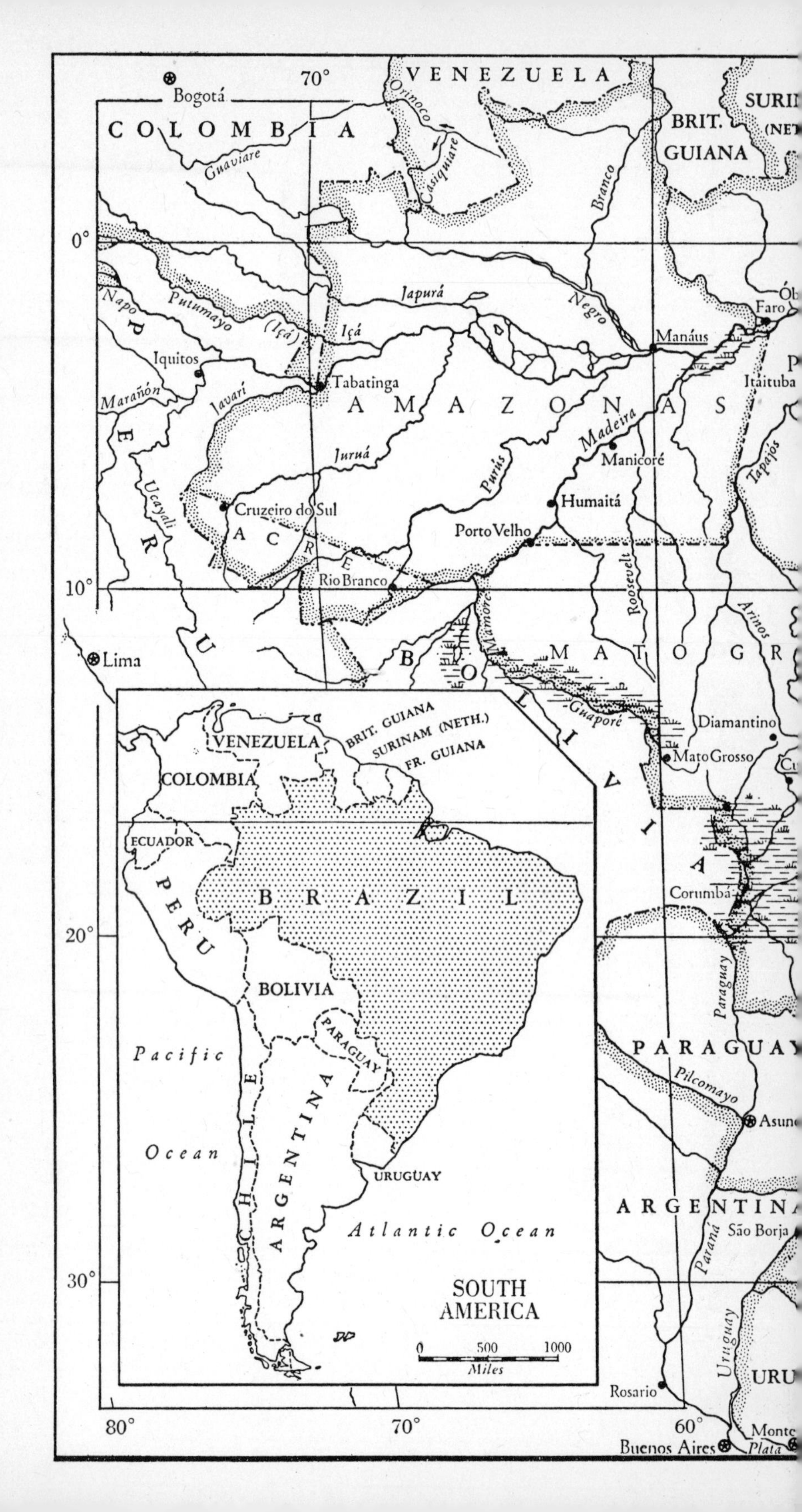

Bogotá
70°
VENEZUELA
Orinoco
COLOMBIA
Guaviare
Casiquiare
Branco
BRIT. GUIANA
0°
Napo
Putumayo
(Içá)
Içá
Japurá
Negro
Manáus
Faro
Iquitos
Tabatinga
Itaituba
Marañón
Javari
AMAZONAS
Madeira
Manicoré
Tapajós
PERU
Juruá
Purús
Ucayali
Cruzeiro do Sul
Humaitá
ACRE
Porto Velho
Rio Branco
Roosevelt
10°
Mamoré
Arinos
Lima
BOLIVIA
MATO GR
Guaporé
Diamantino
Mato Grosso
Corumbá
20°
Paraguay
PARAGUAY
Pilcomayo
ARGENTINA
São Borja
Paraná
30°
Uruguay
Rosario
80°
70°
60°
Buenos Aires
Plata
VENEZUELA
BRIT. GUIANA
SURINAM (NETH.)
FR. GUIANA
COLOMBIA
ECUADOR
BRAZIL
PERU
BOLIVIA
PARAGUAY
Pacific Ocean
CHILE
ARGENTINA
URUGUAY
Atlantic Ocean
SOUTH AMERICA
0 500 1000
Miles